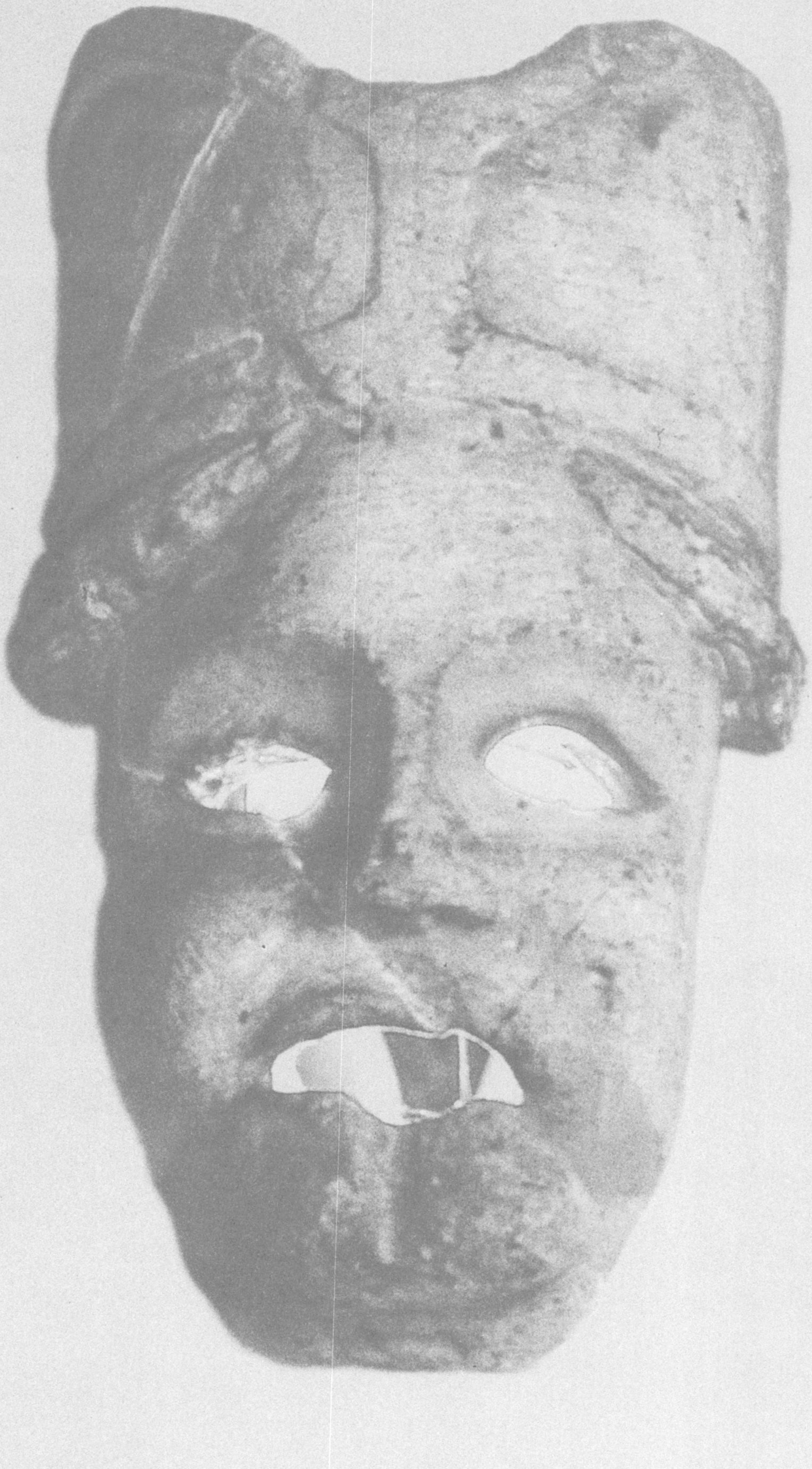

ENGLISH
MANOR HOUSES

ENGLISH MANOR HOUSES

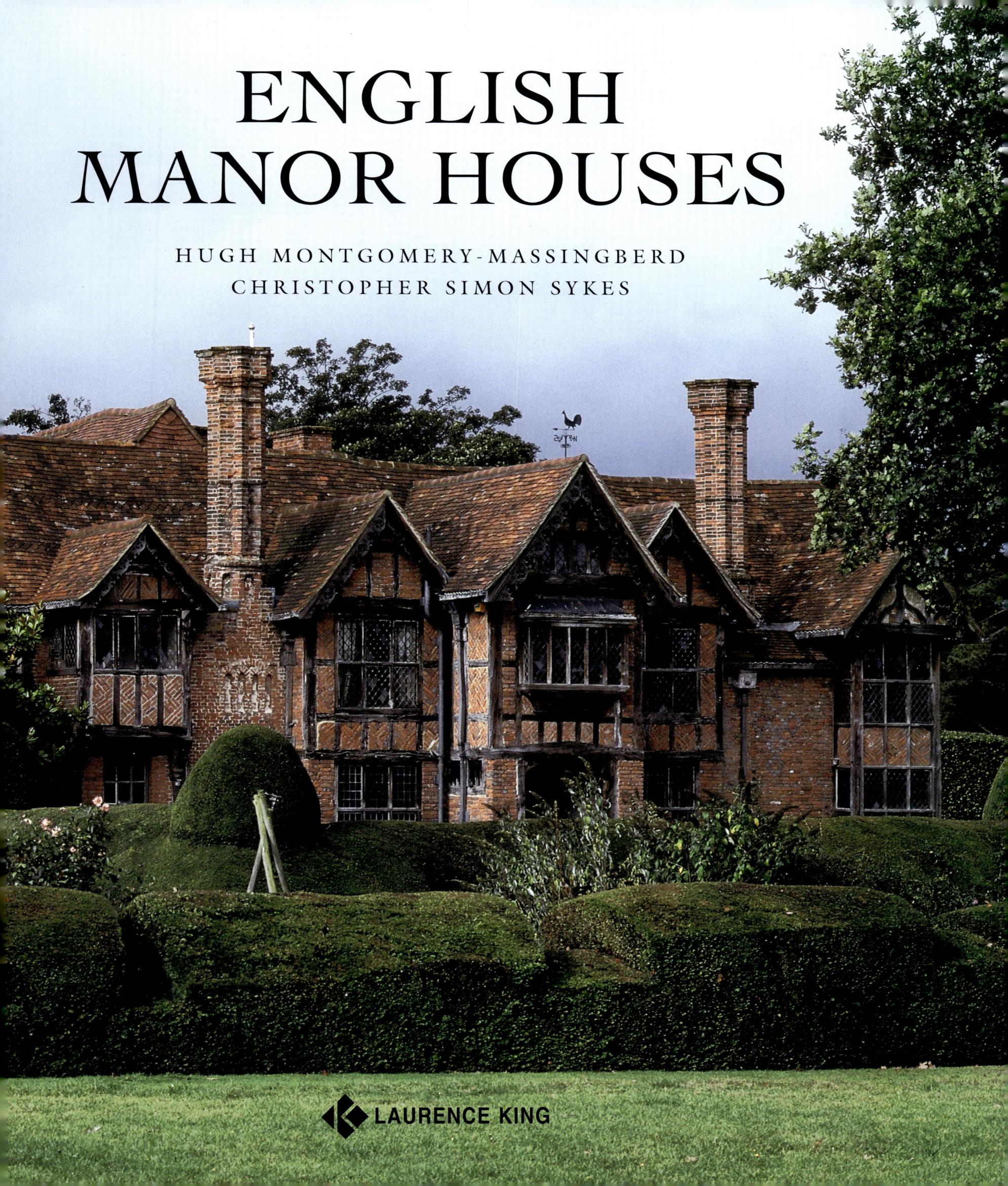

HUGH MONTGOMERY-MASSINGBERD
CHRISTOPHER SIMON SYKES

LAURENCE KING

For Ripples and Isabella

Acknowledgements

WE are very grateful to the owners of the manor houses featured in this book for their generous co-operation and kind support, as well as for their hospitality, guidance and constructive criticism. We also received most helpful encouragement, guidance and sustenance from many friends, relations and experts along the way. In particular, we would like to thank (in alphabetical sequence): Antony and Juliet Alderson, L.A. Alston, Siobhan Anderson, Lady Clare Asquith, Hal and Susan Bagot, Karl and Faith Ballaam, Mr and Mrs Colin Barrow, Jack and Josephine Bellyse Baker, John and Susan Bellyse Baker, Mark and Gillian Bence-Jones, Craig and Frances Brown, the late William Bulwer-Long and Sarah Bulwer-Long, Robin Bush, Guy and Christine Cavenagh-Mainwaring, Michael Cavenagh-Thornhill, Nicholas and Sheila Charrington, the Marchioness of Cholmondeley, Patrick and Andrea Cooke, Simon and Philippa Courtauld, Ann Darracott, Simon and Annabel Elliot, Robert Floyd, Christopher and Catherine Foyle, Crispin and Ann Gascoigne, Christopher Gibbs, Sir James and Lady Graham, Lady Grantley, Maria Carmela Viscountess Hambleden, Michael and Arabella Heathcoat-Amory, Sir John and Lady Guinness, William Hobden, Nicholas and Bethan Howard, John Jolliffe, Mr and Mrs John Langham, Ben and Rose Laycock, the late James Lees-Milne, Martin Little, Candida Lycett Green, Nicholas and Karin Mander, Michael McGarvie, Sir Mervyn Medlycott, Bt, Timothy Mowl, Lord and Lady Neidpath, Christopher Nevile, Lady Nevile, the Earl of Oxford and Asquith, the late Peregrine Palmer and Jill Palmer, Charles and Joanna Peck, the late Anthony Powell and Lady Violet Powell, John Powell, Richard Prideaux-Brune, Shervie Price, James Puxley, Lord and Lady Reay, William Ripley, Mr and Mrs Alastair Robb, John Martin Robinson, Richard and Anthea Roundell, the Earl and Countess of Sandwich, Michael Sayer, William Shawcross, Brian and Jill Stein, Humphrey and Solveig Stone, Sir Tatton Sykes, Bt, Captain and Mrs Nigel Thimbleby, the late Reverend Henry Thorold, Hugo and Elizabeth Vickers, Benjamin Wiggin, Graham Wilde, Oliver William-Powlett, Raymond Williams, Roger and Carol Winlaw, Giles and Mary Wood, and Robert and Nicola Wright.

Luke Massingberd carried out invaluable research both on the road and in the warmth of the London Library. Cynthia Lewis once again battled heroically against the clock to type the manuscript and also to mastermind the administrative side, including the all-important liaison with the owners. Philip Cooper and Elisabeth Faber of the publishers were the souls of patience. It was a privilege once more to work with the excellent editor Elisabeth Ingles and the passionately committed designer Karen Stafford.

HMM
CSS
March 2001

Published in 2001 by Laurence King Publishing
an imprint of Calmann & King Ltd
71 Great Russell Street
London WC1B 3BP

Tel: + 44 20 7430 8850
Fax: + 44 20 7430 8880
e-mail: enquiries@calmann-king.co.uk
www.laurence-king.com

Text © 2001 Hugh Montgomery-Massingberd
Photographs © 2001 Christopher Simon Sykes
This book was designed and produced by Calmann & King Ltd, London

All rights reserved. No part of this publication may be reproduced or transmitted in any form or by any means, electronic or mechanical, including photocopy, recording or any information storage and retrieval system, without permission in writing from the publisher.

A catalogue record for this book is available from the British Library

ISBN 1 85669 222 1

Designed and typeset by Karen Stafford
Edited by Elisabeth Ingles
Printed in China

Note on public opening arrangements

By no means all the houses featured in this book are open to the public. In every case the reader is well advised to consult the annual guide, *Hudson's Historic Houses & Gardens* (published by Norman Hudson & Co., Upper Wardington, Banbury, Oxfordshire OX17 1SP) for precise information as to the opening arrangements (if any).

ENDPAPERS Masks at Great Chalfield Manor, Wiltshire.
HALF-TITLE Porch at Hambleden Manor, Buckinghamshire.
FRONTISPIECE Dorney Court, Buckinghamshire.

Contents

Introduction 6

BEELEIGH ABBEY 12

MARKENFIELD HALL 18

BINGHAM'S MELCOMBE 26

IGHTHAM MOTE 32

JOHNBY HALL 38

STANTON HARCOURT MANOR 42

GREAT CHALFIELD MANOR 50

OCKWELLS MANOR 56

OWLPEN MANOR 64

COTHAY MANOR 70

ATHELHAMPTON 76

NORTON CONYERS 82

COTEHELE 88

FRISTON PLACE 94

DORNEY COURT 100

HERRINGSTON 108

EAST BARSHAM MANOR 116

LAYER MARNEY TOWER 120

WOLFETON HOUSE 124

MAPPERTON HOUSE 132

BECKLEY PARK 138

CADHAY 146

FLEMINGS HALL 152

SANDFORD ORCAS MANOR 158

HIGHFIELDS 166

STOCKTON HOUSE 170

LEVENS HALL 176

STANWAY HOUSE 182

HEYDON HALL 188

MARSTON HALL 194

AUBOURN HALL 198

MELLS 202

CHASTLETON HOUSE 208

HAMBLEDEN MANOR 214

DORFOLD HALL 220

EYAM HALL 226

WHITMORE HALL 232

HONINGTON HALL 236

WELFORD PARK 242

CLIFTON HAMPDEN 246

Glossary 252
Select Bibliography 253
Index 255

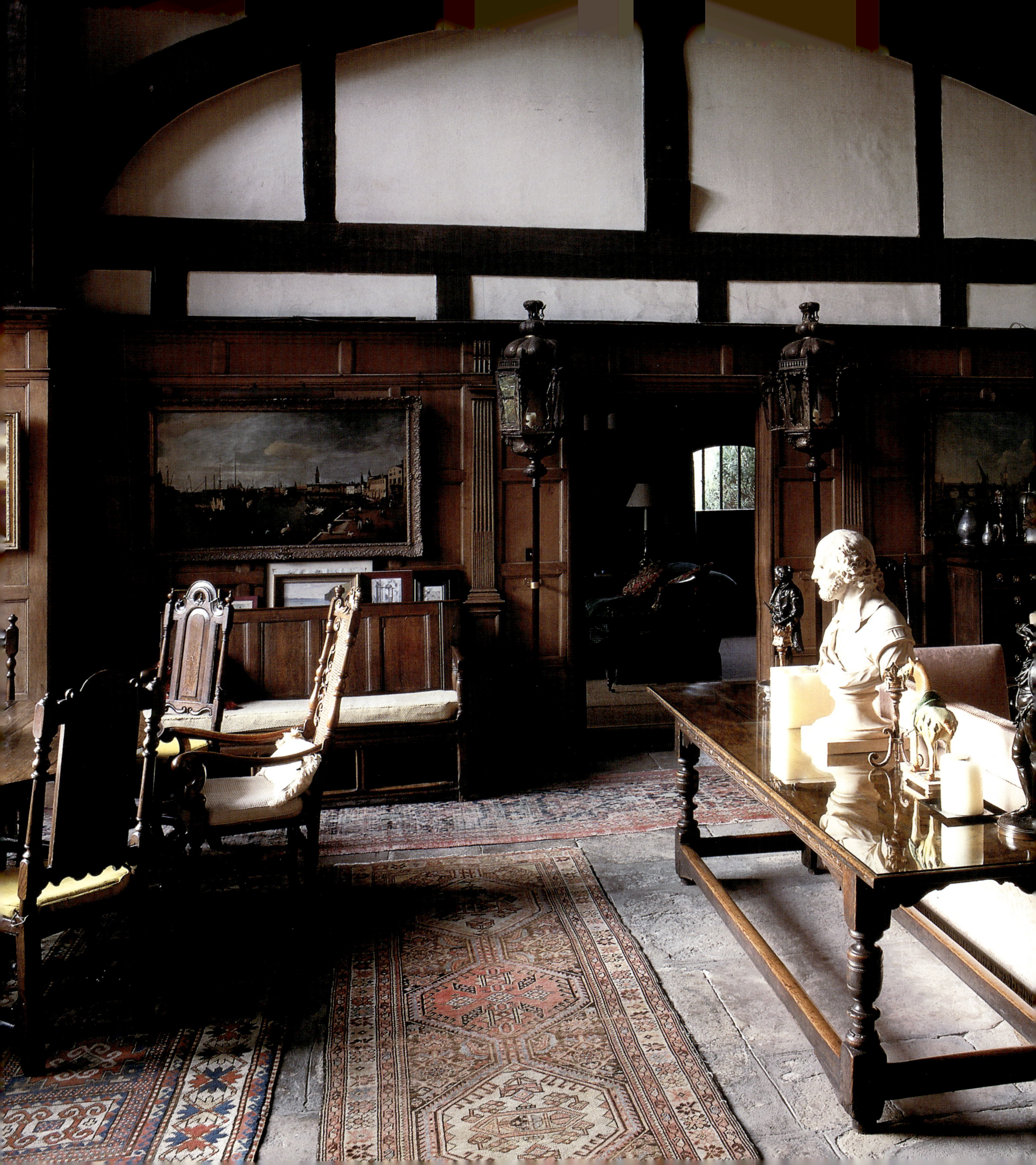

INTRODUCTION

I N *Great Houses of England and Wales*, our first collaboration in this series of illustrated volumes, we quoted Vita Sackville-West's romantic description of Knole, her family home in Kent, which she insisted was

> no mere excrescence, no alien fabrication, no startling stranger seen between the beeches and the oaks. No other country but England could have produced it, and into no other country would it settle with such harmony and such quiet.... It is not an incongruity like Blenheim or Chatsworth, foreign to the spirit of England. It is, rather, the greater relation of those small manor houses which hide themselves away so innumerably among the counties.

After journeying to Scotland and Ireland, we now return to England in order to celebrate 'those small manor houses' in this latest volume. Happily, as Vita Sackville-West intimated, there are plenty of them: our original list of places that might be featured ran to some 300 squirearchical seats. In the event, the exigencies of publishing and printing meant that we were obliged to whittle the number down to 40 of the most picturesque examples of a particularly covetable genre.

A question that we were often asked as we traversed the counties in search of these hidden gems was: 'How do you define a Manor House?' Initially one would be overcome with guilt at past failures to get to grips with the recondite mysteries of Land Law as a student – dread words like *caput manerii*, capital messuage, frankpledge, court leet, serjeanty, copyhold, mortmain, frankalmoign (that's quite enough) floated into the mind as if in a nightmare. Soon, though, we learnt to stiffen the sinews. 'There is actually *no* legal definition for "Manor House" ', the answer would come forth. 'A *manor* is a specific

INTRODUCTION

English territorial unit, originally of the nature of a feudal lordship, but a *manor house*, while traditionally the seat of the lord of the manor, has merely come to be regarded as a romantic synonym for a small country house, particularly of the late-medieval, Tudor and Stuart periods, and that is what we are really concerned with, not all the feudal fiddle-faddle.'

'But then how do you define a small country house?'

By this stage, it is time to move on. For our purpose is not to become bogged down by technicalities but to give an impression of the magical places we visited, to capture something of their romance, history and atmosphere. As Reginald Bosworth-Smith, Harrow master, polymath and squire of Bingham's Melcombe, put it in his Foreword to *Some Dorset Manor Houses* (published in 1907 at the height of the revival of interest in such buildings):

> An Old Manor House is, as it were, a dewdrop from the past – pure, pellucid, peaceful. It seems to breathe the air and esteate [*sic*] the fragrance of Chaucer and the *Canterbury Tales*. It is the survival, the personification of what was most lovable and domestic in the not very lovable or domestic times of the later Plantagenets, the Tudors or early Stuarts.... It is the peace and restfulness of their centuries, and not their turmoil and their progress, that live and breathe and brood around them.

PRECEDING PAGES Friston Place, Sussex: Hall.

Interior view of East Barsham Manor, Norfolk, which was restored in the 1930s.

INTRODUCTION

RIGHT Markenfield Hall, Yorkshire: a bedroom.

BELOW Cothay Manor, Somerset: Oratory.

Dorset has certainly scored well in this selection – as Bosworth-Smith claimed, it is 'rich above all in the number, variety, and beauty of its manor houses'. Apart from Bingham's Melcombe itself, we have included Athelhampton, Herringston, Wolfeton, Mapperton and Sandford Orcas. Yet, without striving consciously for a fair 'regional spread', we seem to have ended up with plenty of variety. In neighbouring Wiltshire, we took in Stockton and Great Chalfield; further west, we ventured to Mells, Cothay, Cadhay and Cotehele. The Cotswolds are represented by Owlpen and Stanway in Gloucestershire and Chastleton in Oxfordshire – a county that can also claim Stanton Harcourt, Beckley and Clifton Hampden. Flying the flag for the Home Counties are Ightham Mote, Ockwells, Dorney, Hambleden and Welford, with Friston on the Sussex coast. In the Midlands we covered Highfields, Dorfold, Eyam, Whitmore and Honington. Up north we went to Markenfield, Johnby, Norton Conyers and Levens. Finally, to the east, we embraced Marston, Aubourn, East Barsham, Heydon, Flemings, Beeleigh and Layer Marney.

The manor houses are dealt with in individual chapters in a fairly loose chronological sequence that reflects the development of English architectural history from monastic times, as at Beeleigh, right up to the Victorian Gothic of Clifton Hampden – which has been included by way of a coda. On the whole, we have concentrated on manor houses that remain habitable, and that have therefore inevitably had to undergo some adaptation, rather than the few pristine survivors of the Early English period.

The traditional 'hall house' had developed by about 1300 to the familiar arrangement of a central Great Hall, with kitchen, offices and family bedrooms adjoining it at one end and the ladies' retiring room, or 'Solar', at the other. The medieval manor houses that we are concerned with here tend to have, at least, a Great Hall range and one or more 'cross wings' incorporating a Great Chamber, bedrooms and storage rooms. Sometimes the Great Hall was placed at first-floor level, as at Markenfield, but was more usually on the ground floor, where it was entered from a porch at one end. Although Markenfield, or rather its owner, was granted a licence to crenellate in 1310, most of the

INTRODUCTION

LEFT Mells, Somerset: Sitting Room.

BELOW Dorney Court, Buckinghamshire: detail of woodwork.

medieval manor houses were unfortified and had to rely on their moats and gatehouses to repel unwelcome callers.

The ideal of the unfortified medieval manor house is to be found at Great Chalfield, where the Great Hall, lit by high windows, is in the centre of the entrance front, defined by its porch, and is flanked by two-storeyed wings on either side. 'The whole arrangement', as Mark Girouard has pointed out, 'is exactly suited to the standing of its builder, an officer from a great household who had set up as a landed gentleman. It is both dignified and sensible: it exudes prosperous hospitality.' In some late-medieval manor houses, such as Cotehele and Ightham Mote, the Great Hall is placed on one side of a courtyard, with chambers and service rooms occupying the other ranges. At Stanton Harcourt, the spectacular surviving kitchen is in a detached structure. Other outstanding examples of this late-medieval period include Ockwells and Cothay. Both were highly praised by Christopher Hussey of *Country Life*, whose articles did so much to open 20th-century eyes to the English architectural heritage – much as the modern-day champion of the manor house at *Country Life*, Jeremy Musson, is doing in the 21st century.

INTRODUCTION

The early Tudor age ushered in the Renaissance style, whereby brick and terracotta detailing characterized such buildings as East Barsham and Layer Marney. Their splendid gatehouses may evoke a medieval spirit of defence, but they were really built for show. Under the Tudors England gained an internal peace and security such as she had never previously enjoyed; fortification was now a thing of the past. While the more prosperous Tudor landowners erected 'prodigy' palaces of Renaissance splendour, the lesser gentry – particularly after the Dissolution of the Monasteries opened up a new territorial opportunity – put up more modest manor houses. None the less, the Elizabethan and Jacobean squires did not stint themselves on comfort and decoration – as evidenced by the sumptuous wood carving and elaborate plasterwork illustrated at such places as Wolfeton, Sandford Orcas, Stockton, Levens, Herringston and Chastleton.

In the 17th century – though as Eyam in Derbyshire shows, as late as the 1670s the lesser gentry continued to build in the old-fashioned manorial style in the more remote parts – the Classical 'double pile' arrangement (with the rooms arranged in a compact block two rooms deep) gradually became the preferred plan for smaller country houses. The late-Stuart Classical façades of Whitmore, Honington and Welford are examples of this handsome 'dolls' house' appearance.

By the 18th century, however, Englishness held less appeal. 'The great Palladian houses of the eighteenth century are in England,' as Vita Sackville-West pithily put it, 'they are not of England...'. In many cases the squirearchical owners of the manor houses either altered their ancestral homes out of all recognition or moved to something grander; the old family seat would often degenerate into dereliction or descend to the status of tenant farmhouse. And so the Old Manor House, like the Sleeping Beauty, fell into a deep slumber.

Eventually, in the late 19th and early 20th centuries, its romance was rediscovered by antiquarians, Arts & Crafts enthusiasts (as at Owlpen) or recently impoverished aristocrats glad to escape from expensive grandeur to something much more snug and cosy. The stories of how the manor houses were lovingly and carefully restored is given as much, if not more, attention in the pages that follow as the original construction. Similarly, the families that created, or recreated, these gems are accorded at least equal status with the craftsmanship and building materials. As Reginald Bosworth-Smith averred, the character of manor houses depends upon these families 'handing on from the Middle Ages the quiet continuity of English country life and of English history'.

It is this 'quiet continuity' that strikes one most when savouring the special flavour and haunting beauty of English manor houses. In several instances the places featured have passed by inheritance since the Middle Ages. The tenacity and commitment of their owners still *in situ* are beyond praise. Yet among the newer owners, not least the National Trust (represented here by Ightham Mote, Great Chalfield, Cotehele and Chastleton), the enthusiasm and sympathy for old manor houses is now so palpable that you cannot fail to rejoice in the prospects for their preservation.

Whitmore Hall, Staffordshire: Staircase Hall.

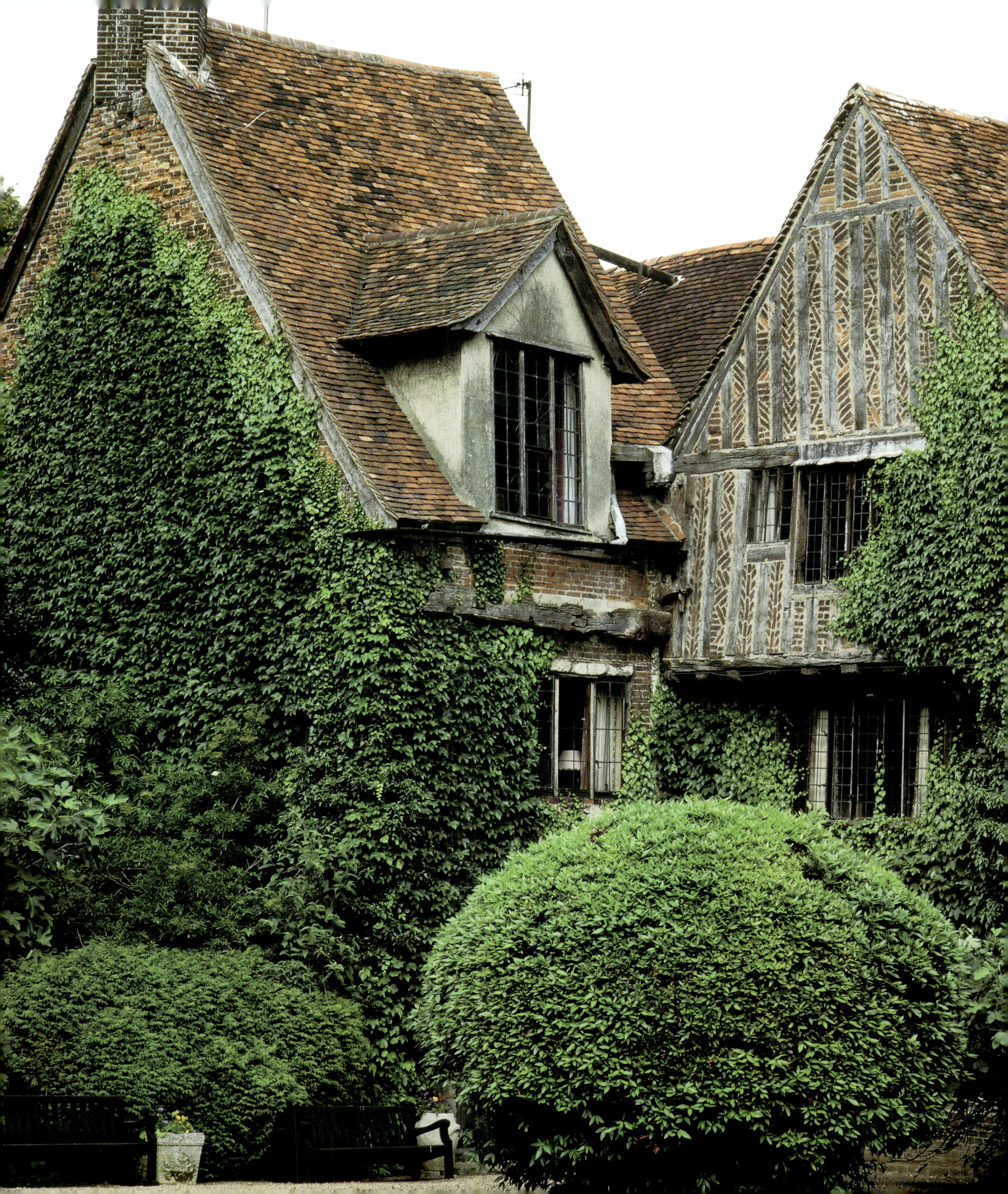

1

BEELEIGH ABBEY

ESSEX

THERE could be no more picturesque place to begin this tour of English Manor Houses than Beeleigh Abbey, tucked away beside the River Chelmer in the Essex Marshes below Maldon. Besides its exceptional beauty, Beeleigh has an instructive history that links medieval monasticism with Tudor expansion, subsequent neglect with early 20th-century restoration. And happily today, at the dawn of the 21st century, Beeleigh is being treated to a sympathetic programme of repair and refurbishment by its present owners, Christopher and Catherine Foyle. Mr Foyle, chairman of Air Foyle and also of W. & G. Foyle Ltd, the celebrated London booksellers, has vivid memories of Beeleigh in its heyday during the long reign of his grandfather, William Foyle, and the Foyles' enthusiasm for recapturing the magic of this enchanted place is refreshingly infectious.

At first glance, as you approach from the south-west, Beeleigh's timber-framed exterior and steeply pitched roof lead one to suppose that this is purely a Tudor manor house. Yet the 'Abbey' in its name is emphatically not a piece of romantic fiction. For the east and south ranges of this lovable agglomeration constitute an important fragment of the Abbey of St Mary and St Nicholas, founded in 1180 by the Premonstratensian Order, better known as the White Canons. Within are some remarkable survivals from the first half of the 13th century, principally the Chapter House and part of the Dormitory, with its Undercroft.

The Undercroft, latterly used as a sitting room, would originally have been the monks' warming house or Calefactory – the only interior part of the Abbey where they were permitted to have a fire during the winter months. An exceptionally healthy order, the White Canons laid particular stress on working in the fields with their hands. Fortunately the fireplace itself is a generous affair, with a wide segmental arch and spandrels panelled with quatrefoils, shields, flowers and so forth. Above is a frieze carved with flowers and half a dozen angels

PRECEDING PAGES 'A picturesque delight': the Tudor west wing of Beeleigh Abbey.

LEFT The Calefactory or Undercroft, with its columns of Purbeck marble and elaborately decorated fireplace.

holding musical instruments. All this elaborate decoration is difficult to explain. One suggestion is that it may be a fragment from the canopy of a niche-tomb in the demolished church – possibly of the Abbey's so-called 'patron', Henry Bourchier, Earl of Essex, who laid claim to Beeleigh after the Dissolution of the Monasteries in 1536. However, Christopher Hussey of *Country Life* considered that the absence of any armorial bearings or symbols renders this unlikely. The way the masonry has been assembled suggested to Hussey that the decoration may have been installed 'at a later date'.

The Undercroft is divided longitudinally by a line of columns of Purbeck marble. The windows, though, are much later than the 13th-century period of the interior. Probably they were the 'new windows' that Bishop Redman, the annual visitor of the English monasteries of the White Canons, is recorded as having admired in 1499–1500. The Bishop had previously been concerned that the Abbey was floundering in debt (£100 was the figure mentioned), but shrewd administration by Thomas Skarlett had enabled the balance to be restored. The new windows may have been installed as a thank-offering.

Whereas the Undercroft is a well-preserved gem for medievalists, the Chapter House is an even more significant survival, since it would have been slightly earlier in date – doubtless following on closely from the original church built by the White Canons – and in style, as Sir Nikolaus Pevsner noted in his *Essex* volume for *The Buildings of England* series, 'more elaborate and elegant'. Its vaulted hall has three Purbeck marble piers of octagonal section. The ribs have deeply undercut filleted roll-moulding. Latterly, the Chapter House has been used by the Foyle family as a private chapel for weddings and christenings, as well as for occasional Sunday services in the summer – when the sound of hymns floating across the lawn on the evening air must be an evocative reminder of Beeleigh's religious origins.

RIGHT A view of the east front, with the Chapter House (now used by the Foyle family as a chapel) on the right, and the Calefactory on the left.

ABOVE Canine security: a labrador guards the door to the Calefactory.

RIGHT A bedroom in the Tudor wing, with its bulbous bed said to have been made for James I of England and VI of Scotland. The carved head and torso of the 'Wisest Fool in Christendom' certainly add a powerful presence.

These were brutally cast aside in Henry VIII's Dissolution of the Monasteries. Lord Essex, who had earlier curried favour with the erratic monarch by writing to the Pope in favour of Henry's divorce from Catherine of Aragon and had acted as 'Carver' at the coronation of Anne Boleyn, pleaded with the King's henchman, Thomas Cromwell, that he might purchase Beeleigh Abbey. After all, he pointed out, it was entirely within his own lands. By now deaf ('except a man speak very loud even in my ear I may not hear a whit', he told Cromwell) and decrepit (a contemporary *Report on the English Nobility* described him as 'an old man, of little wit and less experience, without power'), Lord Essex was cast aside in favour of the ambitious Sir John Gate, or Gates, one of the most active agents of the Dissolution. As the *Dictionary of National*

BEELEIGH ABBEY

Biography notes, Gate 'received valuable grants in Essex for confidential services'.

At Beeleigh Gate promptly demolished the Abbey and the portions of the precincts that he did not require for his own use. The surviving parts were linked together in what Alec Clifton-Taylor described as 'a characteristic example of building in puddingstone rubble'. However rough and ready the transition from monastery to manor house, the consequence moved even the usually dry Pevsner to hail Beeleigh as 'a picturesque delight'.

Like so many manor houses, Beeleigh subsequently fell on bad days, with a constantly changing roster of dim owners. In 1778 it was bought by a local landowner, Abraham Shuttleworth, who settled it on his daughter, Frances Baker. Beeleigh remained in the Baker family for the next century or so, but it was described as having fallen into a desperate condition by the time it was leased in 1912 to Captain F.W. Grantham, who consulted the architect Basil Ionides concerning its restoration. Vital repair work was carried out, and then continued by Mrs R.E. Thomas, who finally bought Beeleigh from the Bakers in 1920.

William Foyle (1885–1963), the bookseller from a long-established West Country family, acquired the Abbey in the 1940s and housed his great collection of old books in the surviving part of the original Dormitory, above the Undercroft. This irresistible interior, now the Library, remains Beeleigh's chief glory, with its wonderful waggon-roof of chestnut, double collar-beams and trussed rafters supported by arched braces. Thanks to Christopher and Catherine Foyle, Beeleigh is currently being restored to the antiquarian atmosphere of his grandfather's day, and among their projects is a revised history of the Abbey – complete with fresh investigation of such traditional tales as the treasure-hunt supposedly led by the Elizabethan magician John Dee and the secret tunnel said to have led to Maldon. Whatever transpires, Beeleigh Abbey seems set fair to regain its prime position among the loveliest houses in England.

The original monks' dormitory, now the Library, with its waggon-roof of chestnut, double collar-beams and trussed rafters supported by arched braces.

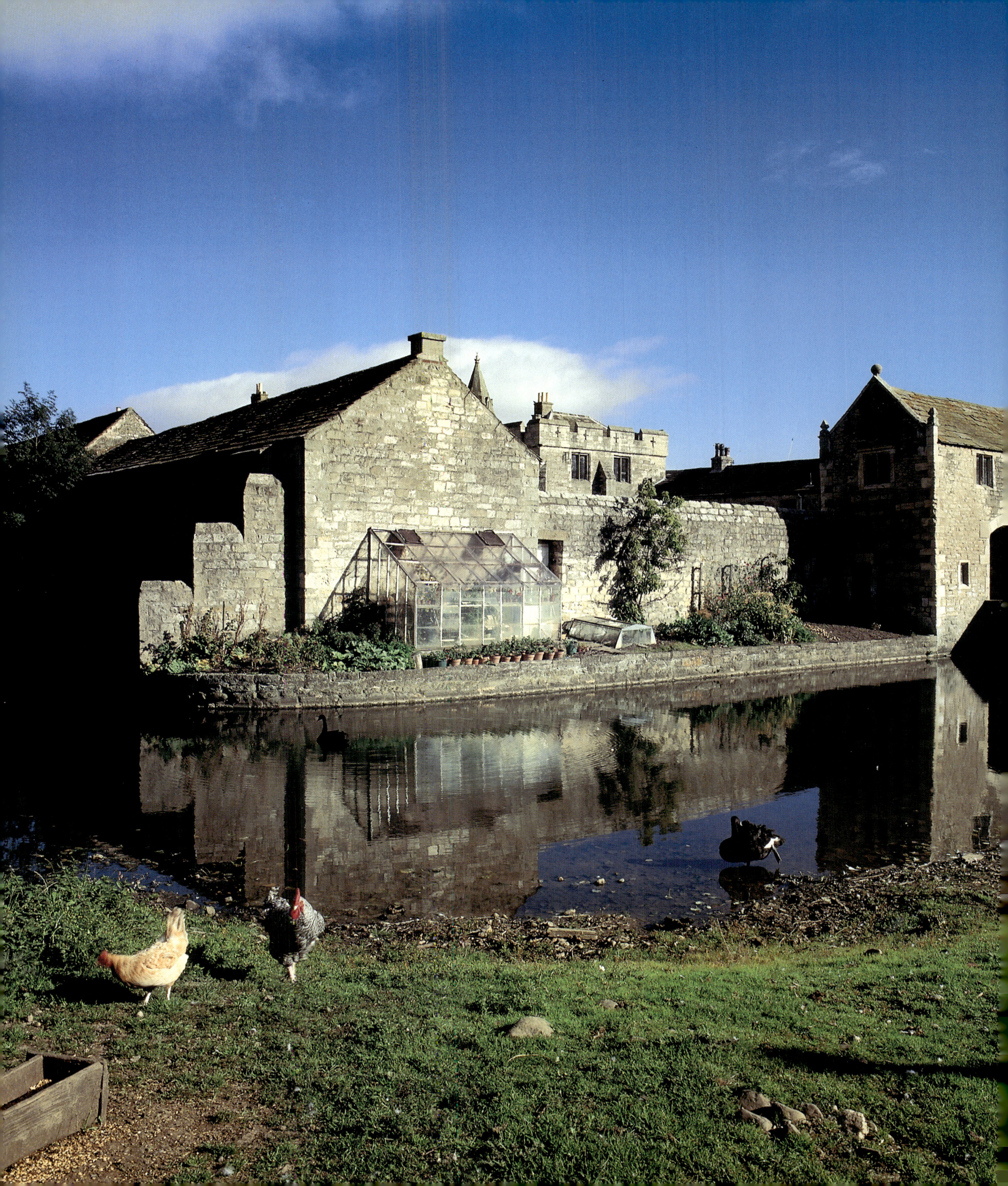

2

MARKENFIELD HALL

YORKSHIRE

ROMANCE and charm, which the moated Markenfield, hidden away among meadows and cornfields south of Ripon, has in abundance, often contain a streak of melancholy and this potently feudal place has no shortage of that either. For it was here in 1569 that, in support of the 'Old Faith', the headstrong young Catholic squire Thomas Markenfield (described by a contemporary as 'rash, daring and too wildely yonge') mustered a local army in the courtyard together with his neighbour, Richard Norton of Norton Conyers (*qv*). Hundreds of Yorkshire warriors gathered under the Norton ensign of the Five Wounds of Christ with the motto 'God Us Ayde'.

This was to be the ill-fated Rising of the North against Queen Elizabeth I, following on from the equally vain, if valiant, 'Pilgrimage of Grace' (for which Thomas's father had been attainted) against the devastation caused by Henry VIII's Dissolution of the Monasteries. After taking the sacrament in Ripon Minster – where young Thomas's ancestor and namesake, a prominent supporter of Henry Bolingbroke against Richard II, is buried in a splendid tomb – the rebels headed south on their mission to replace Elizabeth on the throne with Mary Queen of Scots. Inevitably, it all ended in disaster.

Thomas Markenfield fled abroad. The old family seat was abandoned, eventually being granted to Queen Elizabeth's Lord Chancellor, Lord Ellesmere (who rebuilt the gatehouse). Several of the Nortons went to the scaffold, though Richard's son, Edmund Norton, who had declined to join the rising, escaped the recriminations. And in the 18th century it was his descendant, Fletcher Norton, a successful lawyer known as 'Sir Bullface Doublefees' in his days as Attorney-General, who rescued Markenfield – then long since a farmhouse – from neglect and ruin. 'Sir Bullface', who had taken silk in 1754, entered Parliament two years later as a Whig but had a tendency to cross the floor of the Commons on occasion. He was the subject of the satirical verse:

Careless of censure and no fool to fame,
Firm in his double post and double fees,
Sir Fletcher, standing without fear or shame,
Pockets the cash and lets them laugh that please.

'Sir Bullface' went on to become Speaker of the House of Commons before being created a peer as Lord Grantley in 1782. Although he and his successors were based at Grantley nearby, Markenfield was lovingly restored and after the 7th Lord Grantley's marriage in 1955 to Lady Deirdre Hare, eldest daughter of the 5th Earl of Listowel, it once more became a family home. The 7th Lord Grantley died in 1995, but his widow – whose features are immortalized in one of the decorative bosses that adorn the interior – continues to open Markenfield to interested groups by appointment.

Markenfield's importance as an example of a completely moated English manor house can hardly be overstated. As Christopher Hussey pointed out in *Country Life*, it is a 'key-type in the evolution of the English house'. With its moat and gatehouse, approached through spacious farm buildings, Markenfield gives us an irresistible picture of what so many manor houses, since altered out of all recognition or simply vanished, must have been like 500 or 600 years ago. Here, you feel, is the quintessence of a feudal knight's home in Chaucerian England.

In the *Domesday* survey, Markenfield was recorded as in the occupation of one 'Grim' (presumably a Viking), but its building history begins in the early

PRECEDING PAGES View across the moat at Markenfield to the 16th-century Gatehouse (rebuilt by Lord Ellesmere).

ABOVE Modern boss of Lady Grantley, Markenfield's present châtelaine.

BELOW Another view of the house and its tranquil moat.

– 20 –

14th century when John de Markenfield, a powerful figure in the reign of Edward II who rose to be Chancellor of the Exchequer, was granted a 'licence to crenellate' (or fortify, in other words) in 1310. The house takes the form of a letter 'L'. Originally it would have consisted of two storeys only, but the south wing was subsequently altered and the first floor divided so as to form a third storey.

Hussey considered that the insertion of this floor may have occurred during the time of Sir Ninian Markenfield, who is mentioned in the *Ballad of Flodden* as having worn an 'armour cote of cunynge work' in Henry Clifford's Yorkshire contingent in the decisive victory over the Scots in 1513. Or the alterations might even have been during the Wars of the Roses when the martial Markenfields were also to the fore.

Appropriately enough, the entire house is embattled. The ground floor is divided into a number of rooms, mostly vaulted. At some point the Under-

ABOVE Detail of decorative boss.

RIGHT Vaulted view from the Great Hall to the Chapel.

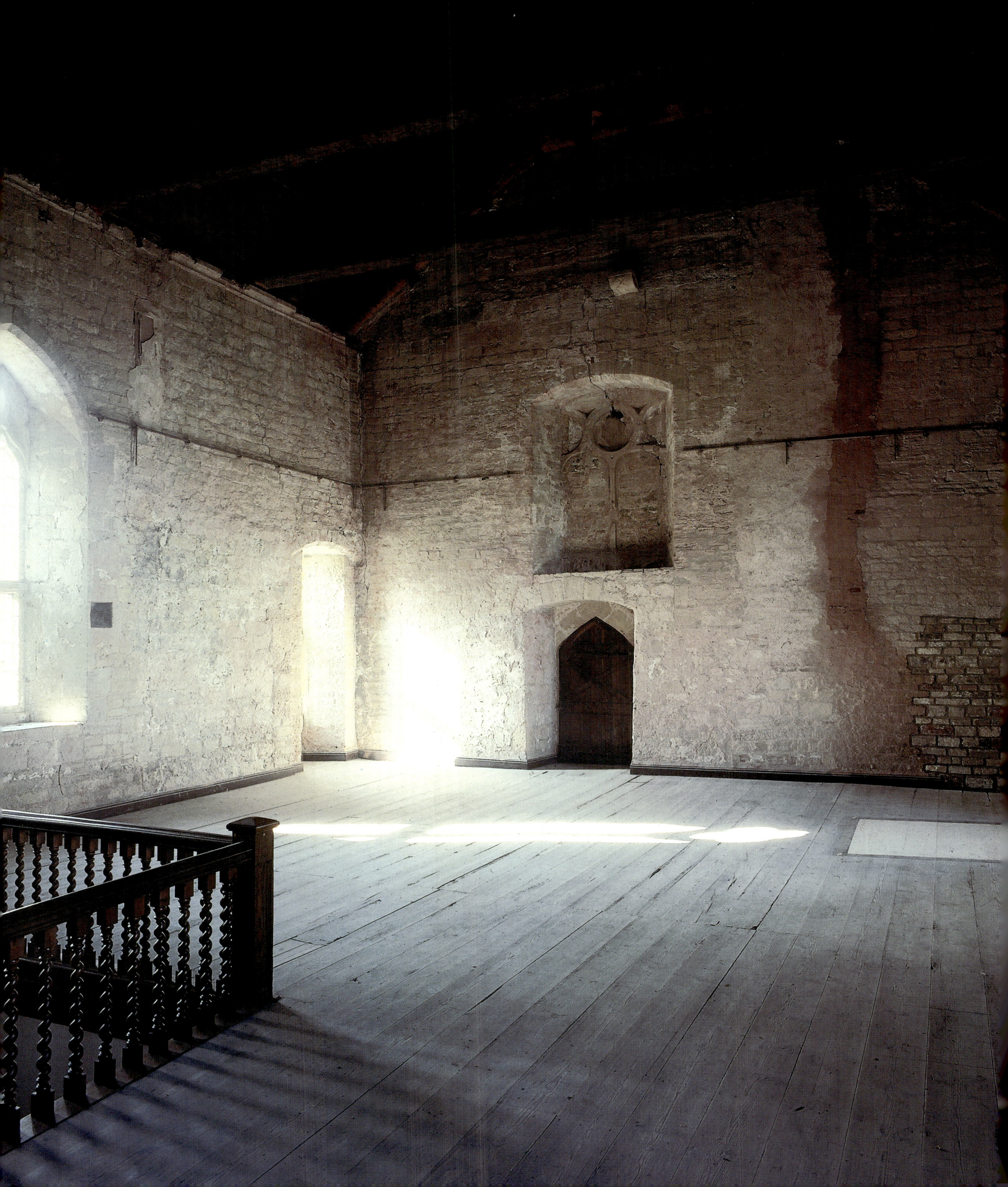

croft must have been converted into a kitchen. The greater proportion of the north wing is occupied by the Great Hall, a noble apartment some 40 feet in length with traceried windows, which look as if they go back to the original date of the licence to crenellate. There is an even more beautiful traceried east window in the Chapel, which also has a piscina, or holy water stoup, bearing the Markenfield family's coat of arms, featuring three bezants.

More heraldry is on display in the courtyard, which is full of character and also contains a 14th-century doorway. The strong agricultural flavour of the myriad structures beyond the moat only adds to Markenfield's extraordinary atmosphere of timelessness. They are solid, handsome and completely in keeping, for the secret of the place's survival is that it has always been a working farm.

That it has been so comprehensively and sympathetically restored yet so sensitively preserved over the last two-and-a-half centuries reflects great credit on the Nortons, Lords Grantley, and, in particular, on their 19th-century architect, J.R. Walbran, whose work, as Hussey noted, was 'very conscientious for that date'. Formerly the haunt of bats and owls, this atmospheric medieval manor house still sits proudly in its hidden landscape, not only, as William Hobden put it in his eloquent guide *The Story of Markenfield* (1971), as 'a monument to its distinguished builders but to a tragic story of bitter religious and political controversy – of bygone struggles, broken monasteries and sad and broken promises'.

LEFT One of the most magnificent medieval interiors in England: the Great Hall, 40 feet long, with traceried windows.

BELOW The Kitchen underneath the Great Hall.

ABOVE Vaulted study.

LEFT Panelled bedroom, hung with armorial banners.

RIGHT A view of the courtyard, showing the Great Hall building in the centre. The position of the original outside staircase to the Great Hall on the first floor is indicated by the chevron to the left of the two traceried windows.

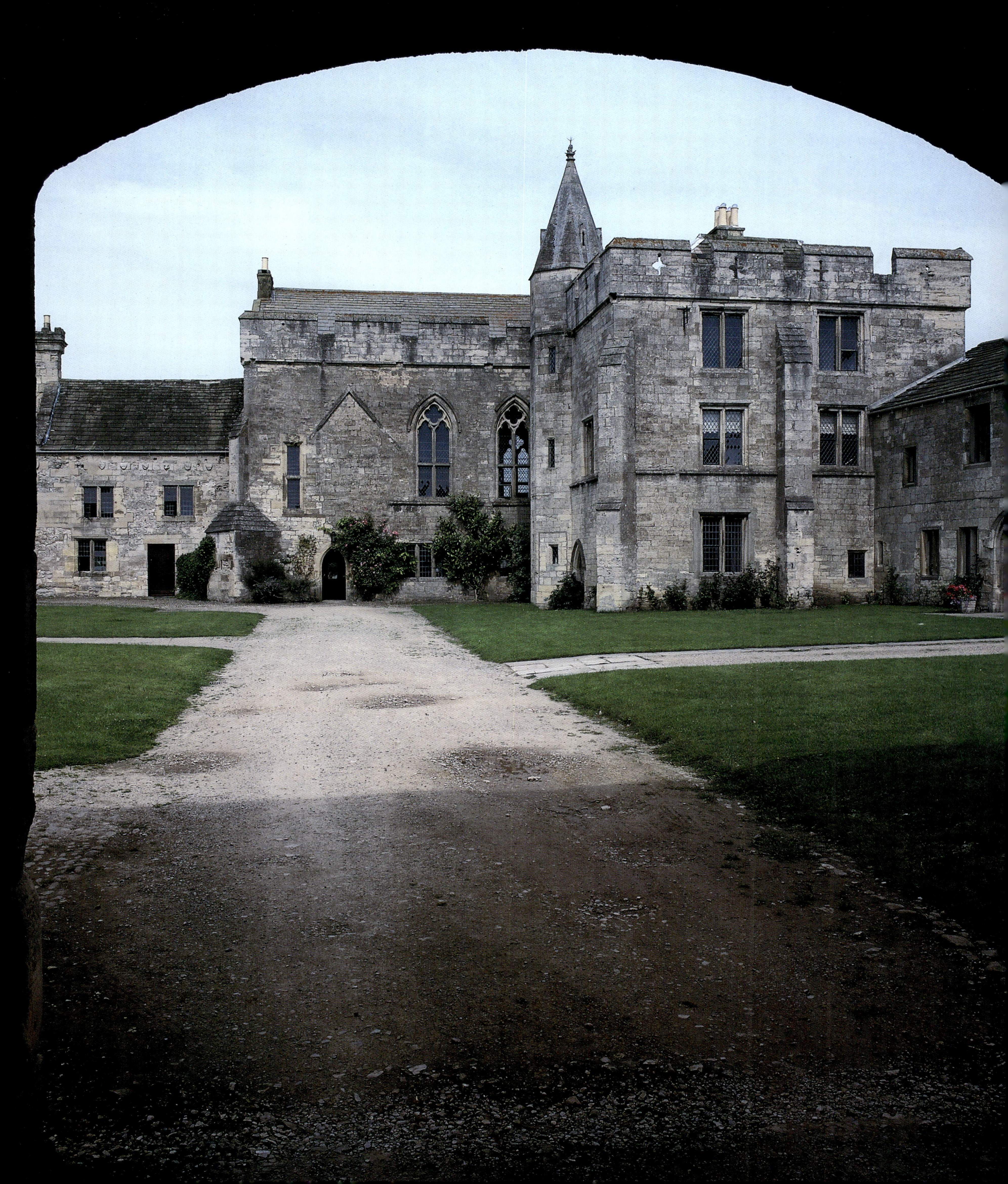

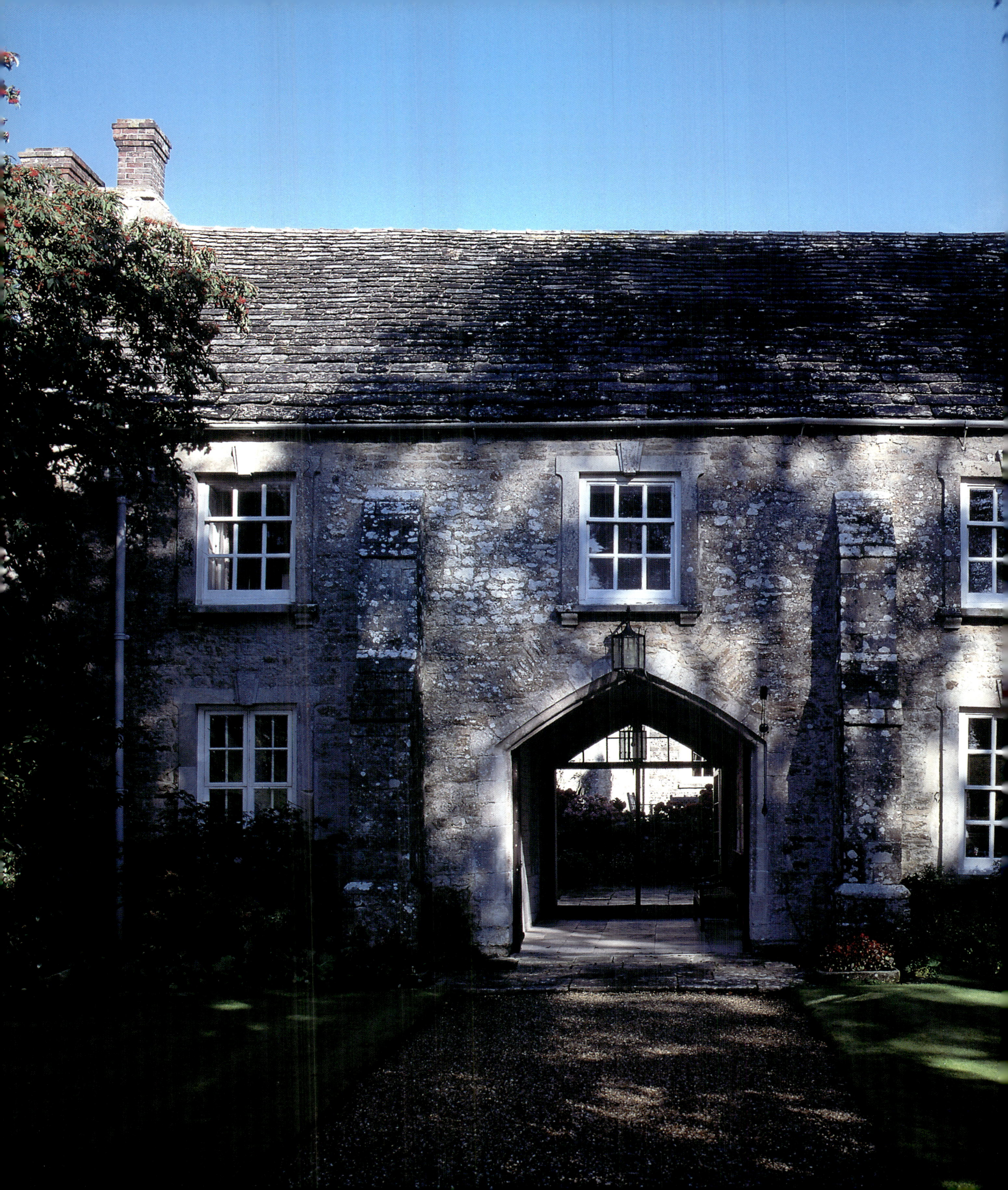

3

BINGHAM'S MELCOMBE

DORSET

NOBODY better captured the extraordinary quality of Dorset manor houses than Thomas Hardy, and the poet's spirit lives on at Bingham's Melcombe, where the west window of the church commemorates the Reverend C.W. Bingham, otherwise 'Parson Tringham' in *Tess of the d'Urbervilles*. The Parson, in real life, was a Victorian scholar who helped revise Hutchins's magisterial history of Dorset, which duly records how this ancient and now remote estate originally belonged to the de Turberville family (the name romanticized by Hardy). In the 13th century their heiress Lucy married Robert Bingham, in whose family it was to remain until the end of the 19th century.

A 'capital messuage' is mentioned in a document of 1317 and it could well be that the earliest part of the present structure, the Gatehouse, dates from this period. Although now of Georgian appearance with its sashed windows, the arched entrance, pair of buttresses and the gable ends, not to mention the stout thickness of its walls, certainly proclaim medieval provenance. Adjoining the Gatehouse in the southern range of Bingham's Melcombe are the present Kitchen and Dining Room. When repairs were carried out by the present owners, Mr and Mrs John Langham, in 1987, it was discovered that this part was built not later than 1500 (possibly earlier) and that it had originally been a typical 'hall house' with a central hearth open to the rafters, and a small sleeping loft at either end.

In the 16th century the west end of this wing was converted into a great Kitchen, complete with fireplace, while across the courtyard Robert Bingham (who died in 1561) rebuilt the present Great Hall to accommodate the magnificent Tudor oriel. This presumably dates from Mary Tudor's reign, as the original armorial glass includes her coat of arms and that of her husband, Philip of Spain. On the outside of the oriel, forming a delightful feature of the ravishingly picturesque courtyard, is an elaborately carved panel of the Bingham arms.

PRECEDING PAGES The old Gatehouse at Bingham's Melcombe; the sash windows are an 18th-century addition.

ABOVE and RIGHT Two views of the Hall, with its oriel.

On the whole, the Binghams of Bingham's Melcombe were a quiet, stay-at-home lot – keeping a low profile was always the secret of squirearchical survival. Yet among Robert's eight sons, two, in particular, made their mark in Ireland. Sir Richard Bingham became Governor of Connaught and Marshal of Ireland before being buried in Westminster Abbey, and Sir George Bingham was the ancestor of the line known to history as the Earls of Lucan.

The manor house continued to remain a peaceful haven and to expand steadily, with a carved ornament here and a gable or two there. Yet even the Binghams could not avoid becoming caught up in the Civil War. In spite of its remoteness, Bingham's Melcombe was chosen as the headquarters of the local Parliamentary forces, and Colonel John Bingham commanded the last siege of Corfe Castle. The Colonel was said to have admired the courage of his gallant foe, Dame Mary Bankes, and to have succeeded in eventually saving the lives of some 140 souls within the blighted hilltop fortress.

The Colonel's nephew and successor at Bingham's Melcombe, Richard Bingham, married Philadelphia Potenger, daughter of the Headmaster of Winchester. To accommodate her 13 children, the practical Philadelphia undertook a thorough modernization of the old manor house in the Rococo style of about 1720, when an upper floor was inserted in the Great Hall, and sash windows replaced the old mullions in various parts of the building. Fortunately the exuberant Tudor plasterwork in the Dining Room, traditionally attributed to a travelling band of Italians, was left unchanged by the improving Philadelphia.

BINGHAM'S MELCOMBE

When the Binghams finally departed in 1895, Reginald Bosworth-Smith, polymath, Oxford don and Harrow schoolmaster, fell in love with this 'very dream in stone' and bought it. 'Everything about it is old world,' he wrote. 'The peace of centuries seems to be brooding over it. They have passed over it with their myriad changes and chances, with their ceaseless ebb and flow, with the racket and the turmoil of all their half-realized hopes and fears, leaving it unchanged – one would almost say unchangeable.'

Happily Mr Bosworth-Smith's successors have echoed his sentiments, not least his daughter, Lady Grogan, who lived on here until 1947. Next, the 3rd Lord Southborough, managing director of Shell, carried out an eminently practical modernization of the manor house, involving the installation of proper sanitation, electricity and mains water. On the north side of the house he also added the notable feature of the original late Tudor (1583) porch from Tyneham, seat of the Bond family, partially demolished when their estate was requisitioned by the military during the Second World War.

This porch, in the form of a temple, now houses, among other memorials, the Queen's Awards for Industry won by Mr Langham's companies. There

ABOVE A characteristic corner of Bingham's Melcombe, with its moulded stonework and stout door.

LEFT View looking back from under the Purbeck stone archway that divides the oriel from the Hall.

are further fascinating mementoes of nautical and shipbuilding life from nearby Portland arranged in the Museum housed in the old guardroom of the Gatehouse. Since they took on Bingham's Melcombe, much of the Langhams' considerable energies have been concentrated on restoring the Tudor gardens, with their elephantine yew hedges. The many pretty features include a bowling green, weirs and bridges and a 17th-century circular dovecote.

Lord David Cecil, who knew the house in several incarnations, considered the gardens better-kept than he had ever seen them before when he revisited Bingham's Melcombe in the early 1980s. As Lord David memorably observed in *Some Dorset Country Houses* (1985), the place 'casts a spell'. Its compelling spirit is 'fabulous and magical', inducing a state of mind in which he was disposed to believe anything that appealed to his imagination. Thus, there is an old tradition that sometimes at midnight the stone eagles on the late-18th-century gateposts flanking the entrance to this enchanted demesne are supposed to spread their wings and fly away to refresh themselves by bathing in a stream beyond the church. Many visitors will echo Lord David's conclusion: 'When I am under the place's influence, this seems to me not wholly incredible.'

ABOVE A corridor indicates the thickness of the walls of the original medieval manor house.

RIGHT The north side of the courtyard, with the porch and, to the left, the most delightful feature of Bingham's Melcombe, the oriel adorned with the Bingham coat of arms.

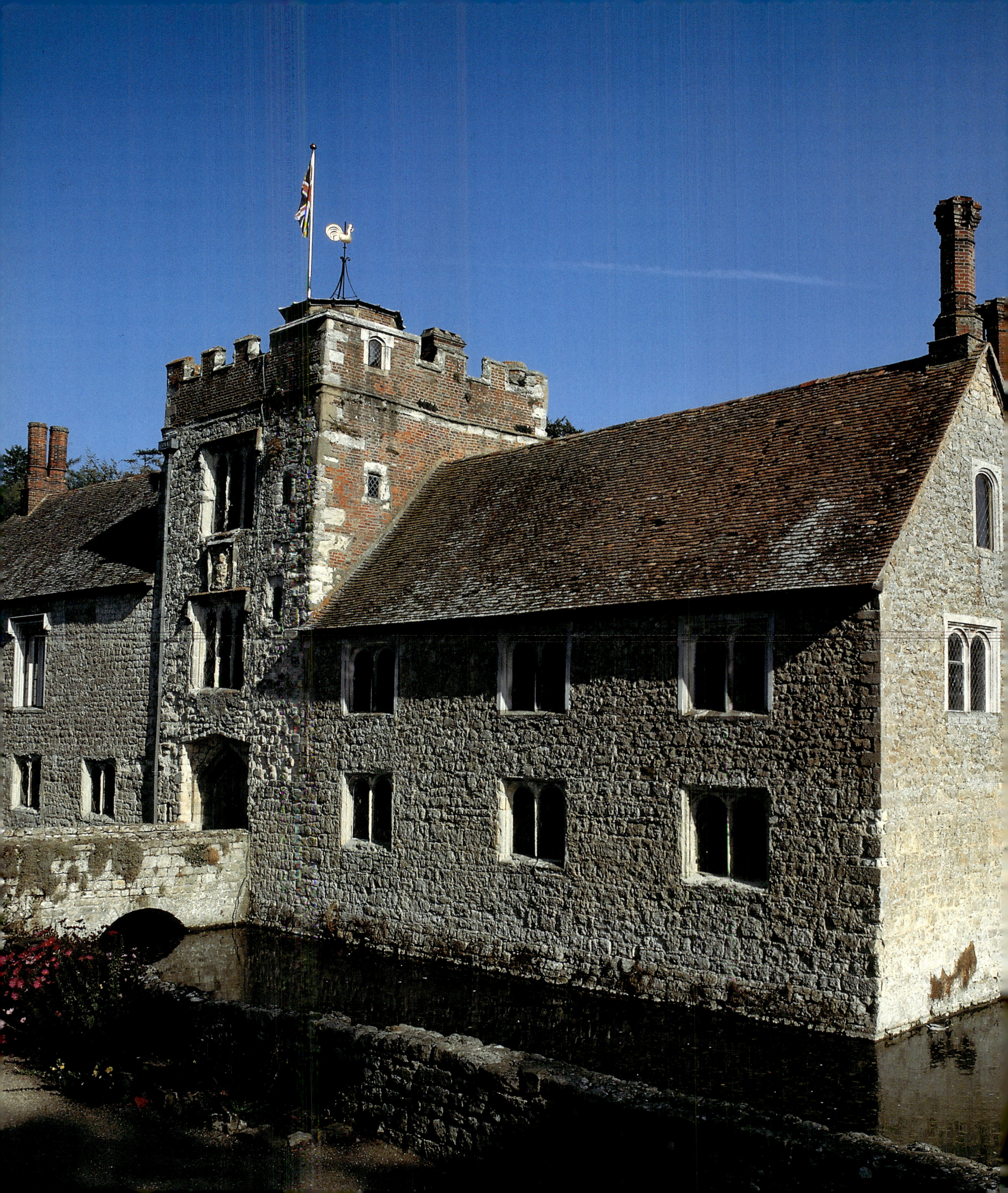

4

IGHTHAM MOTE

KENT

Hidden away in the still rural depths of the Kentish Weald, Ightham Mote is everyone's ideal of a half-timbered moated manor house and is now receiving a sympathetic restoration by its owners, the National Trust. Yet only half a century ago its prospects, even its very survival, were in doubt. Following its sale by the Colyer-Fergusson family in 1951, there was the threat that Ightham Mote might be demolished for the sake of the lead on its roofs.

To their eternal credit, a group of local businessmen stepped in to save the house in the hope that a more permanent solution could be found. For two years Ightham Mote stood empty as minimal repairs were undertaken to keep it waterproof. Fortunately, Charles Henry Robinson of Portland, Maine, a prosperous North American stationer, spotted one of the sale advertisements in a back number of *Country Life*: it struck a strong romantic chord. For many years ago he had fallen in love with this archetypal English idyll when he saw a picture of 'the Mote' (as it has been known since the 14th century) in the window of a London art dealer's shop. Then, by further happy chance, he had unexpectedly come upon it during a bicycling tour of southern England and recognized it as his dream house.

On a wild surmise, after seeing the *Country Life* advertisement, Robinson headed for England and made an offer to buy the Mote. Returning home on the *Queen Mary*, however, he began to have doubts, and wrote a letter withdrawing the offer. It is gratifying to report that the letter was never posted. Robinson duly bought and restored the house, and furnished the interior with 17th-century pieces that he had collected over the years. Upon his death in 1985 he bequeathed the property to the National Trust, who launched a national appeal to secure the future of the Mote. By 2000 this had raised £3 million.

Although it might be reasonable to assume that the Mote derives its name from an ancient spelling of 'moat', it is more likely to refer to 'moot',

PRECEDING PAGES A view of Ightham Mote from the south-west. The Gatehouse is to the left, the south front to the right. The moat runs all round the house, and is crossed by three bridges – one of which was probably a drawbridge leading to the main entrance.

LEFT Jacobean staircase, credited to Sir William Selby, who inherited the Mote in 1612. It was subsequently altered to fit its present position.

OPPOSITE The Great Hall, with its original timber roof of about 1340 and five-light Perpendicular window erected by Richard Haut in the 1480s. The heraldic stained glass was added by Sir Richard Clement in tribute to Henry VIII. The heraldic frieze and the panelling were designed by Norman Shaw and carved by James Forsyth for the Selbys in the 1870s.

BELOW The crest of the Selbys, a Saracen's head, carved on the newel post of the staircase.

or the Anglo-Saxon 'mot', meaning a meeting place where a council is held. The building history has been scientifically established by dendrochronology to date from the period 1330–42 when a widow, Isolde Inge (later Seyntpere, or St Pere), is on record as having owned the manor. Either this lady or one of her husbands presumably built the Great Hall and its solars, as well as the Old Chapel and Kitchen.

Later in the 14th century the Mote became the home of Sir Thomas Cawne, MP, and subsequently it descended to the Haut family, whose profile became dangerously high during the Wars of the Roses. Richard Haut of Ightham was comptroller of the household to the young Prince of Wales, one of the 'Princes in the Tower', murdered in 1483. He had his estates confiscated when Richard III crushed the Duke of Buckingham's rebellion, but they were returned after Richard was routed at Bosworth Field.

The north range of the house would seem to date from Richard's ownership in the 1470s, whereas the entrance wing and the south wing are probably from the period when his son, Edward Haut, was in residence – from 1487 to 1519. The cottages that stand outside the moat were also built by the Hauts, who, among other improvements, modernized the service area south of the Great Hall. Presumably all this building work over-extended the Hauts' fortunes, for by 1518 Edward was obliged to mortgage the house and soon afterwards

– 34 –

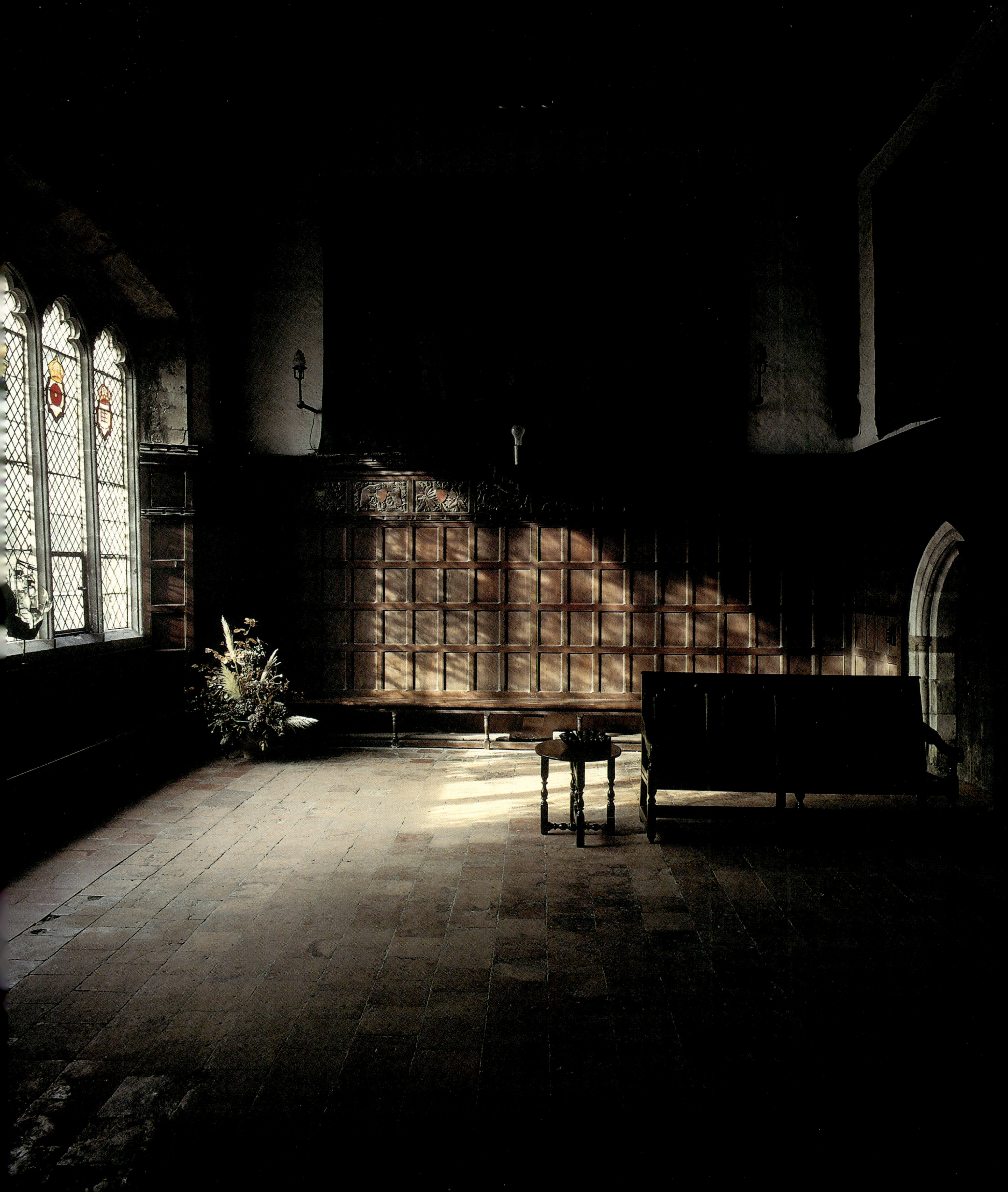

it became the property of Sir Richard Clement, a devoted courtier of the Tudors who adorned the interior with the emblems of Henry VIII and his first Queen, Catherine of Aragon. The roof of the New Chapel, for instance, is a riot of Tudor roses and Aragon pomegranates, and the Great Hall boasts brilliant heraldic tributes in stained glass to Clement's royal master and mistress.

Having had a series of fairly brief ownerships, Ightham Mote was acquired in 1585 for £4,000 by Sir William Selby, described on his memorial in Ightham Church as a 'discreet and valiant soldier', whose family remained here for 300 years. His nephew and namesake, who has a place in history for delivering the keys of Berwick to James VI of Scotland as he travelled south to claim the English throne (as James I), succeeded to Ightham in 1612 and is also commemorated in the church, albeit in somewhat equivocal terms:

> His few failings (if any failings he had), when mingled with the
> dazzling splendour of his divine virtues and accomplishments,
> appear as small atoms in the air….

ABOVE and RIGHT Two of the absurdly grotesque crouching corbel figures who support the arches of the roof in the Great Hall.

LEFT Detail of the painted barrel-vaulted roof in the New Chapel, dating back to the early 16th century. As in the Great Hall, Sir Richard Clement was paying tribute to Henry VIII and his marriage to Catherine of Aragon. The now faded decoration includes allusions to the pomegranate of Aragon, the York, Lancaster and Tudor roses, the French fleur-de-lys and the Beaufort portcullis, as well as the quivers of arrows for Aragon and the castles of Castile.

The epitaph for his widow, Dorothy ('Dorcas'), a legendary needle-woman, is even more eccentric:

> She was a Dorcas
> Whose curious Needle turned th' abused Stage
> Of this leud World into the golden Age...
> In heart a Lydia; and in tongue, a Hanna
> In Zeale a Ruth; in Wedlock, a Susanna.
> Prudently Simple, providently Wary;
> To th' world a Martha: and to Heaven a Mary.

Certainly from the portraits on display in the Great Hall, Dame Dorothy looks a formidable figure. She and her husband were responsible for the Jacobean staircase, with its newel post carved with the family crest of a Saracen's head; for rebuilding the upper storey of the west wing, originally timber-framed, in stone; and for the Jacobean fireplace in the Drawing Room, which bears their arms on the overmantel. In the 18th century subsequent Selbys inserted new windows, including a handsome Venetian number in the Drawing Room.

The changes, though, tended to be easily absorbed into the Mote's seemingly timeless atmosphere. Even Norman Shaw's robust heraldic frieze and panelling of 1872, carved by James Forsyth, now seem an essential part of the character of Ightham's most important interior, the Great Hall, with the arches of its 14th-century roof resting on vividly carved corbels in the form of crouching figures.

After the Selbys came the Colyer-Fergussons, who carried out some much-needed repairs and restoration at the end of the 19th century, including the installation of bathrooms, the re-ordering of the service areas and the rebuilding of the staircase from the courtyard to the Chapel landing. Yet before the arrival of Sir Thomas Colyer-Fergusson, 3rd Bt, in 1889, there was a significant interlude when the colourful General William Jackson Palmer, founder of Colorado Springs, rented the Mote and entertained here such fellow Americans as John Singer Sargent and Henry James – who recorded of Christmas 1887 how 'seventy people were accommodated in the great high-roofed dining hall, with our backs to the Yule log, we carved dozens of roast beefs, turkeys and plum puddings'. Ightham Mote's irresistible appeal to Americans as the epitome of Englishness was to bear joyful fruit a century later.

RIGHT 'Everyone's ideal of a half-timbered moated manor house': the south front of Ightham Mote.

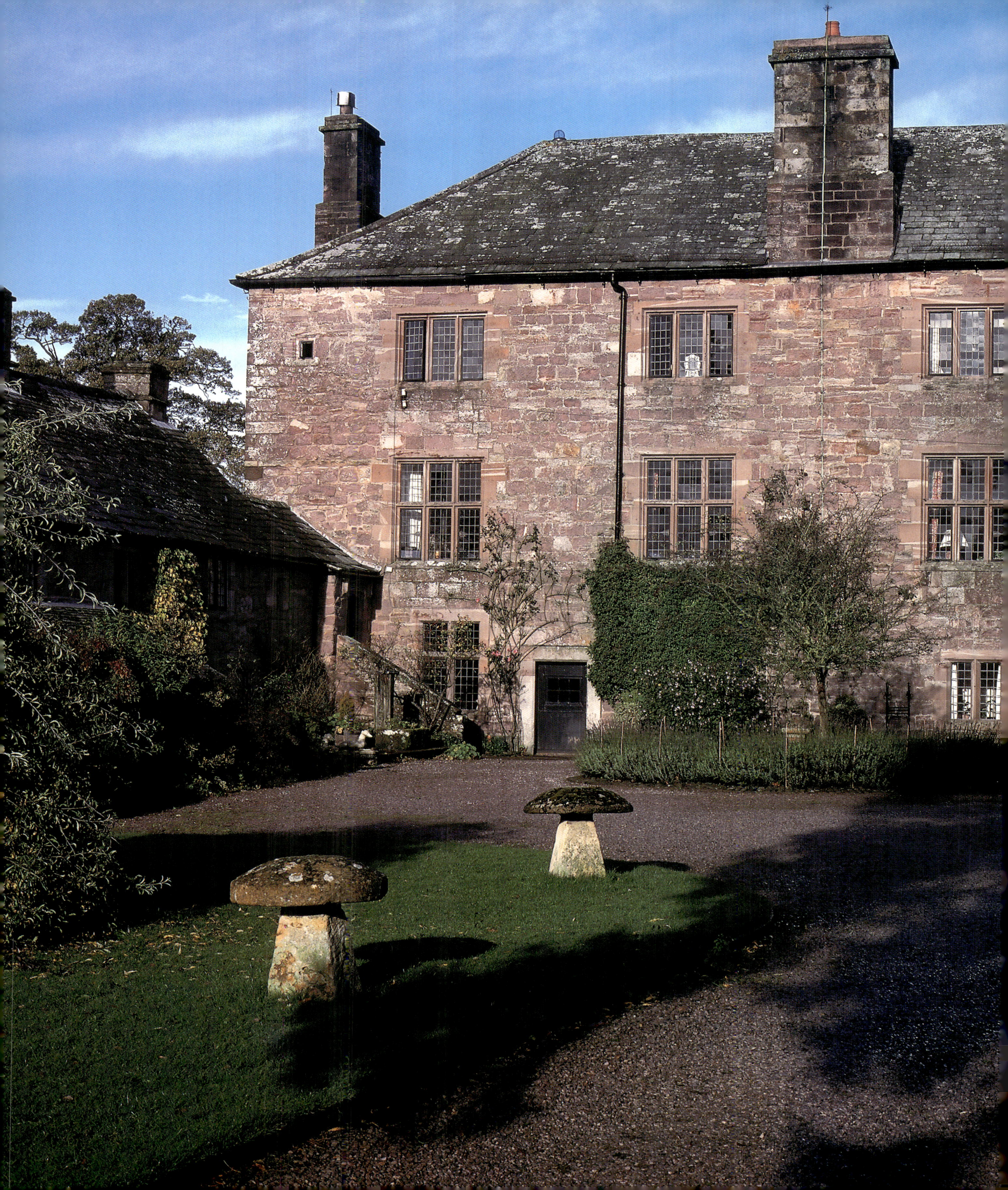

5

JOHNBY HALL

CUMBRIA

THE MANOR house is an essentially English concept and yet, for all its undoubted status as a small dependent manor of the Barony of Greystoke in the north of England (Cumberland to be precise, or rather 'Cumbria', as it is now unfortunately designated), there is something inescapably Scottish about Johnby Hall. The spiral stair, the situation of the principal living rooms on the first floor, and the general atmosphere of the place all combine to suggest that you may have strayed north of the border. Significantly, parish records show that a Scottish mason, Thomas Millar, was working at Johnby in the 1580s.

It was in this decade that Johnby acquired its spiral staircase, and a dated inscription above the entrance door (itself set in a curious egg-timer-shaped framework which looks 17th-century in design) records the pedigree and arms of the Musgrave family, who were responsible for the extension to the east of the original pele tower in 1583. This tower, measuring some 32 feet by 28 feet externally, probably dates from about the middle of the 14th century, following the havoc caused in the Greystoke Barony by the invasion of David Bruce of Scotland in 1346. Consequently the necessity to build stone houses for defence became paramount. Generally, as at Johnby, these comprised a small tower, with a curtain wall (or 'pele') enclosing a courtyard around it.

Originally, long before the building of the tower, the manor of Johnby was owned in the 12th century by William de Johnby, youngest son of Ivo, Baron of Greystoke. William, a troublesome character and jailbird, was memorably summed up by the local historian Nigel Hudleston of Hutton John nearby as 'a damned nuisance'. The tower was presumably built by the de Aubeney family, from whom, through the de Veteriponts and the Stapletons, Johnby descended to the Musgraves.

The Musgraves remained staunch Roman Catholics after the Protestant Reformation and it is recorded that Leonard Musgrave, William's son and successor, maintained a priest at Johnby in the late 16th century. In 1597 the priest, Christopher Robinson, was arrested and executed in barbaric circumstances in Carlisle. A contemporary observer described how the rope broke twice. At the third attempt, when two ropes were employed, Robinson bravely exclaimed: 'By this means I shall be longer a-dying; but it is no matter, I am very willing to suffer all.'

In the early 17th century Leonard's surviving sister-in-law, Winefred Musgrave, was excommunicated three times but she lived on at Johnby ('An Ancient Old Woman') until 1637. This is the date on the west wing, which suggests that this range of the building was intended as a sort of dower house for Winefred and her younger daughter, Grace, when the elder daughter, Mary, married William Wyvell from Yorkshire and came to live at Johnby. The old stable and coach house, adapted from the original dovecote, bears the datestone of 1675, by which time Johnby was owned by the Williams family, who were stewards to the Dukes of Norfolk at Greystoke Castle nearby.

From the Williamses, Johnby descended to the Hasells of Dalemain, another Cumbrian squirearchical dynasty. After the failure of the Jacobite Rebellion of 1745, Edward Hasell decided that the time had come to make Johnby less of a fortress against invading Scots and a builder's contract of 1747 documents how the old battlements and fortifications were to be dismantled and how eight Georgian sash windows were to be installed. From this contract it

PRECEDING PAGES Johnby's entrance front.

ABOVE The inscription above the entrance door recording the Musgraves' extension to the original pele tower in 1583.

BELOW The Great Hall, with its fireplace adorned with wood carvings by Maud Leyborne-Popham.

ABOVE Elegant arches embellish the stout stonework of the spiral staircase in the old tower.

BELOW An indication of the thickness of the walls at this Border stronghold.

would appear that Johnby was then in a ruinous state and it seems safe to assume that the hipped roof we see today was also added at this time. As the present owners, Nicholas and Bethan Howard, point out: 'A visit to the attic shows turrets and spiral staircases summarily "truncated" horizontally, as if with a huge metaphorical cake-slicer.'

Johnby has been owned by the Howard family since 1783, when Charles Howard, 10th Duke of Norfolk, began the great expansion of the Greystoke estate, which was to be continued by his raffish son, 'Jockey', the 11th Duke. 'Jockey' was a crony of the Prince Regent, though his own political views veered towards republicanism – he even named his farms in honour of American revolutionary leaders and their victories. The story goes that he formed a particular friendship with his neighbour, Mr Hudleston of Hutton John, for the reason that when they drank together, the Duke first lost the use of his legs and Hudleston the use of his voice – so that Hudleston could get up and ring the bell for the servant and the Duke, from his chair, could order more wine.

Johnby, only a mile from Greystoke Castle, lay just outside the Duke's great deer-park wall, 10 feet high and 13 miles around. During the 19th century the house fell again into a fairly ruinous state. At one stage the downstairs part of the west wing was occupied by beagle-hounds, and the more habitable parts were occupied by Benson, the estate gamekeeper – recalled as 'a grand old man' in the 1890s by Sir Algar Howard, Garter King of Arms, who was briefly to inherit Johnby after the Second World War.

Like so many old manor houses, Johnby enjoyed a remarkable revival at the turn of the 20th century when Sir Algar's Aunt Maud, previously Mrs Leyborne-Popham of Littlecote, Wiltshire, fell in love with the place and gave it a comprehensive overhaul. The Georgian sash windows were replaced by more sympathetic Elizabethan-style mullions; the fireplace in the Great Hall was rebuilt and adorned with her own talented wood-carvings; and an extraordinary bog-oak fireplace (made from 'the piles of one of the ancient lake-dwellings found in the lake of Neuchâtel in Switzerland') was installed in an upper bedroom. Major improvements were also made to the sanitation and domestic arrangements.

These improvements have been enthusiastically enhanced and embellished by the current owners, who came into possession of the place on their marriage in 1966 when Johnby was handed over by Nicholas Howard's father, Stafford Howard. He, in turn, had been passed the Greystoke property by his brother, Sir Algar, already comfortably seated at Thornbury Castle in Gloucestershire. Since his retirement from Government service, Nicholas Howard and his wife have devoted themselves to making Johnby a lived-in family home once more. When they inherited the house, there was no heating, only primitive plumbing and no furniture. The west wing, though now empty of hounds, was virtually derelict.

The transformation that the Howards have achieved so that the vaulted ground floor is now cosy and convenient, and the upper rooms are full of character and redolent of a long history, is an eloquent tribute to the reverence they feel for this Border stronghold. Johnby, with its potent evocation of northerly spirits, is a most unusual and singularly beguiling place.

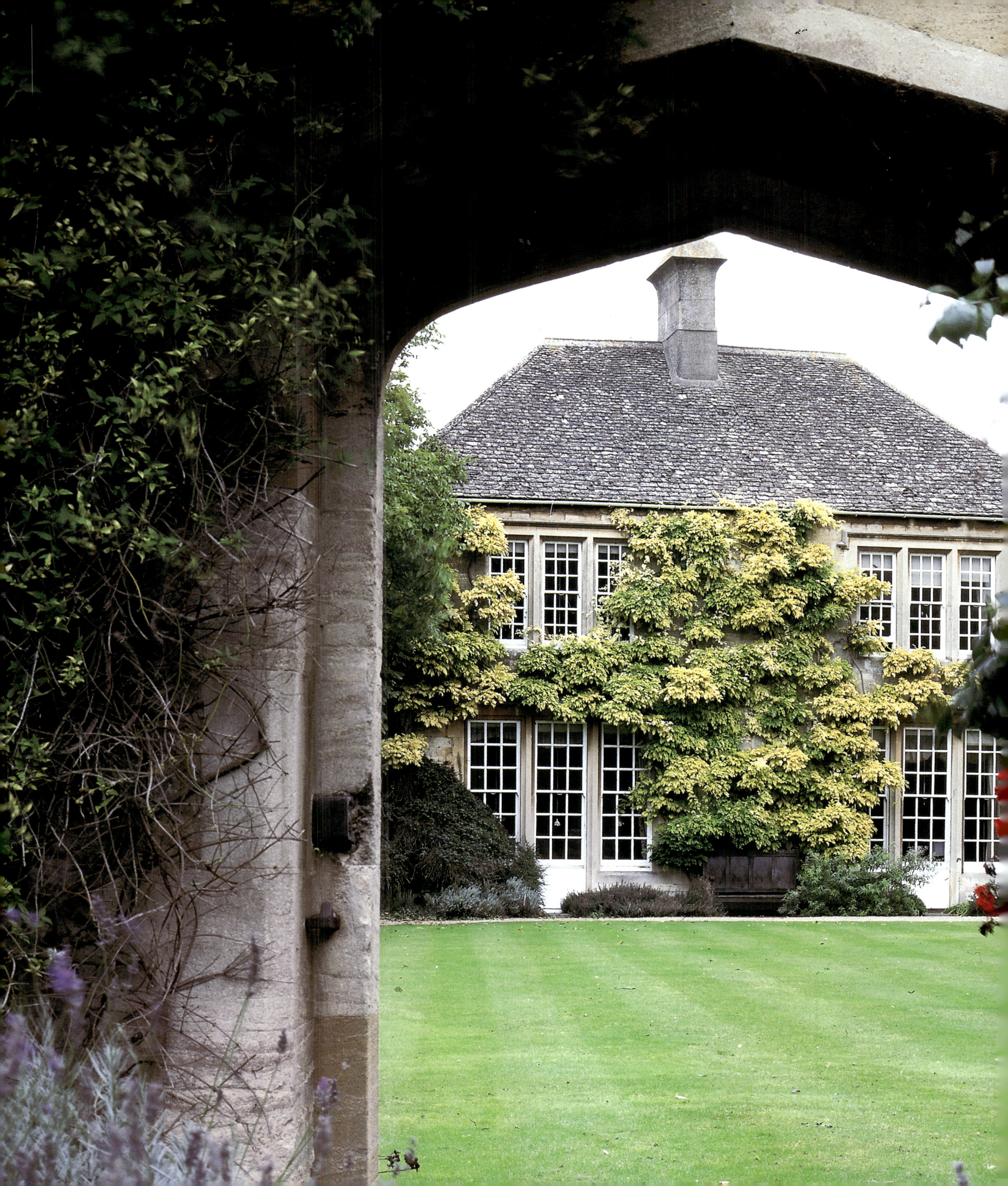

6

STANTON HARCOURT MANOR

OXFORDSHIRE

S O OFTEN with manor houses it is the grouping of the domestic buildings with the parish church that achieves an irresistibly picturesque effect. Nowhere is this better exemplified than at Stanton Harcourt, between the Rivers Windrush and Isis near Oxford, where the medieval ensemble is breathtaking in its beauty. Christopher Hussey of *Country Life* considered that St Michael's Church, a singularly complete cruciform Early English building (in parts Norman, with the 15th-century Harcourt family chapel added), seen from the east across the Lady Pool, with the manor house beyond, 'makes one of the prettiest pictures of a parish church to be seen anywhere'.

That the originally extensive range of buildings, one of the earliest unfortified manor houses in England, now survives only in scattered fragments adds to rather than subtracts from Stanton Harcourt's extraordinarily powerful air of romance. As Candida Lycett Green lyrically described in her collection of *100 Favourite Houses*, there is no pomp and ceremony: the entrance curls in past the Manor Farm to a jumble of farm buildings and then 'you walk through a stone arch into Arcadia'.

The house, mostly built over the period 1380 to 1470, was spaced around an inner court, now represented by the rose garden and vineyard. The principal rooms would have been on the north side. Although the Great Hall and the Great and Little Parlours have disappeared, the easternmost end of the range survives, containing the Domestic Chapel and its tower – known as 'Pope's Tower' after Alexander Pope, a friend of Simon Harcourt, son of the 1st Viscount Harcourt, who lent the poet the rooms in the tower in the summers of 1717 and 1718. Here, as Pope recorded in a graffito on a window-pane, he 'finished… the fifth volume of Homer' (a translation of the *Iliad*).

PRECEDING PAGES 'Through a stone arch into Arcadia...', a view of the garden front of the present house at Stanton Harcourt, extended from the original Gatehouse in the 19th century.

LEFT The manorial ensemble seen from across the fishpond: St Michael's Church is in the foreground, with the Domestic Chapel and its tower (marked by the flag) behind it; to the left, the Kitchen.

OPPOSITE 'The forge of Vulcan, the cave of Polypheme or the temple of Moloch...', the Kitchen, so colourfully described by Alexander Pope, remains one of the most spectacular medieval structures of its type in England.

The poet also chronicled for posterity some remarkably vivid impressions of the already ruinous manor house, which must rank as among the earliest romantic appreciations of an ancient building. He was especially excited by the Great Kitchen, which he described as being

> built in the form of a Rotunda, being one vast vault to the top of the house, where one aperture serves to let out the smoke and let in the light. By the blackness of the walls, the circular fires, vast caldrons, yawning mouths of ovens and furnaces, you would think it the forge of Vulcan, the cave of Polypheme, or the temple of Moloch.

In fact, the Kitchen, which survives, is a square building, with an octagonal roof which in its present form is said to date from 1485. Medievalists cannot agree, however, whether the stone structure and its timber roof are contemporary with one another. If the stone walls are earlier than the roof, then the Kitchen may be one of the earliest parts of the house, dating from about 1380. In any event, it is surely, as Sir Nikolaus Pevsner (not given to superlatives) wrote, 'one of the most completely medieval kitchens in England, and certainly the most spectacular'.

The history of Stanton effectively begins in the early 12th century, when Henry I gave the manor to his second wife, Queen Adeliza (or Adela), who passed most of it on to a kinswoman, Millicent de Camville. It came into the Harcourt family, and thereby acquired the name of Stanton Harcourt, when, at the end of the 12th century, Isabel de Camville married Sir Robert de Harcourt, of the great Norman family in whose possession it happily remains some 900 years later.

The manor house at Stanton Harcourt was most probably built by Sir Thomas Harcourt, MP, who died in 1417. His grandson, Sir Robert, who was installed as a Knight of the Garter by Edward IV and was slain in the Wars of the Roses, built the Domestic Chapel, where the chancel arch incorporates the coat of arms of himself and his wife, Margaret Byron. Sir Robert was

BELOW Heraldic carving on the oriel of the Tudor Gatehouse.

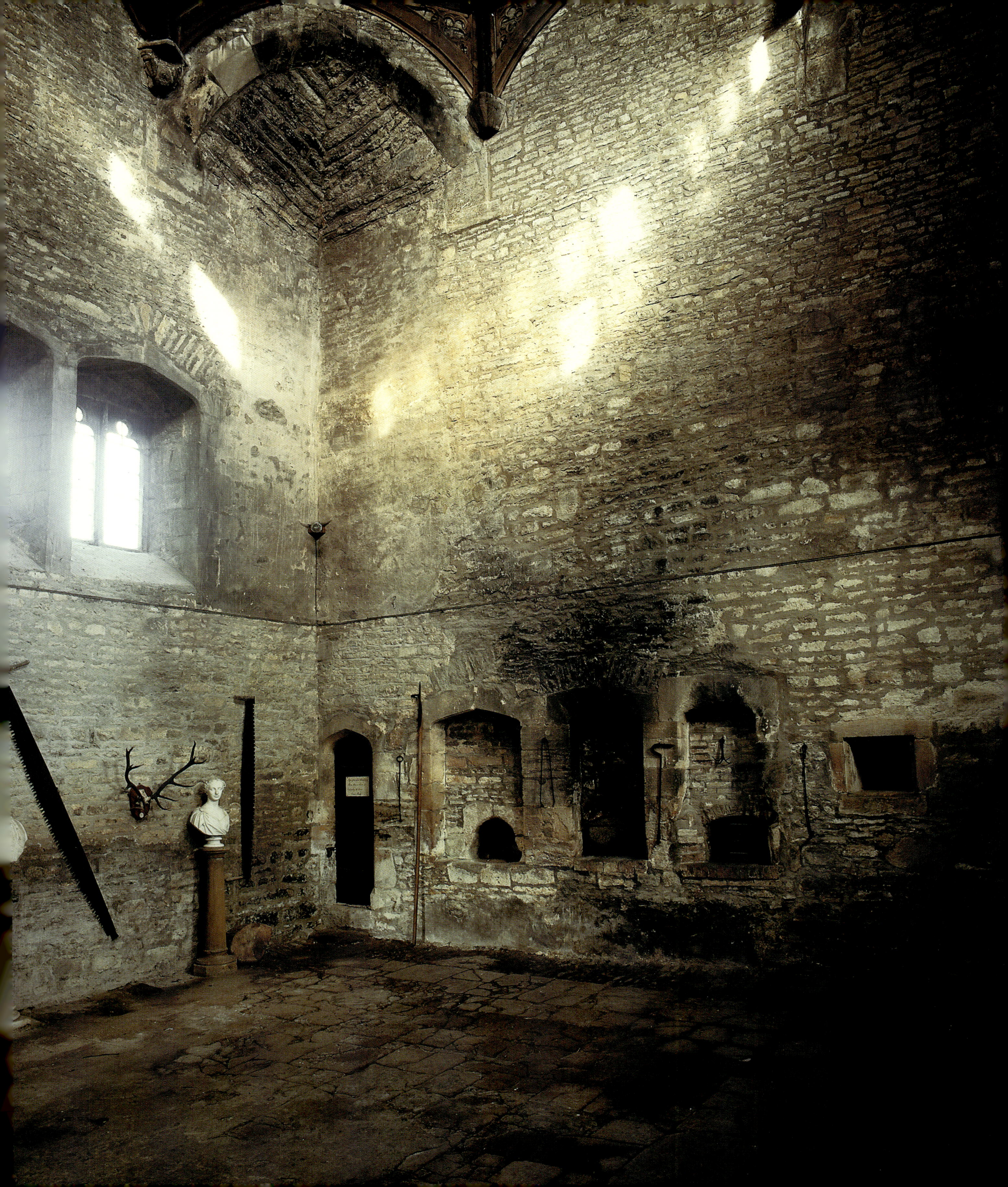

probably also responsible for the Harcourt Chapel adjoining the chancel of St Michael's Church (which was under the patronage of Reading Abbey until the Dissolution of the Monasteries). The magnificent monuments and effigies in this chapel attest to the Harcourts' illustrious family history.

Among the most notable tombs is the painted effigy of Sir Robert's grandson and namesake, who was Standard Bearer to Henry Tudor at Bosworth Field in 1485. He lies in full plated armour and the tomb is decorated with 'weepers' – four black-robed monks telling their beads and two angels.

The core of the present manor house at Stanton Harcourt was originally the Gatehouse, which seems to have been built, or rebuilt, in about 1540 by Sir Simon Harcourt. This structure has subsequently been much altered – the gateway filled in, the oriel window evidently reconstructed – but originally, with its porter's lodge, it would have provided a secure entrance to the outer courtyard, now represented by the lawns between the present house and the Domestic Chapel.

OPPOSITE The Library, added, together with the Dining Room and bedrooms above, to the original Gatehouse in 1868.

BELOW The Staircase Hall of the present house which occupies the old covered carriageway of the Tudor Gatehouse.

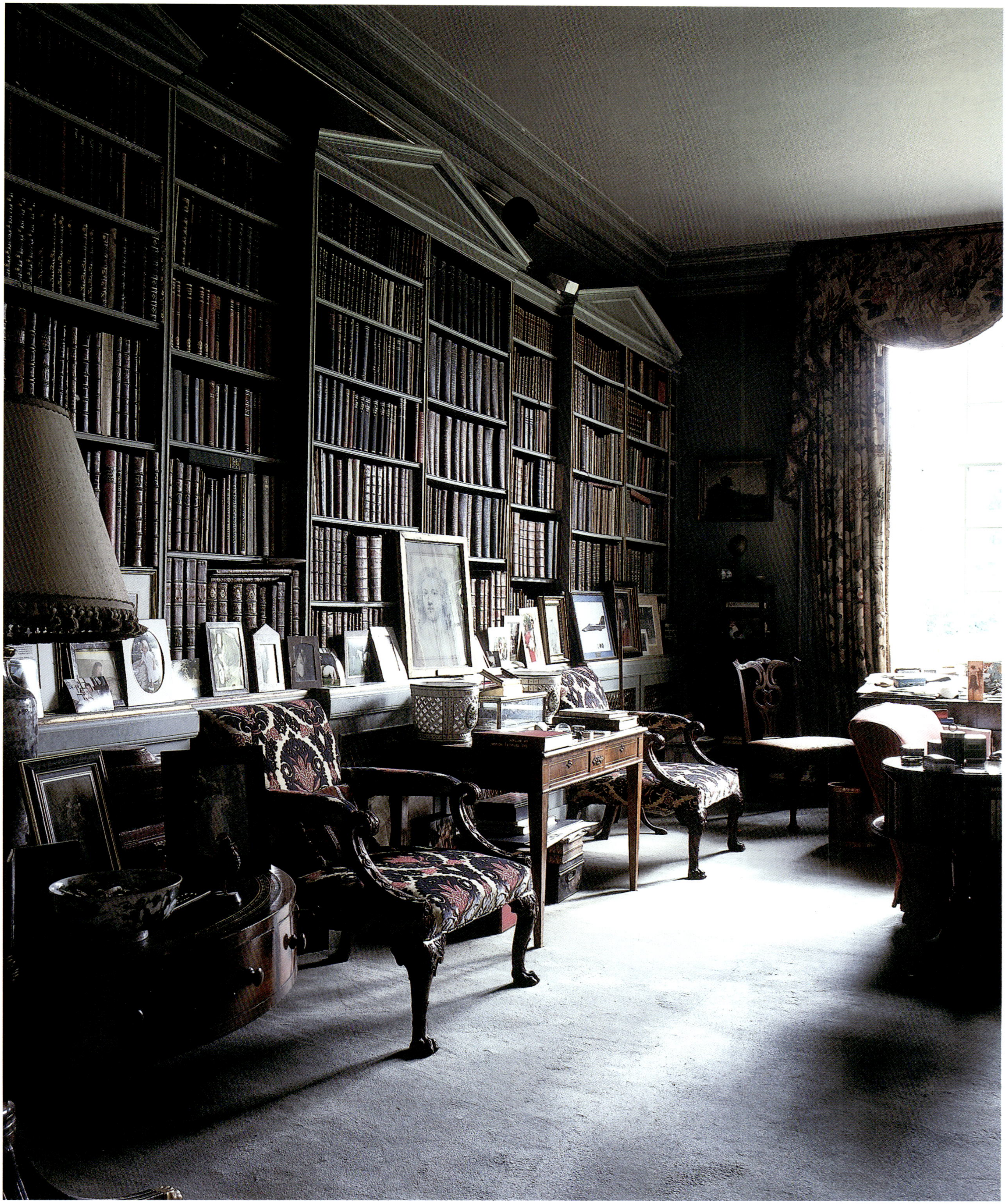

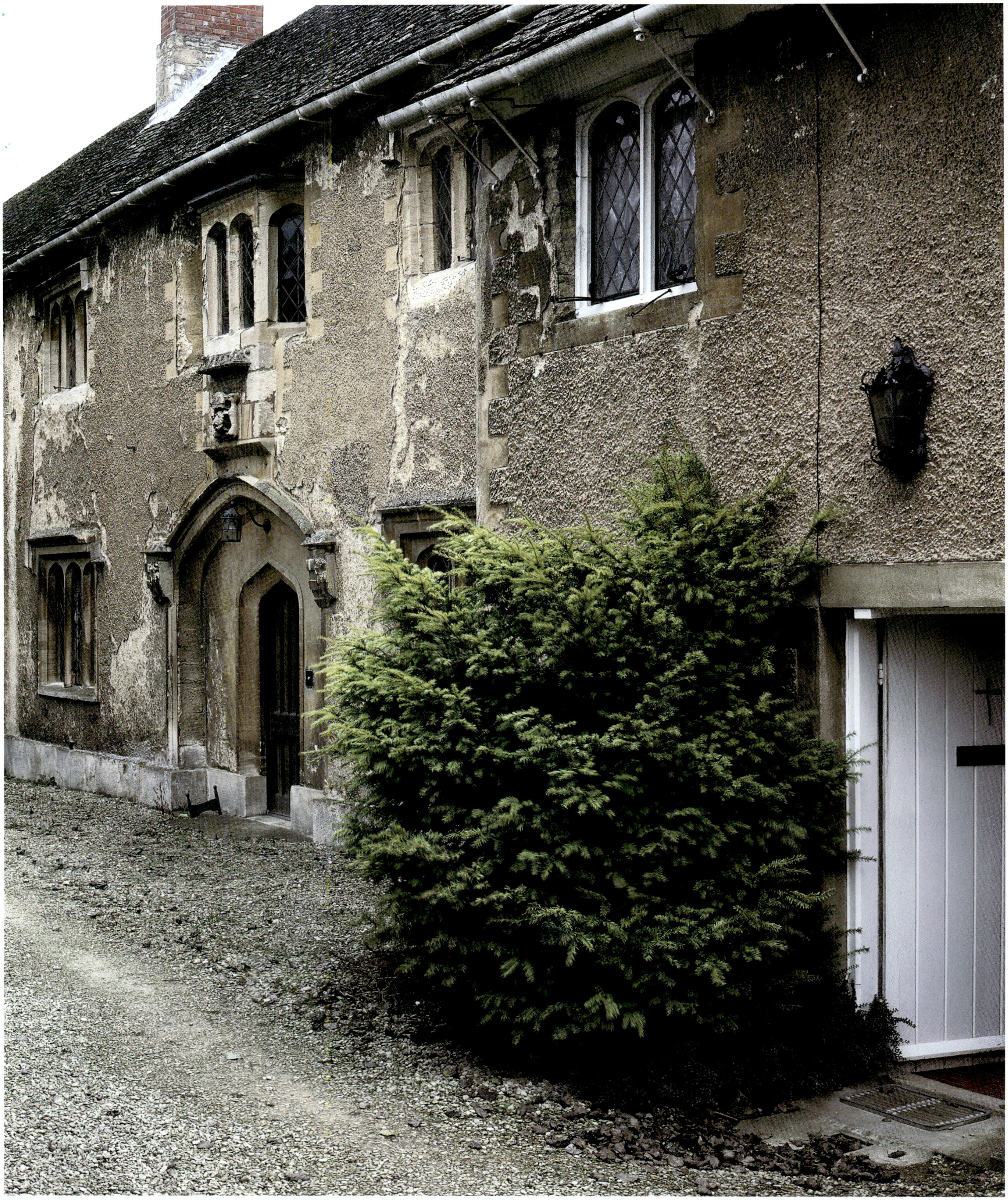

ABOVE The reconstructed doorway of the Gatehouse.

LEFT View of the Gatehouse entrance range, built, or rebuilt, by Sir Simon Harcourt, who married a Darrel of Scotney Castle, Kent. Their coats of arms adorn the stonework.

RIGHT The Kitchen, with its staircase turret to the roof.

Stanton Harcourt remained the home of the family until the death of Sir Philip Harcourt, MP, in 1688. His widow moved out, sold the contents and allowed the old house to fall into serious disrepair. Her stepson, an eloquent lawyer who became Lord Chancellor and then, in 1721, the 1st Viscount Harcourt (of whom an historian observed 'he did not sit on the fence, but always managed to keep the right side of it') settled at Cokethorpe nearby. And later in the 18th century the 1st Earl Harcourt incorporated much of the building material from the demolished parts of Stanton Harcourt into the construction of the great house at Nuneham Courtenay, which was to be the principal seat of the Harcourt family until after the Second World War.

Fortunately, though, Stanton Harcourt had not been forgotten and in 1868 the Dining Room, Library and bedrooms above were added to the old Gatehouse in order to create a comfortable residence. It was here that the late Viscount Harcourt returned with his family in 1948, following the sale of Nuneham, and today it is the home of his eldest daughter, Ann Gascoigne, and her family.

Mrs Gascoigne frequently opens Stanton Harcourt to the public in the spring and summer. The 12 acres of gardens are a delightfully contrasting mixture of formality; fruit, roses and vines; and semi-wilderness enclosing manorial fish-ponds. The largest of these, the Lady Pool, takes its name from a ghost story – which particularly tickled Alexander Pope's fancy – about a lady, supposedly murdered by a priest in the tower, who rises to revisit the scene if the pool ever runs dry. Pope himself features in another traditional yarn associated with this magical place: the Methodist mother of one of the workmen engaged on fitting up the panelled room for the poet misunderstood the name of its intended occupant and was horrified to learn that it was to be occupied by 'the Pope'.

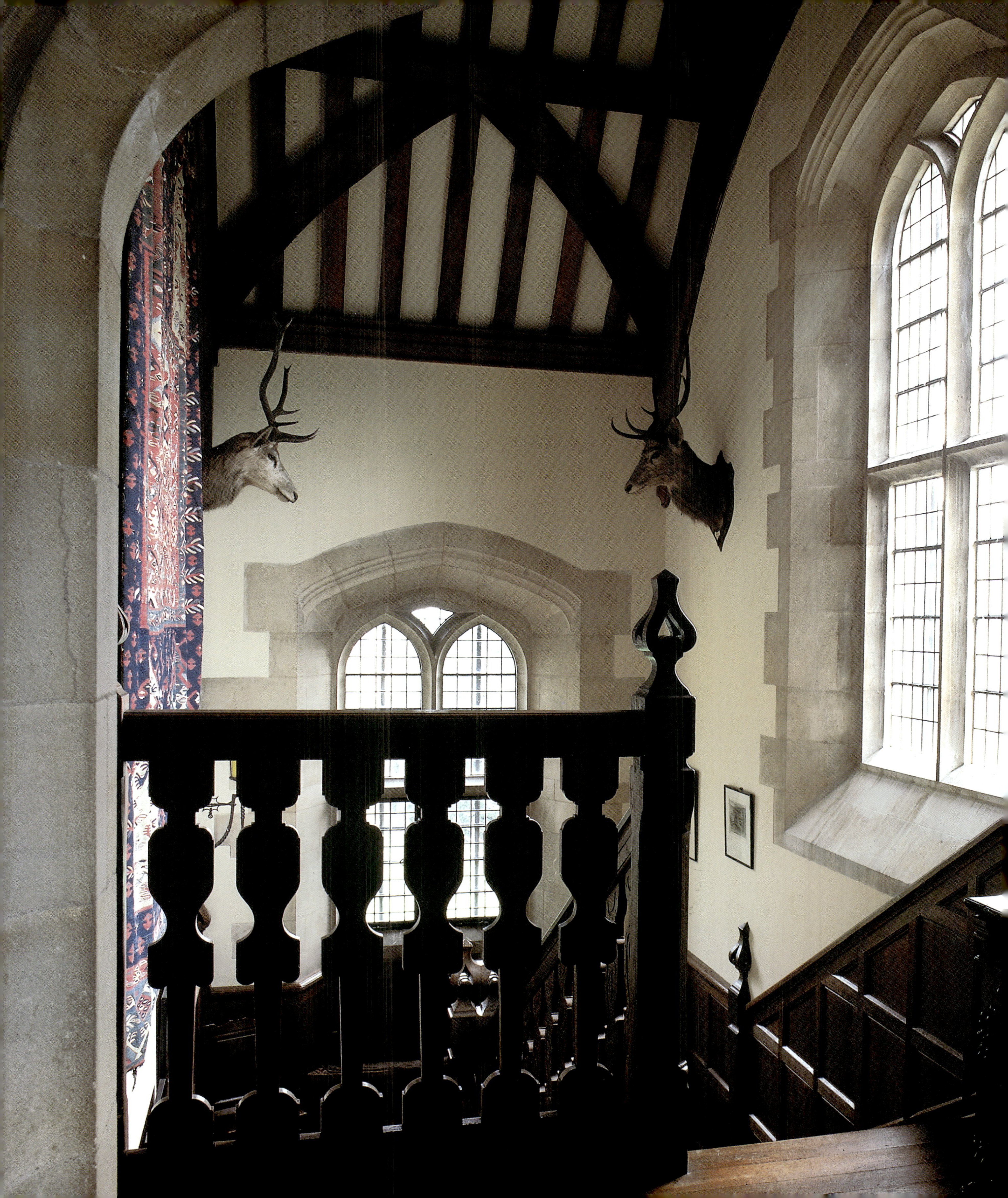

7

GREAT CHALFIELD MANOR

WILTSHIRE

'IT CANNOT be doubted', wrote a correspondent, one Victor, in the *Gentleman's Magazine* in 1838, 'that the curious and reflecting visitor of Chalfield Manor-house and its appurtenances, will feel his imagination somewhat excited, when they carry back his thoughts to the era of freshness; to the inartificial manners of that early age; and to the scenes of hospitality and merriment, which then gladdened the venerable pile.' Even making allowances for a tone of voice that became increasingly sarcastic in its manner, this report provides interesting contemporary evidence that at the dawn of the Victorian age hitherto neglected medieval manor houses such as the pleasingly mellow Great Chalfield were being appreciated afresh for their antiquity and romance.

Indeed, a couple of years before Victor paid his visit to Great Chalfield, the then owners of the estate, Sir Henry Burrard, Bt, of Walhampton, Hampshire (a sailor whose ship had refused to join the Nore mutiny in 1797), and his wife, Grace Neale, employed Thomas Larkin Walker, a pupil of A.W.N. Pugin, to draw and survey the beautifully balanced manor house, then let out to a tenant farmer, with a view to its restoration. In the event, the Burrards did not move in, but the house was duly altered to suit the occupying tenant. And Walker's drawings and descriptions of the house, published in 1837, were to prove an invaluable record when the Fuller family began their joyful restoration of Great Chalfield at the beginning of the 20th century – what might be called the Golden Age of manorial revival.

There was no finer interpreter of this revival than the antiquarian architect Sir Harold Brakspear, who lived nearby and had particular knowledge of medieval churches and houses built in Bath and Cotswold stone, such as Great Chalfield. Besides his work in the cloisters of Lacock Abbey in the

GREAT CHALFIELD

PRECEDING PAGES The staircase landing at Great Chalfield.

LEFT Late-medieval manorial sophistication: gables and oriels in symmetry, with the harmonious composition set off by the church's bellcote and crocketed spire.

BELOW One of the three stone looking-masks, or 'squints', in the Great Hall; this one is in the form of a laughing face.

same county (like Great Chalfield now a property of the National Trust), Brakspear also distinguished himself further afield, as at Haddon Hall, Derbyshire, which he restored for the 9th Duke of Rutland.

Brakspear and his client, Robert Fuller, chairman of the Avon Rubber Co., decided to retain as much original work as possible, but not to resort to imitation or to replacement of detail not shown in Walker's drawings. The happy consequence is that when you look at the house today – which, once you have entered the precinct by a bridge across the moat and negotiated the Gatehouse, forms an inseparable group with the neighbouring church of All Saints – you are struck by how little this lovable buff stone composition appears to have changed since it was built by Thomas Tropnell in the 15th century.

Strictly speaking, that should read 'rebuilt', for the Percy family are recorded as having lived here from the 13th century. The manor subsequently fell into a thicket of family disputes which the shrewd Tropnell, who

BELOW Another Great Chalfield grotesque: a gargoyle on the roof of the north façade.

LEFT Garden front, with half-timbered range.

The Great Hall, the centre of Great Chalfield, 40 feet long and 20 feet wide, with its original timbers in the slightly cambered ceiling. The oak screen is a copy of the original from T.L. Walker's drawings of 1837, and confirmed by J.C. Buckler's watercolour of 1823.

had begun life as a steward for the powerful Hungerford family and risen to become an MP, was able to disentangle to his own advantage. He finally secured possession of Great Chalfield in 1467 and wasted no time in proceeding with building work. Stone was provided from the quarry he had bought at Hazelbury near Box in 1465.

What is so striking about Great Chalfield is its architectural sophistication for a house dating from this late medieval period. This is far from a haphazard agglomeration: the fine gables on either side of the central Great Hall achieve a remarkable symmetry. The semicircular oriel window on the left gable is crowned by exquisite strawberry-leaf ornament, whereas the octagonal oriel window in the right-hand gable is surmounted by Tropnell's coat of arms. The splendidly carved and decorated house is an exuberant, confident statement of the new squire's status. Tropnell balanced the whole composition by adding a bellcote and crocketed spire to the church, where he also built the painted chapel to the south side, with its stone screen.

Inside the house, the Great Hall, 40 feet long and 20 feet in both breadth and height, has pride of place. The timbers of Tropnell's ceiling are all original. The most unusual feature is the set of three stone looking-masks, or 'squints'. One depicts a bishop in his mitre, another a king adorned with asses' ears and the third, a laughing face, looks on to the minstrels' gallery.

The separate Dining Room, an innovation in Tropnell's day, is notable for a curious mural painting depicting a figure with five fingers as well as a thumb on each hand. It has been suggested that this might represent Avarice, or even Thomas Tropnell himself (if so, it could be the earliest known portrait of a commoner MP), though it seems a little unfair to impugn the memory of the builder of one of the most appealing houses in England.

Tropnell died in 1488 and the male line expired soon afterwards with the unfortunate death of Giles Tropnell out beagling ('putting one end of a paire of Dogg Couples over his head running after his sport and leaping over a hedge, the end of ye Dogg Couple which hung at his back took holde of a boughe, kept him from touching ye ground until hee was strangled'). Subsequently Great Chalfield passed through various ownerships including the families of Eyre, Gurney (when it was besieged by Royalist troops in the Civil War), Hanham and Hall before being acquired by the Neales in 1769. At one stage it even formed part of the property portfolio of the 2nd Duke of Kingston, notorious for marrying bigamously the coarse strumpet Elizabeth Chudleigh, who was already the wife of the 6th Earl of Bristol.

Today Great Chalfield remains the home of the descendants of Robert Fuller, who sensitively restored it from 1905 to 1912 and furnished and decorated the house in keeping with Tropnell's original building. In 1943 Fuller gave the manor house, gardens and immediate surroundings to the National Trust and since his death in 1955 it has continued to be a family home tenanted from the Trust. This charming place lives on as the hub of a rural estate complete with its own farms, woodlands, cottages and thriving community.

LEFT The North Bedroom, with its superb roof timbers, nearly all of which are original.

ABOVE One of the carved figures atop the gable ends, a soldier attired in 15th-century armour.

RIGHT The Solar, ingeniously rebuilt to the form in which T.L. Walker recorded it in 1837. The room is dominated by the beautiful semi-circular oriel window. The fireplace, not shown in Walker's drawings (he described it as a 'singular design of meretricious taste'), was probably inserted by the Eyre family.

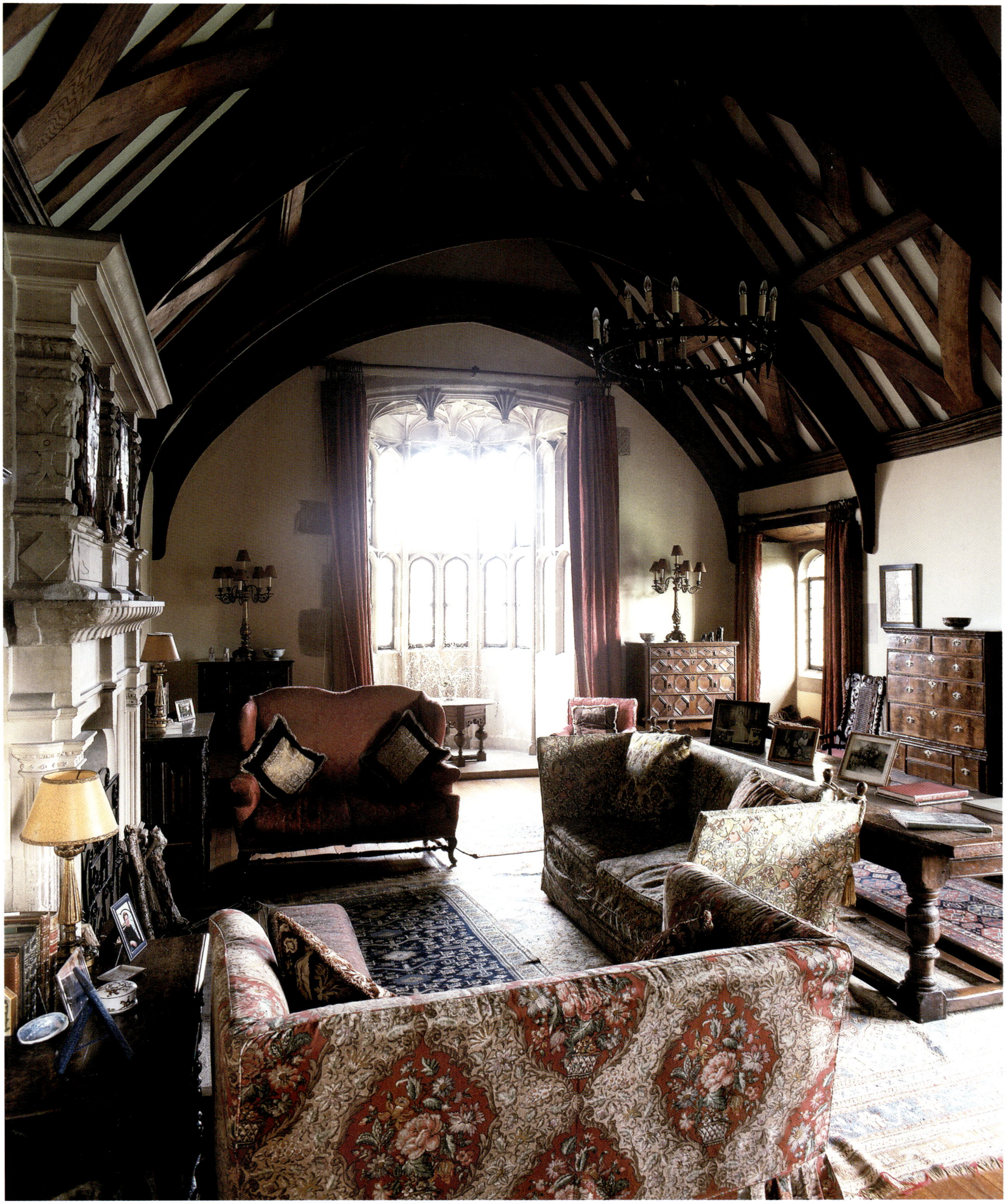

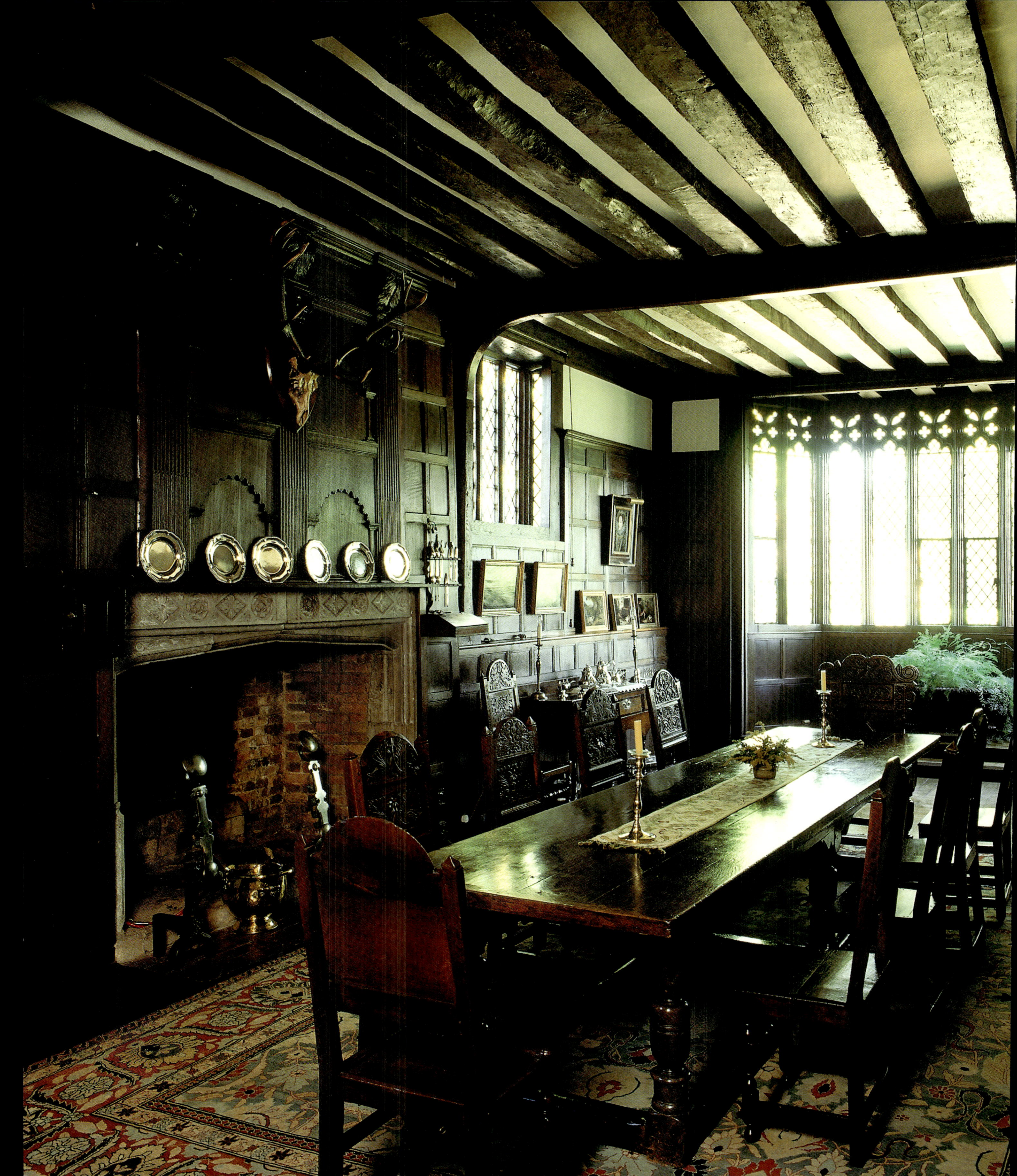

8

OCKWELLS MANOR

BERKSHIRE

NOT dissimilar in general plan and date to Great Chalfield Manor, the subject of the previous chapter, is Ockwells Manor, an astonishing survival on the outskirts of Maidenhead. The obvious difference, though, is that whereas Great Chalfield is of stone, Ockwells is of timber and brick nogging (or 'brickefillying' as it was simply termed in relation to another near-contemporary building not far away, the Horseshoe Cloisters at Windsor Castle). Indeed Sir Nikolaus Pevsner described Ockwells as 'the most refined and the most sophisticated timber-framed mansion in England'.

It was built some time between 1445 and 1466 by Sir John Norreys, Squire of the Body and then Master of the Wardrobe to the unworldly Henry VI. Christopher Hussey of *Country Life* described Ockwells as a typical residence of a courtier of this period and noted how 'it preserves this atmosphere better than any other similar building in the country'.

The manor of Ockwells, or Ocholt as it was then called, was granted in 1267 by Henry III to Sir John's ancestor, Richard le, or de, Norreys, described as 'Coci' (cook) to Queen Eleanor. The Norreys family were principally based in Lancashire and it was only in the 15th century that proximity to the Court at Windsor appears to have reminded them of the potential advantages of having a manor house built at Ockwells. The collegiate buildings at Eton nearby also seem to have influenced the style of the new manor, with its unusual upper cloisters, or corridors – exceptionally early examples of communication galleries in a private house.

Originally the house was built as part of an outer court, comprising the manor house, tithe barn, stables, gatehouse, chapel and fortified wall. The entrance would have been through the gatehouse on the south side of the court.

Despite all the vicissitudes it has suffered, Ockwells is in a wonderful state of preservation, and this reflects great credit on the various owners who have fallen in love with the place since it was described as 'quite ruinous' in 1800

PRECEDING PAGES The Dining Room (formerly a withdrawing room) at Ockwells. The panelling and stone fireplace are mid-16th-century, though the chamfered ceiling beams are original, of the 15th century.

LEFT View of the entrance (east) front from the north.

BELOW The bressumer of the oriel above the entrance porch is carved with coats of arms, including those of Sir Stephen Leech, who began the restoration of the house in 1889.

RIGHT The dais end of the Great Hall, with its original arched collar-braced roof.

BELOW Detail of wood carving.

– most notably Sir Stephen Leech (1889–93); Sir Edward Barry, 2nd Bt (1893–1949); and, of course, the present owners, Brian and Jill Stein (from 1984), who maintain it impeccably.

The chief glory of Ockwells is the Great Hall, as satisfying an interior as one could ever wish to see, with its original arched collar-braced roof and staggeringly beautiful display of armorial glass that fills the windows on one side of the room. If ever there was a demonstration of the joys of heraldry, in all its brilliance and chivalry, this must be it – and, moreover, it predates the foundation of the College of Arms by Richard III. In fact, the glass was probably put up as early as the mid-1440s to celebrate the marriage of Henry VI to Margaret of Anjou. The King's and Queen's arms are among those displayed, along with a gallery of Sir John's friends, patrons and fellow courtiers. The coats represented include those of Sir Henry Beauchamp, Duke of Warwick; Sir Edmund Beaufort, Duke of Somerset; Sir William de la Pole, Duke of Suffolk (who was involved with Sir John in the endowment of Eton College), and Sir James Butler, Earl of Wiltshire.

In the 16th century Ockwells descended to the Fettiplace family and thence to the Englefields, who were probably responsible for installing the

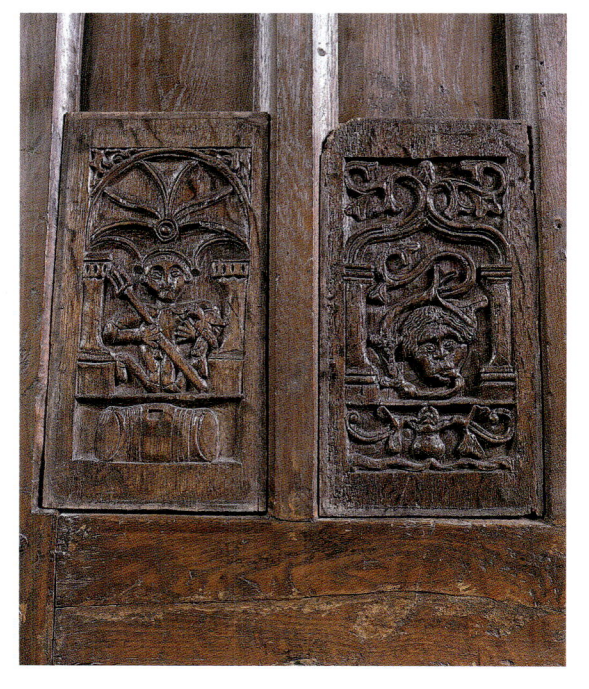

– 58 –

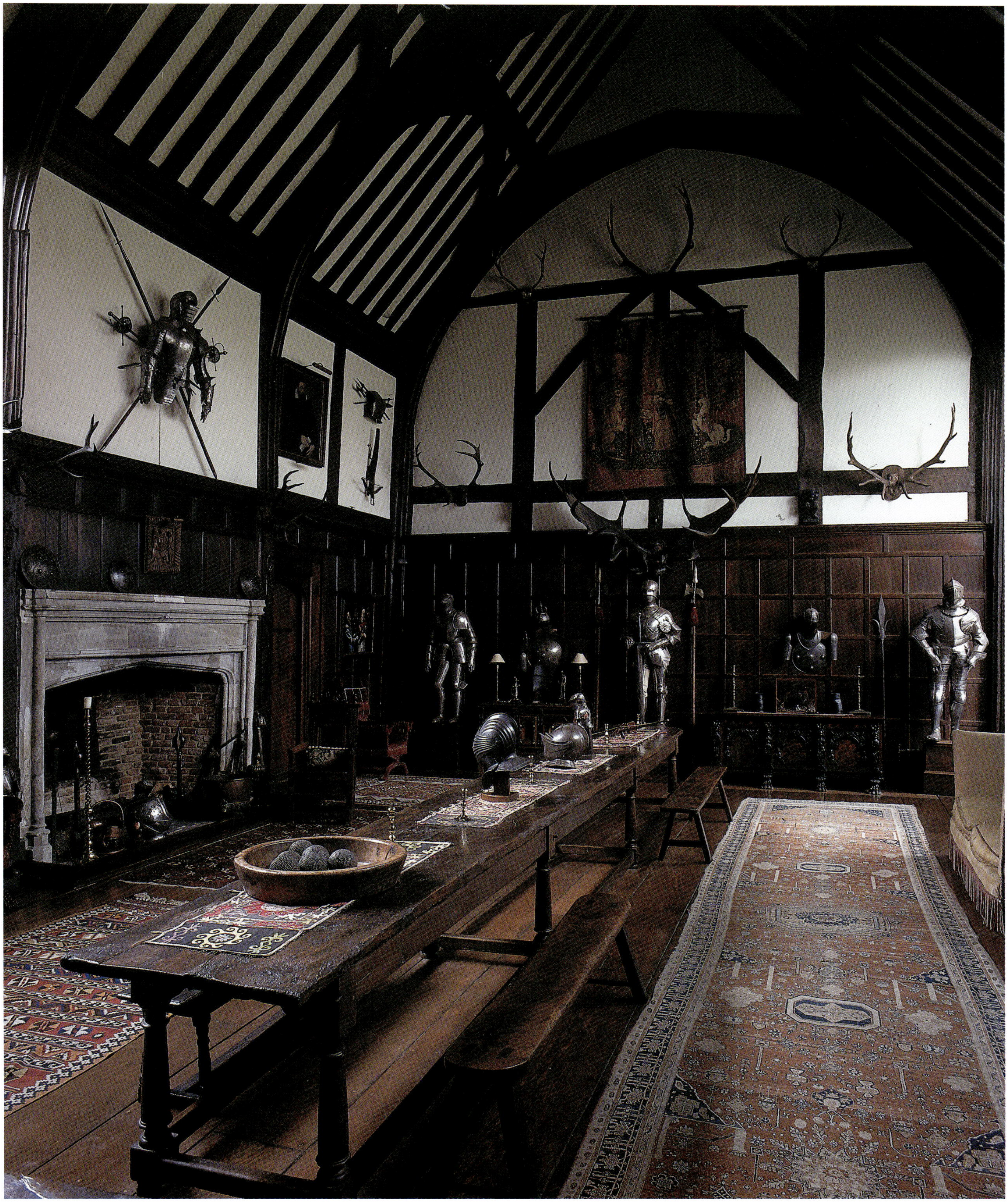

panelling in what is now the Dining Room and also the 'Queen Elizabeth Room', as well as the fireplaces of about 1550 in both rooms. The overmantel in the Dining Room (formerly the withdrawing room), though, was probably installed by the Day family in the 17th century. The Days also inserted the panelling in the Great Hall and the staircase in the internal courtyard (later moved, twice, in the 19th century).

By the end of the 18th century Ockwells was obviously in a bad way. The Chapel is said to have burned down at this period. Indeed, it was only thanks to the foresight of the Grenfell family, who in the 1840s acquired what was by now described as 'a third-rate farmhouse', that the house's greatest treasure, the heraldic glass, survived. Charles Pascoe Grenfell, a neighbouring squire, transferred the glass for safety to his seat of Taplow Court on the other side of the Thames. Then, with splendid generosity, his grandson, Lord Desborough (always held up as the *beau idéal* of a gentleman), gave the glass back to Ockwells on the occasion of its restoration by Sir Stephen Leech and the architect Fairfax Wade.

Among Sir Stephen's many improvements to the house, besides putting it once more in good structural repair, were the installation of the oriel windows in what is now the Dining Room and the removal of a plaster ceiling in the Great Hall which had previously hidden the beams. The bressumer under the porch

ABOVE The Cloister, which connected the screens passage with the pantry, kitchen and buttery – the remarkable original serving hatch of which can be seen in the right foreground.

ABOVE and OPPOSITE Details of stone carving.

LEFT Sitting Room, with carved chimneypiece, probably installed by the Days in the 17th century.

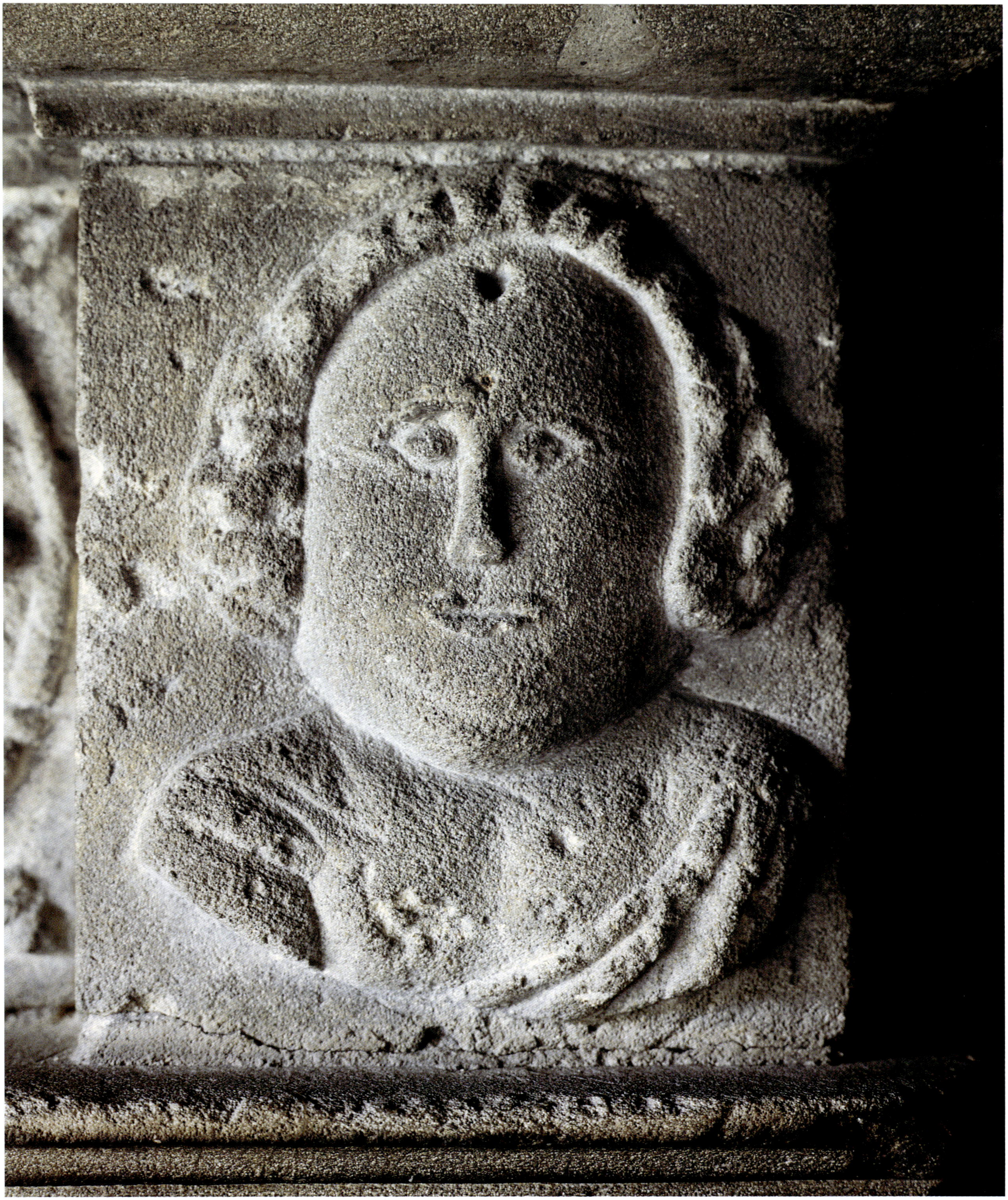

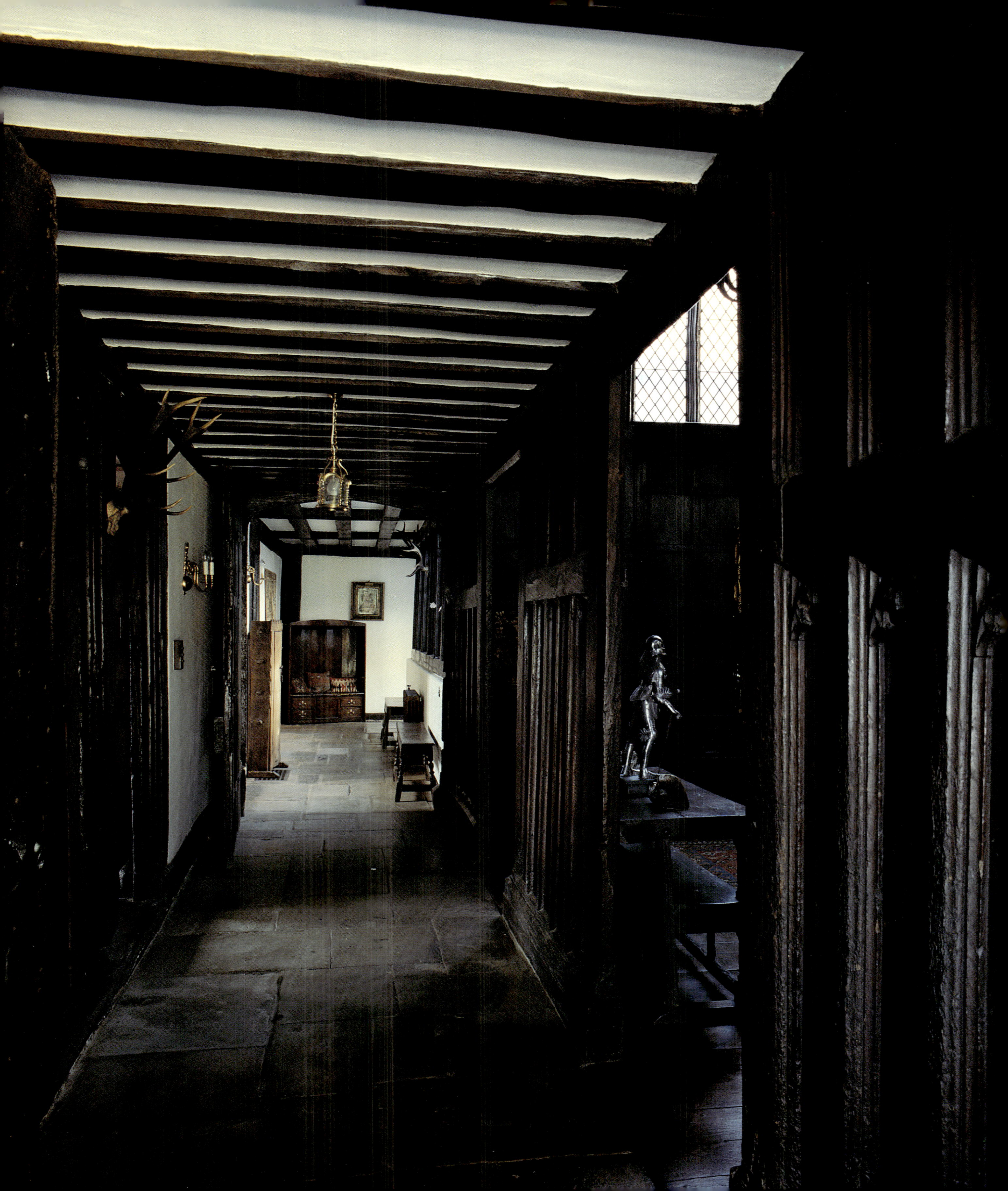

window bears his coat of arms. However, the west wing that Leech added was later demolished, and the changes to the old kitchen area were, in turn, revised by his successor at Ockwells, Sir Edward Barry, son of the local MP.

In the 1890s Barry carried out a thorough overhaul of the property. This included a substantial new extension to the north-west, as well as a new side passage to the old withdrawing room which now became the Dining Room. The large window lets light into the stairwell that was erected to house the 17th-century stair when Barry moved it from the old kitchen. A new downpipe was installed on the east front, the most picturesque façade. The Buttery and Pantry – noteworthy for its remarkably well-preserved Buttery Hatch, with its original metal legs folded out to support the hatch on which provisions would be placed – were knocked together to form a billiard room. And the sitting room on the south side was adorned by Sir Edward (who had strong Iberian connections and was a Portuguese baron) with Spanish leather, said to have originated from the residence of the Spanish Ambassador in Mexico City.

All these changes seem to have been absorbed smoothly into the place's historic ambience, but its troubles were by no means over. Before the arrival of the Steins, the house was empty for 15 years and the current owners have had to undertake a great deal of hard work to give Ockwells the air of serene and courtly perfection, so evocative of the late Middle Ages, that it proudly exudes in the 21st century.

OPPOSITE The screens passage: one of the earliest fixed screens in England.

BELOW 'The most refined and sophisticated timber-framed mansion in England': the unforgettable east front of Ockwells.

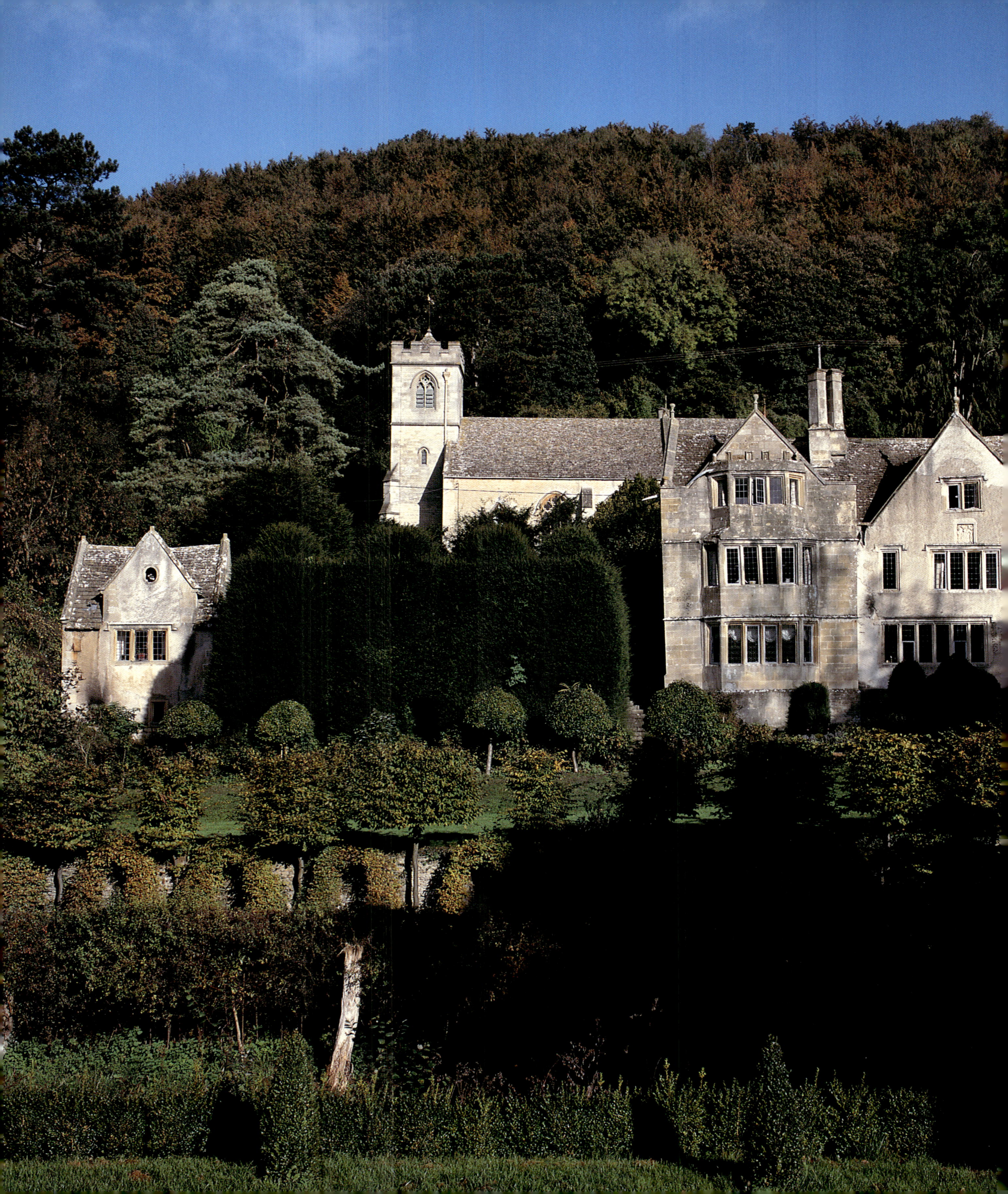

9

OWLPEN MANOR

GLOUCESTERSHIRE

'OWLPEN in Gloucester', mused Vita Sackville-West, 'ah, what a dream is there!' The dream-like quality of this pearl-grey Cotswold manor house has been attested by many other writers. Christopher Hussey of *Country Life* described it as 'a dream made real, yet preserving, with all substance of structure and history, something of a dream's lovely unreality'. For David Verey, author of the *Gloucestershire* volume in *The Buildings of England*, it was 'the epitome of romance'.

As Verey pointed out, Owlpen cannot easily be dated to one century. The eastern service wing, the oldest part of the house, boasts arched-braced cruck trusses. The central portion, containing the Great Hall, dates from a mid-16th-century rebuilding; the western end presumably replaced an earlier solar wing, and is dated 1616. The kitchen and service wings were also added in the 17th century. The sash windows on the eastern bay of the south front, and the wainscoting within, are evidently early 18th-century. And by no means least, the early 20th century played a vital part in Owlpen's history when the architect Norman Jewson's sensitive restoration earned it an important place in the Arts & Crafts movement.

The manor originally belonged to the Olepenne, or Owlpen, family and the name is said to derive from Olla's *pen*, or enclosure, rather than from owls – though the heralds, with their customary love of puns, granted the family an owl as a crest. In 1464 the heiress of Owlpen, Margery, married John Daunt, whose father and namesake was a prominent Lancastrian in the Wars of the Roses. This connection gave rise to Owlpen's ghost story, in which Queen Margaret of Anjou's spirit, attired in a fur gown and wimple, parades in the Great Chamber (or 'Queen Margaret's Room') where she is supposed to have slept *en route* to the fateful Battle of Tewkesbury in 1471.

Owlpen descended through the Daunt family until 1925. The Great Hall retains features of the early Tudor period, including the doorway, the fireplace and the massive timbers of the ceiling. In the Great Chamber above these is an original door, with its hinges and lockplate. Thomas Daunt, who rebuilt the west wing in 1616 (his initials and the date appear on the embattled bay window), had extensive interests in property and the pedigree in *Burke's Irish Family Records* notes that he was also seated at Tracton Abbey and Gortigrenane in County Cork as well as at Owlpen.

The early 18th-century improvements seem to have been made by Thomas's great-grandson and namesake, who married Elizabeth Synge, from an Irish Ascendancy family. Besides the sash windows in the east wing, they included a handsome early Georgian doorway leading from the Great Hall to the Parlour, which gained a shell-headed alcove and a cupboard-recess flanking the chimney breast. Above, the East Bedroom formerly contained Owlpen's most remarkable internal feature, the set of 17th-century painted cloths depicting the story of Joseph and his coat of many colours (once thought to represent the Prodigal Son). These were moved, in the 1960s, to the Great Chamber – where they are, of course, no less remarkable. James Lees-Milne in his book *Some Cotswold Country Houses* remarked that he could not think of anywhere else where such painted cloth wall hangings had survived *in situ*. In Tudor and Stuart times this form of decoration was a cheaper substitute for tapestry – Falstaff, for example, recommends such hangings to Mistress Quickly in Shakespeare's *Henry IV*.

PRECEDING PAGES 'Ah, what a dream is there!' Owlpen in its picturesque setting below the church.

OPPOSITE The Great Chamber, with its painted cloths telling the story of Joseph and his coat of many colours.

ABOVE Plaster detail by Simon Verity in the Dining Room.

LEFT Winding stair.

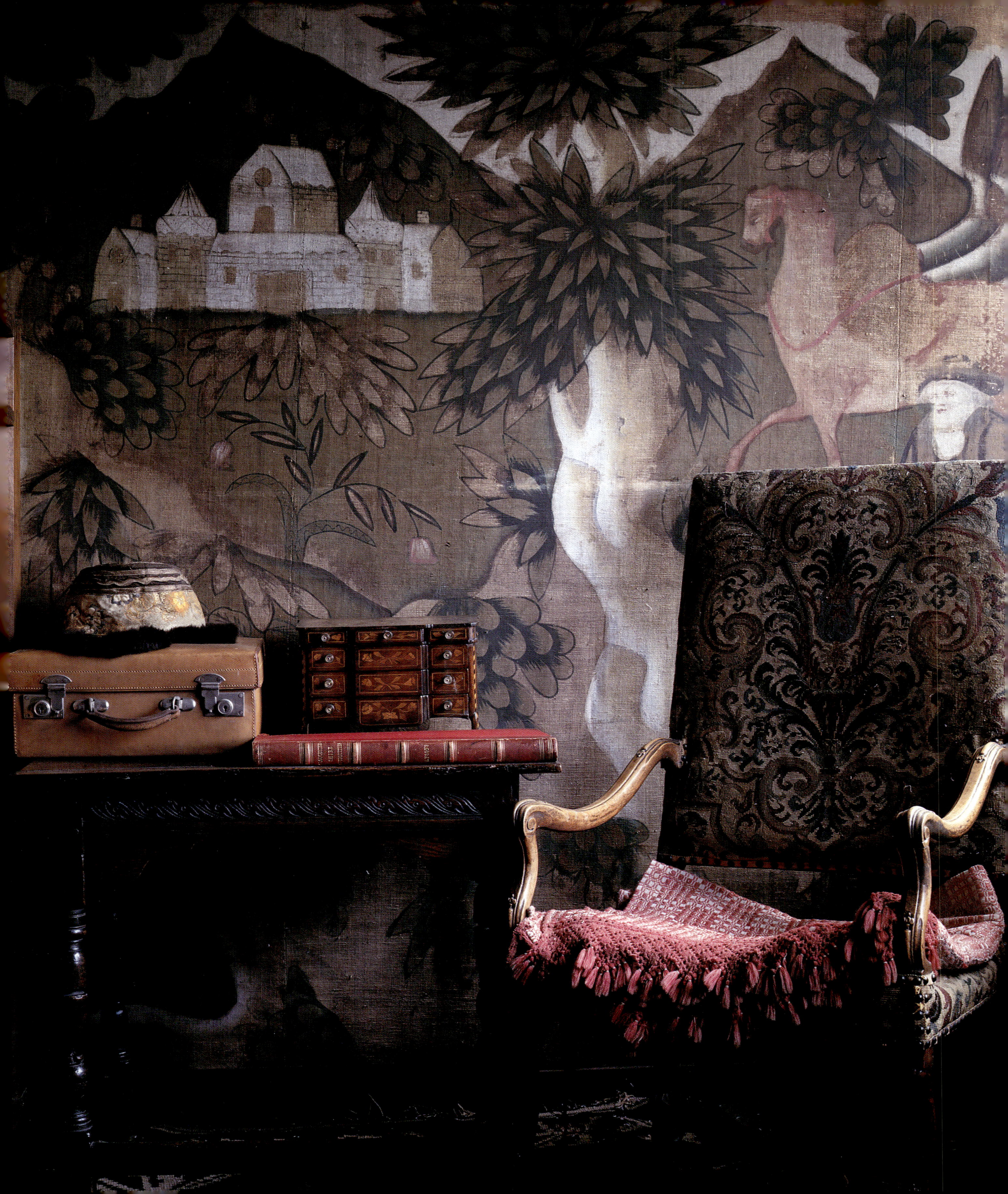

Dining Room, with (to the right) the oak settle bequeathed to the Manders by Norman Jewson. It was made by the Arts & Crafts craftsman Sidney Barnsley and had belonged to another of the Cotswold colony of architects, Ernest Gimson.

In 1815 the Daunt heiress, Mary, married Thomas Stoughton from County Kerry and they later established themselves in a neo-Jacobean pile, Owlpen Park, nearby. The old manor house was abandoned, though a gardener occupied a few of its back rooms and happily the gardens, which retained their early 18th-century features, were faithfully preserved. Indeed, Gertrude Jekyll and Laurence Weaver mentioned Owlpen in the introduction to their *Gardens for Small Country Houses* (1912): 'Among notable examples of little hillside gardens treated in a formal fashion, none is more delightful than that of Owlpen Manor.'

So the house had not completely disappeared from the map. Its eventual saviour, Norman Jewson, recorded his memorable first impressions of it in his autobiography, *By Chance I Did Rove*:

> A very beautiful and romantically situated old house, which has been deserted by its owners for a new mansion.... The house was rapidly falling into complete decay but a caretaker lived in a kitchen wing and would shew some of the rooms to visitors.... In spite of the dilapidation of the house, which was so far advanced that one of the main roof trusses had given way, the great stone bay window had become almost detached from the wall and huge roots of ivy had grown right across some of the floors, it seems to me that such an exceptionally beautiful and interesting old house might still be saved.

ABOVE The handsome early-Georgian doorway which leads from the Great Hall to the Parlour.

Jewson had established himself as a member of the Arts & Crafts colony based at Sapperton in the Cotswolds alongside Ernest Gimson and the Barnsleys, Ernest and Sidney (Jewson married Ernest's daughter). In 1925 he showed great commitment in buying Owlpen for £3,200 from the executors of the previous owner, Mrs Trent-Stoughton. Using the traditional methods so cherished by the Arts & Crafts movement, Jewson carried out thorough repairs. The nobility of this effort is nicely expressed in his friend F.L. ('Fred') Grigg's inscription to his etching of *Owlpen Manor* (1931):

> To my friend Norman Jewson, who, with only one purpose, and at his own cost and loss, possessed himself of the demesne of OWLPEN when for the first time in seven hundred years, it passed into alien hands & with great care and skill saved this ancient house from ruin.

Jewson's 'loss' was such that he was obliged to sell Owlpen immediately after the rescue. The story, however, has a gratifying twist, for in old age he became friendly with Owlpen's new owners, Nicholas and Karin Mander (who had bought the place in 1974) and he was able to advise them in various ways. He bequeathed to the house his oak settle, made by Sidney Barnsley, which had belonged to Gimson.

Mr Mander is an historian of the Arts & Crafts movement; he and his wife have added other appropriately Cotswold pieces to the Owlpen interior. Among the notable paintings they have commissioned of this famously picturesque house is a topographical portrait of Owlpen by 'Boots' Bantock. The Manders open the house and gardens regularly to the public in the spring and summer months, as well as running a restaurant in the old cyder house and letting out cottages for holidays.

BELOW Owlpen's entrance to the east: the earliest part of the house.

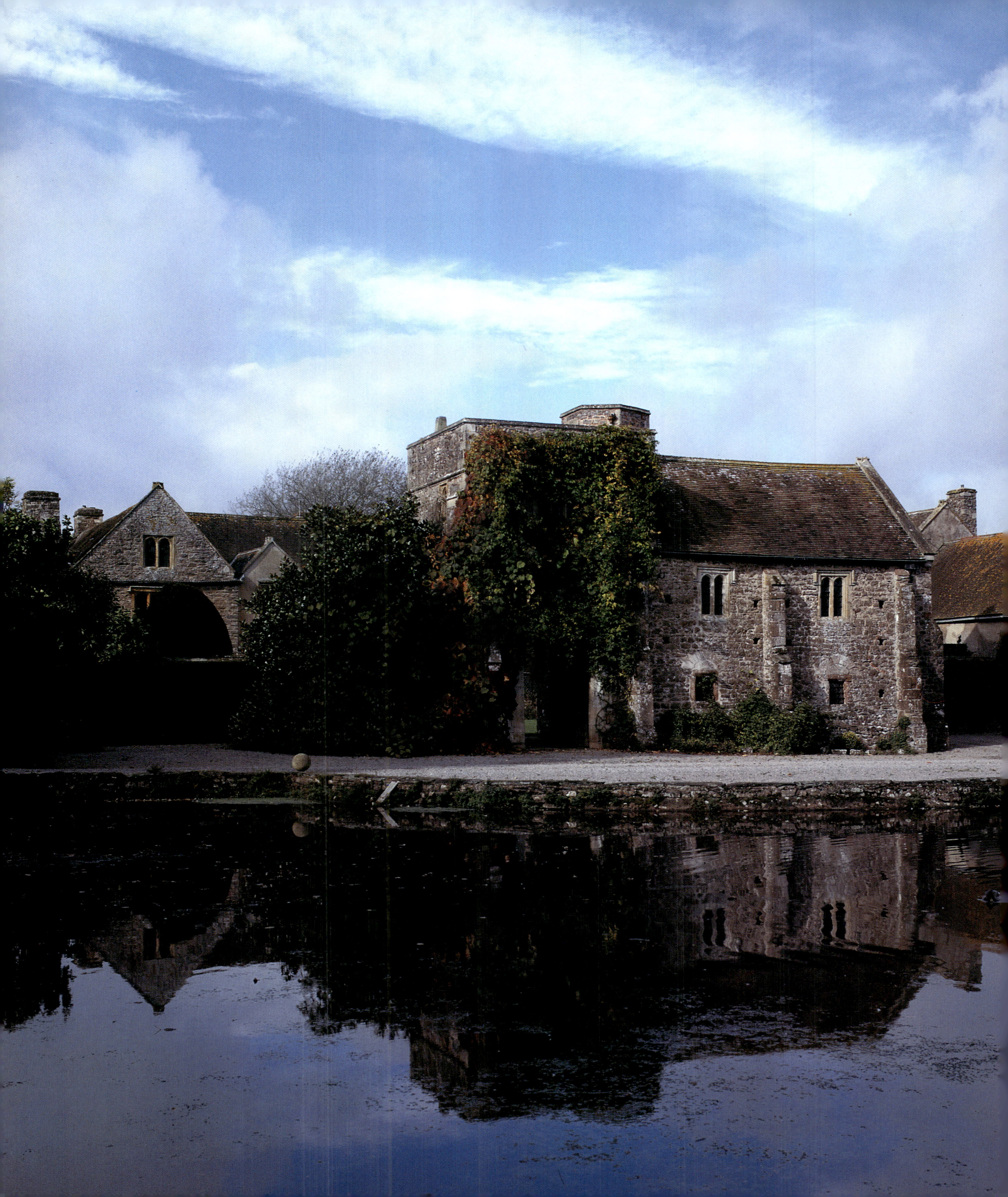

10

COTHAY MANOR

SOMERSET

N O ONE did more to open people's eyes in the 20th century to the beauty of English country-house architecture than Christopher Hussey of *Country Life*. So when one comes across a description by him in 1927 of Cothay as 'the most perfect small fifteenth-century country house that survives in the kingdom', attention naturally turns to Somerset to discover how this paragon is shaping up for the 21st century.

Finding the place, buried among a series of high-banked lanes that appear to lead nowhere and are generally clogged with rich, red mud, is by no means easy. Its well-concealed situation on the Devon/Somerset border near Wellington has doubtless contributed to its remarkably intact survival. Indeed, originally it was even more inaccessible, being positioned on what was then an island bounded by a brook and a ditch connecting to the River Tone – hence the name Cothay, meaning 'cot on the ey', or eyot.

Cothay originally lay within the manor of Kittisford, or 'Kydeforde' as it is called in old documents. In the early 13th century we find that Richard, Lord of Kydeford, granted to William de Cotthehee and his heirs, in return for his homage and services, and a rent of four shillings a year, the lands of Cotthehee, or Cothay, which William's ancestors had held from Richard's ancestors – an arrangement that had presumably already been in place for some centuries. In the 15th century the Bluett family, who had acquired the manor of Kittisford, eventually managed to buy out the Cothays. In 1465, we learn, Walter Bluett determined to settle 'all the landes and tenementes in Cottehays, together with his manors of Kittisford and Almsworthy' on his younger son, Richard. Although Richard found himself with a dispute on his hands after Walter died in 1481, when the elder son, Nicholas, laid claim to the property, matters appear to have been settled by 1485 when Richard set about building the present house.

PRECEDING PAGES 'The most perfect small 15th-century country house that survives in the kingdom': Cothay, as described by Christopher Hussey of *Country Life*. The restored Gatehouse is in the foreground.

LEFT The east front.

Thus with Cothay we reach the very end of the Middle Ages in our tour of English manor houses – and there could be no better example of its type, especially as it is so extraordinarily unchanged and 'unrestored' (as Christopher Hussey shrewdly noted when writing about Lieutenant-Colonel Reginald Cooper's supremely sympathetic repairs in the 1920s: 'Nor are there any new old fireplaces or new old panelling'). The building follows the conventional form of small manor houses of this period, as exemplified by Great Chalfield (*qv*). It is of local sandstone, harled and washed yellow ochre on the east front. The north and west sides are of purplish hue, though the little Elizabethan wing has an orange wash. As Hussey put it, Cothay looks 'as though it had been moulded by thick fingers out of the soil'.

None the less, all the dressed features are of the superior Ham Hill stone and the windows are, for the most part, mullioned and transomed. An unusual touch is the flamboyant roundel in the west gable of the north wing. The porch arch, curiously, looks as if it predates the house – perhaps it is a remnant of the earlier building on the site. On the other hand, the Gatehouse – splendidly restored in 1926–27 by Colonel Cooper from drawings supplied by Sir Harold Brakspear, who had previously worked at Great Chalfield – appears to date from towards the end of Richard Bluett's time at Cothay. He died in 1524 and is commemorated, together with his wife Alice Verney, by some magnificent brasses in Kittisford church. The armorial stone on the Gatehouse duly features the arms of Bluett and Verney.

By the early 17th century, if not earlier, Cothay had become the home of the Every family. Certainly William Every was responsible for adding the fine panelled Dining Room, with its elaborately carved heraldic chimneypiece. He also wainscoted the dais end of the Great Hall and the Parlour, with its walnut graining. William went on to serve as High Sheriff of Somerset in 1638 and died in 1652; but subsequent generations of Everys mainly seem to have been absentees and Cothay, like so many old manor houses, declined to the status of tenanted farmhouse during the 18th and 19th centuries.

Fortunately, in 1925, Colonel Cooper came to the rescue, when he bought the place from the Sweet family. 'To him', wrote Christopher Hussey, 'a real debt is owed by all lovers of English architecture and craftsmanship for his preservation and skilful treatment.' Not the least of the Colonel's exciting discoveries were a phenomenal series of wall paintings, hitherto covered in

ABOVE View from the porch looking east, towards the Gatehouse.

RIGHT Detail of elaborately carved heraldic chimneypiece in the Dining Room, added by William Every, High Sheriff of Somerset in 1638.

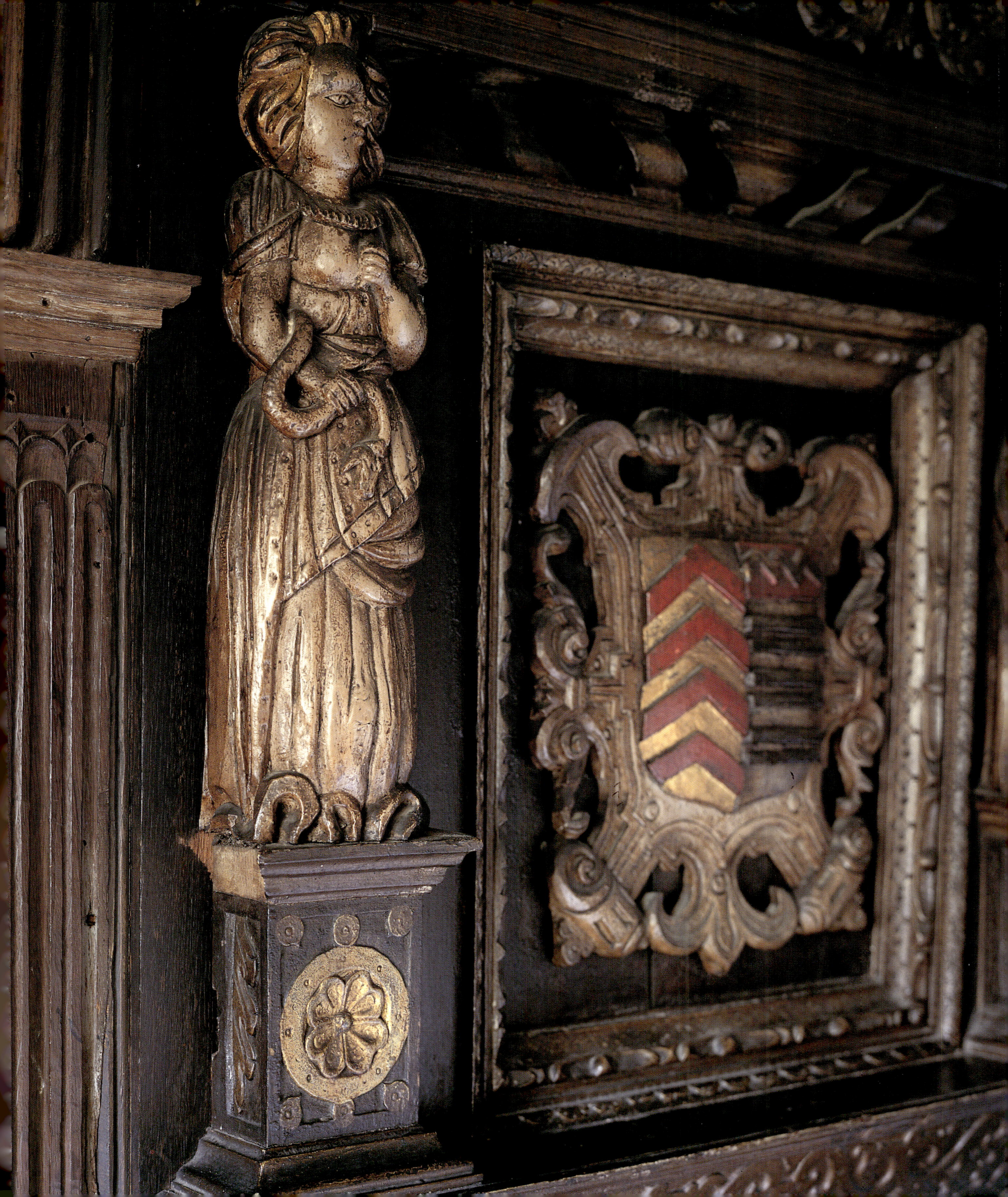

ABOVE View from the entrance arch, inside the porch, down the screens passage.

LEFT The Great Hall, with its original high-walled gallery of plastered lath plus central windows – an unusual survival.

BELOW The light and airy Solar, with its broadly timbered roof and cheerful decoration.

OPPOSITE 'The Immaculate Conception': one of Cothay's remarkable series of medieval wall paintings.

successive coats of plaster, and sufficient traces of the original interior decoration in several of the rooms for it to be satisfyingly completed. Professor E.W. Tristram, author of the classic three-volume work *English Medieval Wall Painting*, wrote that he knew 'of no other domestic work with which one could make any real comparison, and in this way the Cothay paintings appear to me unique'.

Besides some fascinating fragments in the Great Hall, the outstanding surviving wall paintings include a frieze in the Parlour and, in the bedrooms, a Madonna and Child and the Immaculate Conception. Other notable interior features at Cothay are the refreshingly light and airy Solar, with its rose window, broadly timbered roof and cheerful decoration; the exquisite little Oratory, and the unusual gallery above the Great Hall which not only still serves its original purpose of giving access to the bedrooms but has its original high wall of plastered lath, with central window.

The present owners of Cothay, Mr and Mrs Alastair Robb (who acquired the place after the departure of Sir Edward Du Cann, the former Conservative politician, in 1993), are happily following in the expert footsteps of Colonel Cooper, both inside and out. The gardens, which achieved renown in 'Reggie' Cooper's day, between the World Wars, have been redesigned by the Robbs and replanted within the original framework of yew hedges. A white garden, scarlet and purple garden, herbaceous borders and bog garden are but a few of the delights to have attracted horticultural enthusiasts to this increasingly sought-after showplace. The Robbs also open the house, and their enthusiasm for this magical domain is irresistibly infectious.

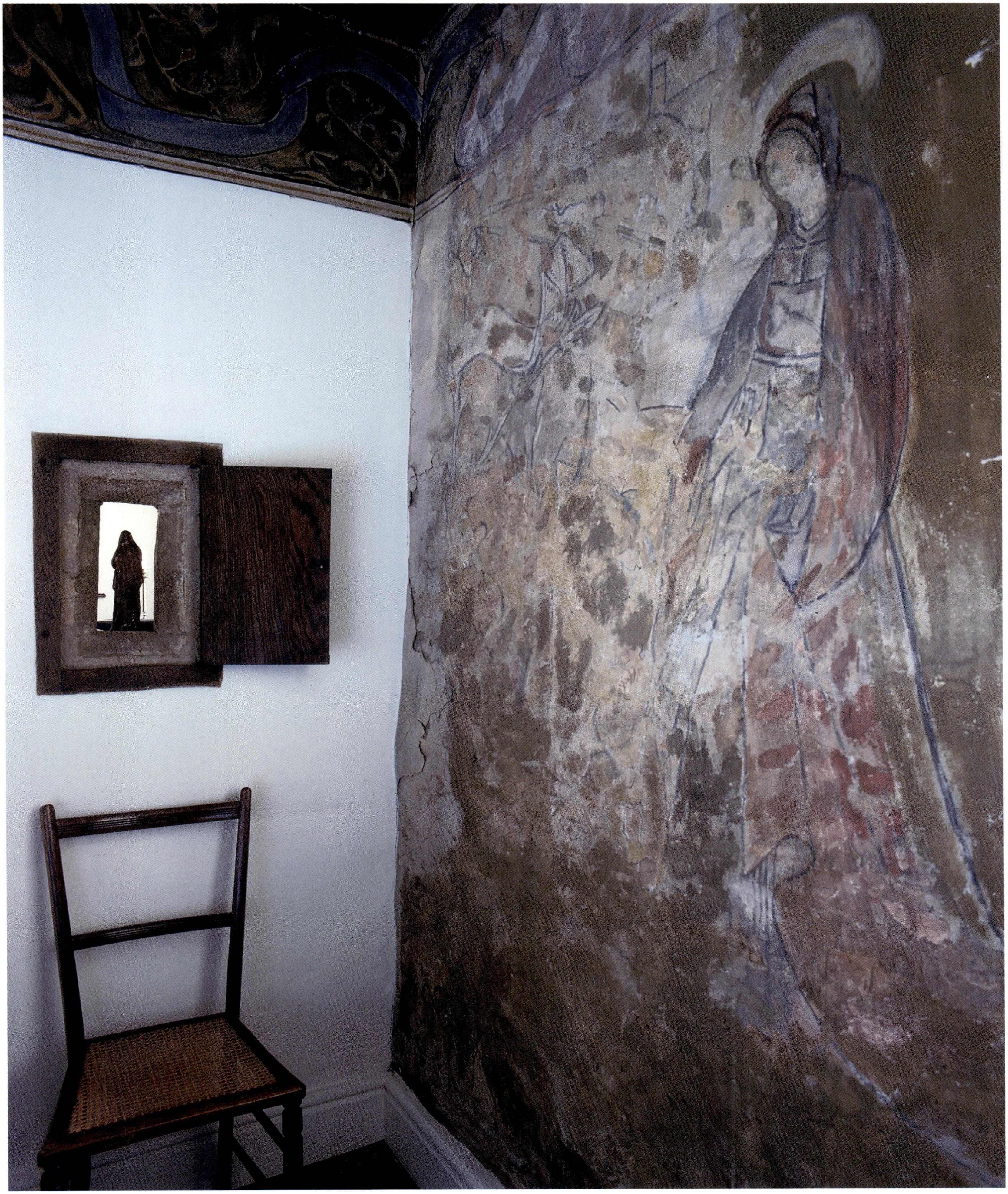

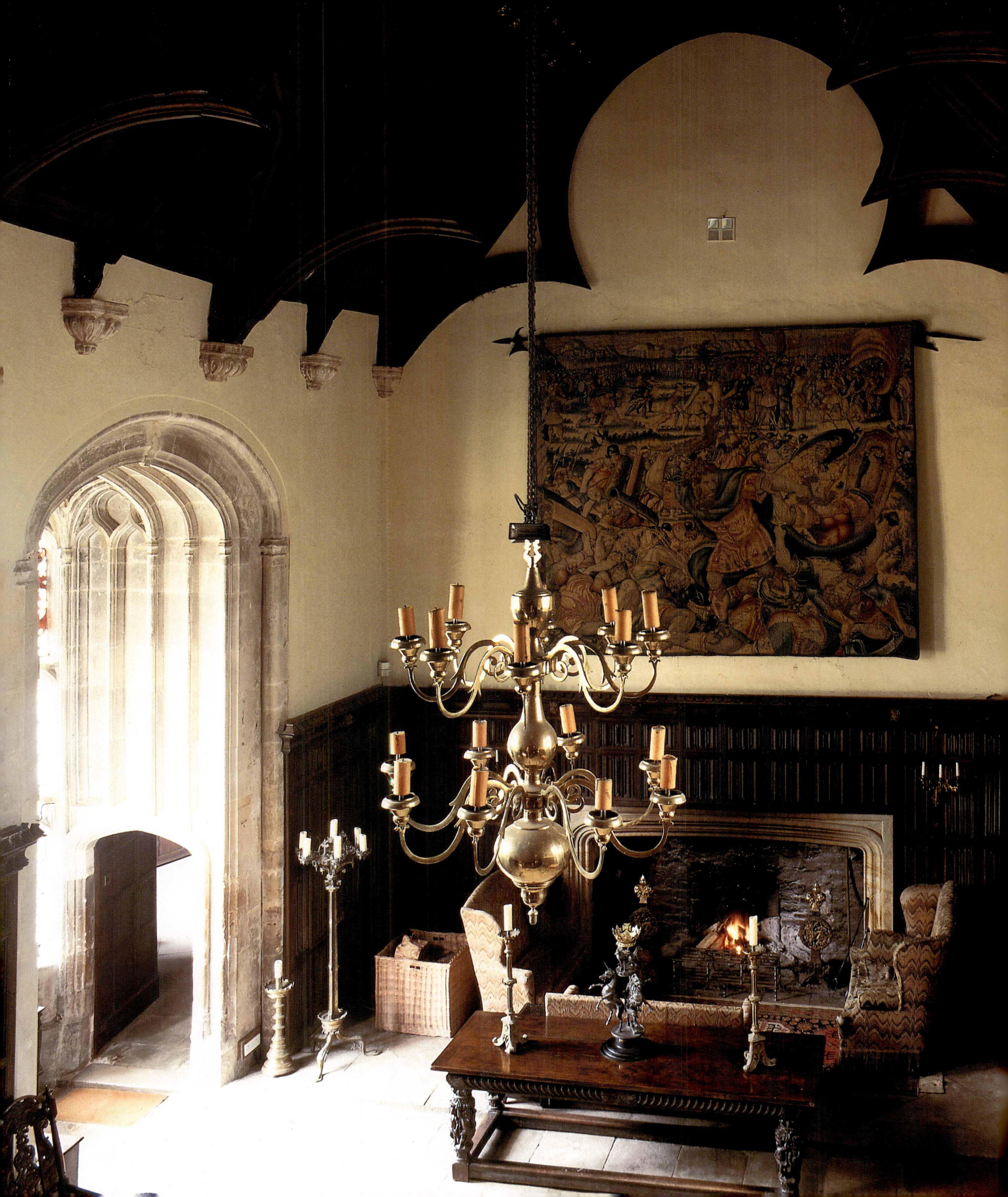

11

ATHELHAMPTON

DORSET

As with all the best Dorset manor houses, the name of Thomas Hardy is associated with Athelhampton, by the River Piddle near Dorchester. The poet featured the place as 'Athelhall' in his poems *The Dame of Athelhall* and *The Children and Sir Nameless*, and there is a particularly evocative description of the Great Hall, Athelhampton's outstanding interior, in his macabre short story, *The Waiting Supper*. Its roof, wrote Hardy, of 'braces, purlins and rafters made a brown thicket of oak overhead'.

This 'brown thicket' is notable for the immense cusps given to the arch-braces of the principal trusses so that they appear as a series of bounding trefoil arches. At first glance, this astonishing roof seems to belong more to a medieval aisled hall of the 14th century rather than to a house well documented as early Tudor.

Certainly the history of the estate stretches back into the Middle Ages, when the manor of Pidele was recorded in *The Domesday Book* as being held by the Bishop of Salisbury, though in Saxon times it had been held by one Aethelric. The name 'Aethelhelm' does not crop up until the 13th century. Subsequently Athelhampton ('the verie name intimates Nobilitie', asserted John Coker in his *Survey of Dorsetshire*, 1732) belonged to the de Loundres and de Pydele families, from whom it passed to the Martyns.

The builder of the present house, Sir William Martyn, made his fortune in wool and became a prominent London merchant, ending up as Master of the Skinners' Company and Mayor of London. In 1495 he was given licence to crenellate Athelhampton (or 'Adlampston', as it was spelt in the document) and to enclose 160 acres of deer park. Built of whitish limestone with Ham Hill stone dressings, the new house followed the traditional medieval arrangement of porch, battlemented hall, oriel and service wing in a broadly asymmetrical grouping.

Over the entrance arch is an heraldic ape or 'martin sejant' holding a looking-glass. This was the family crest of the Martyns and complements the family motto: 'He who looks at Martyn's ape, Martyn shall look at him'. The ape is a recurring motif throughout the house (it also features in the coat of arms of the current owners, the Cooke family), and the story goes that in the 16th century one of the Martyns kept an ape here. Inevitably, a ghost story arose,

PRECEDING PAGES 'A brown thicket of oak overhead...', Thomas Hardy's description of the roof of the Great Hall at 'Athelhall', alias Athelhampton. The immense cusps of the arch-braces of the principal trusses give them the appearance of bounding trefoil arches.

LEFT The east front.

wherein the ape can be heard trying to escape from the secret staircase and cellar in which it is trapped.

In cold fact, the 16th century at Athelhampton was notable for the addition of the projecting west wing and the gatehouse (unfortunately dismantled in 1862) by Sir William's grandson, Robert Martyn. There are interesting stylistic similarities between this new wing (which contains the Great Chamber) and the manor house at Sandford Orcas in the north of the county (*qv*), such as the lozenge-shaped panels and the octagonal shafts at the angles. The links between the two houses were further strengthened when Robert's granddaughter,

ABOVE 'He who looks at Martyn's ape, Martyn shall look at him': the family crest of the Martyn family, who built the present house at Athelhampton where the ape is a recurring motif.

LEFT View across the entrance forecourt (with the porch of the late-15th-century house to the right) to the west front, added in about 1540. The lozenge-shaped panels are echoed at Sandford Orcas (*qv*).

ABOVE Detail of the carved figures that adorn the external walls of Athelhampton.

ABOVE RIGHT A corner of the labyrinthine interior.

Catherine, married Edward Knoyle of Sandford Orcas. The Martyn male line at Athelhampton expired in 1595 – when, or so the story goes, the ape roamed the house searching for its new master only to find four daughters.

The consequently divided ownership ensured that Athelhampton declined to the fate suffered by so many old manor houses in the 17th and 18th centuries, that of a tenanted farmhouse in poor order. Ultimately, in the 19th century, the estate passed to Catherine Tylney-Long, wife of the notorious 4th Earl of Mornington, whose obituary in the *Morning Chronicle* in 1857 did not mince words: 'Redeemed by no single virtue, adorned by no single grace…'. And *The Annual Register* noted: 'Of the miseries which followed this marriage, and of the subsequent scandals of the deceased's career, it is better to say nothing.' None the less, it proceeded to chronicle how 'The vast property he had acquired by marriage and all that came from his own family, was squandered; and, after many years of poverty and profligacy, he subsisted on a weekly pension from his relatives, the late and present Duke of Wellington.'

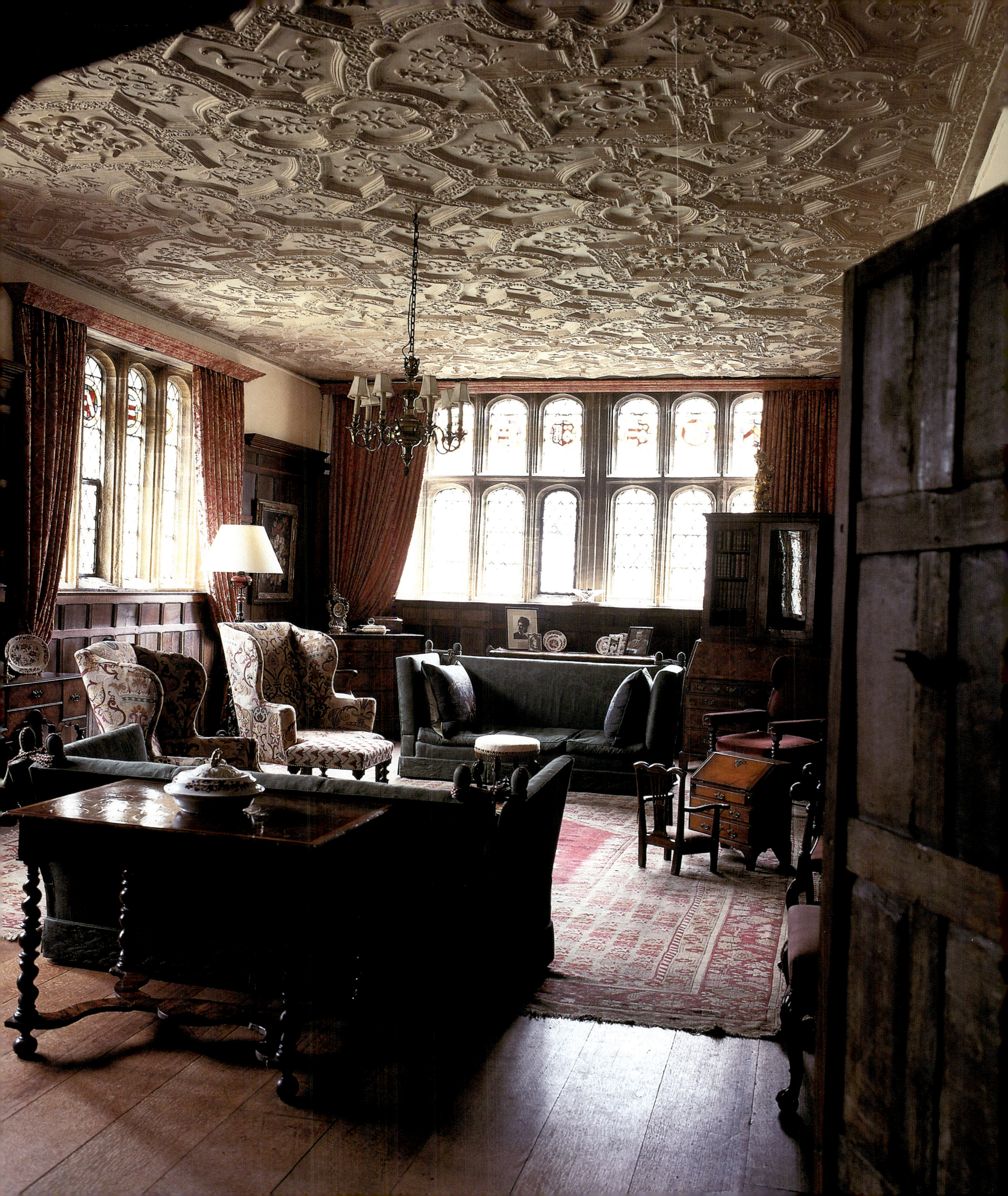

ABOVE Screens passage.

OPPOSITE The Great Chamber, rescued from use as a granary, with its ceiling of 1905, installed by Alfred Cart de Lafontaine and executed by G. Giuntini, in the 16th-century 'Reindeer Inn' pattern from Banbury in Oxfordshire.

BELOW View through to the small Chapel in the south-east tower adjoining the State Bedroom.

Part of the fallout from this unhappy alliance saw the 5th Lord Mornington sell the Athelhampton estate in 1848 to George Wood, an upright Nonconformist farmer and businessman who began the long process of restoration. By all accounts, it desperately needed attention. 'I remember it a deserted and seemingly ruined building used as a farm,' recalled Lady Dorothy Nevill of her childhood nearby in the 1830s. 'The garden was a wilderness through which cattle roamed right up to the door.'

Athelhampton's great revival came under the ownership of Alfred Cart de Lafontaine from 1891. On arrival, he recalled, he found the roof of the Great Hall 'almost white with neglect and mildew', though 'luckily beyond cleaning and oiling I had little to do to it'. The Great Chamber, once used as a granary in Athelhampton's wilderness years, was given a new plaster ceiling in the 16th-century 'Reindeer Inn' pattern from Banbury, and the Library (now a billiard-room) was panelled in oak under a new ceiling described by Clive Aslet in *Country Life* as being 'more Art Nouveau in feeling'. Cart de Lafontaine's principal achievement, though, was to create the splendid Ham stone courts of the formal gardens which make a visit to Athelhampton so unforgettable. It is said that 40,000 tons of stone went into the walls and architectural features of this paradisal haven.

Sadly, the First World War ruined Cart de Lafontaine's continental business interests. The next owner, George Cockrane, added the north wing in the early 1920s; but it was not until the 1950s that Athelhampton really came into its own during the ebullient ownership of the Cooke family. First, Robert Victor Cooke, a surgeon and connoisseur, then his son Robert or 'Robin' (later Sir Robert, MP and indefatigable champion of the Heritage movement) and his wife Jenifer (a descendant of the Martyns, incidentally), and latterly their son Patrick and his wife Andrea, have all played significant parts in improving the house and gardens.

Patrick Cooke had to cope with a seemingly disastrous fire in 1992, but since then he has successfully co-ordinated the restoration of the east wing and completed the conversion of the Coach House into a popular restaurant and function-room. After all its vicissitudes, Athelhampton now exudes an informal *joie de vivre*, as well as a soothing sense of the past. There is much to enjoy, both inside and out, from a wide range of English furniture and 19th-century works of art to an intriguing series of 'garden compartments'.

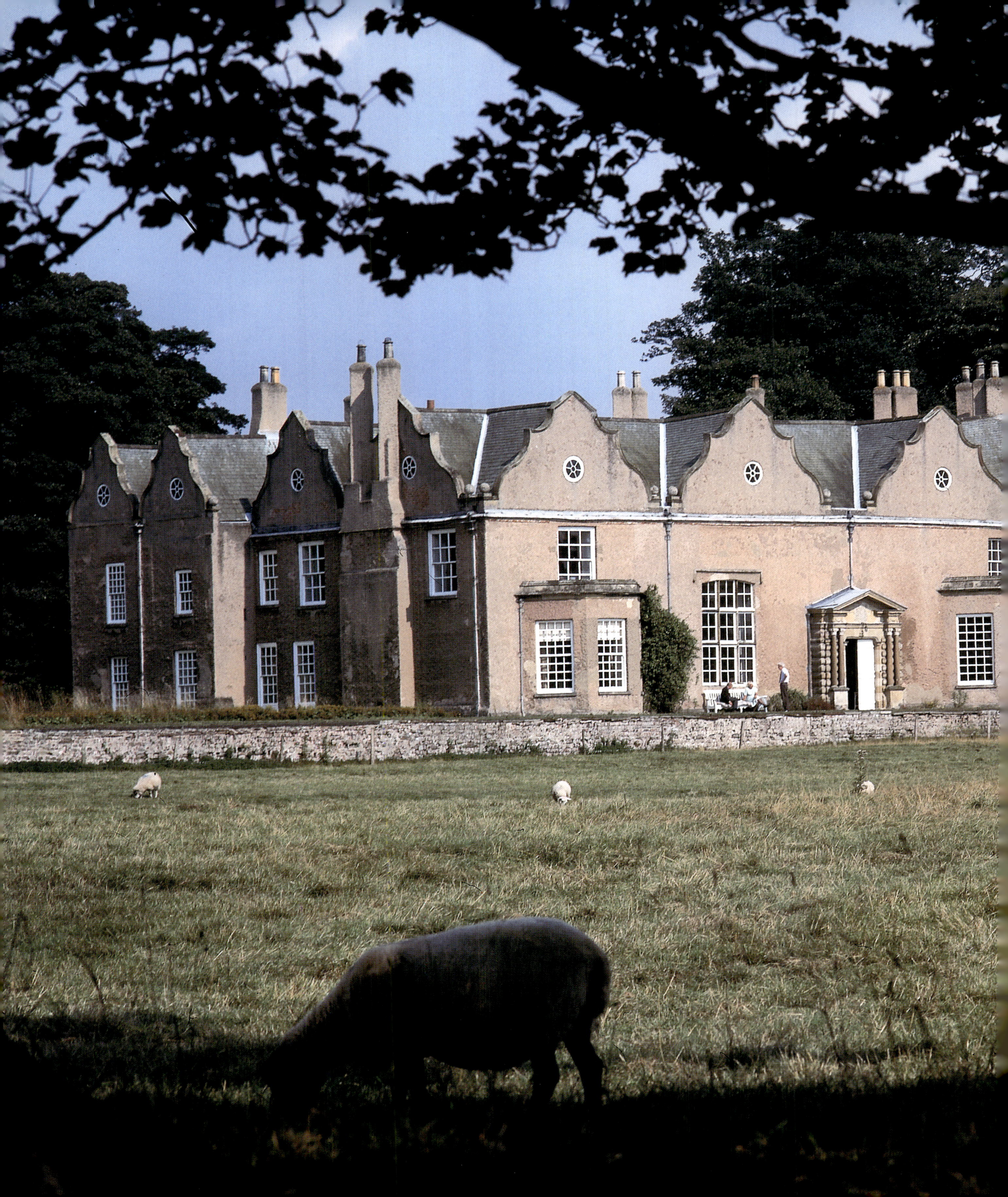

12

NORTON CONYERS

YORKSHIRE

'IT WAS three stories high, of proportions not vast though considerable: a gentleman's manor house, not a nobleman's seat…'. The description, as every student of English literature will know, is of Thornfield Hall in *Jane Eyre*. It also fits Norton Conyers in the North Riding of Yorkshire, which the novelist Charlotte Brontë is known to have visited in 1839 when, as governess to the 'riotous, perverse, unmanageable cubs' of the Sidgwick family, she accompanied them to this seat of the Graham Baronets. According to Charlotte's friend, Ellen Nussey, Miss Brontë was much impressed by the story she heard at Norton Conyers about the Graham family legend of the 'Mad Woman'.

Apparently some time in the 18th century an unhinged female is supposed to have been confined in the remotest corner of the attics – a room still known as 'the Mad Woman's Room'. It seems reasonable to assume that this story gave Charlotte the idea for the crazed Mrs Rochester in *Jane Eyre*. Certainly there are striking similarities between Thornfield and Norton Conyers, such as the rookery ('whose cawing tenants were now on the wing'), the sunk fence, the broad oak staircase lit by a high latticed window and the high square hall covered in family portraits.

The history of this highly atmospheric place goes back to *The Domesday Book*, where it appears as 'Norton' – Anglo-Saxon for 'North Village'. In the early 12th century it was acquired by a Norman family called Conyers – hence the name Norton Conyers. The date of the present building is uncertain; recent research suggests most of it dates from the late 14th or early 15th century, with further additions in the 16th, 17th and 18th centuries. The exterior has been much altered; the gables, for instance, were added some time in the 17th century, and the main front's prominent bow windows in the late 18th. The house is brick throughout; the peachy roughcast that covers the brick is a relatively recent addition. An interesting discovery was made some years ago when an archaeological survey revealed traces of a previously unknown late medieval garden to the north-east of the house.

The Great Hall, the predominant interior, still has something of the flavour of the medieval house, and its sheer size is an indication of how powerful the Nortons, who succeeded the Conyerses, had become. Yet, as we saw in the chapter on the neighbouring Markenfield (*qv*), they were to become spectacularly unstuck in the 'Rising of the North' of 1569. One year (1567–68) Richard Norton was High Sheriff of Yorkshire; the next, he was attainted and stripped of his lands. He died in exile in Flanders in 1585.

Meanwhile, Norton Conyers was acquired by the Musgrave family, who entertained James VI of Scotland on his way south to be crowned King James I of England. The King crops up again in the house's history: he granted Richard Graham, a protégé of the Duke of Buckingham, the crest of a pair of wings on account of the speed with which Graham returned to London from Madrid with despatches of the unsuccessful mission to win the hand of the Infanta of Spain for the Prince of Wales (later Charles I). Graham married Catherine Musgrave and bought the Norton Conyers estate from his father-in-law for £6,500. He subsequently bought another estate at Netherby in Cumberland, where, as at Norton Conyers, his descendants still live.

Family tradition portrays Sir Richard (created a baronet by Charles I) as a loyal and gallant Cavalier during the Civil War. (Contemporary records, however, suggest that his conduct was far from distinguished.) The story goes that he was wounded at the battle of Marston Moor, near York. His horse subsequently galloped him all the way home to Norton Conyers, in through

PRECEDING PAGES 'A gentleman's manor house, not a nobleman's seat…': Charlotte Brontë's description of Thornfield, alias Norton Conyers. The exterior shows an interesting mixture of different dates and styles.

OPPOSITE The arch leading from the Hall to the staircase.

BELOW Detail of the supposed hoof-print burnt into the wood of the staircase by the steed of the Cavalier Sir Richard Graham after their escape from Marston Moor in 1644.

LEFT The Hall, as remodelled by William Belwood in the early 1780s. The vast canvas by John Ferneley (at the far end) of the Quorn Hunt in the 1820s was won at dice by Sir Bellingham Graham, 7th Baronet.

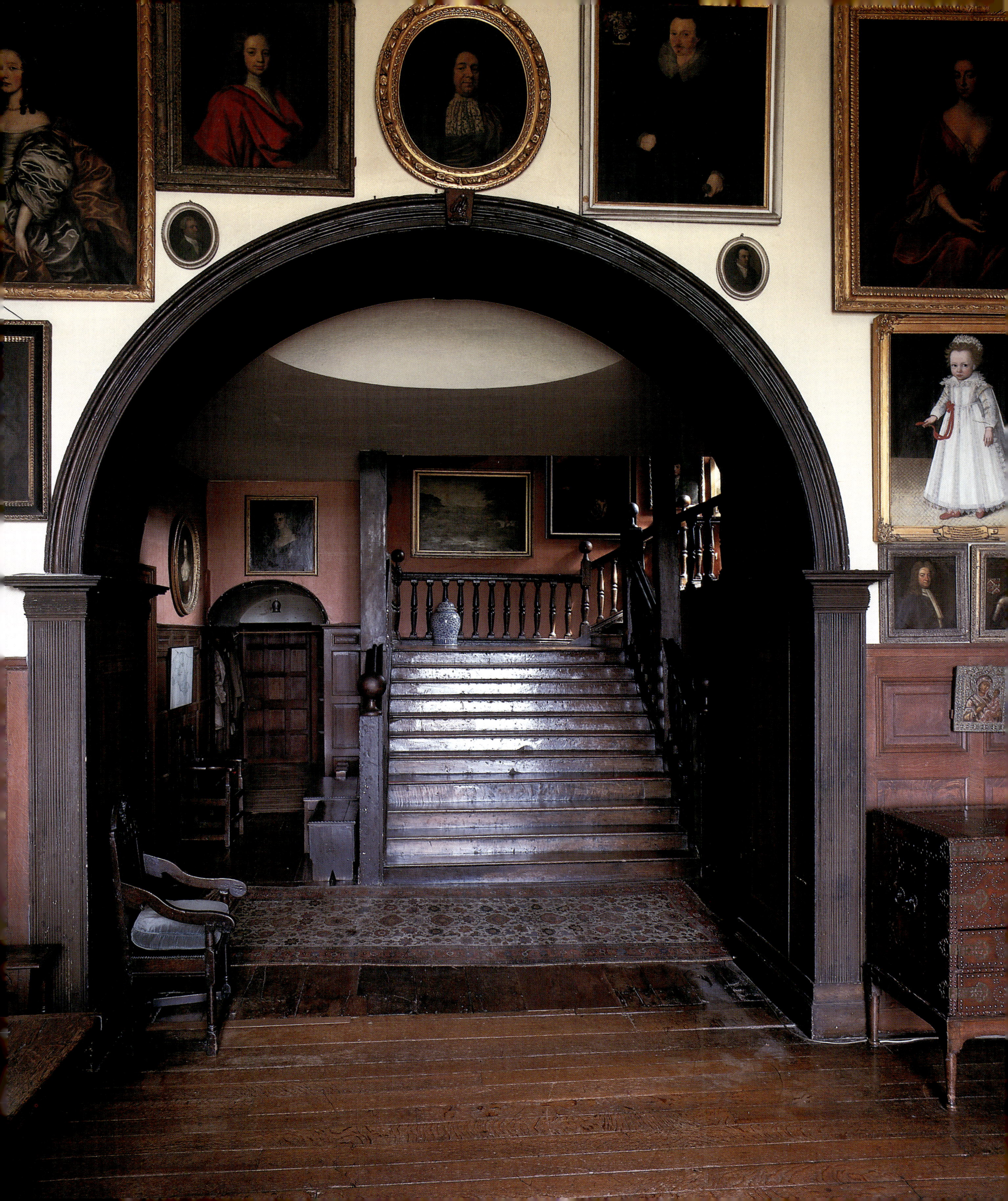

the front door, across the Great Hall (then paved with stone flags), before coming to a halt at the foot of the staircase. This gallant steed then planted one of its fore-hooves on the bottom tread. The iron shoe, hot from the long ride, burned its way into the wood. The hoof print (subsequently removed to another, less exposed part of the staircase) can still be seen - even if spoilsports claim that it is merely a knot in the wood.

They might also argue that the present staircase itself was more likely to have been installed by the next Sir Richard Graham than by his father, though the evidence for this is inconclusive. None the less, the major remodelling of Norton Conyers in the second half of the 17th century can safely be attributed to this younger Sir Richard, whose arms, together with those of his wife, Elizabeth Fortescue, are carved above the central doorcase on the south front. Gervase Jackson-Stops considered in *Country Life* that its 'curiously bulgy rustication' might have been inspired by Francini's *New Book of Architecture* (1669), and Dr Richard Hewlings has suggested the master-mason Robert Trollope as a possible executant.

The next significant remodelling, a century or so later, was carried out by a hitherto underrated local architect, William Belwood (who was Robert Adam's clerk of works at Harewood and Newby), for Sir Bellingham Graham, 5th Baronet, described by a contemporary as 'cheerful and hospitable'. Sir

ABOVE Manorial security: detail of door-locks.

BELOW LEFT 'Curiously bulgy rustication': the central doorcase on the south front, possibly inspired by Francini's *New Book of Architecture* (1669) and executed by Robert Trollope. The armorial bearings are those of Sir Richard Graham, 1st Baronet of Norton Conyers (son of the Cavalier) and his wife, Elizabeth Fortescue.

BELOW The Red Hand of Ulster, the symbol of the Order of the Baronetage, on a downpipe.

Bellingham's father and namesake, the 4th Baronet, had met an unfortunate end in 1755 when he drank a cup of poisoned tea intended (by whom history does not relate) for his mistress, otherwise the unpopular Irish housekeeper.

After a hiccough when the 7th Baronet, another Sir Bellingham (the absentee squire when Charlotte Brontë came to call), squandered the family fortunes on the turf, the hunting field and the *boudoirs* of Paris, Norton Conyers had to be bought back for £28,000 in 1882. Happily, more than another century further forward, the place remains the much-loved family home of the historian Sir James Graham, 11th Baronet, and his wife Halina, a distinguished museum curator. They regularly open to the public the house and gardens, with their 18th-century walls and orangery, plus herbaceous borders. It is a place full of good stories and fascinating things, including portraits by George Romney, Pompeo Batoni and Sir William Beechey (a dashing study of Sir Bellingham 'the Black Sheep' in his 10th Hussars uniform), as well as a vast canvas by John Ferneley depicting the Quorn Hunt in 1822. This was won, in characteristic style, by the 7th Baronet, then Master of the Hunt, on the throw of a dice.

LEFT The staircase landing. The portrait shown in the upper right is thought to represent the younger Sir Richard Graham (1st Baronet of Norton Conyers and second son of Sir Richard Graham, 1st Baronet of Esk, the Cavalier) and his bandaged horse, Brown Bushel, after their escape from the notorious Faw Gang on Hutton Moors, whom he later brought to justice.

RIGHT 'The Mad Woman's Room': a reminder of the Graham family legend that is said to have inspired Charlotte Brontë's idea for the crazed Mrs Rochester in *Jane Eyre*.

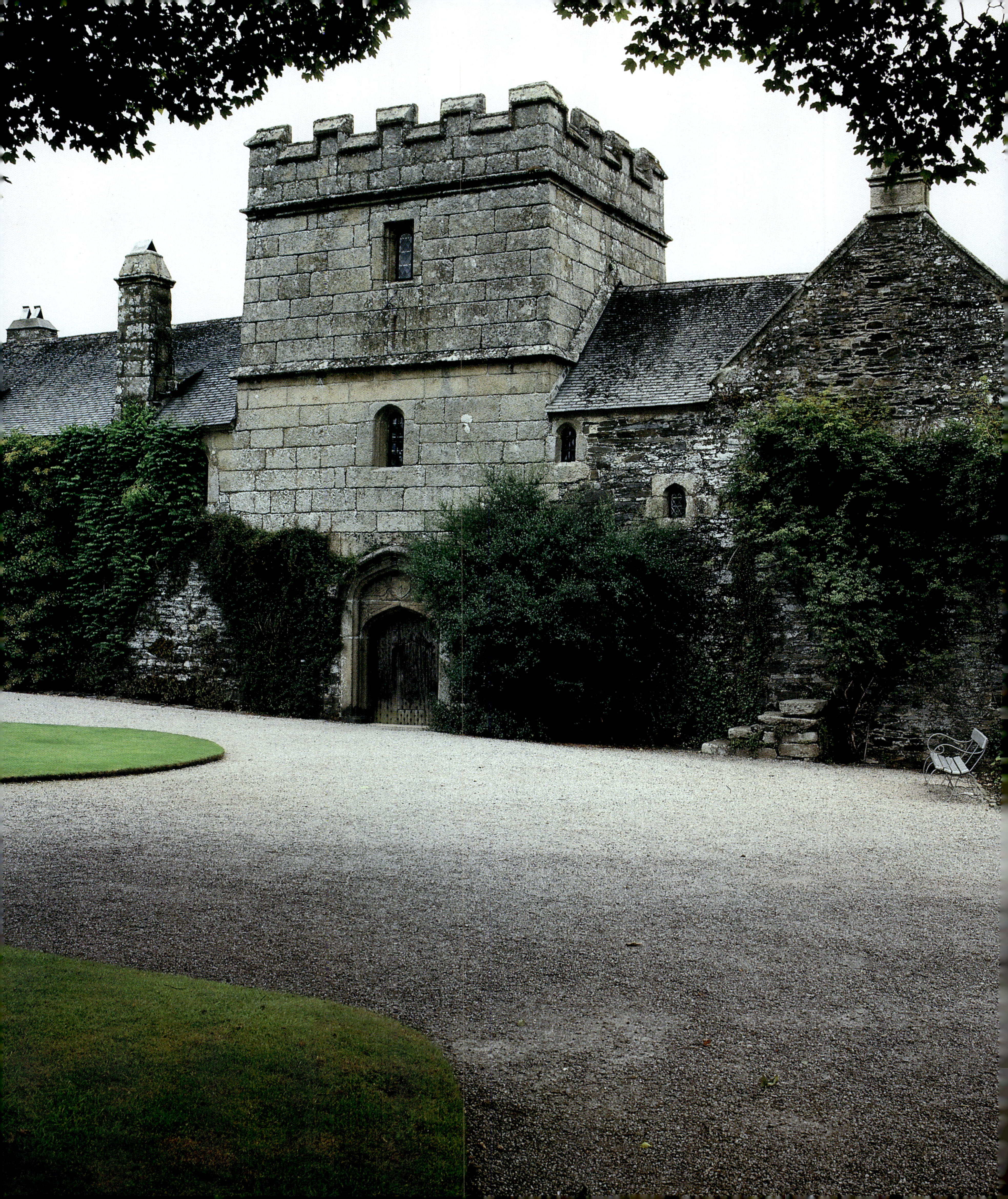

13

COTEHELE

CORNWALL

A FAMILIAR pattern in the history of manor houses is for the family who built the house to develop grand ideas, move away to a statelier pile and leave the old house to degenerate into a dilapidated farmhouse. And then, when the cash runs out, the family suddenly rediscover the quaint delights of the 'sleeping beauty' of their ancestors, lovingly restore it and move back in. The story of Cotehele, nestling into the hillside high above the Cornish bank of the River Tamar, follows some of this pattern, but there are some instructive twists along the way.

For although the Edgcumbes, who were responsible for Cotehele's various stages of construction between 1485 and 1627, subsequently based themselves at their principal seat of Mount Edgcumbe overlooking Plymouth Sound, their original family home was far from neglected. As James Lees-Milne put it, giving a sympathetic description of how Cotehele came into the ownership of the National Trust in his book *People and Places*: 'The Georgian owners came to regard the strange old house as a specimen of antiquarian interest and *virtu*'. The Edgcumbes, by now barons and earls, would bring their guests up from Mount Edgcumbe to admire Cotehele's curiosities by way of a day's diversion. In 1789, for instance, as the Queen recorded in her diary, King George III and Queen Charlotte came to see this intriguing tourist attraction:

> [We] landed at the woods of Cotehill half hour after 10 where we found Lord and Lady Mount Edgecombe ready to receive Us. We went in their coach up to this Old Family seat of theirs... At Breakfast we Eat off the Old Family Pewter, used Silver knives Forks Spoons which have been Time immemorial in the Family have always been kept at this place....

Queen Charlotte's description took in the Great Hall, 'full of old armour & swords and old carved chairs of the times, the drawing room and closets hung with old tapestry, the skirting board which is straw, the chair seats made of

PRECEDING PAGES The battlemented late-15th-century Gatehouse of Cotehele.

LEFT The east front, facing the garden.

the prince's vestments', and many other points of detail, such as the glass in the Chapel. Nor did 'the decanter… of the year 1646' escape her notice.

In 1840 the 3rd Earl of Mount Edgcumbe commissioned Nicholas Condy, a Cornish watercolourist, to illustrate a folio-size volume recording the exterior and interior of Cotehele. The sumptuous result provides a remarkable documentation of the contents, complete with tapestries, bed-hangings and furniture, which a visitor can still easily identify today. As you look at these beautiful pictures, it is tempting to become carried away and hail Cotehele as an unaltered 'time capsule', but in his account of the house the peerless architectural historian Mark Girouard reminds us that 'one needs to be gently sceptical'. As he points out, Cotehele was arranged by the antiquarian Edgcumbes as they 'thought an old-fashioned house ought to be arranged'. The way the old tapestries are used 'almost like wallpaper' is more typical of the 19th than of the 16th or 17th centuries. By the time Condy set up his easel in 1840, 'the stage had already been set'.

A century later, James Lees-Milne described his first impressions of Cotehele in his diary:

> The situation is romantic, wild and wooded… It is uniformly old,
> late medieval with pointed windows, all of granite. The great hall is
> as fine as any I have seen, with curved windbraces in the roof and
> plastered white-washed walls, hung with armour.

In the text that accompanied Condy's illustrations, the Reverend F.V.J. Arundell suggested that the name 'Cotehele' was derived from 'coit', meaning a wood, and 'hel', a river, in Old Cornish. Certainly the woods over the Tamar give the place its distinctive flavour, memorably summed up by Lees-Milne as 'russet roofs, lichened walls, ferns, rills and sodden leaves'.

Yet the original Cotehele was doubtless far from romantic. Its principal builder, or strictly speaking, re-builder, Sir Richard Edgcumbe (whose family had acquired the property in the 14th century through marriage to Hillaria, the de Cotehele heiress), was, as Mark Girouard pithily puts it, 'a tough professional soldier living in a tough part of the world and he built a tough house'. In 1483 Edgcumbe, who had joined the Duke of Buckingham's rebellion against Richard III, was besieged by Sir Henry Bodrugan, the King's representative at Cornwall, but escaped through the woods to the river. Here he hid behind some bushes, weighed down his hat with a stone and threw it into the water. His pursuers, noticing the Edgcumbe headgear floating downstream, came to the conclusion that he had drowned. Edgcumbe fled to France.

BELOW The White Room, with its attractive bedhangings.

'As fine as any I have seen...': James Lees-Milne's first impression of the Great Hall, with its curved windbraces in the roof and plastered white-washed walls hung with armour.

When the King was defeated at Bosworth Field two years later, Sir Richard (as he now became) assumed the role of Comptroller of the Household to Henry VII and had the satisfaction of taking over the estates of Sir Henry Bodrugan, whom he literally chased into the sea – at what is now called Bodrugan's Leap, near Mevagissey. Understandably, Cotehele's battlemented exterior was not made particularly welcoming. Virtually the only ornamental feature on the outside is the bell-turret on the Chapel. One of its bells is also the bell of the original 1480s clock – the earliest clock in England still in working order in its original position. It predates the invention of the pendulum and the clock-face, being regulated by the horizontal balance known as a foliot.

Once you step inside the courtyard, however, Cotehele's special charms reveal themselves. Sir Richard's son, Sir Piers Edgcumbe, another soldier, completed the Great Hall range, with its fine timber roof, together with the second courtyard, by 1520. The tall tower was added a century later by Sir Thomas Coteel (father-in-law of the then Edgcumbe squire), who had taken up residence here, while his daughter was installed at Mount Edgcumbe.

Later in the 17th century, during the Civil War, the Cavalier Colonel Piers Edgcumbe returned to Cotehele, as Mount Edgcumbe was inconveniently close to Parliamentary Plymouth. Charles I stayed at Cotehele in 1644 – an event commemorated in the virtually unchanged Charles I Bedroom. According to Richard Polwhele's *History of Cornwall*, the Colonel's daughter-in-law, Lady

COTEHELE

Anne, 'died' and was placed in the family vault at Cotehele. A sharp-eyed sexton tried to pull a gold ring off her finger, whereupon the 'corpse' sat upright and the sexton fled in terror.

During the Second World War, when Mount Edgcumbe was bombed by the Germans, the Edgcumbes once more sought sanctuary at Cotehele. In 1947, while arranging for the transfer to the National Trust in lieu of the estate duties due to the Treasury (the first property to come to the Trust by this means), James Lees-Milne observed the Countess of Mount Edgcumbe's Cairn puppy eat 'a good slice of Queen Anne's tatting from the famous needlework sofa in the Punch Room'. 'You naughty little thing' was all the admonition Lady Mount Edgcumbe uttered as the terrier scuttled off with a mouthful.

Today Cotehele is a splendidly preserved and very popular National Trust showplace. There are formal gardens and a richly planted valley garden, with medieval dovecote, stewpond and Victorian summerhouse. Cotehele Mill has been faithfully restored to working condition and down at the quay there is an outstation of the National Maritime Museum. The refurbished Tamar sailing barge Shamrock is moored alongside.

The Kitchen: another atmospheric interior in this popular National Trust showplace.

– 93 –

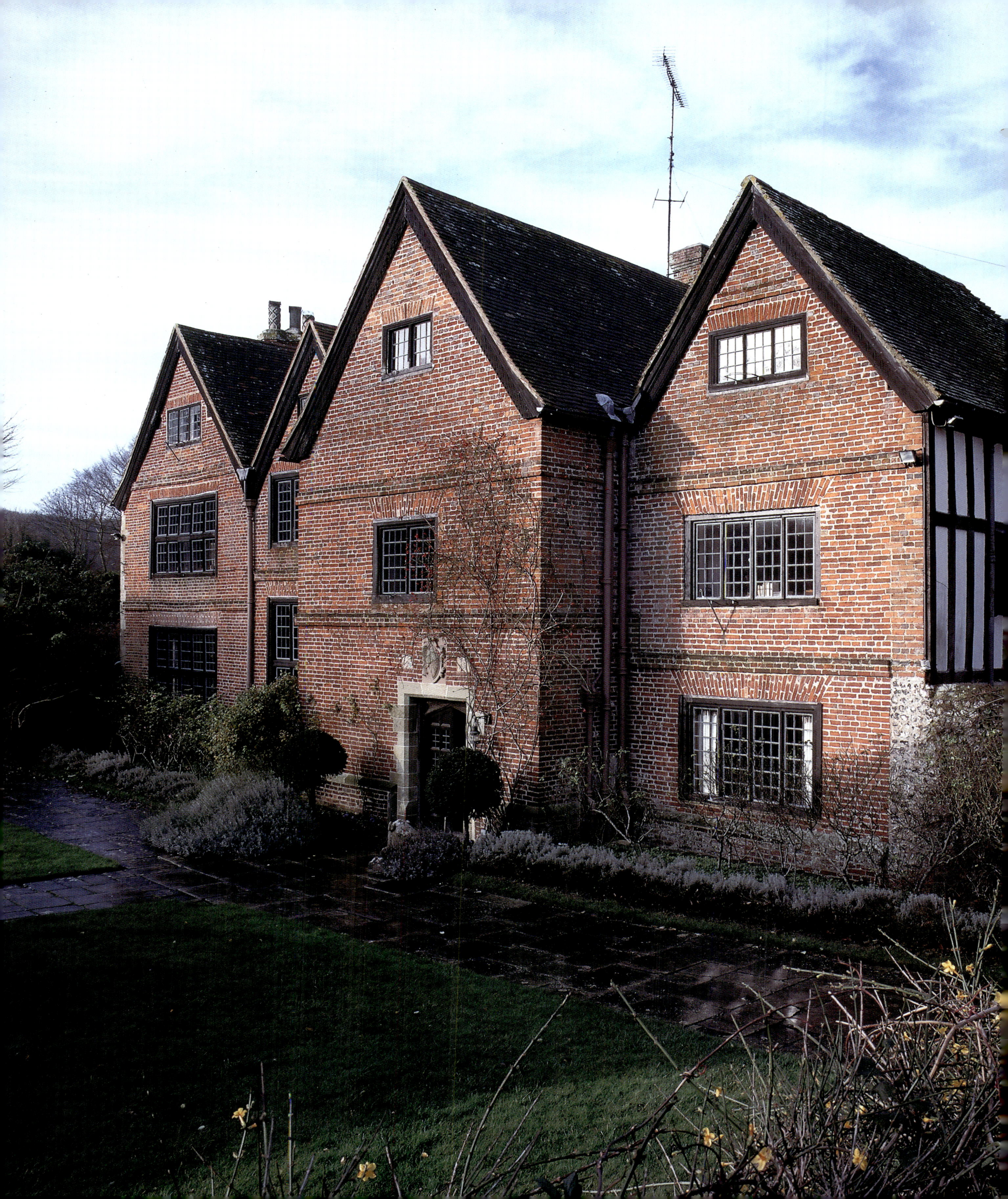

14

FRISTON PLACE

SUSSEX

THE EARLY 20th century saw the apogee of the Manor House Revival. Hitherto neglected old farmhouses, medieval and Tudor halls would be rediscovered and enthusiastically restored, their woodwork lovingly burnished along with their romantic legends of 'Olden Times'. The *Sussex County Magazine* of that period ran a series of articles on 'Historic Houses' by Viscountess Wolseley (spinster daughter and successor of the celebrated late Victorian soldier, Sir Garnet Wolseley, 1st Viscount Wolseley) which perfectly capture the manorial mood of the time.

In 1936 (the year of her death) the indefatigable Lady Wolseley, author of *Gardening for Women*, led her readers down a carriage drive, sheltered by overhanging trees, to a 'many-gabled house, its rose-tinted brick walls alternating with older portions where massive stonework predominates'. To her ladyship's mind ('perhaps due to its position, shut away from where the Eastbourne holiday-makers frequent'), Friston Place was 'one of the unspoilt gems of Sussex'. Happily today, half a century or so later, the same can be said thanks to the sympathetic ownership of the Shawcross family, who have been here since the late 1950s.

So evocative is Lady Wolseley's descriptive style ('As we descend from the car and follow the flagged walk through the Forecourt Garden to the front door... of this creeper-clad, cheerful looking house') that it is hard to resist quoting her *in extenso*. Modern architectural and historical scholarship, though, as exemplified by Clive Aslet's excellent account of Friston Place in *Country Life*, demands a more rigorous approach.

None the less, in fairness to Lady Wolseley, she was canny enough not to be misled by the two datestones – 'T.S. 1613' and 'F.S. 1634' – beside the oak front door. She noted that these were actually removed from the stables by the grandfather of the then owner, Major A.F. Maitland, who was himself largely responsible for rescuing the house from dilapidation. Certainly, as

Lady Wolseley remarked, 'the first impression is that we are looking at a seventeenth century home, where ornate barge-boards and mullioned windows betray a Jacobean touch'.

Yet hidden away behind this 17th-century façade is a fascinating timber-frame structure described by Clive Aslet as 'one of the most impressive to survive in the Downs and Weald'. The earliest part of the present building is the Great Hall, built about 1500. It retains its original roof – which, quite understandably, moved Lady Wolseley to raptures:

> Here, in a comparatively small space, is some of the finest timbering that can anywhere be seen. The great over-spanning arch of massive oak that supports a beautifully-moulded king post is wonderfully fine. The Hall, in its good proportions and general finish is said to be one of the most perfect in this country.

Ah, how the manorial enthusiasts loved their king-posts!

Clive Aslet classifies Friston's original timber-frame structure, which partially survives within the shell of the 17th-century building, as an example of the 'Wealden' house which originated in Kent around 1400, a type that was built in great numbers between 1450 and 1530. As Aslet points out, these houses 'represent the late-medieval and Tudor carpenter's first attempt to give a balanced architectural form to his work'.

After the Great Hall range came a new wing behind its service end, traditionally said to have housed a chapel. The Chapel Room, on its first floor, boasts a muscular moulded crown-post beam. Then, probably at the

PRECEDING PAGES 'One of the unspoilt gems of Sussex': Viscountess Wolseley's description of Friston Place.

OPPOSITE The Great Hall, of about 1500, which retains its original roof. The handsome panelling is a 17th-century addition.

ABOVE Detail of wood carving.

LEFT Friston's interior contains intriguing evidence of the original timber-frame 'Wealden' structure within the shell of the 17th-century building.

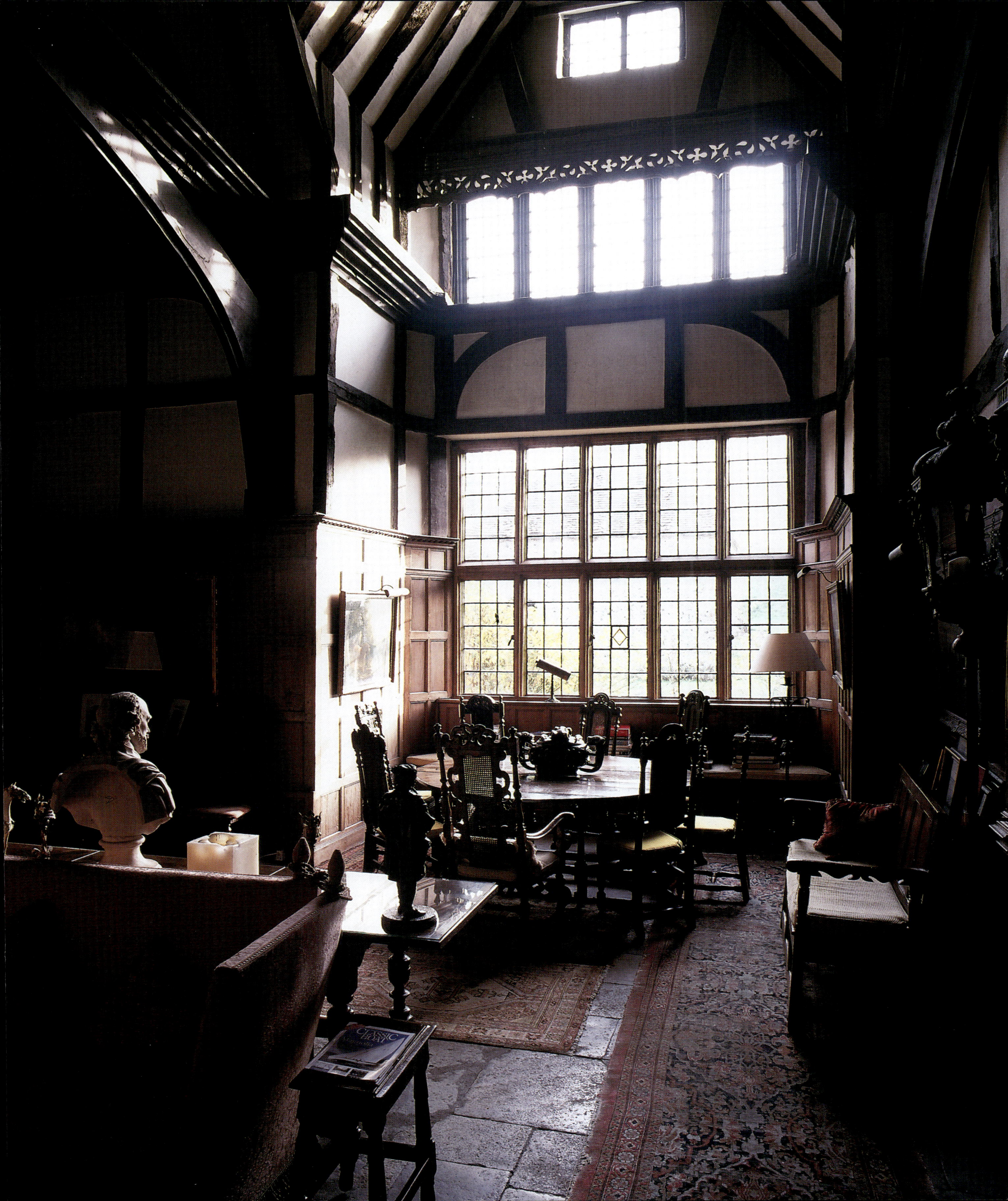
CLASSIC
BOAT

ABOVE Panelled bedroom.

BELOW The comfortable Drawing Room in the original solar area at the west end of the Great Hall.

end of the 16th century, the original solar area at the west end of the Great Hall was replaced by the present cross wing – which provided a Parlour and a Chamber, as well as a staircase and lobby. Much of the timber-framed exterior was covered in walls of flint, with stone quoins and windows.

Also of flint is the Well-House on Friston's front lawn. This contains one of the place's special treasures, a vast wooden donkey-wheel. Within this contraption a tethered ass would tread and tread and tread in order to make it revolve, thereby raising the water from a depth of 136 feet – according to Lady Wolseley, who recalled seeing a similar device at Carisbrooke Castle on the Isle of Wight.

Lady Wolseley and other early historians of Bechington (as the house was originally called) assumed that it was built by the Potman family, who owned the property in the early 15th century. It was greatly enlarged by Thomas Selwyn, from a prominent Sussex family of landowners; he married Margery Adam, whose mother Alice had been the ultimate Potman heiress.

The 'T.S.' alluded to by the front door must be Thomas's descendant and namesake who died in 1613 and whose effigy is at Friston Church. This later Thomas may well have been responsible for the west wing, which contains the Dining Room. On the first floor is a bedroom adorned with some remarkable wall paintings of detailed, colourfully exuberant hunting scenes. The costumes of the figures date the work to the first or possibly second quarter of the 17th century.

The 'F.S. 1634' can only be Francis Selwyn, a moderate Parliamentarian in the Civil War, who presumably added the brick entrance façade and may also have done up the Great Hall, with its handsome panelling. The screens passage has Tuscan pilasters and lozenge-shaped fielded panels. This centrepiece frames a picture of a drum. By this time the Great Hall had been divided into two storeys, though the false ceiling was removed during the 19th century.

More research needs to be carried out into the full extent of the changes made in that century and the one that followed, particularly by the Maitlands, who initially rented the property from the 7th Duke of Devonshire, a substantial landowner around Eastbourne, and by Mrs Young, who owned the property between 1938 and 1945.

The eminent jurist and politician Sir Hartley Shawcross (created a life peer in 1959) and his second wife, Joan, arrived at Friston in 1958 and took special pleasure in developing the garden. Faithfully maintained by his family, it provides a romantic setting for what Lady Wolseley characteristically, but by no means inaccurately, called 'the jewel of a house within its happy Downland surroundings'.

ABOVE The wooden donkey-wheel in the Well House on Friston's front lawn. Water could be drawn up from a depth of 136 feet thanks to the exertions of the ass on the treadmill.

RIGHT and BELOW Details of the remarkable early-17th-century wall paintings in a first-floor bedroom.

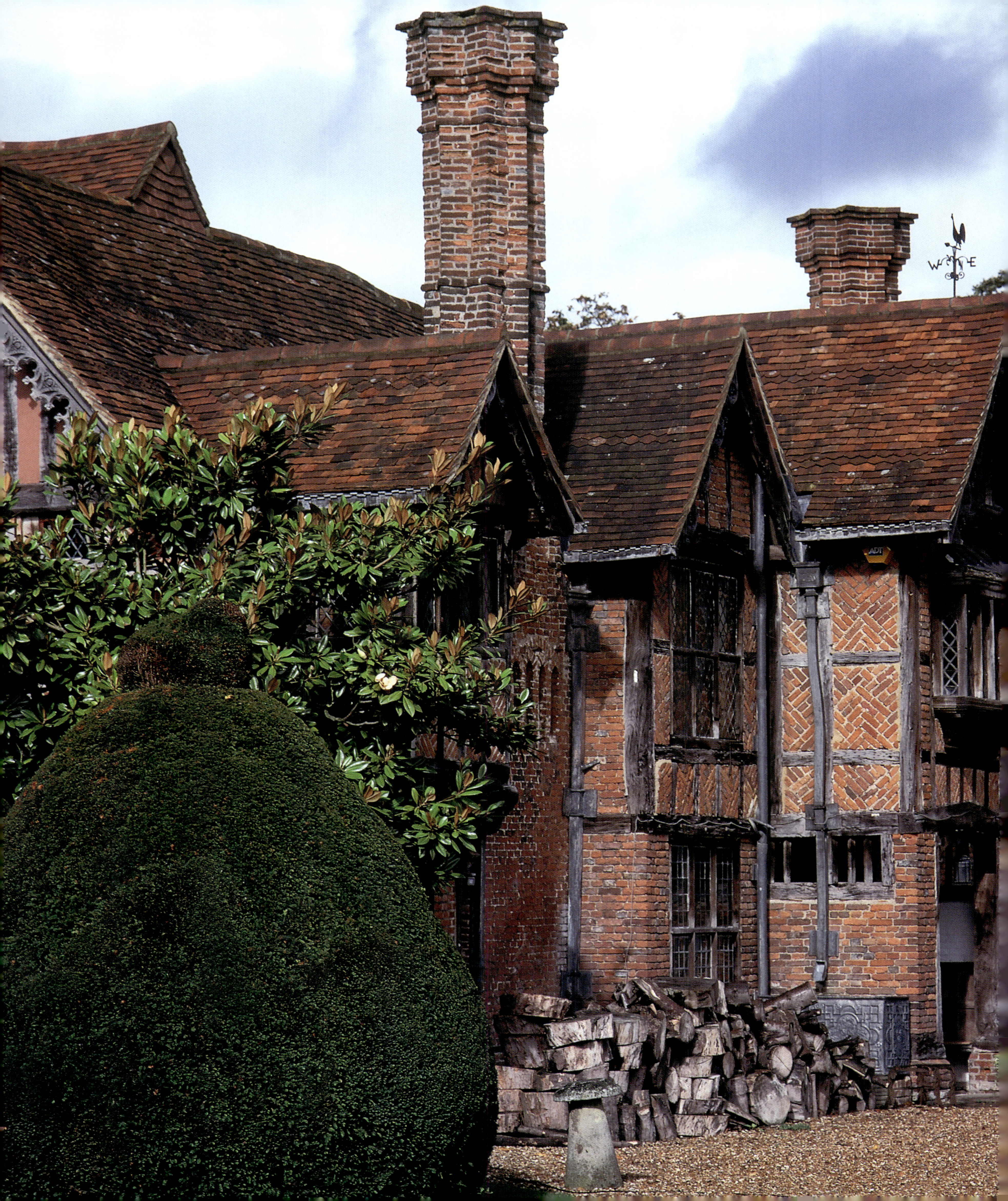

15

DORNEY COURT

BUCKINGHAMSHIRE

A T FIRST blush the gabled pinkish brick and timbered vision that is Dorney Court, with the church tower behind, appears almost too good to be true. By the time it shimmers into view you have already been transported into a dream world by the approach through ancient woodland, although you are only a few miles from the Slough conurbation and the M4. Somehow you half expect Ronald Colman to emerge from behind a yew hedge puffing on his pipe, strolling nonchalantly towards Greer Garson who is graciously dispensing tea on the lawn.

As metaphors become mixed in this fantasy, one imagines Rupert Brooke making earnest inquiries about the availability of honey. And, unlike Peter Sellers in his famous sketch parodying Brooke ('Honey's off'), he would not have been disappointed, for the name Dorney means 'island of bumble bees' and Dorney Court's own honey, celebrated for its delicate flavour, is still on sale here.

For this is emphatically no mirage. Dorney Court is the genuine article (give or take some sympathetic restoration work here and there to remove ill-judged 18th-century 'improvements'): an authentic early Tudor manor house of quite exceptional quality. And what makes it even more extraordinary is that the place has not been on the market – as the estate agents say – for nearly 500 years.

The last time it was the subject of a property transaction was when Sir William Garrard, or Gerrard (as in Gerrards Cross, elsewhere in the county), a grocer and Lord Mayor of London, bought the manor of Dorney and 600 acres from the Hill family in 1537. Sir William's son and namesake had a daughter, Martha Garrard; she married Sir James Palmer, in whose family it has remained ever since. Since 1600 Dorney has passed from father to son in succession – a squirearchical survival that is surely unique in such a built-up area close to London.

Dorney, the most southerly village in Buckinghamshire, lies on a slight rise in the Thames flood plain and is separated from the river by water-meadows, where remains of prehistoric life can be found in the damp peat. Recent excavations at Dorney have revealed that the manor house was once fairly substantial. Although it is dated by dendrochronology in the Great Hall about 1510 and first mentioned in a document of 1513 (when the Lytton family sold it to Richard Hill, but retained a life interest), some of the structure is manifestly earlier.

There are marked similarities between Dorney and Ockwells (*qv*), only a few miles away across the Thames. However, Ockwells, strictly speaking, is classified as a medieval (that is to say, pre-1485) manor house, whereas Dorney is regarded as early Tudor. Christopher Hussey in *Country Life* considered it probable that the greater part of the existing house was built by the Lyttons during their tenure from 1504 to 1514, though it is possible that the west block, enclosing the courtyard, was a reconstruction of an earlier building. As Hussey wrote, the appearance of these western gables is 'picturesque in the extreme'.

The outstanding interior at Dorney is, of course, the galleried Great Hall, which remains an atmospheric example of early Tudor architecture notwithstanding its 'improvement' in the 1840s. Unfortunately the changes included the removal of two large antique windows of stained glass (which must have accentuated the similarity to Ockwells). None the less, the 17th-century woodwork (which replaced the vanished screen), the linenfold panelling from Faversham Abbey and the brought-in 15th-century chimneypiece have all proved sympathetic additions.

Much good antiquarian work was done by Colonel Charles Palmer around the turn of the 20th century, a period particularly sympathetic to English manor houses of this character. The Queen Anne-style brick façades that had bizarrely defaced the west and east sides of the house were, sensibly, removed, though the Dining Room retains its William-and-Mary character. The Colonel

PRECEDING PAGES 'Picturesque in the extreme': Dorney Court.

OPPOSITE The Great Hall: looking towards the dais end. The linenfold panelling came from Faversham Abbey.

BELOW The porch on the east front.

BOTTOM A ravishing manorial ensemble, with the church tower setting off the composition.

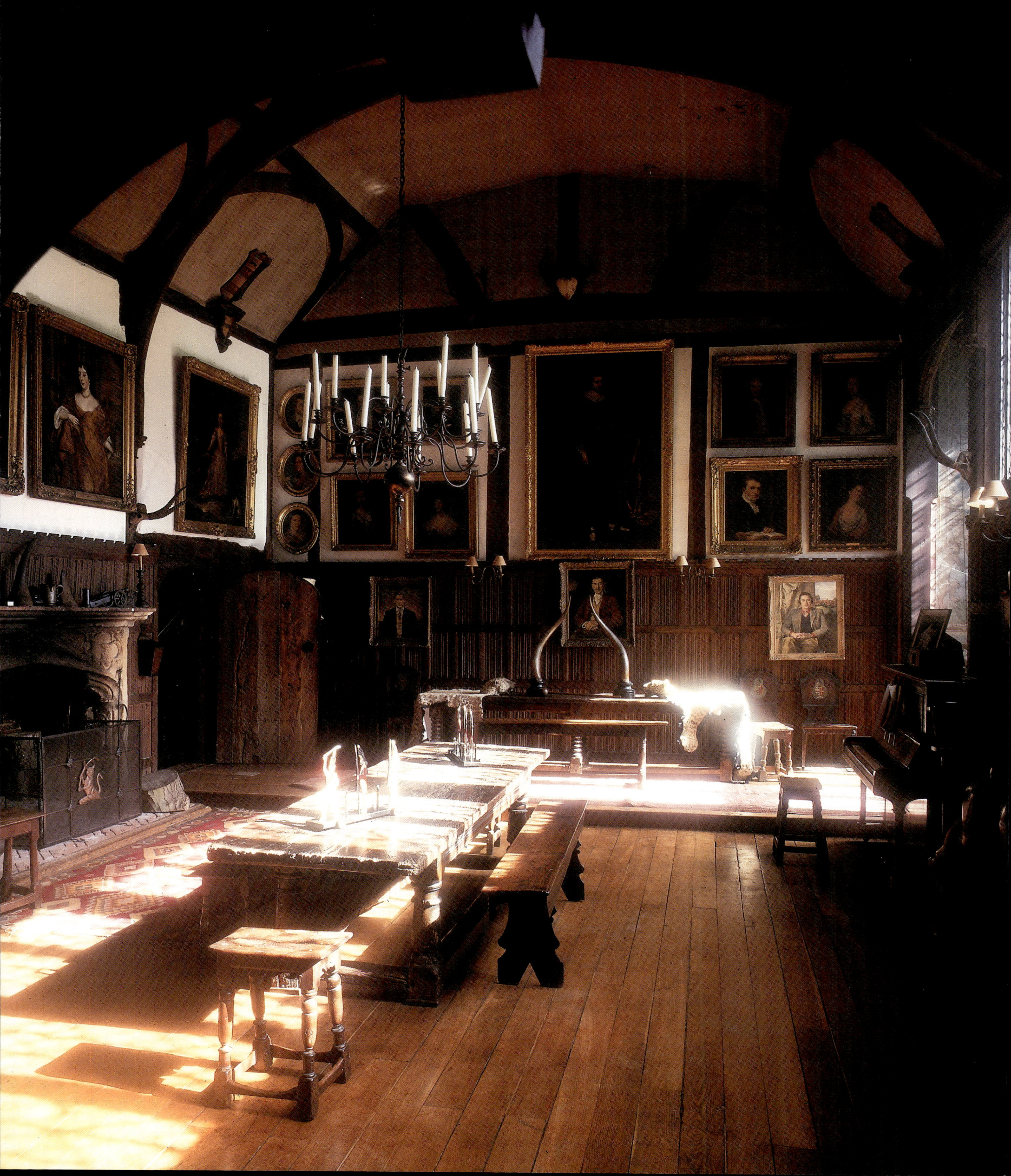

Sʳ IAMES·PALMER·CHANCELLOR·
OF·Yᵉ·GARTER·3ᴿᴰ·SON·OF·Sʳ·THOMAS·
PALMER·BARᵀ·HE·MARᴰ·MARGARET·
DAUᵗ·OF·Sʳ·WILLIAM·GARRARD·Kᵗ

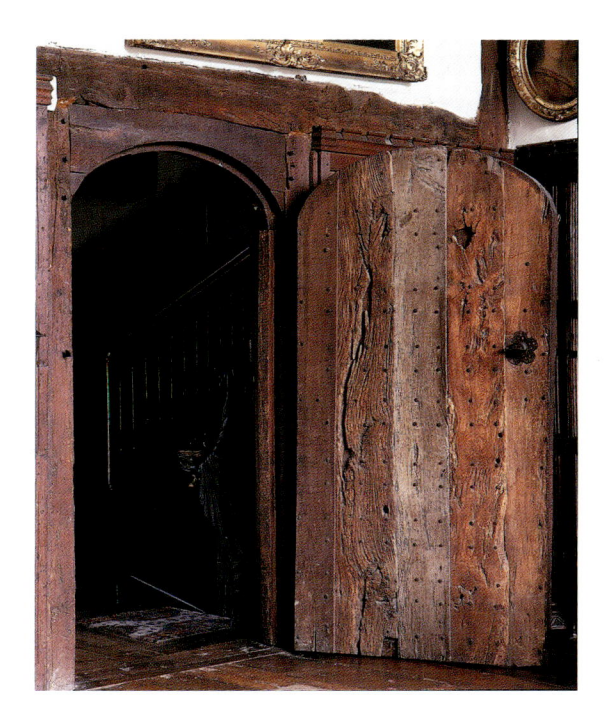

ABOVE Ancient doorway.

OPPOSITE Light on the past: the heraldic record of Sir James Palmer's marriage to Martha Garrard, the Dorney heiress.

RIGHT One of the bedrooms.

BELOW The carved stone pineapple, in the Great Hall, commemorates the first pineapple ever to be grown in England – according to tradition, by the Palmers at Dorney.

did such a sound job of restoration that now it is difficult, if not impossible, to untangle the various changes and counter-changes.

There is so much to catch the eye at Dorney that a precise account of its detailed architectural history becomes rather irrelevant. Among the treasures on display is the Palmer Needlework, dating from about 1624, which traditionally depicts the phenomenon of the Palmer triplets – born on three successive Sundays in 1489. And the carved stone pineapple in a corner of the Great Hall commemorates the first pineapple ever to be grown in England – the story goes that it was grown at Dorney Court.

Legend has it that at a dinner at the Mansion House in London Charles II cut the top off a pineapple which had been brought over from Barbados, and gave it to Roger Palmer, soon to be created Earl of Castlemaine and the husband of the King's notoriously athletic mistress, Barbara Villiers, Duchess of Cleveland. Roger's gardener at Dorney, Rose, planted the top and the pineapple that grew from it was duly presented to the Merry Monarch in 1661. A garden in the village is still known as Pin Garden.

Roger was also responsible for bringing back the early portrait series *Seven Eminent Turks* from Constantinople, though sadly the fine collection of miniatures assembled by his father, Sir James Palmer, himself a distinguished artist in that exquisite medium, was stolen during the Civil War

– 105 –

when the Cromwellians pillaged Dorney. Yet in most other respects the house appears as if nothing much has changed since Sir James's time.

The Palmers, who open the place to the public, generate a delightfully informal atmosphere at Dorney Court which sits well with the unpretentious charm of the surroundings. Hardly surprisingly, it is in steady demand as a film and television location. The oddly shaped octagonal Parlour and the panelled Great Chamber, for instance, were used to memorable effect in Channel Four's adaptation of Tom Sharpe's *Porterhouse Blue*.

Jill Palmer, widow of the late squire, Peregrine Palmer, is doing a sterling job of stewardship for the next generation. Peregrine died, far too young, in 1998 after devoting his life to preserving Dorney Court for posterity. His simple gravestone beside the church (which houses the Garrard Chapel and some noble tombs) reads:

> Wonderful Glorious Days
> Do not cry that they are gone
> But smile that they have been.

OPPOSITE Pipe-dreams amid the timbered paradise of Dorney.

BELOW Corridor through history.

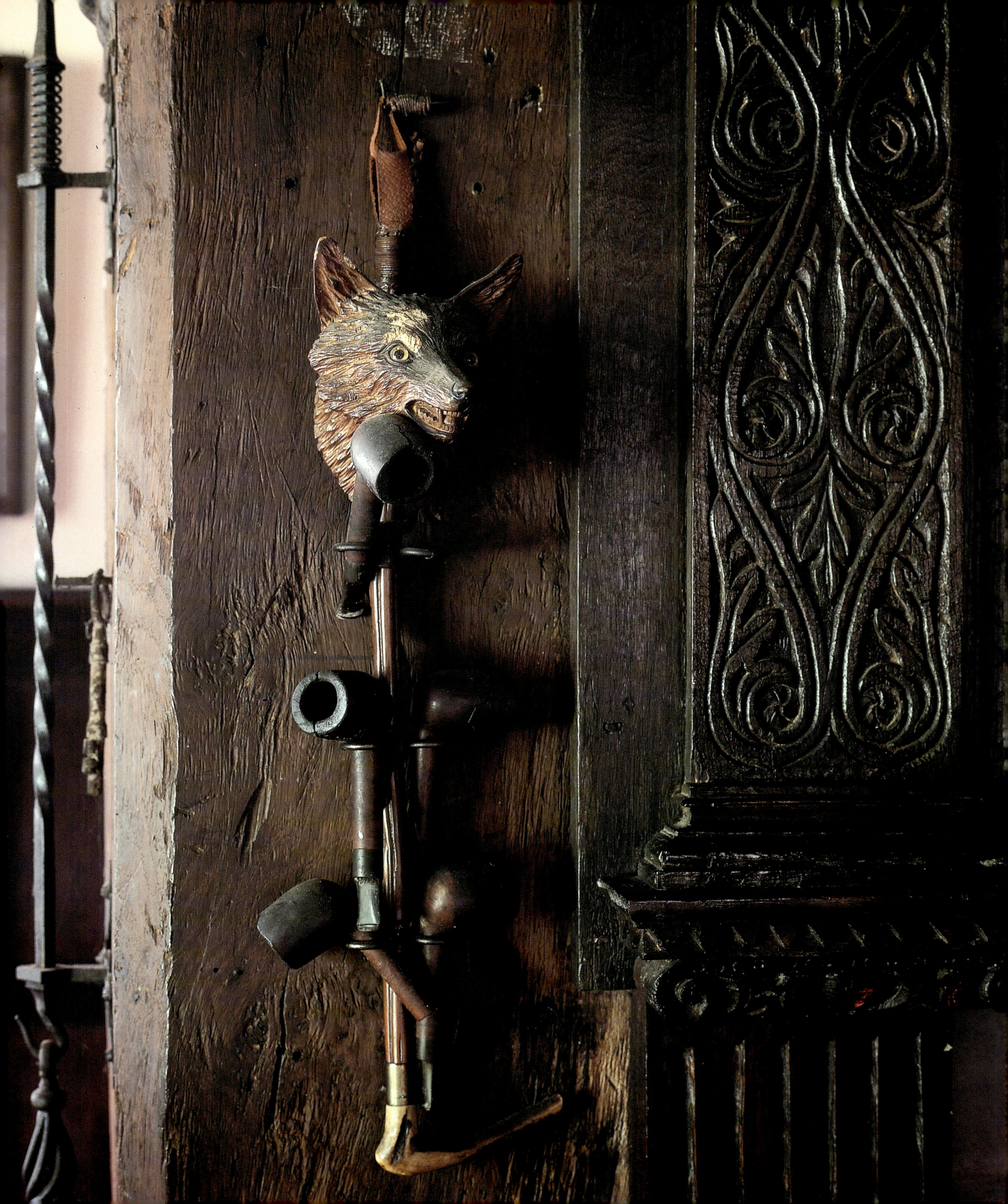

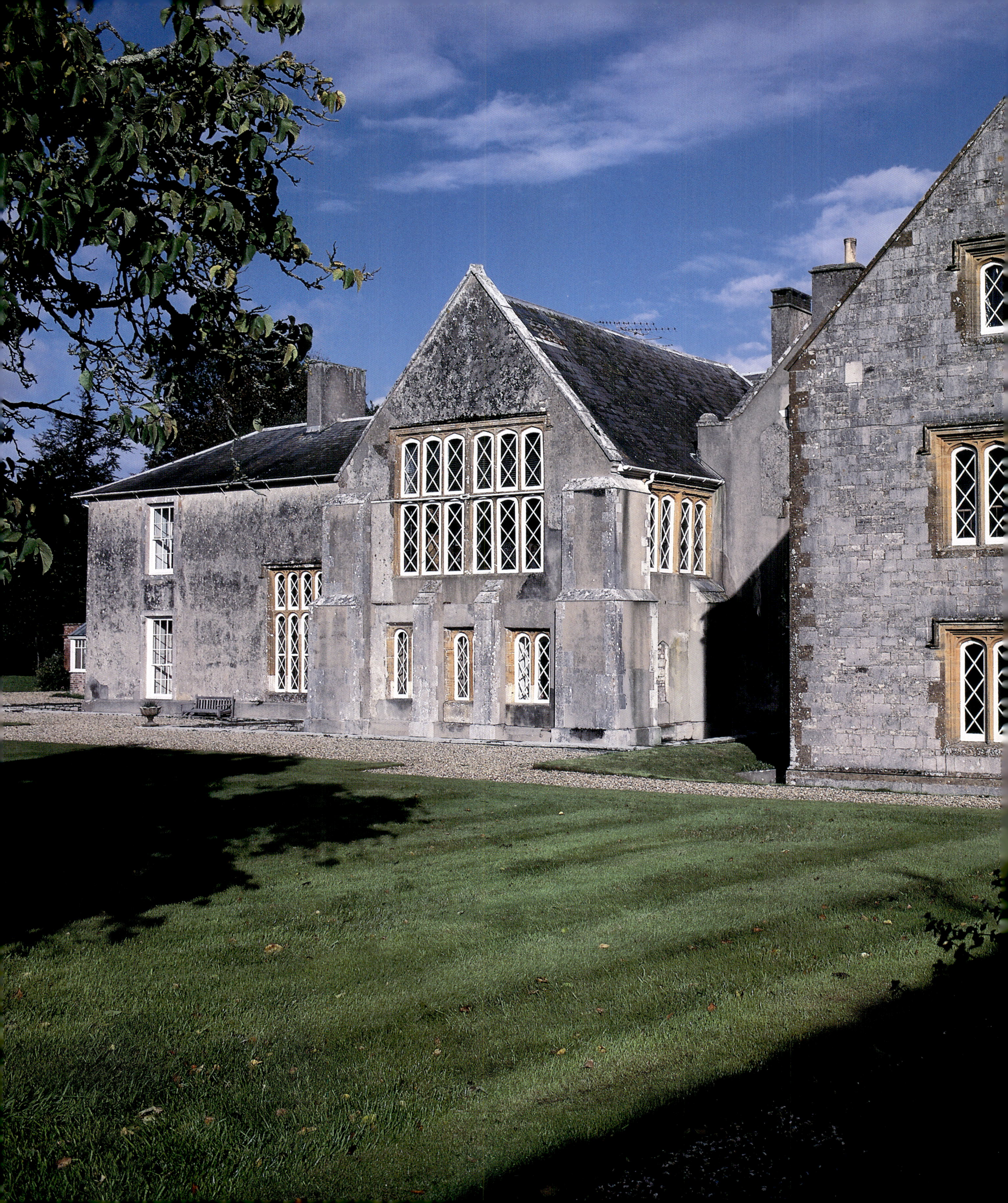

16

HERRINGSTON

DORSET

FOR A FANCIER of family seats the fact that the family in question is still *in situ* after many generations of ownership adds a vital dimension to the appeal of a manor house. Whereas at Dorney Court, in the previous chapter, we saluted the squirearchical survival of the Palmers, whose inheritance by descent can be traced back to 1537, here at Herringston, just south of Dorchester, the county town of Dorset, we can rejoice at the staying power of the Williams family, whose unbroken tenure stretches back at least to a deed of 'common recovery' dated 1513 for a sum of £360.

Whatever the precise starting date, one can only echo the sentiments of Lord David Cecil, who commented, in his account of Herringston in *Some Dorset Country Houses*, that 'the Williams family are surely to be congratulated by posterity for so quietly maintaining their position for over 400 years [now nearer 500] as a leading Dorset family, prosperous and respected…'. As ever, their comparatively low profile – though the pedigree includes several MPs and an unfailing supply of local worthies – has been a key factor in their 'getting the trip', to employ the parlance of the turf.

The house reflects the continuity of the family who own it. The present Herringston mainly dates from the 16th century when the Williams family built, or rather 'rebuilt', it round a quadrangle. Inside, some of it was redecorated during the 17th and 18th centuries to suit the changing tastes of the times. Then, at the beginning of the 19th century the London architect Thomas Leverton was brought down to remodel Herringston by turning the old quadrangle house into a solid block fronted by the present mildly Gothick façade. The garden front, though, still has a strong flavour of the original house. And finally, at the end of the 19th century, there was the addition of a nursery wing.

Herringston takes its name from the ancient Dorset family of Herryng, Herang or Haryng (medieval spelling might be said to be beyond inconsistency), originally settled at Chaldon Herring. These Herryngs, or Herrings, apparently exchanged lands at Chaldon for Winterbourne (which became known as Winterbourne Herringston) with the Abbot of Bindon in the 13th century.

PRECEDING PAGES The gabled garden front of Herringston.

OPPOSITE and BELOW Two views of the spacious interior.

In the 14th century Walter Herring was given licence to crenellate and fortify Winterbourne with stone walls. By the 15th century the manor was held by the Filiols (possibly by inheritance from the Herrings) and in 1449 John Filiol granted a lease to John Hogies whereby the tenant was to 'well and fully maintain support and repair all the Houses and buildings of the aforesaid manor of whatever sort they may be, and shall preserve and keep them from wind and Water, especially one building called the Gatehouse'.

This was the property acquired by the Williams family at the beginning of the 16th century. The Williamses were already prominent landowners in Dorset. John Williams, father and namesake of the purchaser, was High Sheriff of the county in Henry VII's reign and his son's personal property was assessed, in a subsidy roll of Henry VIII's time, at a higher sum than any other manor in Dorset.

No trace of the original house of the Filiols or Herrings can be discerned, but a manuscript history of Herringston written in 1820 describes how the Tudor house of the Williams family surrounded a square court, with a gatehouse on the north side (presumably a replacement for the one highlighted in the lease of 1449). This 'large semicircular gateway' bore the datestone of 1582.

Croker's chronicle tells us that Sir John Williams, MP and twice High Sheriff of Dorset (knighted by James I at Salisbury in 1607), was 'a very worthie Man and a good Patriot, who by his Building and other ornaments much beautified the Place, and commendablie lived a faire age and left it to his grand childe John'. Sir John died in 1617 and is buried under an arched canopy in the north chapel of St Peter's, Dorchester – a gilded effigy in full armour.

Sir John's outstanding, not to say breathtaking, legacy at Herringston is the sensational room on the first floor known as the Great Chamber. This lofty,

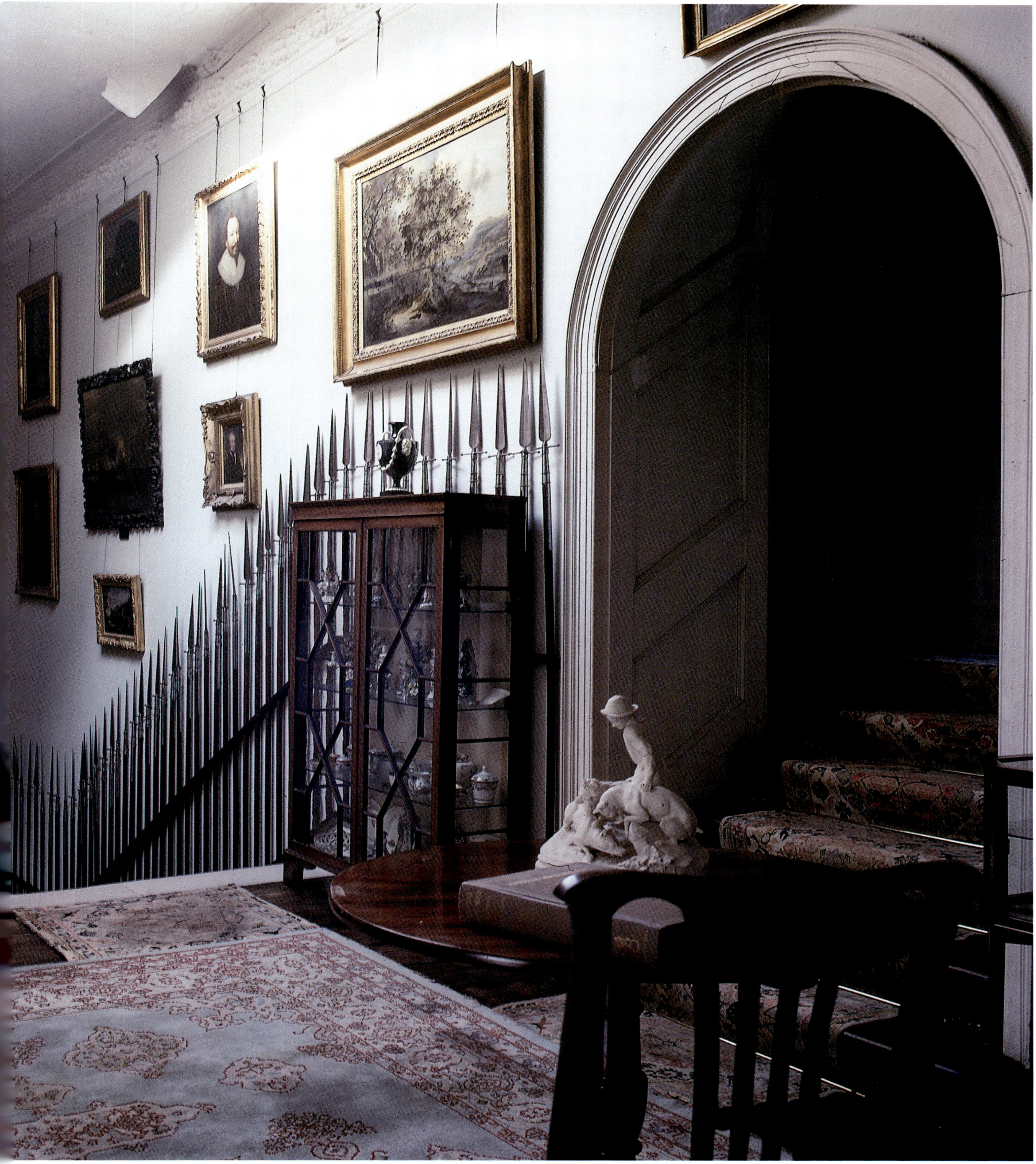

OPPOSITE The sensational barrel-vaulted Great Chamber on the first floor at Herringston, with its exuberant early 17th-century decoration.

A selection of details of the Great Chamber's extraordinary, child-like carvings, in plaster and wood.

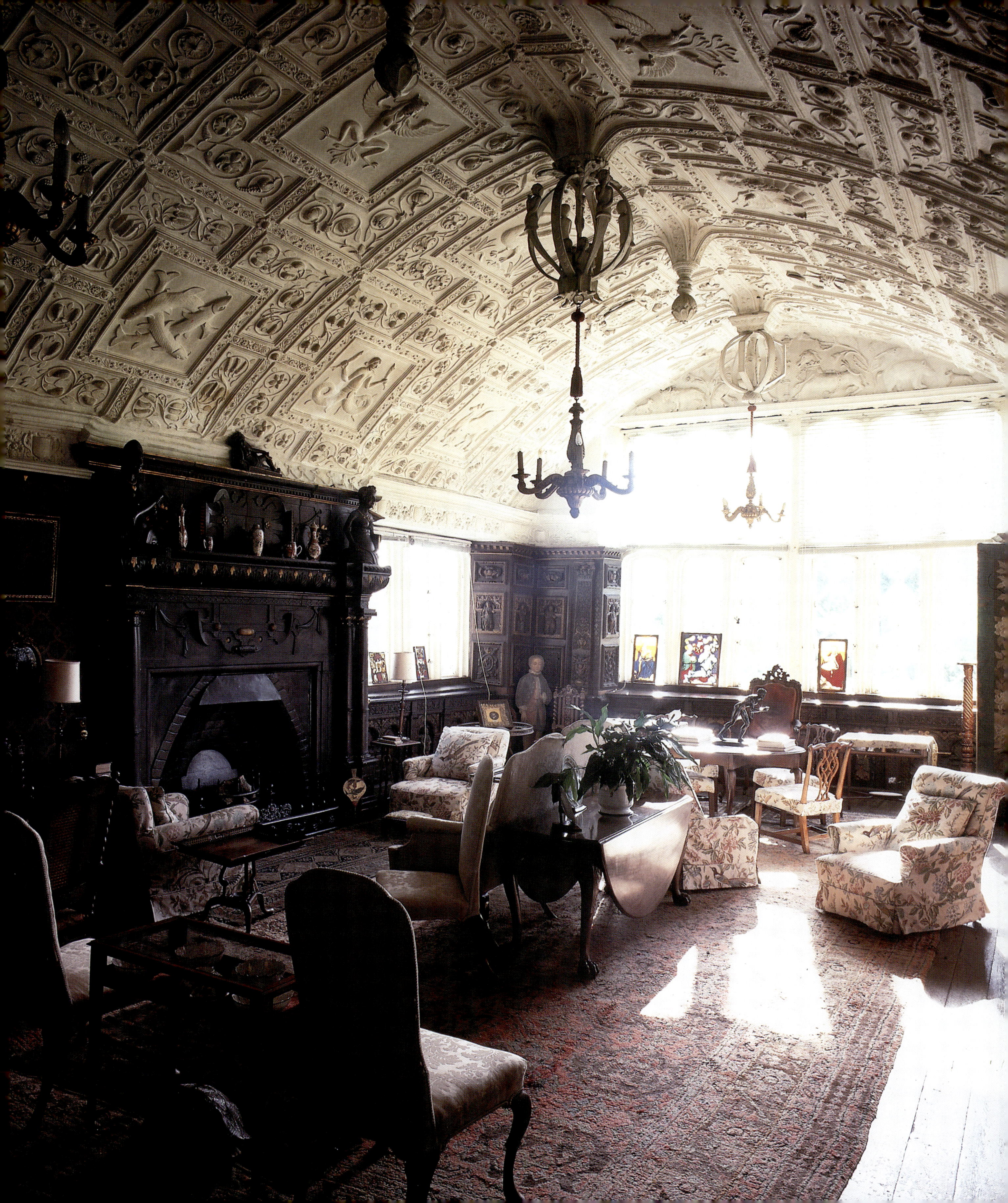

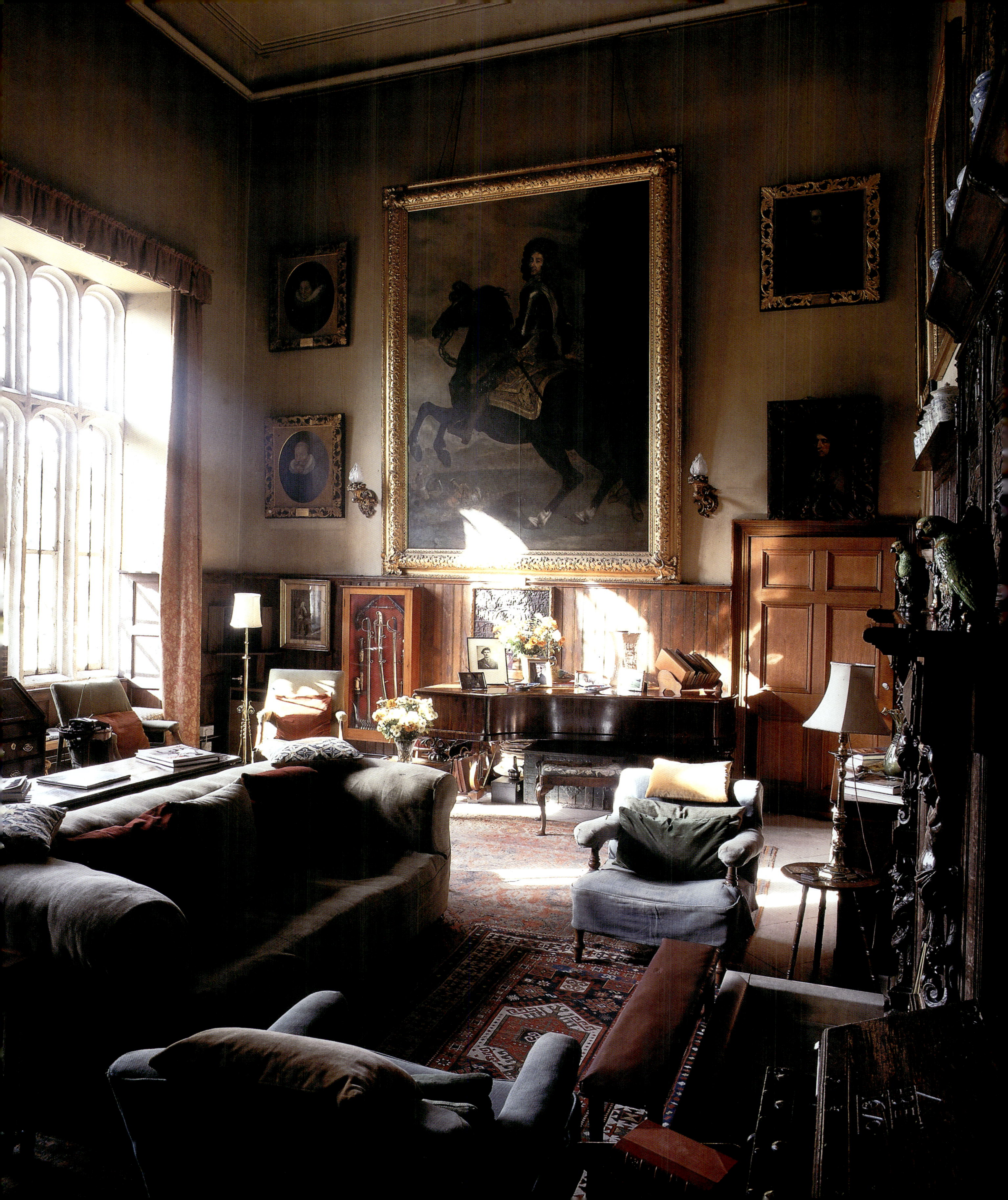

spacious, thrilling apartment has a barrel-vaulted ceiling and is lit by a solarium, a vast three-faceted window jutting due south out of the wall. There is a robust stone chimneypiece featuring the demi-figures of Faith and Charity with a diminutive Hope recumbent on the pediment. But the eye is drawn irresistibly to the exuberant riot of plasterwork on the ceiling – two dozen square panels bursting with Jacobean symbolism. There is a cornucopia of flowers and leaves and a bizarre menagerie of strange-looking creatures, from a rhinoceros and an elephant to mermaids and mythological figures. Lively carvings also cover the wainscot and continue above the dado: biblical allusions, allegorical personages such as Geometry and Geology. You find yourself smiling with joy at the sheer fun of it all. As Lord David Cecil observed, 'the effect is sometimes naif and even comic', like a child's drawings. Yet the carvings also have 'the child's fertility and a child's wealth of fancy and invention and are done with a childish unquestioning conviction that more accomplished works of art often lack'.

A useful clue to the dating of the Great Chamber is contained in one of the ceiling panels, which illustrates the ostrich feathers of the future Charles I when Prince of Wales. He succeeded his stylish brother Henry in the Principality in 1612, which means that the decoration of the room was probably carried out between then and the death of Sir John Williams in 1617. It is possible, though, that it might have been completed by Sir John's son.

Although the Great Chamber dominates the interior, there are other rooms of character at Herringston, including the spacious Hall, which retains a 16th-century flavour. Family portraits – deliciously summed up by Lord David Cecil as 'bearded Jacobeans, ringleted Cavaliers, periwigged Georgians, bewhiskered Victorians' – speak evocatively of generations of Williams ownership. The white-panelled Parlour takes us on to the reign of Queen Anne; the Gothick Dining Room is a reminder of Leverton's remodelling for Edward Williams in the early 1800s.

Edward, incidentally, succeeded to Herringston at the age of ten in 1775 and in turn was succeeded by his grandson and namesake, who lived on until 1913 – so from the reign of the third George to the fifth there were only two squires of Herringston. The present squire, Raymond Williams, a hard-working farmer, maintains the unassuming modesty of his family. To enthusiastic praise for the special continuity and charm of Herringston he simply responds: 'I just think of it as home.'

ABOVE A corner of the Great Chamber.

OPPOSITE The Hall, which retains a 16th-century flavour.

BELOW The north (entrance) front, remodelled by Thomas Leverton at the beginning of the 19th century for Edward Williams in the Gothick style.

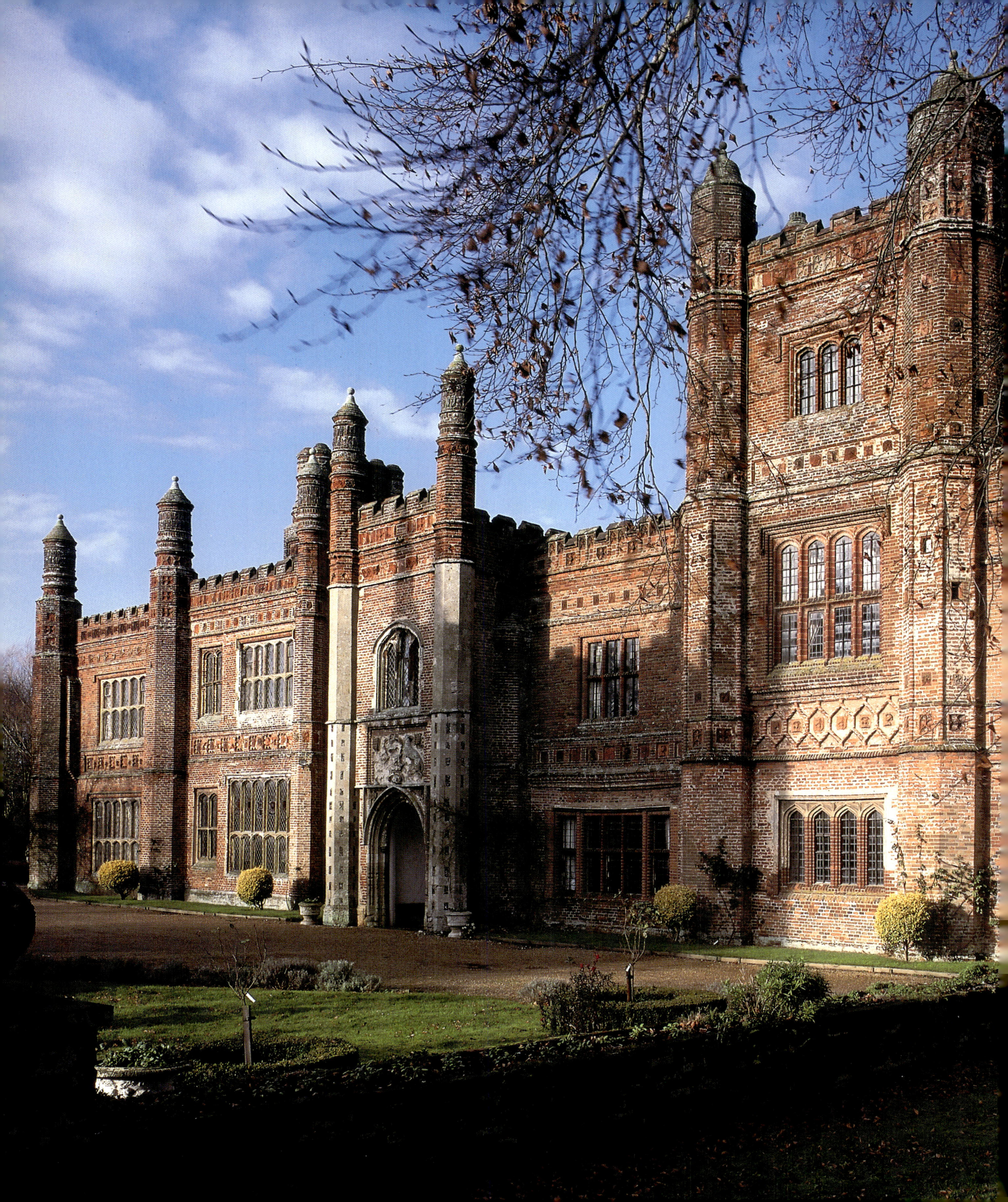

17

EAST BARSHAM MANOR

NORFOLK

WHEN SO much history tends to be forgotten, the early Tudor age still has the power to excite, doubtless due to the larger-than-life personality of 'Bluff King Hal', Henry VIII, who has somehow projected himself through the ages. East Barsham Manor was built by the Fermors, father and son, Sir Henry and Sir William, in order, so tradition has it, to tempt the King to stay here on his way to Walsingham. The idea was for the house to look as grand as possible.

Even in its reduced state – and the old place has suffered many indignities over the centuries – East Barsham still has a thrilling element of grandeur about it. As Sir Nikolaus Pevsner observed in the *Norfolk (Norwich and North-East)* volume of his magisterial *Buildings of England* series, it is 'the picture-book ideal of an early Tudor house'. The mellow brick, the twisted and adorned chimneys and finials are glorious. Indeed, the house boasts probably the richest example of early Tudor brickwork in England, and is chiefly remarkable for its lavish use of terracotta ornament – the height of fashion in the early 16th century.

The early history of East Barsham is set out in Blomefield's *History of Norfolk* (1769). The original owners of the estate, the de Barshams, were followed by the de Woltertons, when the place became known as Wolterton Manor. Roger de Wolterton was the squire in Henry III's reign. In the 15th century it passed to the Wode family, one of whom, John Wode, was elected Speaker of the House of Commons in 1482. Tradition has it that John Wode began building the present house in the reign of Henry VII (who died in 1509), though architectural historians including H. Avray Tipping of *Country Life*, Pevsner and Nicholas Cooper tend to the expert view that it properly dates from the 1520s.

The use of terracotta, which did not come into vogue until that decade, is a significant clue to the building history. Deductions made from the heraldry displayed on the manor and its no less important Gatehouse, however, have tended to confuse the issue. Thus the presence of the griffin and greyhound as supporters to the Royal Arms (as used by Henry VII) and also the armorial bearings of John Wode himself led to the earlier attribution. Yet, in fact, Henry VIII continued using the greyhound as one of his supporters until 1527, when he replaced it with a lion.

None the less, the Royal Arms over the porch, carved out of the stone *in situ*, have the griffin and the greyhound, those over the Gatehouse the griffin and the lion. So the Gatehouse would appear to have been built after the main house, but, judging by its architectural style, only slightly after. The plot thickens when Pevsner frankly admits that the porch of the main house, a two-centred stone arch, does look 'decidedly earlier than 1520'.

In any event, John Wode died in 1496 and his widow, the former Margaret Stapleton, married Sir Henry Fermor, a local tycoon who was recorded in 1521 as owning more than 15,000 sheep in 20 flocks distributed across Norfolk. The previous year he had been up before the Court of Star Chamber for 'depredations' in Thorpland near Fakenham and what sounds like generally beastly behaviour towards his tenantry.

PRECEDING PAGES 'The picture-book ideal of an early Tudor house': East Barsham Manor.

BELOW The Great Hall, given a new plaster ceiling in the 1930s.

ABOVE The Gatehouse, adorned with the Royal Arms (after 1527).

ABOVE and BELOW The mysterious arched labyrinths of East Barsham's interior.

By this stage Sir Henry had secured ownership of East Barsham from the Wode heirs (payments of £35 a year are mentioned). He lived on until 1536 and there can be little doubt that he is the builder of the house. However, Blomefield attributed it to his son, Sir William Fermor, an official of the Court of Augmentation and grantee of church lands who was publicly criticized by Sir Thomas More for avarice. Heraldry (again, possibly misleadingly) suggests that Sir William may well have had a hand in the Gatehouse, for on its inner side the arch displays his coat of arms impaling those of his wife, who was a Knevet or Knyvett.

Inside the main house, little original decoration survives, apart from the huge fireplace and the oriel arch and its windows in the Great Hall and various details which beg for precise identification. Of the house as it now stands, only the east part of the exterior up to and including the porch can be said to be wholly original. Of the west part it is merely the façade and the chimneys – culminating in the magnificent group of ten twisted shafts adorned with different patterns of terracotta decoration – that remain as they were built in the 1520.

From the Fermors East Barsham passed in the 17th century to the Calthorpes, but in the 18th century the Calthorpe heiress, Anne, married Sir Thomas Le Strange, 5th Baronet, who preferred to live at his family's ancient manor house of Hunstanton nearby. Subsequently East Barsham Manor fell on hard times. The eastern half was occupied by tenant farmers and in 1808, when John Adey Repton came to see it, the western half was a set of derelict walls and a grand chimneystack. Repton was surprised at finding the remains of what, as he put it, 'I believe, in richness of moulded brickwork, exceeds anything of its kind in England'.

Eventually, a century later, this romantic ruin was partially restored by the Coleman family, who had bought the property in 1914 from the 21st Lord Hastings, a descendant of the Le Stranges. A more ambitious programme of restoration was undertaken in the late 1930s by a Count Hapsburg-Lothringen (irreverently nicknamed by his Norfolk neighbours 'the Perhapsburg'). This included the installation of plaster ceilings, chimneypieces brought in from elsewhere and the insertion of a splendid staircase from the demolished Thursford Hall nearby. Fishers of Fakenham were the builders responsible for what Pevsner called 'conscientious and judicious' work. The Count was assisted in the restoration by a champion swimmer from Hungary, George Lanyi, later Colonel George Lane, MC of The Buffs, who married, as his first wife, Miriam Rothschild, the eminent botanist.

Since the Second World War East Barsham has passed through a bewildering series of different ownerships but today, after a history as chequered as its Tudor brickwork, it is the home of Sir John and Lady Guinness, whose scholarly enthusiasm for the place encourages one to predict a rosy future for this great manor house. Sir John is chairman of the Reviewing Committee on the Export of Works of Art and his wife Valerie, a porcelain expert, was a North from Rougham not far away, a family connected with the Le Stranges, East Barsham's former owners. The Le Stranges rather neglected the manor, but a visit to East Barsham leaves one in no doubt that the present owners will not make the same mistake.

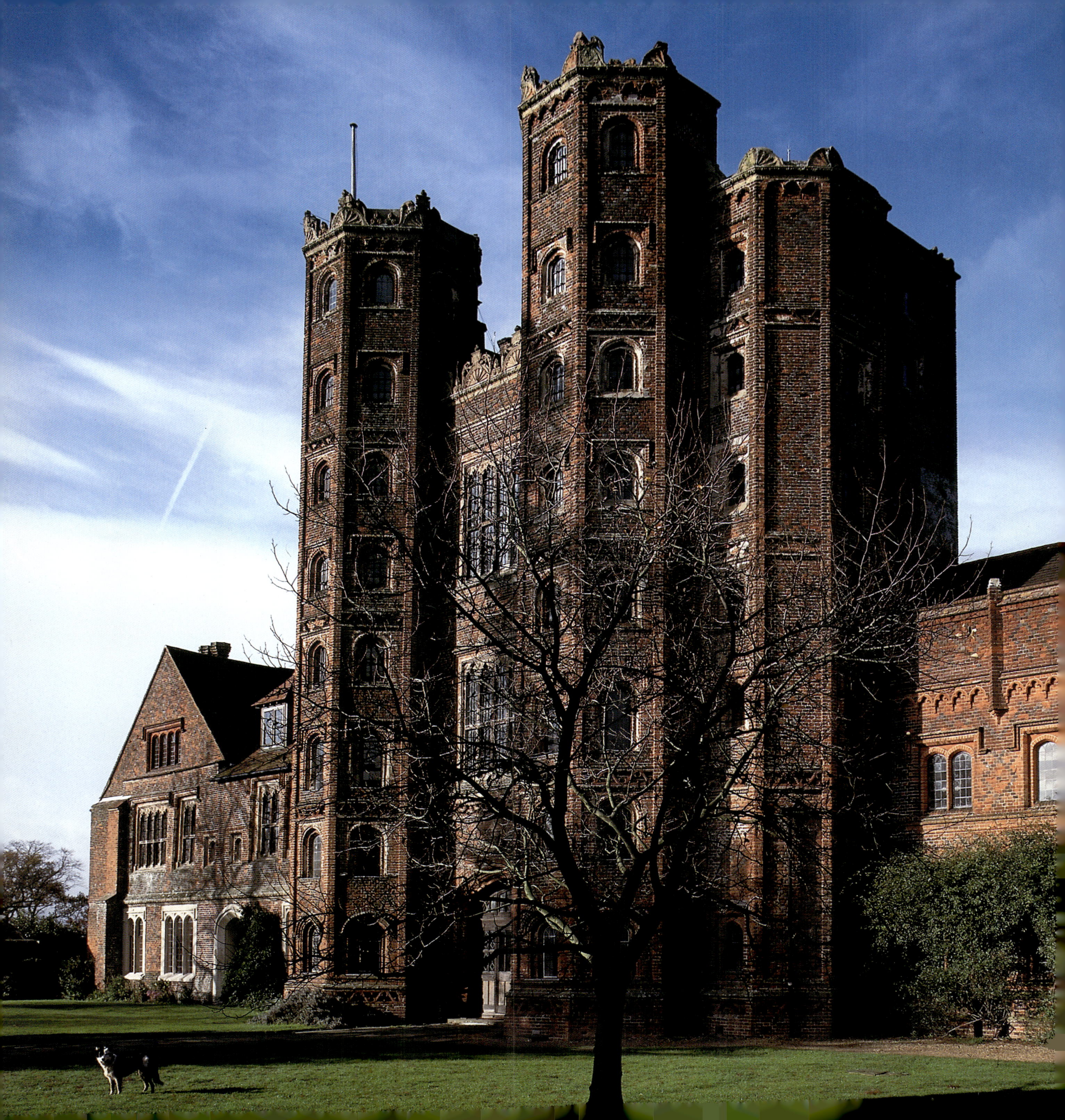

18

LAYER MARNEY TOWER

ESSEX

TERRACOTTA, one of the glories of the Renaissance style of building which became *le dernier cri* in Court fashion in England during the early years of Henry VIII's reign, featured significantly in the previous chapter concerning East Barsham Manor (*qv*). Yet it surely achieved its apotheosis in the construction of the spectacular Layer Marney Tower, south of Colchester. Indeed, the way terracotta was used for window mullions and crestings, so that the buff-coloured clay resembles stone, is unparalleled.

The sheer height of the Tower, which is the tallest brick gatehouse built in England during the 15th and early 16th centuries, and the quality of the moulded brickwork would make Layer Marney remarkable enough, but the Renaissance flourishes in terracotta elevate it to a very special category of importance. In the church there are further superb examples of terracotta work surrounding the tombs of the 1st and 2nd Lords Marney.

The peerage was created in 1523 for Sir Henry Marney, a Knight of the Garter, described by Henry VIII as 'a scant well-borne gentleman of no grete lande'. In 1522 he had been promoted to Lord Privy Seal, crowning a career that had marked a steady ascent up the Tudor power ladder beginning with his appointment as a Privy Councillor to Henry VII back in 1485 after the Battle of Bosworth. Yet six weeks after receiving his Barony the 1st Lord Marney died (being buried in great state at Layer Marney), and within two years the peerage and the Marney line expired on the death of his son John, the 2nd Lord Marney.

As H. Avray Tipping wrote in *Country Life* in 1914, the Marneys (an ancient if never particularly grand dynasty known to have held the manor since the 12th century) came to an end, 'not amid the din of the battlefield or the crowds on Tower Hill, but silently in their beds at the very moment when they seemed to be grasping greatness. But for their "tower", standing like a beacon above the Essex flats, they would be forgotten.'

This 'tower' was, of course, merely intended as the gatehouse to a complete courtyard house that would have rivalled Hampton Court in splendour. The History Room in the Tower houses a modern model by Paul Wells showing how the house might have looked if it had been completed. The architecture is an instructive example of the transition from the defensive, embattled style to a more domestic approach. Although Layer Marney was to show few similarities to traditional fortified manor houses, it retained the principle of a great gateway and flanking towers.

The gatehouse was clearly designed to outdo the not dissimilar though plainer tower at Oxburgh Hall in Norfolk – to whose owners, the Bedingfelds, the Marneys were related by marriage. There is another link with their kinsmen in that the terracotta tombs at Layer Marney are strongly reminiscent of those at Oxburgh. This lends support to the idea that the terracotta work may have been carried out not by Italian craftsmen (such as Giovanni da Maiano, who worked at Hampton Court, and Pietro Torrigiano, who worked in Westminster Abbey) but by Flemish or English craftsmen trained by the Italian masters. For all its fineness, the Layer Marney terracotta work often reveals a shaky grasp of the classical vocabulary of architecture.

Behind the great central terracotta windows of the Tower there could probably have been found the Royal Apartments. The tradition is that Queen Elizabeth stayed here with the Tukes (who had acquired the property) in 1579 on one of her royal progresses around the country. In the late 17th century the

PRECEDING PAGES 'Like a beacon above the Essex flats...': Layer Marney Tower, the tallest brick gatehouse built in England during the 15th and early 16th centuries.

BELOW Detail of brickwork set off by an obliging dove.

ABOVE Roofscape, with stepped gables and twisted chimneystacks in the Tudorish manner.

LEFT One of the great central terracotta windows of the Tower.

ABOVE Up and up twists the stairway to the top of the Tower.

BELOW LEFT The roof of the restored medieval barn.

BELOW RIGHT The Long Gallery, with its timbered Tudor roof and curious pincer-shaped posts and beams. Originally the old stable block, this was restored in the early 1900s by Walter de Zoete, who installed the windows, oak floor and Jacobean-style fireplace.

manor of Layer Marney was bought by Nicholas Corsellis, a London merchant, for £7,200. This family's ownership is commemorated by the refurbished Corsellis Room above the stables constructed by Walter de Zoete in the 20th century.

Until the arrival of de Zoete, in many ways the Tower's saviour, Layer Marney was in the doldrums. During the early part of the 19th century it drifted into decay as a tenanted farmhouse. Later, some restoration work was done by the Peache family, who also added the north-west wing.

Walter de Zoete, of the well-known London stockbrokers De Zoete Gorton, bought Layer Marney in 1904 and set about a thorough overhaul. Bricked-up windows in the Tower, which presented a sad sight in early *Country Life* photographs, were opened up; new oak panelling introduced; 17th-century Flemish chimneypieces brought in. The old stable block, lying to the south of the gatehouse in the original forecourt (now the garden), was ingeniously converted to the Long Gallery. De Zoete removed the partition ceiling to reveal a splendid timbered roof with curious pincer-shaped posts or beams. This and the attractively diapered brickwork is authentically Tudor and original; the raised and sprung oak floor, as well as the three large windows with Kentish ragstone surrounds, the south porch and the Jacobean-style fireplace are all de Zoete additions. The result is a very handsome reception room, which now houses wedding receptions, dances, operas, concerts and conferences. De Zoete also sensitively restored the church.

Walter de Zoete's excellent work at Layer Marney has been sympathetically continued by the present owners, the Charrington family, who bought the place in 1958. Major Gerald Charrington and his bride Susannah Tidbury from Layer de la Haye nearby had been married in Layer Marney Church the previous year and when the Tower came up for sale shortly afterwards they could not resist the opportunity. Today it is the home of their son Nicholas, his wife Sheila and their children.

The Charringtons open Layer Marney regularly to the public. Besides the Tower itself, there is an enjoyable ensemble of outbuildings to explore, including the restored medieval barn, which now houses some of the home farm's collection of rare breed farm animals. Within the Tower, the History Room lucidly sets out a feast of genealogy and colourful heraldry under a recently finished ceiling, complete with 24 oak bosses carved and gilded by two East German craftsmen, Michael Kastner and Chris Danneggar. It is well worth climbing to the very top of the Tower to enjoy the majestic views across the Essex countryside to the sea.

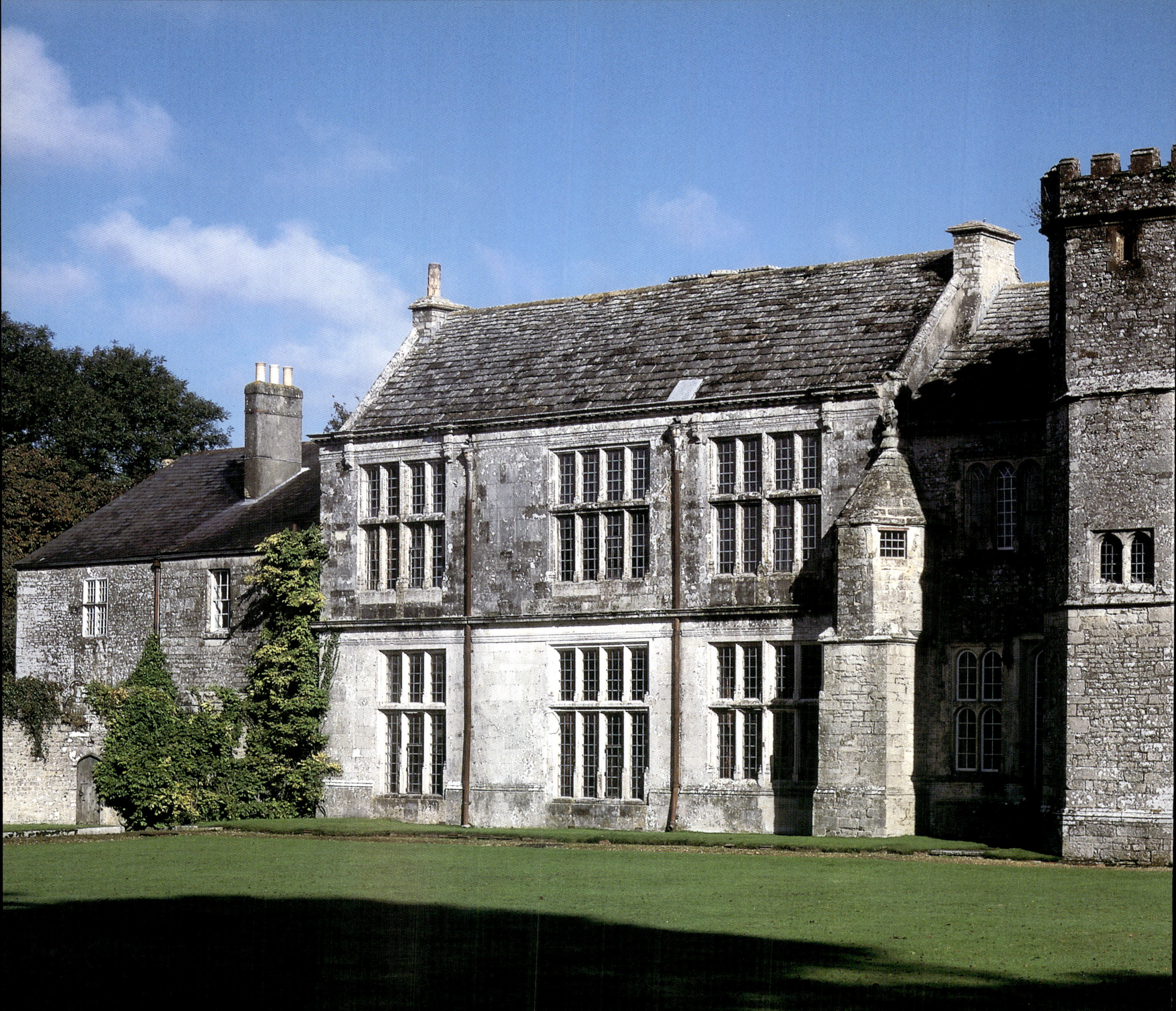

19

WOLFETON HOUSE

DORSET

WE MANAGED not to invoke Thomas Hardy in the description of the previous Dorset manor house on our tour, Herringston (*qv*), where the exuberant style of carving is reminiscent of work at Wolfeton, but there is no escaping the county's great bard here. In *A Group of Noble Dames*, Hardy wrote:

> In going out of Casterbridge by the low-lying road which eventually conducts to the town of Ivell, you see on the right hand an ivied manor house, flanked by battlemented towers, and more than usually distinguished by the size of its many mullioned windows. Though still of good capacity, the building is somewhat reduced from its grand proportions; it has, moreover, been shorn of the fair estate which once appertained to its Lord, with the exception of a few acres of parkland immediately around the mansion. This was formerly the seat of the ancient and knightly family of the Drenghards, or Drenkhards, now extinct in the male line…

For 'Casterbridge', of course, read Dorchester. For 'Drenghard' read Trenchard. Take away the ivy (which indeed was removed to reveal the silvery stonework), and you are left with a pretty serviceable description of Wolfeton, now the home of Captain and Mrs Nigel Thimbleby, whose love of this beautiful, romantic house immediately communicates itself to visitors.

Hardy wove a story around Wolfeton about a Lady Penelope who jokingly told her three suitors that she would marry them 'all in turn' (and duly did so). Yet, as Lord David Cecil sagely remarked, such fiction is 'less gripping to the imagination than the traditional legends of the place, or the impression made by the house itself'. One, unfortunately anonymous, observer likened Wolfeton to 'a shell held to the ear full of the memory of waves that have gone'.

No bigger waves were made than by the house's most celebrated visitors, Archduke Philip of Austria (unlike 'the Perhapsburg' at East Barsham [*qv*], this was the genuine article) and his wife, Joanna of Castile, who were invited to stay in 1506 by Sir Thomas Trenchard after the ship carrying them from the Netherlands to claim the throne of Castile was forced by storms to put in at Weymouth. The illustrious guests spent several days at Wolfeton before proceeding to Windsor. Although the house then existing must presumably have been comfortable enough for royalty, little is known of its architecture except possibly the two surviving circular or 'drum' towers, of unequal size, that flank the Gatehouse.

On the centre of the Gatehouse is the date 1534. What remains of Sir Thomas Trenchard's original courtyard house can be seen on the garden front – namely a stair-tower and a garderobe projection, with windows in between. The rest of the garden front is Elizabethan, as rebuilt by Sir Thomas's great-grandson, Sir George Trenchard, who, curiously enough, succeeded to the property a mere seven years after the death of his great-grandfather in 1550. Sir Thomas had reigned at Wolfeton for 55 years, but Sir George was to better this, notching up 73 years as squire.

During Sir George's time, the Blessed Cornelius, an Irish Roman Catholic priest bound for the gallows, was incarcerated at Wolfeton and traditionally his footsteps are sometimes heard climbing the old oak spiral staircase. John Aubrey records another Wolfeton legend in his *Miscellanies*: on 3 November 1640, the day the Long Parliament began to sit, the sceptre fell from the hand of the carved figure of Charles I which formerly adorned the Great Hall in the house. And a mid-17th-century Wolfeton dinner party ended in disarray when a visiting Judge of Assize thought he saw the figure of his hostess standing behind her chair with her throat cut and her head under her arm.

PRECEDING PAGES 'Manor house, flanked by battlemented towers, and more than usually distinguished by the size of its many mullioned windows…': Thomas Hardy's description of 'the seat of the ancient and knightly family of the Drenghards, or Drenkhards', alias Trenchard. This view is of the south front of Wolfeton, with Sir George Trenchard's late-16th-century building to the left.

BELOW A view from the south-east, showing the Gatehouse, with its two drum towers to the right.

TOP and ABOVE Details of corbel figures carved in the stone.

ABOVE RIGHT The internal archway of the Gatehouse.

During his hurried return to Dorchester, a messenger overtook the carriage to inform his lordship that Lady Trenchard had committed suicide.

On a more cheerful note, it is said that a member of the family won a handsome wager in the 18th century by reaching the top of the monumental stone Great Staircase (of about 1580 and possibly, according to Mark Girouard, decorated by Allen Maynard, who worked at Longleat) in a horse and carriage. Apparently this sportsman's ascent has been repeated many times by his ghost.

By the end of the 18th century Wolfeton had fallen into a sorry state. The Trenchards removed themselves (and the heraldic glass) to a house at Lytchett Matravers and in 1822 the subsequent owners, the Hennings, cousins who were lawyers, partially demolished Wolfeton, including the back parts and the eastern portion of the south range. The surviving parts were let out as a farmhouse.

In the 1860s a new owner, Mr W.H.P. Weston, who was also related to the Trenchards, saved the place from ruin and made a brave stab at restoring it. This involved giving the staircase tower a battlemented top; building a matching tower to the north-east; erecting a Tudor-style porch on the north

WOLFETON HOUSE

ABOVE View through the screens passage.

BELOW Details of carved figures.

OPPOSITE The Parlour, with its robust plaster ceiling and giant oak overmantel featuring the figures of Hope and Justice.

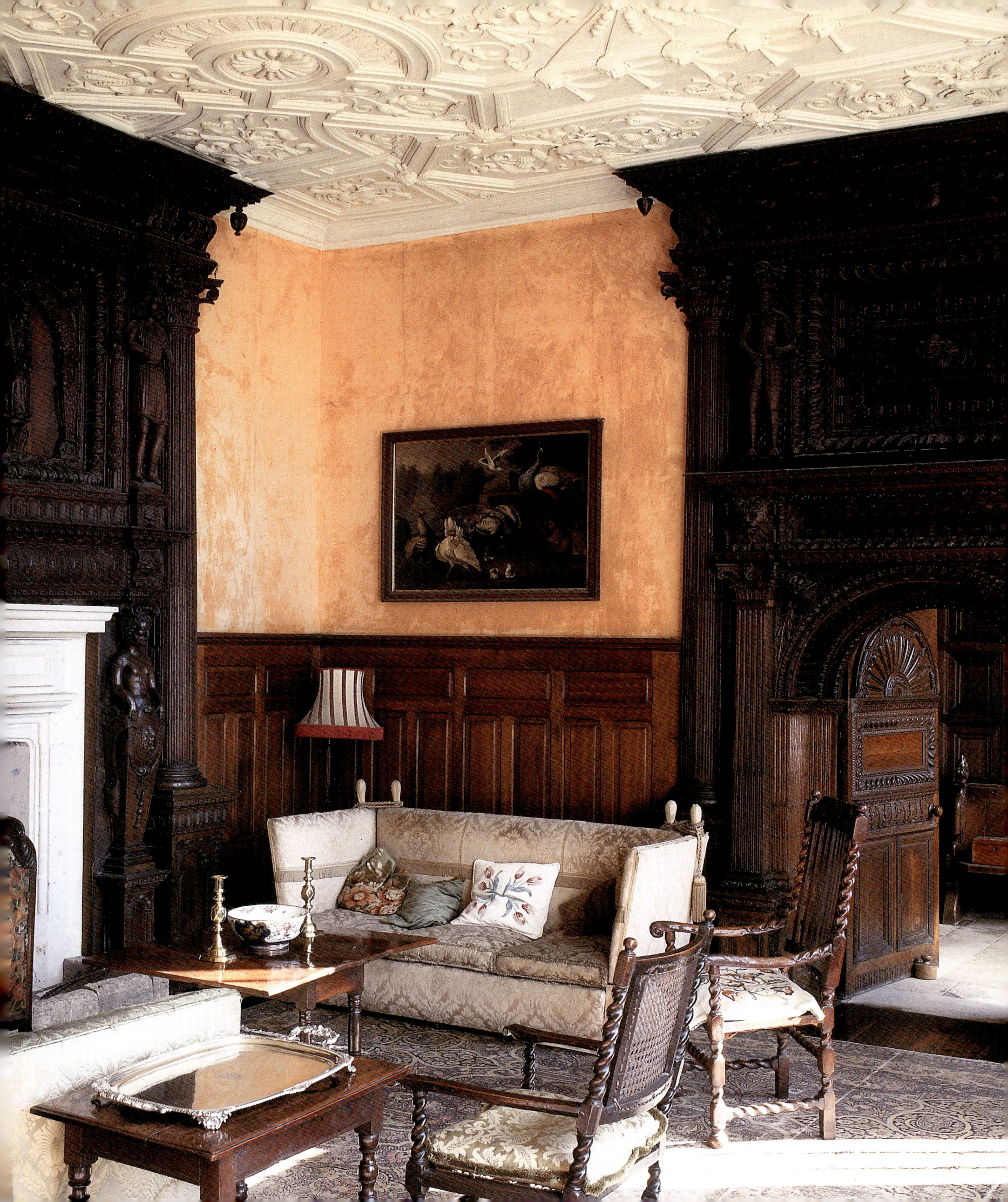

side; and extending the screen wall to connect the main building to the Gatehouse. Inside, some old woodwork was rearranged.

The Great Hall, from which all the original decoration had disappeared, was repanelled by Weston and given a new moulded plaster ceiling. The Parlour, though, retains its jolly late-Elizabethan ceiling ornamented with robust scrolling, foliage, masks, grotesques and reliefs of creatures ranging from unicorns to billy-goats. The assorted sheep remind one that the Trenchard fortunes derived from wool.

The giant oak overmantel in the Parlour features the figures of Hope and Justice, and the equally imposing doorway boasts figures of a king and queen. The superb overmantels in the Dining Room and the Great Chamber upstairs were shown by Arthur Oswald in *Country Life* to be similar in style to work at Montacute, the great late-Elizabethan house near Yeovil (now a property of the National Trust).

ABOVE The Chapel.

LEFT Carved stone chimneypiece of about 1600 in the upstairs Great Chamber which was shown by Arthur Oswald in *Country Life* to be similar in style to work at Montacute, Somerset (now a property of the National Trust).

RIGHT Staircase.

BELOW Doorway to the Great Chamber.

BOTTOM A corbel head.

The present owner, Captain Thimbleby, is himself a kinsman of the Trenchards and their predecessors, the Mohuns (whose arms, together with those of the Jurdains, adorn the Gatehouse). He has already achieved a *tour de force* of restoration. Visitors (the house is open regularly to the public) should not miss the Chapel, where there is a magnificent series of carved Gothic panels depicting the signs of the Zodiac and the occupations of the Months.

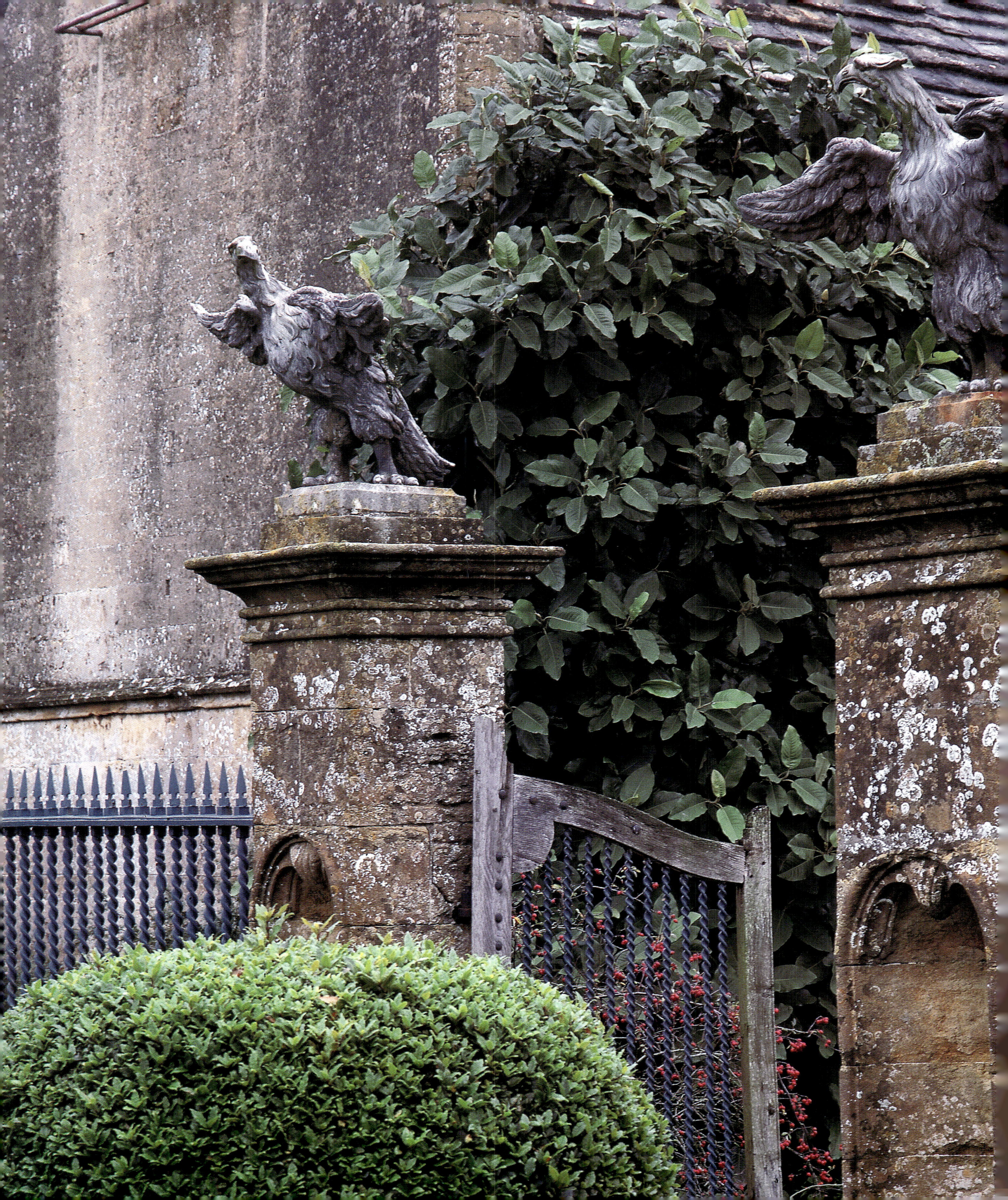

20

MAPPERTON HOUSE

DORSET

S TILL in Dorset (a county which any manorial enthusiast finds almost impossible to leave), we reach just about the halfway point of our tour of English manor houses at Mapperton, above Beaminster, in surely the most beautiful corner of the county – nicely described by Candida Lycett Green as 'like an English Tuscany'. And there could be no lovelier spot at which to take stock than this golden vision, nor one which so epitomizes the manorial ideal.

In *Country Life* Arthur Oswald considered Mapperton 'the apotheosis of the Domesday manor, achieved after centuries of civilising influence in building as well as manners'. Lord David Cecil hailed its harmonious composition, 'a complete group of manorial buildings; house, church, stables, barns and dovecote'. Candida Lycett Green likened the entrance courtyard to 'a hamlet huddling around the house'. Even Sir Nikolaus Pevsner's series on *The Buildings of England* broke free of the shackles of dry architectural history: 'There can hardly be anywhere a more enchanting manorial group than Mapperton'. For the happy ensemble of different dates and styles has a natural charm that no doctrinaire architect working at his drawing-board could ever achieve. And the present owners, the Earl and Countess of Sandwich, have succeeded in making Mapperton even more liveable, with an air of comfortable informality.

Mapperton was entered in *The Domesday Book* as 'Malperetone', held by William de Moion (ancestor, incidentally, of the Mohuns of Wolfeton, *qv*). Subsequently the manor passed by descent, through a maze of female lines, to four families – the Bretts, Morgans, Brodrepps and Comptons – right up until 1919, when it was purchased by Ethel Labouchere. On Mrs Labouchere's death in 1955 it was acquired by the Montagu family, Earls of Sandwich.

The Morgan pedigree is enlivened by two curious royal dispensations to allow a brace of Robert Morgans (one in 1425, the other in 1522) to keep their hats on in the presence of the King. The first explains that 'diverse infirmities which he hath in his hedde cannot convenyently without his grete daungier be discovered of the same'. If the second behatted Robert Morgan had a cold head, his son John evidently had a hot one. He killed one Anchret Palmer, but was pardoned on a plea of self-defence. A later John Morgan, however, was hanged in 1580 for stabbing his brother-in-law Nicholas Turberville to death (apparently during a theological discussion).

By this time the original manor house at Mapperton had been rebuilt by Robert Morgan (son of the first, hot-headed John), who succeeded to the property in 1535 and died in 1567. His building work in the luscious Ham Hill stone is usually dated about 1540. What we see today, the gabled north wing with its twisted chimneys and spiral finials, is all that remains of the house as it was in the last years of Henry VIII's reign. The uncusped arched heads of the windows on the north wing are reminiscent of those at such other Dorset manor houses as Bingham's Melcombe, Athelhampton and Sandford Orcas (*qqv*).

Heraldic lions and griffins, the armorial symbols of the Brett and Morgan families, are featured in the original Tudor ceiling in the Drawing Room, echoing the stone figures on the roof. The bedroom above has a remarkable

PRECEDING PAGES The eagle gate-piers of Mapperton at the entrance to the inner courtyard. The shell-headed niches are features characteristic of the early 17th century; the eagles themselves are a later addition, probably mid-18th century.

BELOW The 17th-century entrance façade of the manor house even Sir Nikolaus Pevsner felt moved to hail as 'enchanting'.

ribbed pendant ceiling with the recurring motif of another Morgan emblem, the fleur-de-lys.

In the 17th century Mapperton was adorned with some handsome Jacobean panelling. The Great Plague of 1665 hit the place hard; in its wake, as Hutchins notes in his *History of Dorset*, 'the tenements fell into the lord's hand, and have all been pulled down'. Shortly afterwards, the new owner, Richard Brodrepp, rebuilt the hall range on the west front and added the two ravishing ranges of stables that flank the outer courtyard (the date 1670 appears on a keystone). This Richard was also responsible for installing the stone gate-piers (the eagles, gates and railings are later additions), and finally in 1704 (two years before his death), rebuilt the nave of All Saints Church, which neatly forms the south wing of Mapperton. In the middle of the 18th century, a later Richard Brodrepp added the balustrade to the house, remodelled the garden front of the north wing and created the surprisingly grand Georgian staircase hall.

The changes wrought during the Compton ownership included the installation in 1908 of two splendid Jacobean overmantels from Melplash Court nearby which date from the time Melplash belonged to the Paulets, Marquesses of Winchester. By the end of the First World War, however, Mapperton – though something of a rarity among manor houses in never having descended to farmhouse status – was showing signs of decay. Mrs Labouchere gave the place a face-lift in the 1920s and introduced the Renaissance-style ceilings in the Hall and Dining Room. Most of her energies, though, were channelled into creating the elaborate Italianate garden, complete with grottoes, stone ornamental birds and animals, and a fountain court.

TOP Mapperton's menagerie: the gable end of the Tudor wing.

ABOVE Lichen on the 18th-century balustrade.

RIGHT Roofscape.

LEFT Bedroom with ribbed pendant ceiling.

OPPOSITE The surprisingly grand mid-Georgian staircase hall.

BELOW Detail of stonework.

The next owner, Victor Montagu, sometime MP for South Dorset (and, by a happy coincidence, a descendant of the Paulets) brought with him from the family seat of Hinchingbrooke near Huntingdon some of the important Montagu collections of pictures and furniture which add such lustre to a tour of the house. His son and daughter-in-law, the present Earl and Countess of Sandwich, open the house to groups by appointment, and the celebrated gardens are open regularly to the public.

Besides Mrs Labouchere's creation, there are 17th-century fish ponds and an orangery added by Victor Montagu, who also extended the lower garden with specimen shrubs and trees in the 1950s. The dramatic contrast between this valley garden and the house has not proved to everyone's taste. Lord David Cecil found that 'its foreign formality jars with the rural situation and even more with the character of the house itself'. However, John and Caroline Sandwich have recently made the garden much blowsier and more luxuriant than it was, with a wider range of planting. Candida Lycett Green has acclaimed it as 'a magical garden worth travelling a hundred miles to see'.

When it comes to summing up this adorable manor house, however, the last word must go to Lord David: 'Throughout the house, 16th, 17th and 18th centuries meet each other at every turn. Yet – and this is notably characteristic of Mapperton – they do not quarrel. Diversity never means discord. Rather the different ages combine to create an unexpected and richer harmony.'

ABOVE Screens passage.

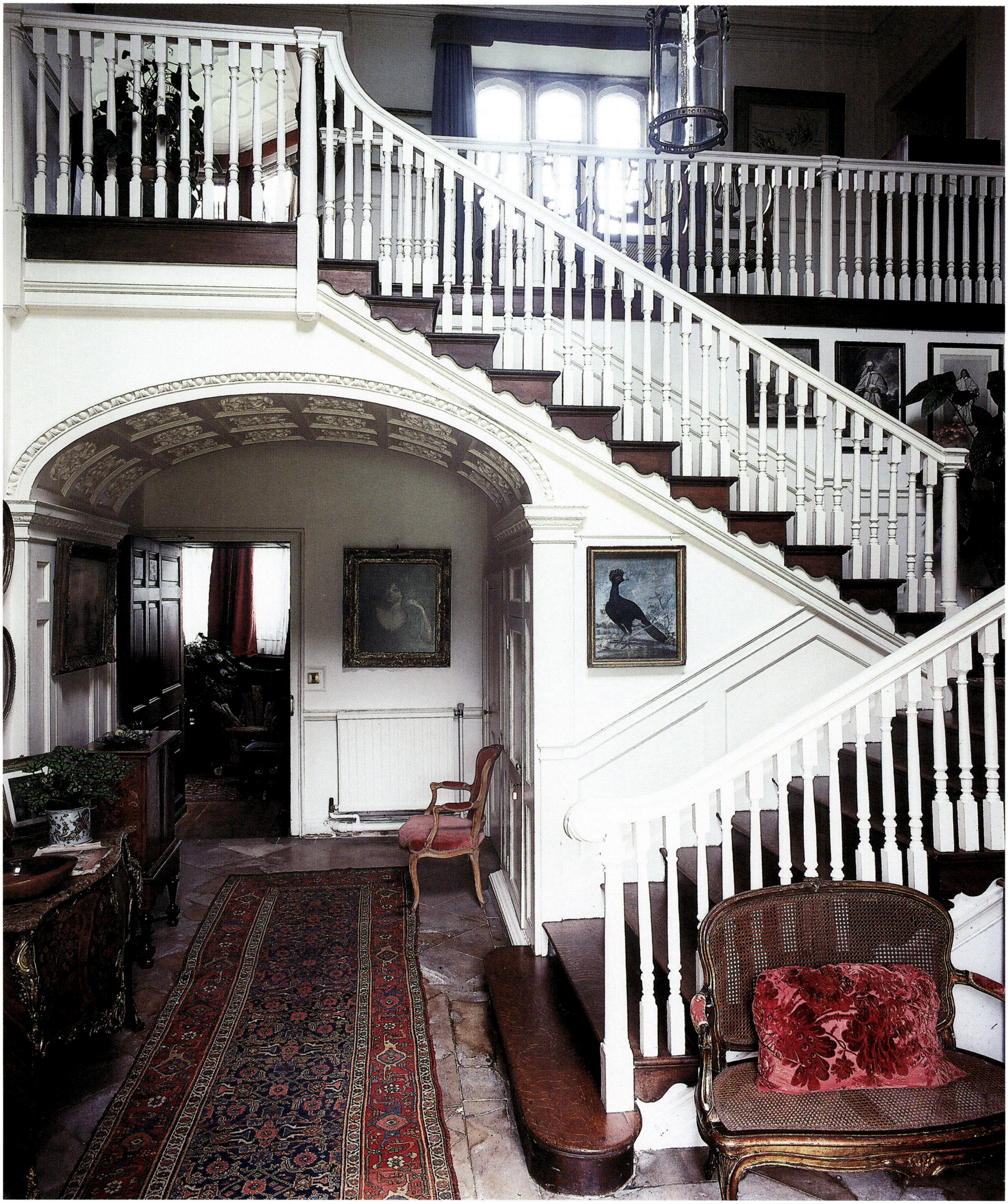

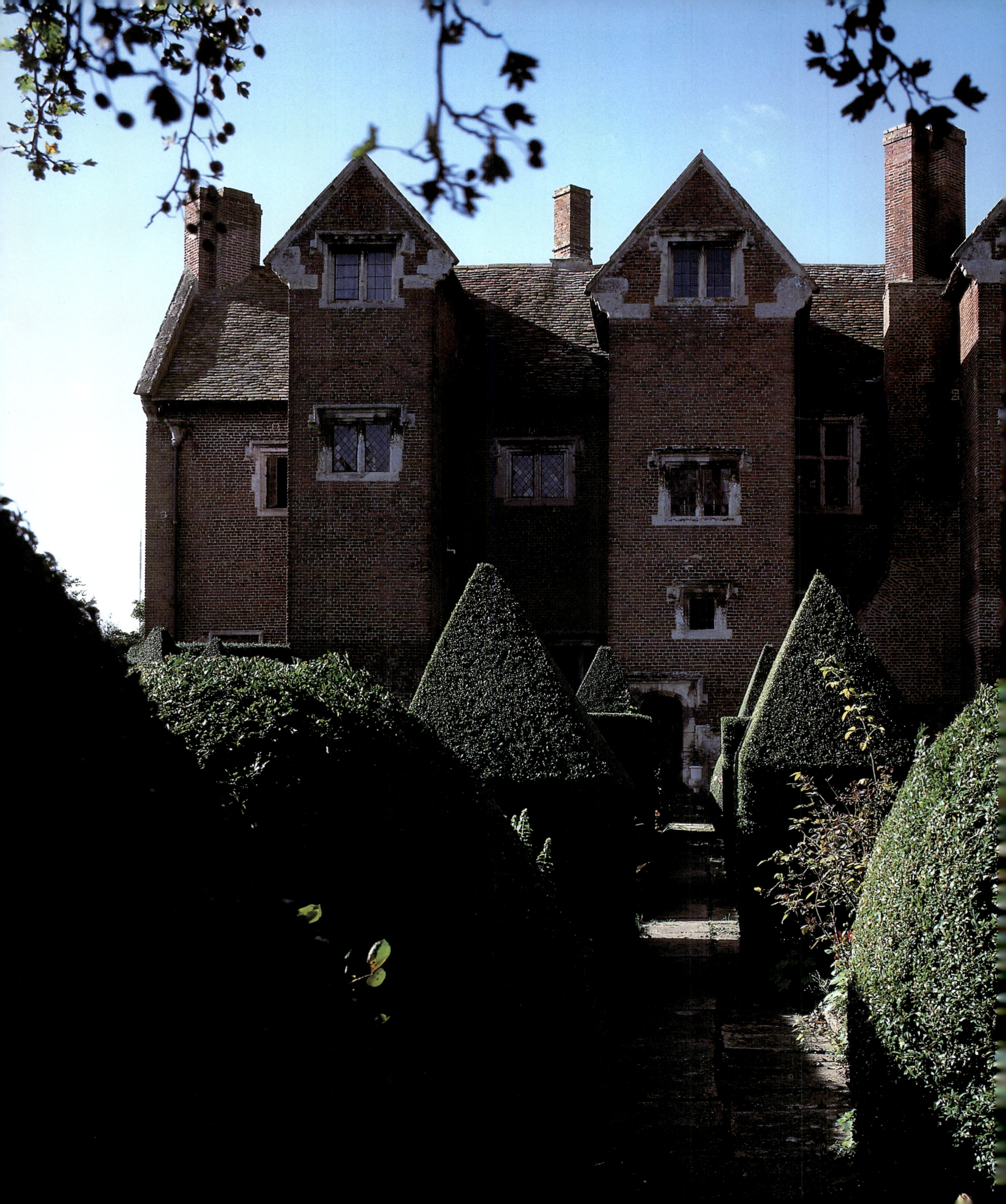

21

BECKLEY PARK

OXFORDSHIRE

OTMOOR, a wonderfully strange and remote area of marshland, remains remarkably inaccessible for a place that, geographically, is merely half-a-dozen miles from Oxford. Until it found itself in the news in the 1970s and early 1980s Otmoor was deliciously unknown, as was the nearby Beckley Park, whose then owners, Mr and Mrs Basil Feilding, braved publicity in pursuance of their fight to prevent the peaceful setting of the area being destroyed by the M40.

Indeed, the Feildings devoted their lives to preserving Beckley's special character. 'One of the hallmarks of this place', Mr Feilding told *The Field* in 1982, 'is the amazing quietness and how extraordinarily still it is'. This captivating sense of secrecy was precisely what the proposed motorway threatened to ruin.

Fortunately the Heritage lobby rallied to the cause. For Beckley is a high house of haunting beauty and mystery, a fascinating example of Tudor architecture. Of mellowed brick the colour of a ripe plum and diapered with black headers, the building is quite exceptional for its three gaunt gabled towers, its encircling rings of moats, and the fact that it has scarcely been altered since it was built in about 1540 by Lord Williams of Thame, a powerful and adaptable Tudor operator whose posts included the keepership of the King's Jewels.

As Mark Girouard explained in defence of Beckley and Otmoor at a public enquiry into the route for the M40, Beckley has been an enclosed park since the 12th century: the Black Prince kept his horses there, and Richard, Earl of Cornwall (the only Englishman ever to be elected Holy Roman Emperor), built a hunting lodge that was later enlarged. The old lodge was surrounded by a triple ring of moats; these still survive in part, but the lodge was replaced by Lord Williams. He kept to the low medieval site at the bottom of the hill, where his house still rises out of topiary hedges and moats.

BECKLEY PARK

PRECEDING PAGES The dramatic north front of Beckley, with its three projecting gables.

LEFT The placid serenity of the entrance front.

BELOW Doorway.

    The topiary hedges, so lovingly tended by Percy Feilding (Basil's father and a kinsman of the Earl of Denbigh), who bought Beckley in 1920, also featured in the public enquiry at Banbury. The designer David Hicks, who lived not far away at Britwell Salome, described Beckley's formal garden of clipped box and yew as 'one of the three most important gardens in Britain'. And it was pointed out, too, that Beckley has a place in literary history, as Aldous Huxley is said to have used the house as the model for Crome in his novel *Crome Yellow*.

    At least one of the three rings of moats around the manor house must have been in existence in the 9th century, the days of King Alfred, who bequeathed 'Beccaule' in his will to his kinsman Osferth. After the Norman Conquest Beckley came into the hands of Robert d'Oilly, a local landowner. Subsequently it passed to the families of d'Ivry and St Valery (when it acquired the romantic name of 'the Honour of St Valery'). Then, in the 13th century, Richard, Earl of Cornwall, arrived to stock the park with deer, add another couple of moats and build his hunting lodge. The 'Honour' was eventually subsumed

– 140 –

BECKLEY PARK

RIGHT The Hall; the window high up to the right of the fireplace still retains its original glazing.

BELOW View of the topiary garden.

BOTTOM Corridor: note the uneven floor.

into the Duchy of Cornwall and passed by descent to the Princes of Wales, heirs to the throne. By Henry VIII's time, though, the old house was in ruins.

The present house stands on the narrow strip of ground between the inner and middle moats. Traditionally, some of the stone from the original building was incorporated into Lord Williams's new brick construction. The south-facing entrance façade, with its stone-dressed windows, is approached across the middle moat by a double-arched stone bridge contemporary with the house. This front has a placid serenity, but the dramatic beauty is to be found at the back.

Here, three closely packed projecting gables soar upwards. The effect is breathtaking. The reason, however, could hardly be more prosaic. The gables were built in this way in order to accommodate three *garderobe* flues. If this was, as seems likely, built as a hunting lodge, then it was fitted out with the most sophisticated sanitation system. Lord Williams, who had recently built the great house of Rycote nearby, obviously liked to entertain his hunting companions in luxurious style.

– 141 –

ABOVE The Main Bedroom, with delicate linenfold panelling on the door and the wall hung with tapestry.

OPPOSITE The Oak Room, formerly the Parlour, with Jacobean panelling.

Lord Williams died in 1559 (his effigy at Thame is so detailed as to show a mole upon his cheek) and Beckley was inherited by his descendants, the Earls of Abingdon, who let it out. Miraculously, it escaped alteration in the 18th and 19th centuries, so that the *Oxfordshire* volume in Sir Nikolaus Pevsner's *Buildings of England* series could describe it as 'the best preserved small house of this date in the county'. Today it is the cherished home of Basil Feilding's youngest daughter, the artist Amanda Feilding, who is married to Lord Neidpath, himself the owner of Stanway in Gloucestershire (*qv*).

Inside, Beckley is cool and dark. Shafts of sunlight pierce the shadows. The plan, or arrangement of rooms, follows the usual manorial pattern for a house of this date: Hall, Parlour, Buttery and Kitchen. The Hall, 16 feet wide (the total width of the house) and 22 feet long, is lit by two large windows, one of which retains its early 17th-century glazing. At what was the screens end of the Hall, a sturdy double-leaved door leads into the old Buttery. Beyond the Buttery was the old Kitchen, now used as a Dining Room, still with its original fireplace.

The former Parlour, now the Oak Room, has Jacobean panelling and the staircase is a perfect newel stair of solid oak, hardly blemished after more than 450 years. Upstairs, there is some delicate linenfold panelling on the door of the Main Bedroom. And there is an intriguing piece of joinery in another bedroom: a casement window with a wooden frame set into it, within which

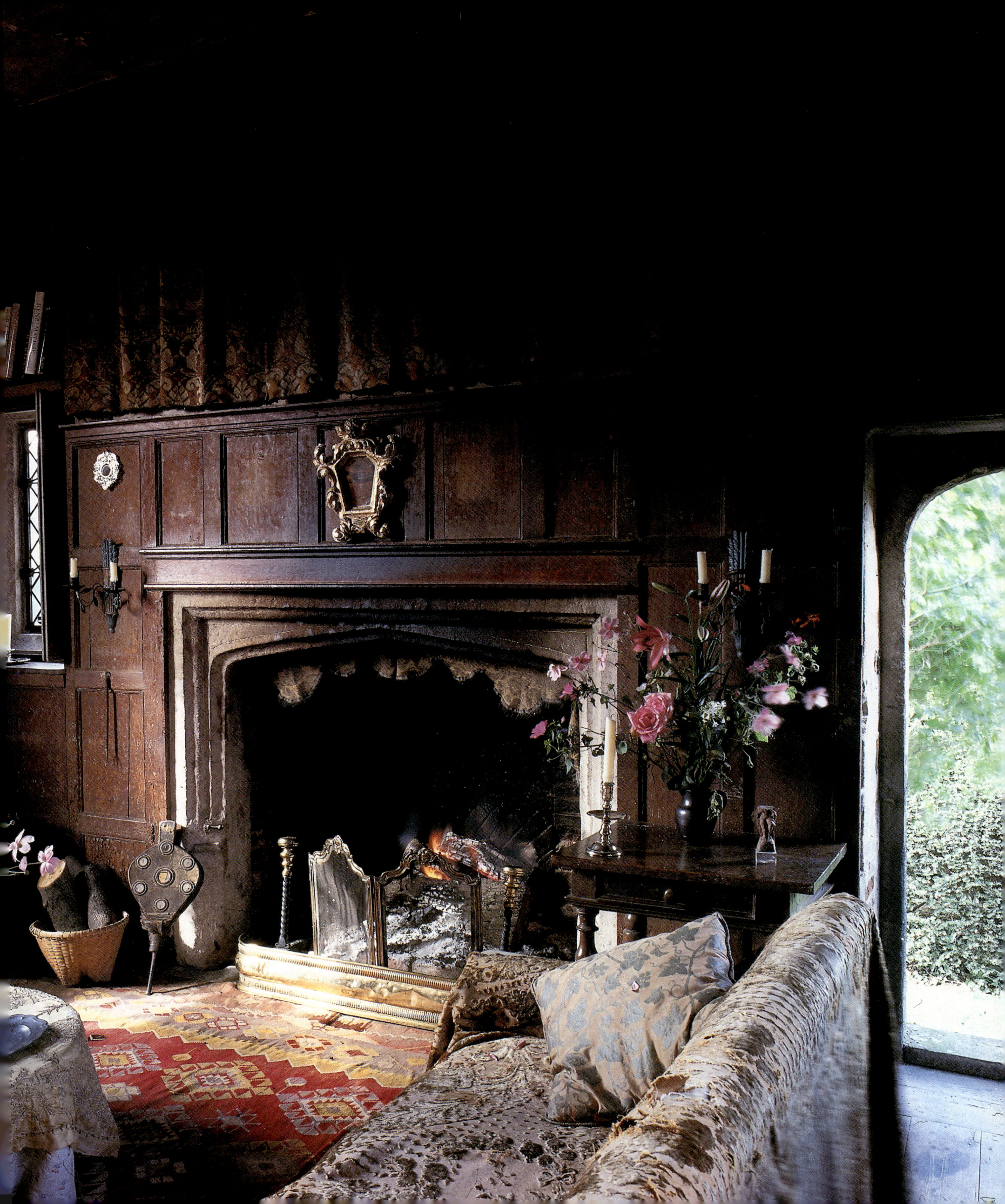

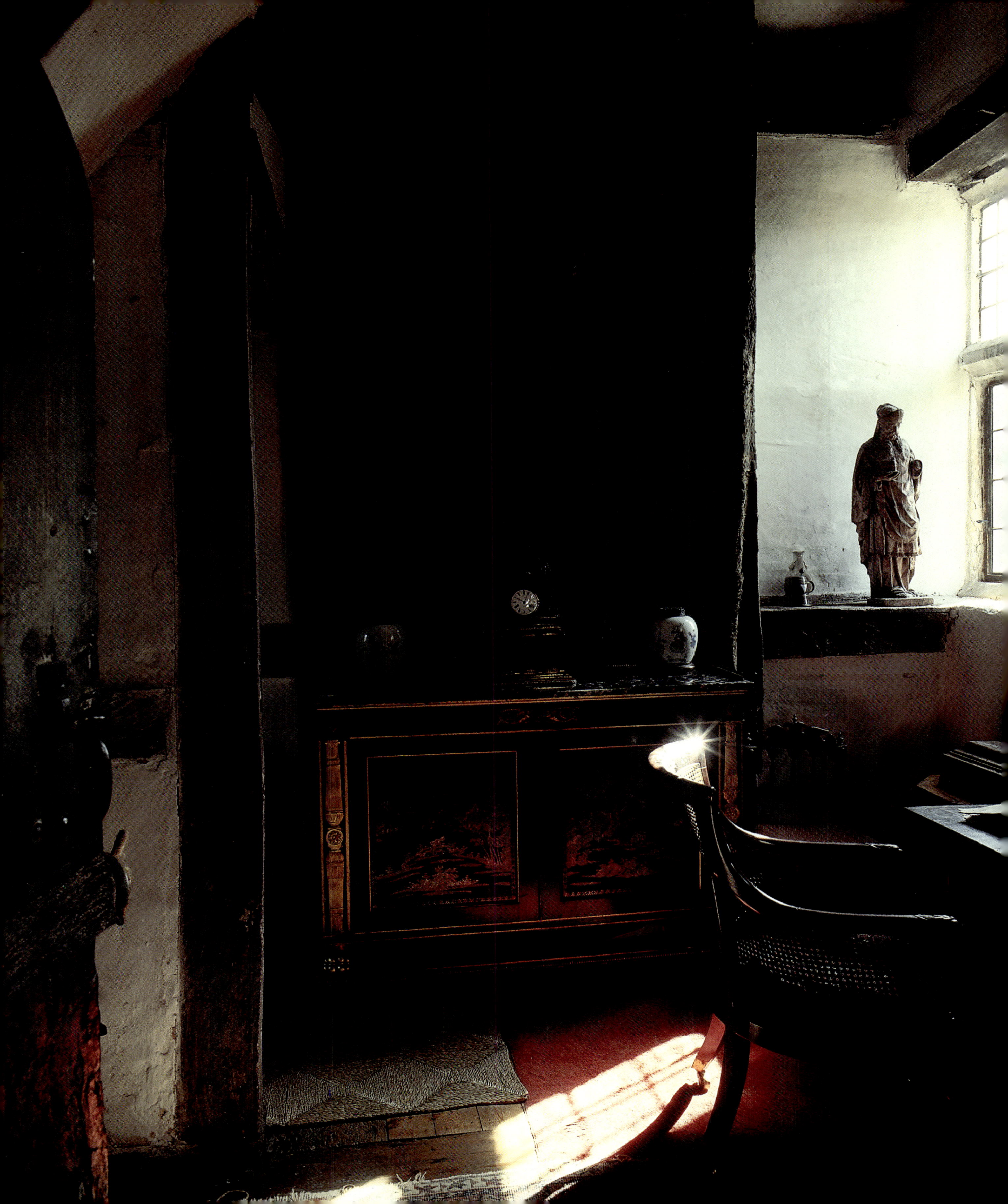

ABOVE The old kitchen, now the Dining Room, with its ancient fireplace and the remnants of an ingenious device for turning spits by means of hot air passing up the chimney.

OPPOSITE The former buttery, once used for the storage of ale.

is hinged another frame that contains a shutter and is grooved for the reception of glazing.

An evocative vignette of what it was like to grow up at Beckley is recalled by a daughter of the house: 'In winter, the house was so cold that nobody came near us. When my hot-water bottle fell out of bed it was frozen in the morning. We lived in our overcoats. The Oak Room was kept warm, and from there we would make a run for the kitchen. I remember the cosiness of the winter evenings, when the wind raged outside, sitting huddled in front of the big fire, with one of my parents reading. With the wind, and the trickle of water falling from the outer moat into the inner one, the outside world seemed very far away.' Long may it remain so.

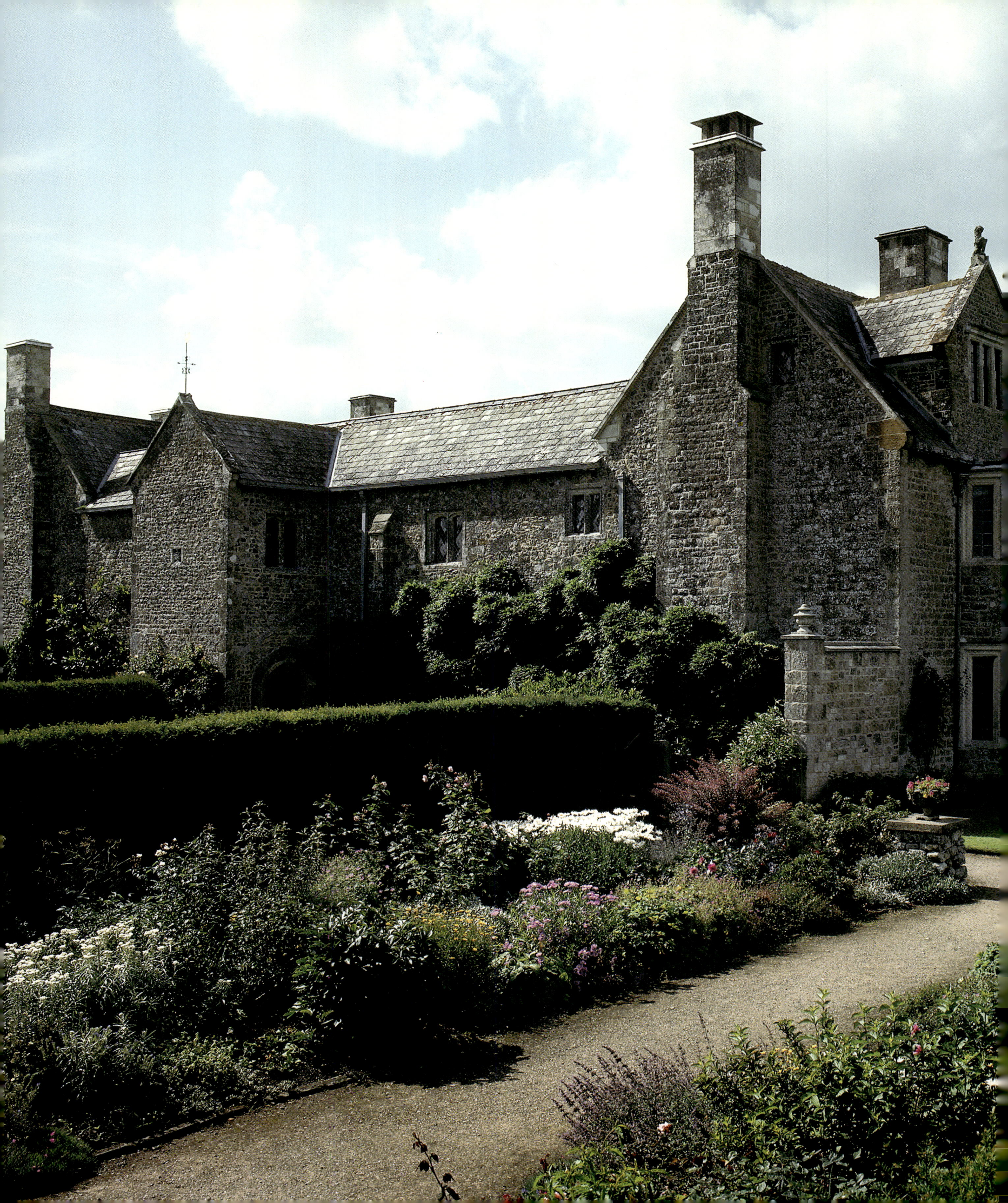

22

CADHAY

DEVON

DEVON is a deceptively large county, well stocked with old manor houses, but among the surviving Tudor seats none is so delightful as Cadhay, near Ottery St Mary. As Laurence Weaver put it in *Country Life* in 1913, the house 'stands four-square on its ancient site, a typical example of three of our greatest periods of English building'.

The 'ancient site' was first mentioned in the reign of Edward I as a sub-manor of the manor of Ottery St Mary held by the de Cadhaye family. The eventual heiress, Joan, married Hugh Grenville and their granddaughter, another Joan, had the Cadhay estate settled on her in 1527 at the time of her marriage to John Haydon, a prosperous lawyer and legal adviser to the City of Exeter. We learn from Risdon's *Survey of Devon* (1620) that 'John Haydon, esquire, sometime bencher of Lincoln's Inn, built at *Cadhay* a fair new house and enlarged his demesnes'.

This 'fair new house' is thought to have been built between about 1546 and 1550. Medieval stone fragments in the walls appear to have been brought in from the College of Priests in Ottery St Mary, of which John Haydon became a governor on its surrender to Henry VIII in 1545. Haydon is known to have profited from the Suppression of the Monasteries, though, in fairness, it should be added that he was a considerable philanthropist. He and his wife built the attractive bridge between Ottery and Cadhay, which is traditionally supposed to have borne the following inscription:

John and Joan built me
Pray good people repair me.

It is possible that John Haydon's Great Hall, with its handsome chestnut roof (a significant portion of which survives), may have incorporated part of an earlier house on the site dating from the 15th century. John Haydon seems to have completed three sides of the courtyard at Cadhay before his death in 1587. The fourth, narrower, side, containing the Long Gallery, was almost certainly added by his great-nephew and successor, Robert Haydon.

PRECEDING PAGES John Haydon's 'fair new house' of 1546–50: a view of Cadhay from the gardens, showing the south and east fronts.

LEFT The Dining Hall, with its Gothic fireplace adorned with the coats of arms of Robert Haydon (John's successor at Cadhay from 1587) and his wife, Joan Poulett.

Robert married yet another Joan, eldest daughter of Sir Amyas Poulett, a powerful Elizabethan courtier seated at Hinton St George in Somerset (and, incidentally, a kinsman of the William-Powlett family, the present owners of Cadhay). The arms of Robert and Joan adorn the fine fireplace in the Hall (now the Dining Hall), a notably Gothic affair. Indeed, one of the most striking points about Cadhay's architectural history is how the late 16th-century building work perpetuated the Gothic style of some 40 years before, at a time when it was generally supposed to be on the way out of fashion.

Cadhay's most celebrated feature, the Court of Sovereigns, is also attributed to Robert Haydon's time. Faced in chequerwork of sandstone and flint – a style more associated with East Anglia than Devon – this Court is adorned

BELOW The south front across the park.

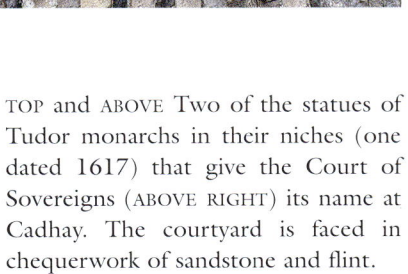

TOP and ABOVE Two of the statues of Tudor monarchs in their niches (one dated 1617) that give the Court of Sovereigns (ABOVE RIGHT) its name at Cadhay. The courtyard is faced in chequerwork of sandstone and flint.

with four ornamental niches, one of them dated 1617. Each niche contains an elaborately executed statue of a Tudor monarch: Henry VIII, Edward VI, Mary and Elizabeth. The sovereigns stand rather stiffly, in bulky cloaks with top-heavy crowns perched somewhat precariously on top of their heads. They present an unforgettable picture.

The sandstone used for the Haydons' house came from Salcombe, but the corners and dressings are of limestone from Beer (the same material as was used at Exeter Cathedral). The closed oblong courtyard is flanked by long sides to the north (where the ground floor is mainly filled by the present Dining Hall) and the south (with the Long Gallery on the first floor). To the east are the living rooms; to the west, the kitchen and service rooms.

During the Civil War the Haydons proved ardent Royalists. In 1649 one of the family, Nicholas Haydon, was fined £69 4s 6d 'for delinquency in

LEFT The Long Gallery: a charmingly simple interior from a time (late Elizabethan and early Jacobean) when decoration tended to the ornate.

BELOW Stairway.

catering to the forces raised against Parliament'. Perhaps they celebrated the Restoration of Charles II too extravagantly, for later in the 17th century they were floundering in mortgages. Finally, in 1736, Cadhay was sold for the first time to a John Brown, who promptly sold it on the following year to William Peere Williams of Gray's Inn.

Williams divided the original Great Hall into two rooms. Although the former hammerbeams and arched braces are no longer extant in the chestnut roof, the sweeping arches are still there to support the principal rafters. The residual timbers, which can be admired in the present waggon-vaulted Roof Chamber, undoubtedly remain Cadhay's most important internal feature.

The Georgian improver also remodelled the entrance front, which he gave an imposing façade of Beerstone ashlar, stepped gables and a front door in the manner of the architect James Gibbs. The Williams heiress married Admiral Lord Graves, second-in-command to the 1st Earl Howe at the battle fought against the French on 'the Glorious First of June', 1794. Lord Graves died at Cadhay in 1802 and the estate passed to his daughter, Mrs Thomas Hare of Stow Bardolph, Norfolk, who preferred to stay in East Anglia.

Thus, as at so many manor houses, the 19th century saw Cadhay in decline. The house was divided up: the west end was adapted for occupation as a tenant farmhouse and the east end let as a small residence. Eventually, in

The Roof Chamber, with its chestnut timbers and sweeping arches supporting the old rafters from the original Great Hall.

1909 Sir Ralph Hare sold the property to W.C. Dampier Whetham (later Sir William Dampier), a Cambridge don and polymath, who carefully restored Cadhay with the help of the architect H.M. Fletcher. Excellent repair work was carried out to put it into sound structural condition. The old fireplaces and roof were revealed once more.

The William-Powletts' connection with the place began in 1924 when the present owner's grandfather, Major B.N.W. William-Powlett, rented Cadhay from Dampier Whetham. Then, in 1935, he bought it outright. Subsequently it became the home of his son, Captain N.J.W. William-Powlett, RN, and his wife Barbara (who as a widow married her husband's younger brother, Vice-Admiral Sir Peveril William-Powlett). Today it is immaculately preserved by the Captain's son, Oliver William-Powlett, who opens Cadhay regularly to the public in the summer months when Devon is a popular holiday destination.

Besides the house, with its appealing combination of Tudor architecture and family collections, visitors can enjoy the very pleasant gardens, with their herbaceous borders, yew hedges, avenue of lime trees and soothing views over the original medieval fish ponds of the de Cadhayes.

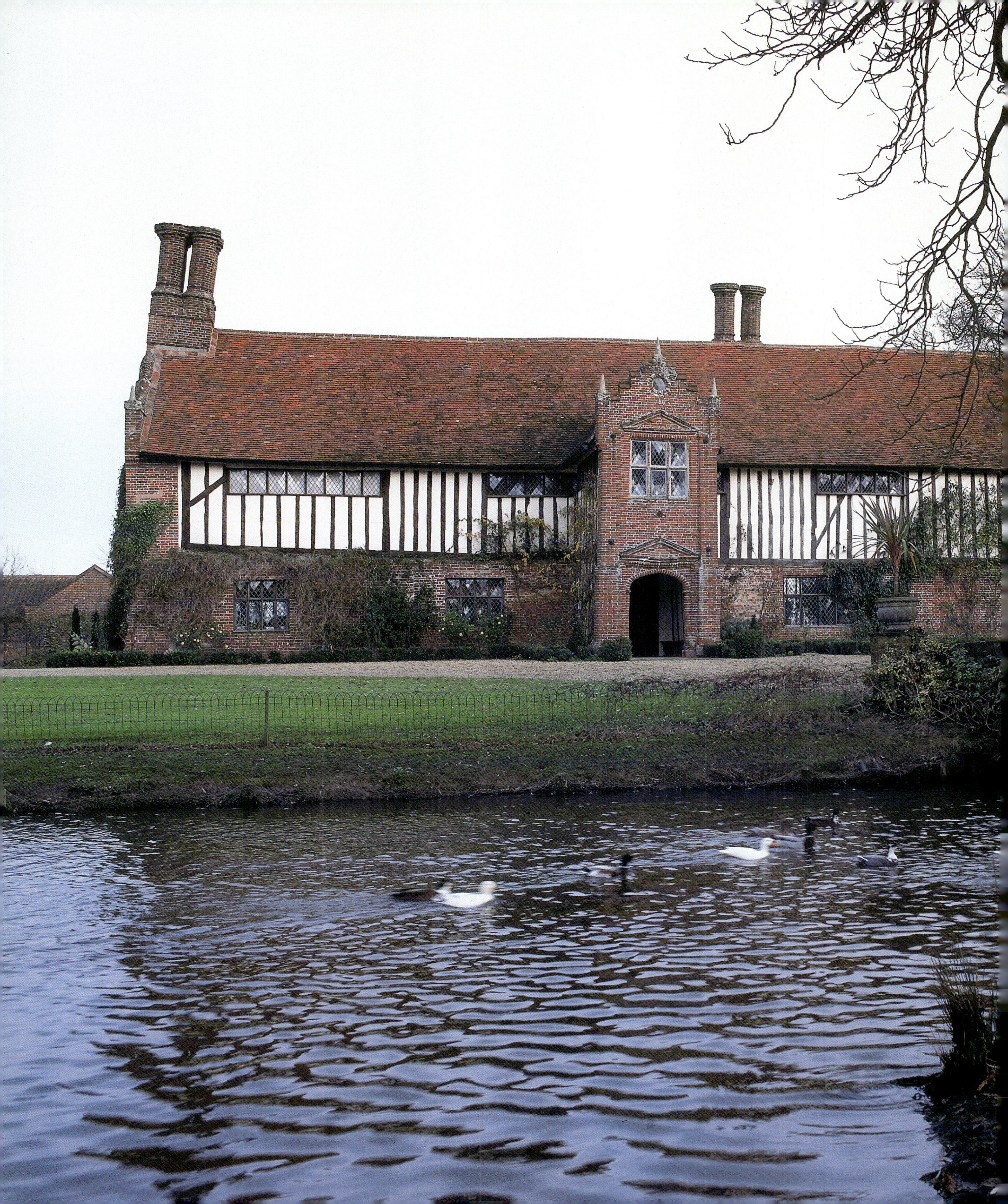

23

FLEMINGS HALL

SUFFOLK

THIS exceptionally attractive moated manor house in brick and half-timber is a photographer's dream – and that is precisely what it was under the ownership of the late Angus McBean, the celebrated stage photographer, who turned that dream into a remarkably practical reality. Although Flemings has a long history, stretching back to medieval times when the builders of this important house, the Bedingfelds or Bedingfields, took their surname from the village with which they were to remain associated until the 20th century, what we see today owes almost everything to McBean's extraordinary eye and personality.

As a boy McBean, already fascinated by art and architecture, won a folding Kodak camera in a raffle in the Welsh Valleys. Installed in London, he began his career in the antiques department of Libertys, the half-timbered emporium of Art Nouveau design. Following a violent altercation with a lady customer, young Angus turned to theatre photography in the mid-1930s and grew the luxuriant, spade-like beard that was to become his trademark. His style of photography was noted for its increasingly surreal effects; among the stars he immortalized were Vivien Leigh and Audrey Hepburn (whom he spotted in a chorus line for a cold cream commercial).

Suffolk, with its beautiful light and gentle landscape, had long proved a magnet for creative bachelors such as McBean seeking solace away from London. Among the confraternity to have settled happily in these parts were the composer Benjamin Britten and the singer Peter Pears, the ballet-dancer and choreographer Frederick Ashton and the novelist Angus Wilson. In the early 1960s McBean's younger partners started an antiques business at Debenham and the veteran photographer decided to find a home in Suffolk. He sold his house in Islington to the chef Robert Carrier (who was later to convert Hintlesham Hall, near Ipswich, into an hotel) and for a 'very modest price' bought Flemings.

From the outside, at least, the place looked a picture. As Norman Scarfe put it in his *Shell Guide* to Suffolk, 'with a great moat, a porch of smouldering brick and silhouetted dutch gables, it is one of the most romantically beautiful houses in Suffolk'. It seemed far from 'the lovely ruin' described in Arthur Mee's frequently fanciful *King's England* volume on the county (published in 1904), with its 'solitude broken only by the scurrying of rabbits as we disturb their haunts'. In fact, the Edwards family are recorded as being in residence in the 1890s and it seems that the Bedingfelds' connection with the place did not finally end until the 1920s; a subsequent owner was said to have spent a considerable sum on restoration work.

When McBean first saw Flemings, he found the external fabric in good order. The tradition was that the basic structure had been medieval; it was enlarged by the addition containing the present staircase and three rooms over one another. The major rebuilding work was done about 1580, or perhaps slightly earlier, including all the brickwork, which not only embraces the gable ends, chimneys and projecting porch but also the front elevation right up to the roof (the woodwork here being false). By this stage the Bedingfeld family were at their zenith. Sir Edmund Bedingfeld, who married a daughter of the 1st Lord Marney, builder of Layer Marney (*qv*), was custodian of Catherine of Aragon after her divorce from Henry VIII. His son, Sir Henry, a Privy Councillor and MP for both Suffolk and Norfolk (where the family were seated at Oxburgh, now a property of the National Trust), fulfilled a similar role towards the young Princess Elizabeth during Mary Tudor's reign.

The local architectural historian L.A. Alston has noted of Flemings: 'Built as an unusually large and high status manor house during the first half of Queen Elizabeth's reign, it was improved and maintained at the highest county level until the later years of the 17th century when it was allowed to slip into fashionable obscurity and eventually into a probable state of near collapse.' By present-day standards, of course, Flemings does not seem all that large: it is just over 100ft long and, like many Elizabethan houses, one room thick.

The interior must have come as something of a shock to McBean. It was stripped bare of all ornament, empty and forlorn. As he himself recalled: 'Gone was the panelling described in an old guide as notable, all the doors

PRECEDING PAGES 'One of the most romantically beautiful houses in Suffolk': Flemings Hall, seen across its moat.

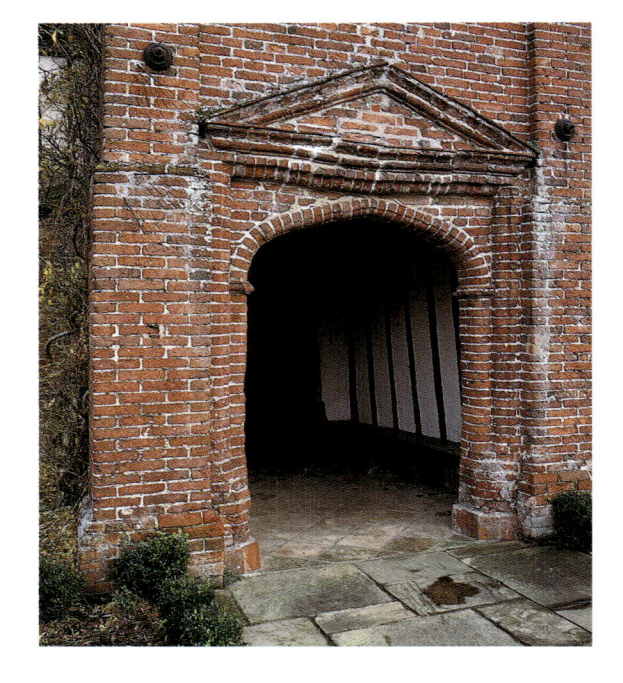

ABOVE The projecting porch, which dates, like most of the brickwork at Flemings, from about 1580.

LEFT The Great Hall, restored as a living room by Angus McBean, with its notable fireplace (complete with linenfold panelling) rescued from a bombed-out house in London.

Upstairs corridor: a maze of half-timbering.

and even the staircase. All had been ripped out, sold and shipped to Australia.' Only the structural wood remained, and this had been stained dark. For the rest the interior was just, as McBean put it, 'a huge cream-washed barn'.

Nothing daunted, McBean determined to restore this empty shell to 'something similar to what it had formerly been in 1580'. The result is astonishing. Far from looking like a lot of trumped-up fakery or a painfully purist exercise in architectural archaeology ('We did not want a museum,' stressed McBean, 'we wanted a home'), Flemings has a robust, potent character all of its own. Whatever the precise origins and provenance of the myriad constituents

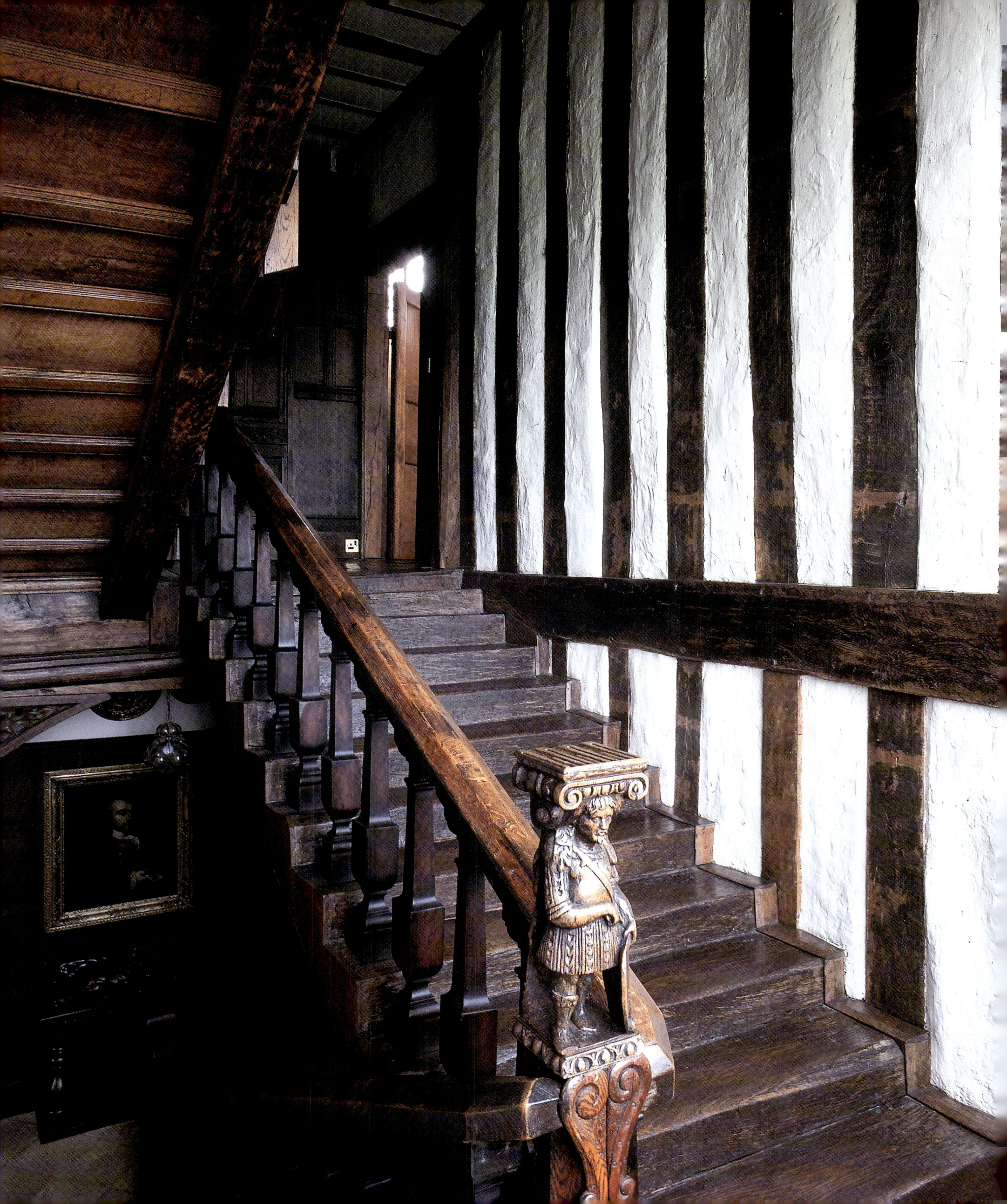

ABOVE Detail of carved woodwork.

OPPOSITE The staircase, as reconstructed by McBean – self-styled 'bodger of genius'.

RIGHT Bedroom under the rafters.

of this by now probably indecipherable jigsaw, somehow it just looks and feels right. As Elizabeth Lambert has written, 'a McBean improvisation is worth more than an authentic original'.

What is so impressive is that McBean did it all with his own hands. He laid aside his lens to concentrate on becoming, as he put it in true Suffolk style, 'a badger of genius'. The rotten wooden bridge over the moat was replaced by one built of old bricks; the roof was rehung with peg tiles and a warren of Victorian service rooms at the back was replaced by a back porch panelled with old oak.

The search for suitable old oak for doors and panelling occupied much of the indefatigable McBean's time. The fine early panelling in the Parlour came from an antique shop at Bakewell in Derbyshire. The magnificent ceiling-high fireplace was constructed from a ruined Elizabethan court cupboard. The Hall, which at least retained most of its original beams from the 1580 remodelling, was also given some brought-in old panelling. The splendid surround that frames the fireplace was rescued from a bombed house in London.

Upstairs, McBean took justifiable pride in hanging a wall covering of his own design, adapted from a 15th-century painted room in Florence, screen-printed on to hessian. When he confessed to a grand antique dealer that he had made his spectacular four-poster bed himself from bits of carved Jacobean oak, this personage replied: 'Dear boy, we *all* have to these days.'

Today Flemings is the home of Mr and Mrs Colin Barrow, who cherish Angus McBean's truly superb achievement of transforming 'a lovely ruin' into a manor house that has managed to improve on reality.

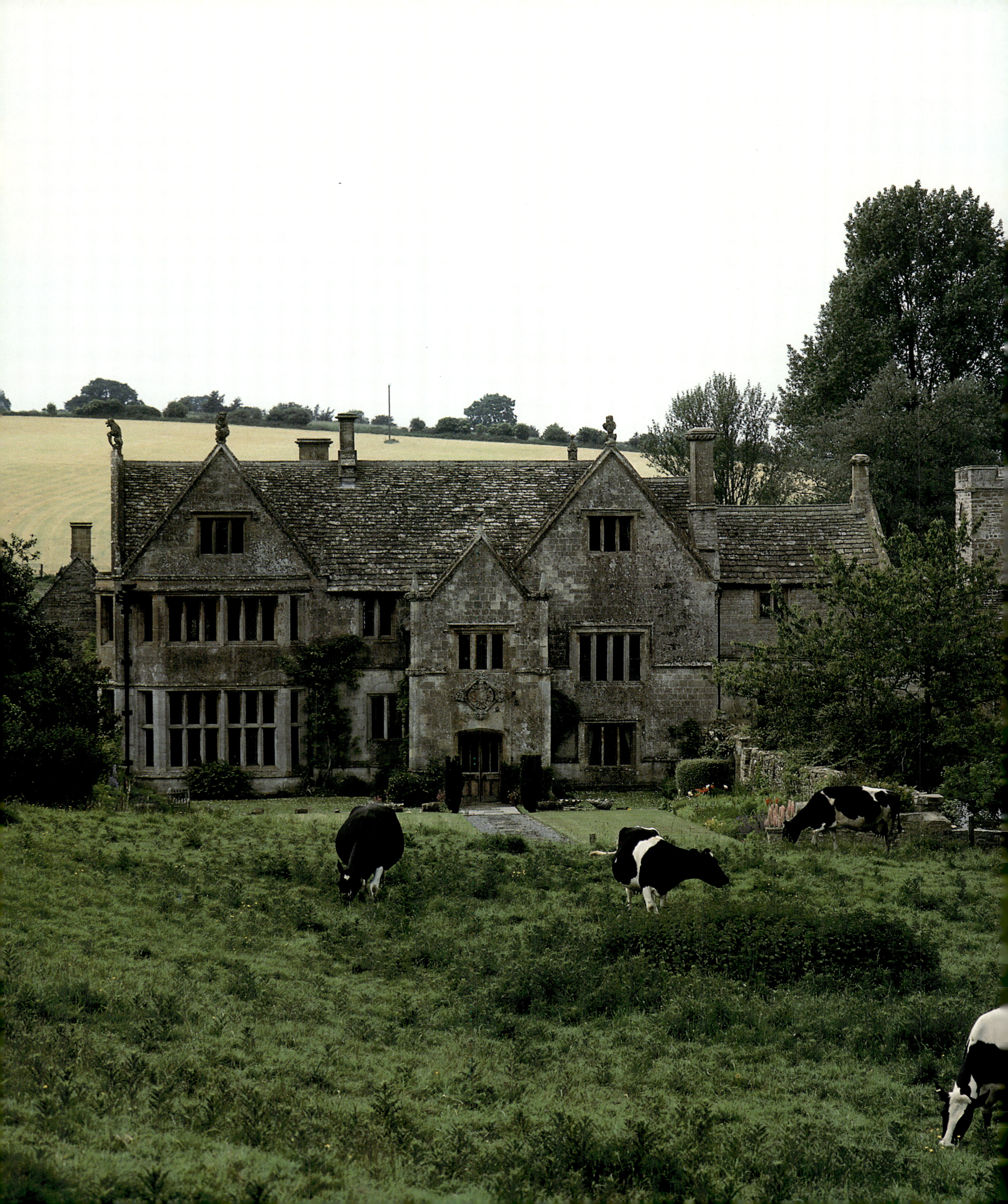

24

SANDFORD ORCAS MANOR

DORSET

As you negotiate the narrow, winding lanes near Sherborne you feel that you are travelling blissfully back in time, and the first sight of the honey-coloured Sandford Orcas Manor lives up to every expectation. Next to the church is a beguiling gatehouse through which you enter a courtyard and then turn to find the entrance front of Ham Hill stone facing away from the road on to an idyllic pastoral landscape. As Lord David Cecil wrote of his visit here, 'Passing through its gateway, I feel myself to be leaving the active populous world to enter a region dedicated to solitude and memory.'

Yet for all its captivating charm, Sandford Orcas is not just a pretty picture postcard of a building. Its architecture represents an unusually good example of this mid-16th-century type. As the present squire, Sir Mervyn Medlycott, 9th Baronet, a respected genealogist and president of the Somerset and Dorset Family History Society, points out on the authoritative tour he gives visitors, Sandford Orcas is one of the earliest houses in Britain to employ straight heads to the mullioned windows; the only Tudor house to attach a gatehouse to the side of the main front; and one of the earliest Tudor buildings to have a Great Hall with a flat ceiling and a Great Chamber over it. Most remarkable of all in a house of about 1550 was the substitution of the traditional oriel window in the Great Hall with a thrilling two-tiered splay of glass – thereby predating such celebrated 'lantern houses' as Longleat. In fact, the ground-floor windows at the south-east corner of the house are twice the height of those on the first storey; this creates a memorable effect.

Such a brilliant scheme reflects great credit on the daring of the house's builder (or, to be precise, 're-builder'), Edward Knoyle, who married a Miss Martyn of Athelhampton (*qv*) and clearly picked up a few pointers from his in-laws' house. The property had been in the Knoyle family since the early 14th century, having descended from the original owners, the family of de Oresculitz ('Orcas' being a pleasantly West Country corruption of this Norman name),

PRECEDING PAGES The entrance front of Sandford Orcas, facing an idyllic landscape, with the church to the right.

LEFT The Gatehouse.

RIGHT Detail of wood carving on the fireplace in the Great Hall.

ABOVE Detail of the lozenge-shaped panel (shades of Athelhampton – *qv*) on the porch at Sandford Orcas, which displayed the arms of Knoyle and Fry. Note the straight heads to the mullioned windows above – Sandford Orcas was one of the earliest houses in Britain to employ this feature.

RIGHT The vigorously carved Jacobean screen in the Great Hall, notable for its pierced strapwork cresting.

through the female line. Although doubtless there had been some sort of dwelling on the site since Saxon times, the first hard evidence of a house here crops up in the will of Edward Knoyle's great-grandfather, William Knoyle or Knoyel, in 1501, which refers to a hall, kitchen, guest chamber and brewhouse, as well as to his volumes of Boccaccio and Chaucer.

It is uncertain how much, if any, of the present house might date from the well-read William's time, though the ground-plan is typically medieval. Perhaps Edward built on his great-grandfather's foundations? And some sections of walling from the old house may have been incorporated into the new building.

The Knoyles, staunch Roman Catholics and Royalists, suffered for their allegiances. The Civil War shattered their financial stability. None the less, an inventory of the effects of the Cavalier Captain Thomas Knoyle compiled upon his death in 1684 (by which time he was merely a life tenant at Sandford Orcas) noted 'one clock, one great table board, one livery cupboard, six joynt stooles, two wicker chairs and a leather chair, three forms and three coffers' in the Great Hall and 'eleven leather chairs' in the Parlour.

There is another fascinating record of Sandford Orcas in the map of 1702 made by the cartographer Joel Gascoyne for the then owner, Sir Thomas Webster. A bird's eye view, it shows the elevation of three gables with porch, just as it is today, though the gardens were laid out with parterres at least an acre in extent. Soon afterwards, however (perhaps as a result of the Great Storm of 1703), the gables over the Great Hall were dismantled and the windows rather bizarrely ornamented with a hipped roof.

Fortunately, in 1873, when the house was sympathetically restored by Hubert Hutchings and his architect Henry Hall, the gables were lovingly put back – exactly in the pattern of the 1702 map. The Hutchings family had actually acquired Sandford Orcas in 1736 from Sir Thomas Webster but had let it out as a farmhouse in the meantime. Such a 'Sleeping Beauty' period occurs in the history of many manor houses, with the consequent beneficial effect that the place remains substantially unaltered. In the case of Sandford Orcas, Hubert Hutchings – a connoisseur of Tudor architecture, collector of Jacobean woodwork and medieval stained glass, a correspondent of the architect Edward Blore and the Gothic specialist John Henry Parker – proved the perfect Prince to awaken the Sleeping Beauty. He and Hall cleverly transformed the cottage and stable blocks, previously in agricultural use, with Tudorish touches, and added a west wing.

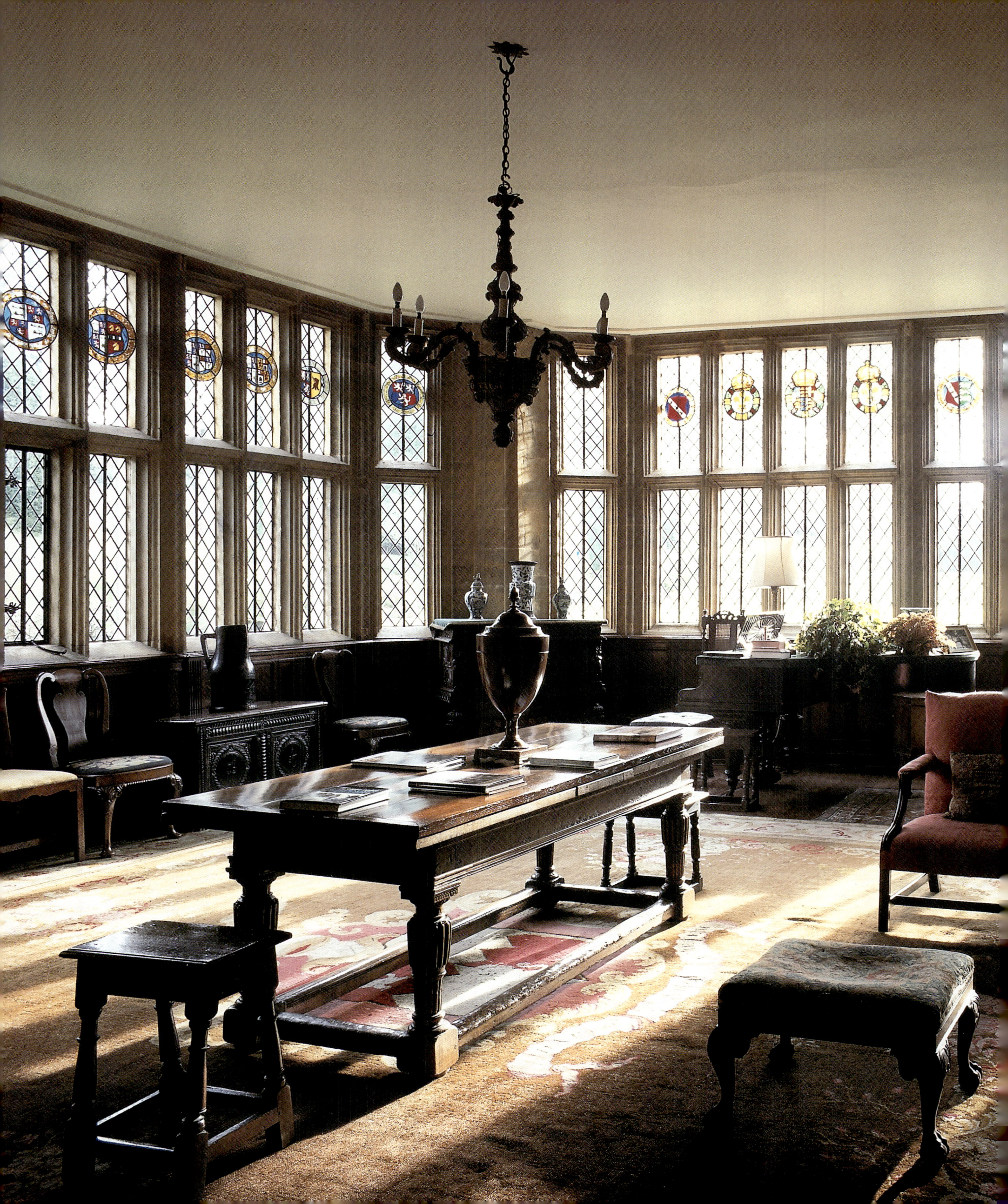

ABOVE An elephant, looking more like a giant pig with a bizarrely looped trunk, painted on a glass pane hanging in a window.

LEFT Sandford Orcas's *pièce de résistance*: the Great Hall, with its lantern of glass decorated with heraldry. This wonderfully light interior is, as Lord David Cecil observed, 'at once spacious and intimate'.

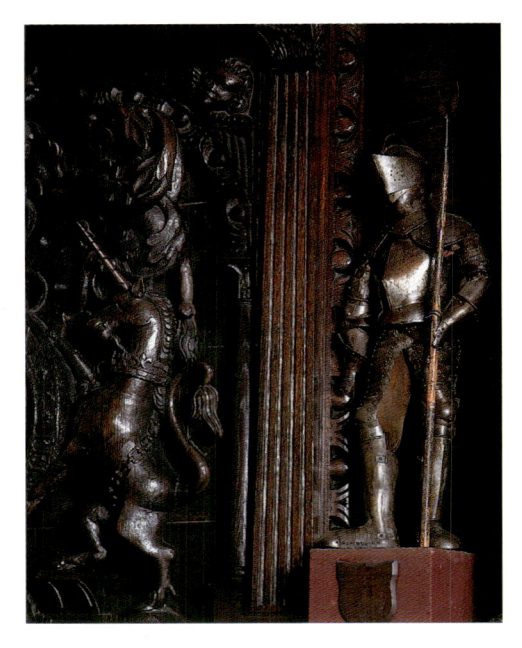

ABOVE Detail of carved wooden overmantel in a bedroom.

LEFT Bedroom, which like other rooms in this well-maintained manor house is full of good furniture and china.

The house's present immaculate order owes everything to Sir Mervyn Medlycott, whose family inherited Sandford Orcas from the Hutchingses in 1916. Since 1978 Sir Mervyn has undertaken a major programme of restoration work in the house and has also created a delightful garden – complete with a herb garden copied from the old map of 1702. During the work he discovered a cannonball of Civil War vintage and a pair of possibly 16th-century children's shoes which had been placed behind a lathe and plaster wall, presumably as a good luck charm.

Sir Mervyn opens the house and gardens regularly to the public, and there is much to see. The Great Hall is an unforgettable experience, with its vigorously carved Jacobean screen, giant fireplace and massive mullioned windows decorated with heraldic glass. As Lord David Cecil observed, this wonderfully light interior is 'at once spacious and intimate'.

Upstairs, one finds oneself slightly confused by the rabbit warren of nooks and crannies on different levels. Yet everywhere the eye is taken by an outstanding collection of Jacobean and Queen Anne furniture of the highest standard, a goodly set of family portraits, china, carpets and medieval stained glass. There is an especially fine overmantel in the Porch Room, depicting the arms of James I, which came from the Joiners' Hall in Salisbury (now a property of the National Trust).

The joy of the place is that Sandford Orcas remains a lived-in house, not a museum. There are no dreaded druggets or guide-ropes, and Sir Mervyn's personally guided tours are a pleasure not to be missed. One of the telling details he points out is that no less than ten of the ancient oak-studded doors survive in the house, together with their locks and keys. These, as Lord David Cecil remarked, are 'heavy and majestic enough to be used by St Peter to open and shut the gates of Paradise' – a most fitting observation.

ABOVE Nooks and crannies at different levels upstairs.

RIGHT At the head of the south newel stair.

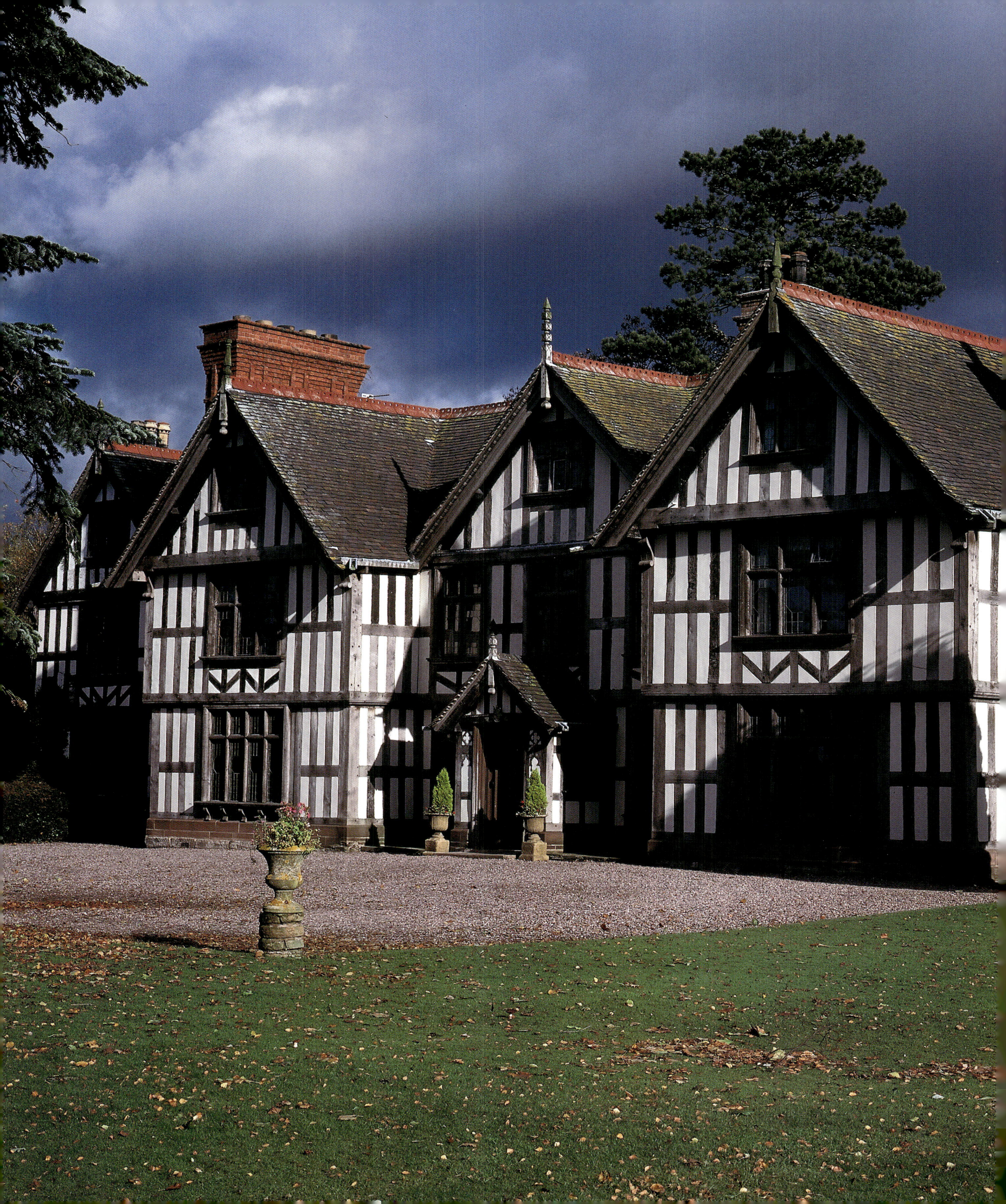

25

HIGHFIELDS

CHESHIRE

THE NORTH-WEST of England, and Cheshire in particular, is celebrated for its timber-framed manor houses in the 'Black and White' style, but most of the best-known examples now tend to have become museums. Highfields, near Audlem, is both lesser known and very much still a family home. The Bellyse Bakers, who live here, are direct descendants of William Dod, who erected the house 'on the Highefields pasture' in about 1585.

William Dod's father and namesake, himself a scion of one of the longest-established landed dynasties in Cheshire, the Dods of Edge and Cloverley, had inherited the Highfields estate in 1553 from Hugh Chester. In 1615 the third William Dod remodelled the house. He is the 'W.D.' referred to on the porch and the fine carved fireplace in the 'Best Parlour' or Oak Room, where he was responsible for the handsome panelling. The principal staircase in the house, with its double-twisted balusters, rises behind the Oak Room; the other staircase, though, which rises behind the original kitchen (now the Dining Room), is hardly inferior, with its singular barley-sugar pattern. The half-panelled Hall boasts another good carved fireplace, thought to date from about 1660.

A particular point of architectural interest about Highfields is its association with William Baker, a leading architect in these parts in the mid-18th century. In 1736 he married Jane Dod, the heiress or rather the actual proprietress of Highfields (her parents had both died when she was a baby), and managed to combine his prolific architectural practice with his squirearchical responsibilities. In the 1740s Baker duly extended Highfields to the east (or rear), adding the present Drawing Room. This extension is remarkable for its harmony with the original house. Baker's faithful rendition of the Black and White style ranks, as John Martin Robinson pointed out in his *Guide to the Country Houses of the North-West*, as 'an exceptionally early example of this kind of revivalism'. (The Black and White Revival was not to reach its peak in Cheshire for well over another century.) Baker's pleasant new Drawing Room, half-panelled in oak with a large bay window and a brought-in, elaborately carved oak fireplace (apparently of Welsh origin), is much lighter and loftier than the interiors of the older part of Highfields.

Baker's account book from 1748 to 1759 has been preserved and provides an absorbing insight into the life of a provincial Georgian architect. The names of many familiar country houses crop up in it, including the nearby Dorfold (*qv*) and Whitmore in the neighbouring county of Staffordshire (*qv*). We learn that Baker kept a kiln at Highfields and sold bricks. Household and farming details are juxtaposed with architectural matters or pithy notes on his clients ('Died Mr Prince Astley... by the effect of drinking').

William Baker's son and successor, Richard, was also an architect-squire. His daughter, Hannah, caused paternal consternation when, in the time-honoured manner, she climbed down from a bedroom window at Highfields into the arms of her lover and eloped in a post-chaise. The object of her affections was John Bellyse, a local sporting doctor who was one of the founders of the Waterloo Cup for coursing. The following morning Squire Baker decided that a call upon the young medic's father, 'Cockfighting' Bellyse of Audlem, would be in order. When the squire had finished his tirade on the subject of the Cockfighter's errant son, the old sportsman – a formidable-looking bruiser, to judge from the portrait hanging at Highfields – put down the book he had been reading and merely observed: 'The gander's as good as the goose, sir.' He then continued with his book.

The eloping couple were soon forgiven and their elder daughter, Louisa, married her first cousin, William Baker, squire of Highfields from 1863 until his

PRECEDING PAGES 'Black and White': the entrance front of Highfields.

ABOVE Detail of the porch, showing the arms of William Dod, who remodelled the house in 1615.

LEFT The principal staircase, with its double-twisted balusters.

HIGHFIELDS

death in 1876. To this day the old Cockfighter's collection of equipment for his favourite sport (in its day as much a national pursuit as racing and foxhunting) remains one of Highfield's treasures. To an 18th-century sportsman the checklist of this esoteric apparatus must have read like poetry – wooden troughs, tin troughs, copper flash, spur saw, burnisher, leather and spur sticks, bag of small padded boxing-gloves, balls of twine, cord, steel and a set of scales and weights.

The agricultural depression of the 1880s hit Highfields hard; John Bellyse Baker sold up and emigrated to New Zealand. Happily, however, the present squire's father was able to buy the place back in 1944 and since then the Bakers have retrieved many of the objects associated with their much-loved family seat.

In the interregnum Highfields was the home of Charles Kellock, a Liverpool ship-breaker, who built the present north wing, to the left-hand side of the entrance front. A photograph taken before this addition shows the house with a temporary stuccoed finish, so it would seem that Highfields, like so many houses in Cheshire, was to benefit from the Black and White Revival.

More recently, the present squire, Jack Bellyse Baker, and his son John have undertaken an impressive restoration, including the retimbering of the south front, with the assistance of an English Heritage grant and the services of Mottershead of Crewe. A former member of the Historical Manuscripts Commission, Mr Bellyse Baker is an enthusiastic conservationist. Thus the fireplace commemorating the great Duke of Wellington's visit to the vicarage at Audlem on Christmas Eve 1820 was rescued following that building's deplorable demolition by the Church Commissioners, and was installed in a bedroom at Highfields.

Since retiring from the chairmanship of the Manchester cotton firm founded by his father, Jack Bellyse Baker has been able to concentrate on his flourishing career as a sporting artist. His colourful hunting scenes adorn several of the walls at Highfields and his upstairs studio is one of the house's most atmospheric interiors. He and his wife, Josephine, share the house with their son John, an estate agent, and his wife Susan and their family. Its design, with the two staircases, makes the place ideal for such multiple occupation.

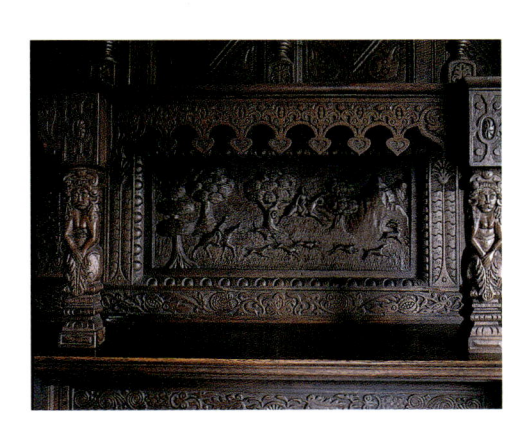

BELOW Detail of wood carving on the chimneypiece in a bedroom.

ABOVE The chase – an appropriate image in a sporting household – as depicted in the elaborately carved oak overmantel (apparently of Welsh origin) in the Drawing Room.

RIGHT Bedroom which also serves as a studio for the present squire, Jack Bellyse Baker, a sporting artist.

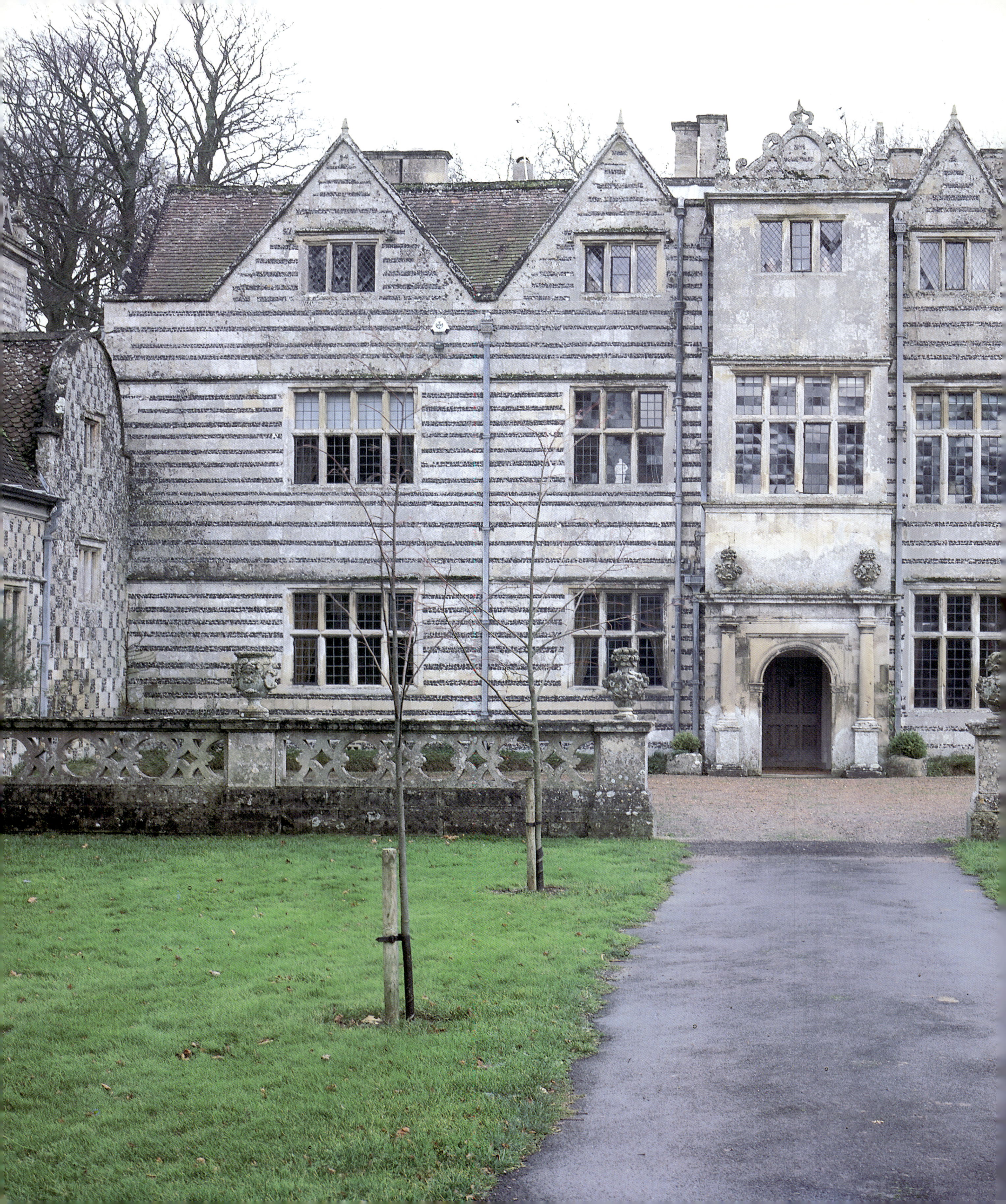

26

STOCKTON HOUSE

WILTSHIRE

THE WYLYE VALLEY in Wiltshire has changed little since the early 19th-century rural rides of William Cobbett, who described its 'watered meadows nearest to the river on both sides; then the gardens, the houses, and the cornfields. After the cornfields come the Downs.' Even the proximity to one of the main routes to the South-West, the A303, does not spoil the singular charm of the village of Stockton, with its thatched cottages, 14th-century church and many other attractive buildings. The *pièce de résistance*, though, lies beyond the gates: Stockton House, a delectable late-Elizabethan creation faced in bands of flint and stone, crowned by three gables and containing within some of the finest early Jacobean plasterwork in England.

What strikes you first is the house's joyfully stripy effect, achieved by the alternating bands of flint and lichen-covered Chilmark stone. In the sunlight Stockton exudes a silvery shimmer which is quite bewitching. More prosaically, the architecture is noted for its immaculate symmetry, a feature that was becoming increasingly important as the 16th century drew to a close.

The principal façade, the west front, is completely balanced, with a three-storeyed porch reaching up into the gable zone. The entrance is flanked by Tuscan columns with vases; above is a transomed four-light window, then a mullioned one and a cresting of strapwork with a pierced ring at its centre. The east front has four gables and the north and south fronts both now have three. The north formerly had Victorian additions, now pulled down except for the square water-tower. The chequerboard Chapel wing was also a later addition to the original house: it is said to date from Cromwellian times when, according to one account, 'some of the ejected clergymen were sheltered at Stockton by the Topps'.

The Topp family seem to have acquired the Stockton estate in 1585, though they had been living hereabouts for some considerable time before that. John Topp, described in the deed of conveyance as 'Merchant Tailor in

London', bought the manor from the 2nd Earl of Pembroke (whose Countess, Mary Sidney, châtelaine of Wilton, was described by the Wiltshire antiquary John Aubrey as 'the greatest patroness of wit and learning of any lady of her time'). Before the Reformation and the Dissolution of the Monasteries, Stockton had belonged to the monks of St Swithun in Winchester.

Judging by the sumptuousness of their new house and their local philanthropy, which extended to improving the church of St John the Baptist in the village and building the mid-17th-century almshouses, the Topps must have prospered in the clothing trade. Nor, in the most robust Elizabethan and Jacobean traditions, were they ashamed of their origins. For example, the plasterwork in the ground-floor Parlour features spindles between the ribs where they spring from the cornice, while on either side of the blank shields in the upper frieze are to be seen teasels, which were used to draw out the wool.

Splendidly restored and preserved by the current owners, Stockton appears very much as it was when John Topp built the house at the end of the 16th century and the beginning of the 17th. A clue to the building dates is given in the decoration of one of the bedrooms; it includes both the arms of James I (who acceded to the English throne in 1603) and the monogram of his predecessor, 'ER'.

The only significant alteration came at the end of the 18th or the beginning of the 19th century, when the owners at the time, the Biggs family

PRECEDING PAGES Stripy, symmetrical Stockton, with its alternating bands of flint and lichen-covered Chilmark stone.

BELOW Hand knocker.

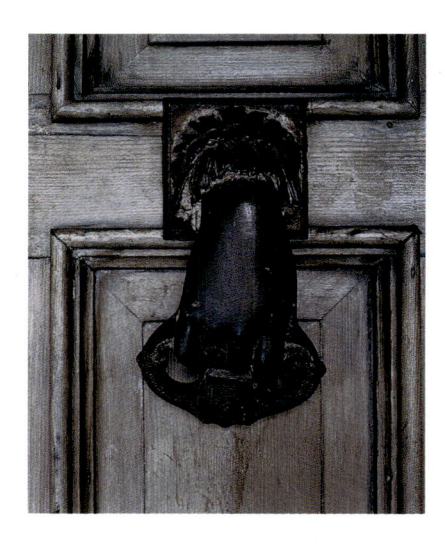

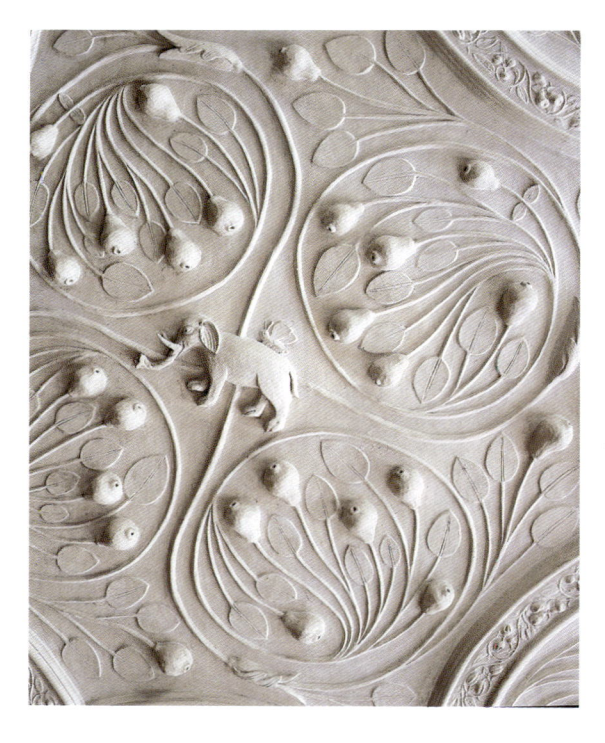

ABOVE and TOP RIGHT Details of the outstanding plasterwork on the ceiling of the Music Room, or Great Chamber. The bulbous pendant, with faces carved on each side, hangs in the oriel.

RIGHT The Music Room, or Great Chamber, with its Adam and Eve fireplace.

LEFT The richly carved porch (similar to one at Broughton Castle, Oxfordshire) in the south-west corner of the Music Room, surmounted by Diana, Cupid and Athena.

(who, then called Yeatman-Biggs, continued to live in the house until 1898), are thought to have roofed over the original open central court. The staircase is an ingenious composition designed to fit into a long narrow space: it starts in two flights, unites in a 'flying' middle piece and divides again to reach the first floor. It probably dates from about 1800 and has been variously attributed to James Wyatt, who worked at Salisbury Cathedral nearby, or to his nephew, Sir Jeffry Wyatville.

The stairs lead to the most spectacular plasterwork. Above the porch and the Parlour is the marvellous Music Room or Great Chamber, with its brilliant ceiling of broad bonds and panels abounding in long-stalked flowers. Each panel is different and the eye feasts on a cornucopia of delights. Especially endearing is the menagerie of exotic animals – boldly carved swans, wild boar, hounds, deer, mythical beasts such as unicorns, and an irresistible elephant with a huge butterfly bizarrely perched on its back. In the oriel there are fish to be found in the ponds, and at its centre a bulbous pendant with faces carved on each side. The east wall is dominated by an imposing chimneypiece with coupled columns in two tiers and detached heads of Adam and Eve in the overmantel.

For its size there can be few rooms so elaborately decorated as the bedroom known as the Shadrach Room. It takes its name from the relief in the overmantel above the towering two-tiered chimneypiece, carved with a vivid

LEFT The Parlour, with its Elizabethan fireplace of stone and plaster.

OPPOSITE The Shadrach Room, which is dominated by its chimneypiece recording the biblical saga of the Three Youths in the Fiery Furnace.

BELOW Detail of the overmantel and frieze in the Parlour.

representation of the story of the Three Youths in the Fiery Furnace as related in the Book of Daniel in the Old Testament. As the Bible tells us, Shadrach, Meshach and Abednego, three Israelites, were 'bound in their coats, their hosen and their hats, and their other garments, and were cast into the midst of the burning fiery furnace' by the deranged Nebuchadnezzar, King of Babylonia, but they would not burn. The scene is flanked by two outsize soldiers. Underneath are two caryatids, arms akimbo.

The Shadrach Room also contains a richly detailed ribbed ceiling, its variously shaped panels exuberantly filled with emblems of the Tudor rose, the Scottish thistle and the fleur-de-lys. A frieze of pairs of winged horses runs round the room. Downstairs, there is another fine frieze in the Parlour, which features the initials 'I.M.T.' for John (Ioannes) Topp and his wife Mary, a Hooper from Boveridge in Dorset. There are recumbent effigies of John and Mary in the church, with their three children kneeling at the back. There is also a memorial plaque to John the Younger and his wife Elizabeth, with the inscription (translated thus): 'They set up so many living temples of God, and daily fed and clothed the Lord of the Temple himself'.

During the Second World War soldiers were billeted at Stockton and subsequently it was the home of Lady Lacey, widow of a long-serving secretary of Marylebone Cricket Club and mother of Rob Walker, a celebrated figure in Grand Prix motor-racing. The present owners have imaginatively redecorated the Parlour in the Knole manner and among their admirable plans for the future is the creation of a knot garden in the forecourt on the west front. Stockton's special character is evidently in sympathetic hands.

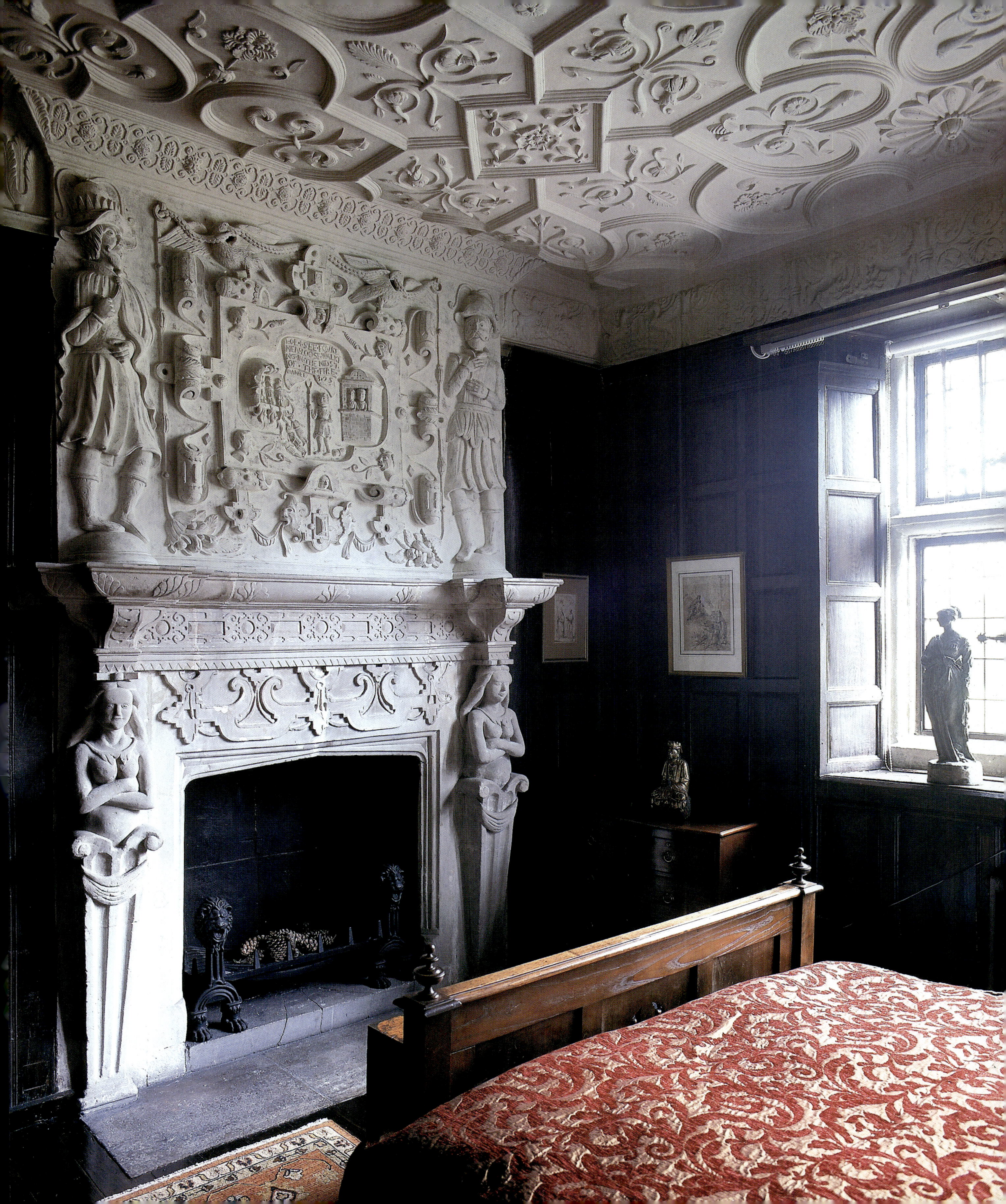

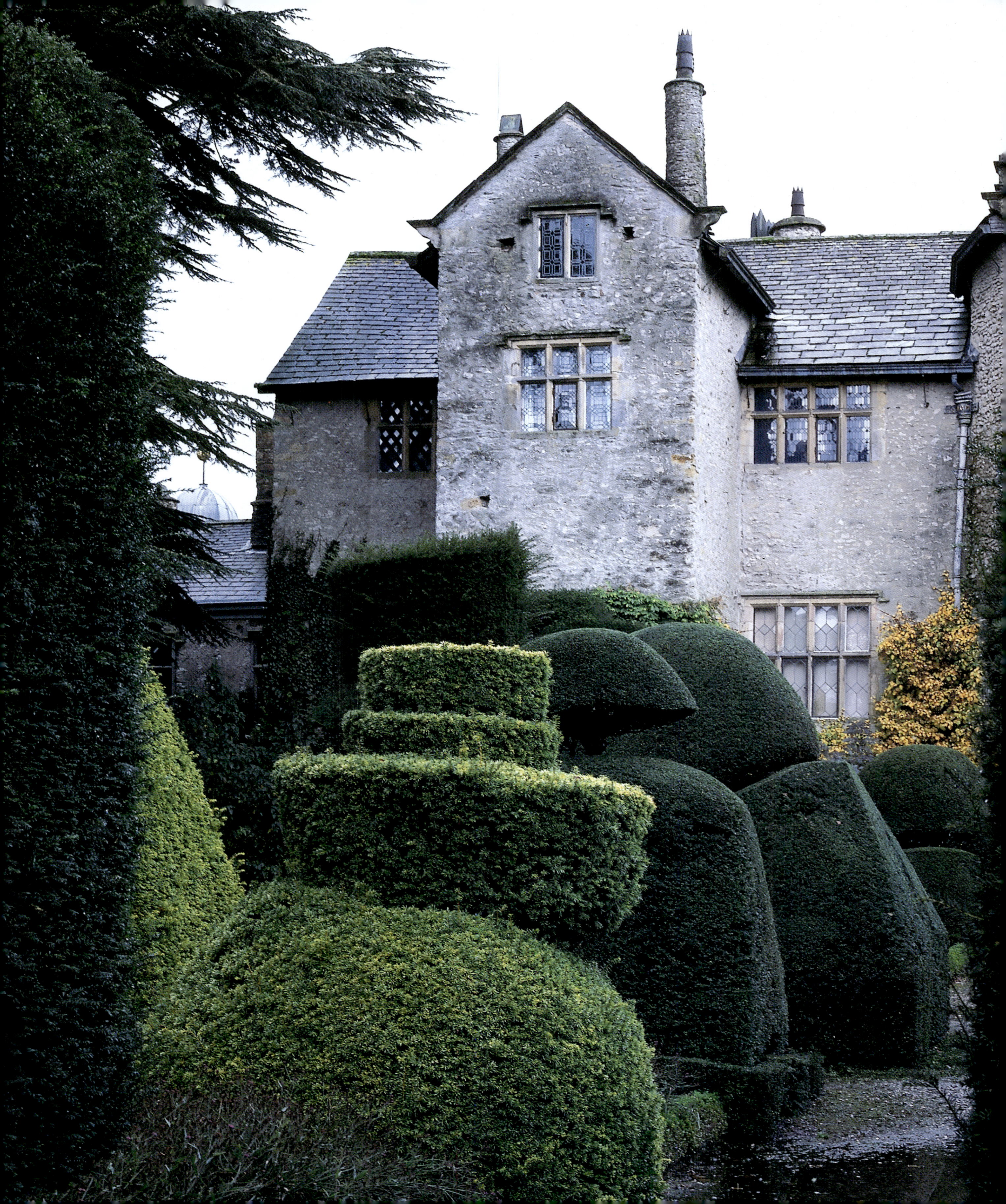

27

LEVENS HALL

CUMBRIA

GREY-GABLED Levens, with its fantastic formal topiary gardens, on the edge of the Lake District, is such an intensely romantic house that the visitor is inclined to indulge the legends associated with the place. One of these says that it was won with the turn of the Ace of Hearts at cards – and by the front door the visitor will not fail to spot that the downpipes are decorated with gilded hearts and the initials of James and Dorothy Grahme, or Graham.

Colonel Grahme, Privy Purse and Keeper of the Buckhounds to James II, certainly acquired Levens in 1688 when the trustees of his kinsman, Alan Bellingham, a notorious gambler described by a contemporary as 'that ingenious but unhappy young man', sold off the estate in Westmorland (now dumped in the unhistorical county of 'Cumbria'). However, it seems that Grahme refused to pay for the timber, which was valued at £2,300, and as he later claimed the timber from Alan Bellingham's heirs, it is possible – as the present châtelaine of Levens, Susán Bagot, points out – that this sum was indeed taken in settlement of a gambling debt. So the tradition may have some foundation in fact.

Grahme duly completed the third stage in the development of Levens. The first dated from medieval times, when the de Redman family constructed a house along the typical local plan of pele tower and hall. The second stage was the rebuilding of the house in about the 1580s by the Bellinghams, who transformed Levens from a grim medieval fortress to an Elizabethan gentleman's residence.

James Bellingham, the rebuilder, completely refurbished the old house and added all available comforts. These included a separate Dining Room (adorned with Cordova leather in the 17th century) and servants' hall, Drawing Room and built-in kitchens. (In the original house the kitchens had been kept apart from the pele tower to lessen the risk of fire.) The interior was copiously panelled in local oak or hung with tapestry and given colour with brilliant heraldic plasterwork. In the place of honour in the Great Hall James

LEVENS HALL

PRECEDING PAGES The gabled façade of Levens above its topiary garden.

LEFT Entrance front, with the old pele tower to the right of the front door.

ABOVE The Ace of Hearts on the downpipe. The tradition is that the house was won at cards in the late 17th century.

OPPOSITE View looking back to the front door from the Great Hall.

Bellingham loyally installed the coat of arms of Queen Elizabeth, with her supporters of a lion and a Welsh dragon.

After the death of the Virgin Queen in 1603, Bellingham was among those who went to welcome James VI of Scotland on his entry into England to be crowned James I, and he was knighted at Durham. Sir James's pistols, dated the same year and some of the earliest English-made pistols in existence, are among the treasures exhibited in the Great Hall. The two Drawing Rooms each boast elaborate chimneypieces exuberantly carved in oak. The inscription in the Small Drawing Room tells us that 'Thus the Five Sences stand Portraited Here, The Elements Foure and Seasons of the Yeare, Samson supports the one side as in Rage, the other Hercules in like equipage'.

Sir James Grahme's improvements at the end of the 17th century included the addition of the south wing, to contain new offices (including servants' bedrooms and the brewhouse), and the glorious collection of contemporary furniture. These pieces make a significant contribution to the harmonious accumulation of treasures that gives Levens so much of its character – a delightfully random mixture of Old Masters and armour, miniatures and family portraits, furniture and needlework, porcelain, silver and glass. The key to the charm of the contents is that Levens, broadly speaking, has remained in the same family's hands throughout its history.

Yet Grahme's chief legacy to Levens is, of course, the great topiary garden, the finest surviving example of its kind in England – indeed, without equal in Europe. Its formality makes a ravishing contrast with the distinctly informal – one might even say organic – architecture. Sir James was responsible for bringing in a former colleague from the Household of James II, Guillaume (or William) Beaumont, to create an intricate parterre, complete with clipped yew topiary and gargantuan beech hedges.

Miraculously, Beaumont's grand design remains as it was laid out in the 1690s. Somehow it survived the 18th-century fashion for 'naturalization'. In

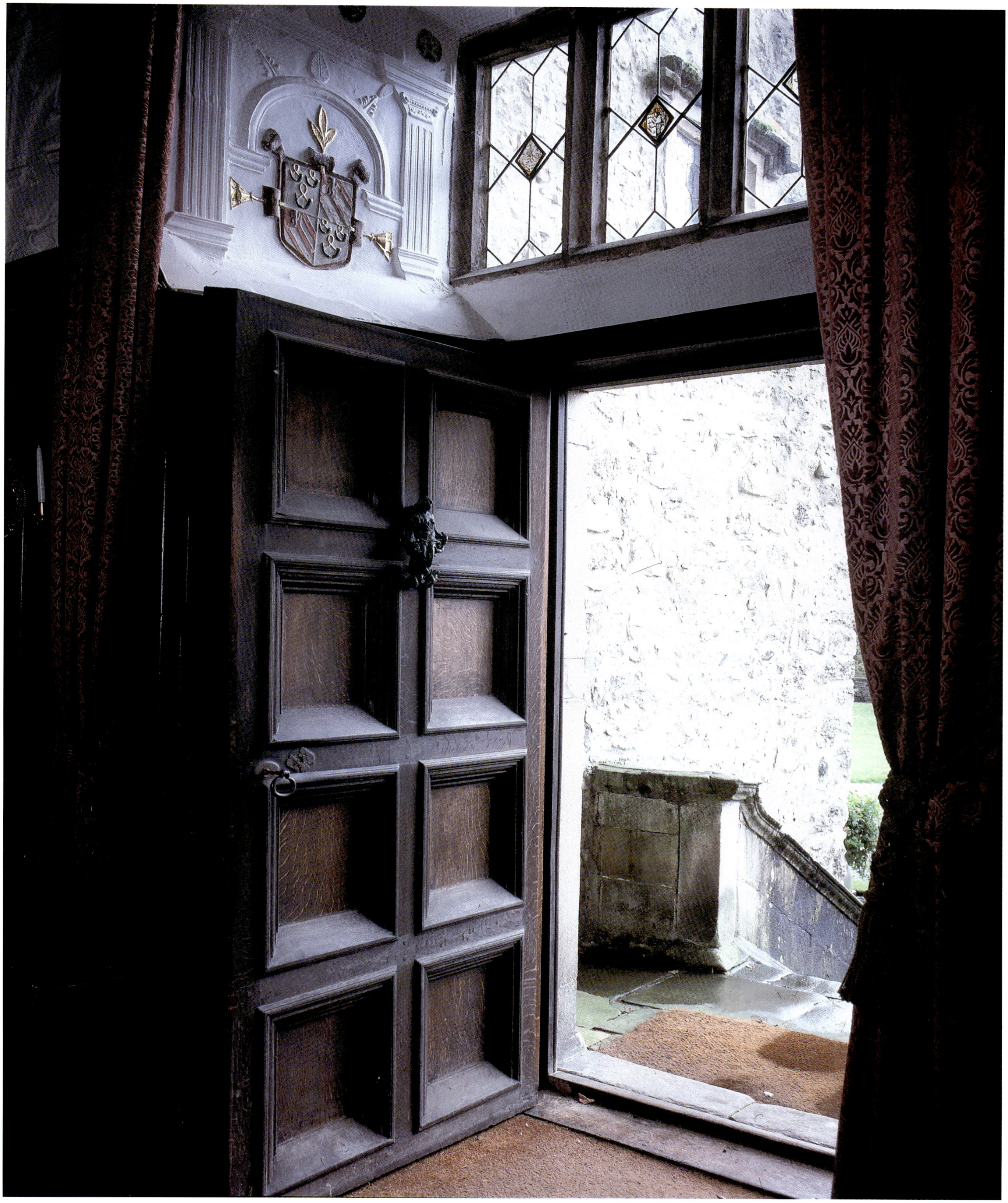

his *Guide to the Country Houses of the North-West*, John Martin Robinson explains that Levens was used as a dower house for most of the 18th century, so it 'escaped unscathed into an age which admired its Picturesque beauty for its own sake'.

The park, which is separated from the house and gardens by the 18th-century turnpike road (now the A6), was laid out by Sir James and Beaumont at the same time, with an impressive oak avenue over a mile long focusing on a pretty view of the River Kent – an early example of the appreciation of landscape. The park's survival owes everything to the efforts of Robin Bagot, an artist and harpsichord-maker, who fought long and hard in the 1960s to prevent it being mutilated by the M6.

It is said that whenever a white fawn is born into the herd of black fallow deer in the park, some change will take place in the house. There must have been very few white fawns, for Levens appears remarkably unchanged. None the less, some sympathetic alterations were carried out about 1810–20 to the designs of Francis Webster, including the panelling in the Library and some of the bedrooms, as well as the bathroom tower. This was fitted up with a marble bath and water closets made by Gillows. 'I, of course,' remarked the estate agent at the time, 'have no Experience of such Conveniences.'

Today Levens is the much-loved family home of Robin Bagot's son Hal (who applied the gold leaf to the hearts himself, not only on the downpipes but also to the ball on the top of the tower) and his wife Susan. They open the house and the famous gardens regularly to the public, and take the legends of Levens very much in their stride.

Apart from the Ace of Hearts and the White Fawn, these include the Grey Lady, the ghost of a gypsy woman who was refused admission to Levens and died of starvation. Her dying curse was that no son should inherit the house until the River Kent ceased to flow, and a white fawn was born in the park. Sure enough, Levens passed through a labyrinth of female lines until the birth of Alan Desmond Bagot (Robin's uncle) in 1896 – when the river duly froze over and a white fawn was found in the park.

On a more homely note, the Pink Lady, attired in a pink print dress and mob cap, is apparently spotted fairly frequently in the Great Hall, while the Black Dog, a little woolly creature, tends to run in front of guests' legs and up the stairs. Nothing, though, can detract from the affection that all visitors feel for Levens.

ABOVE Carved chimneypiece in the Small Drawing Room.

OPPOSITE The Drawing Room, which boasts another elaborate overmantel.

RIGHT Doorway from the Drawing Room to the Small Drawing Room.

BELOW LEFT and RIGHT Details of carved figures.

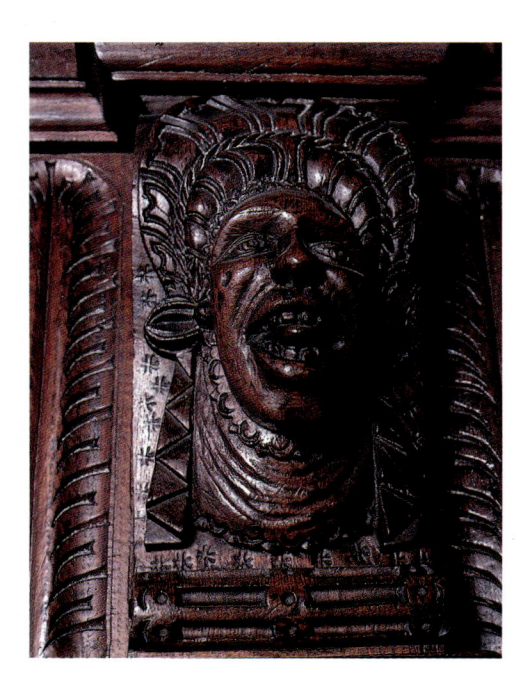

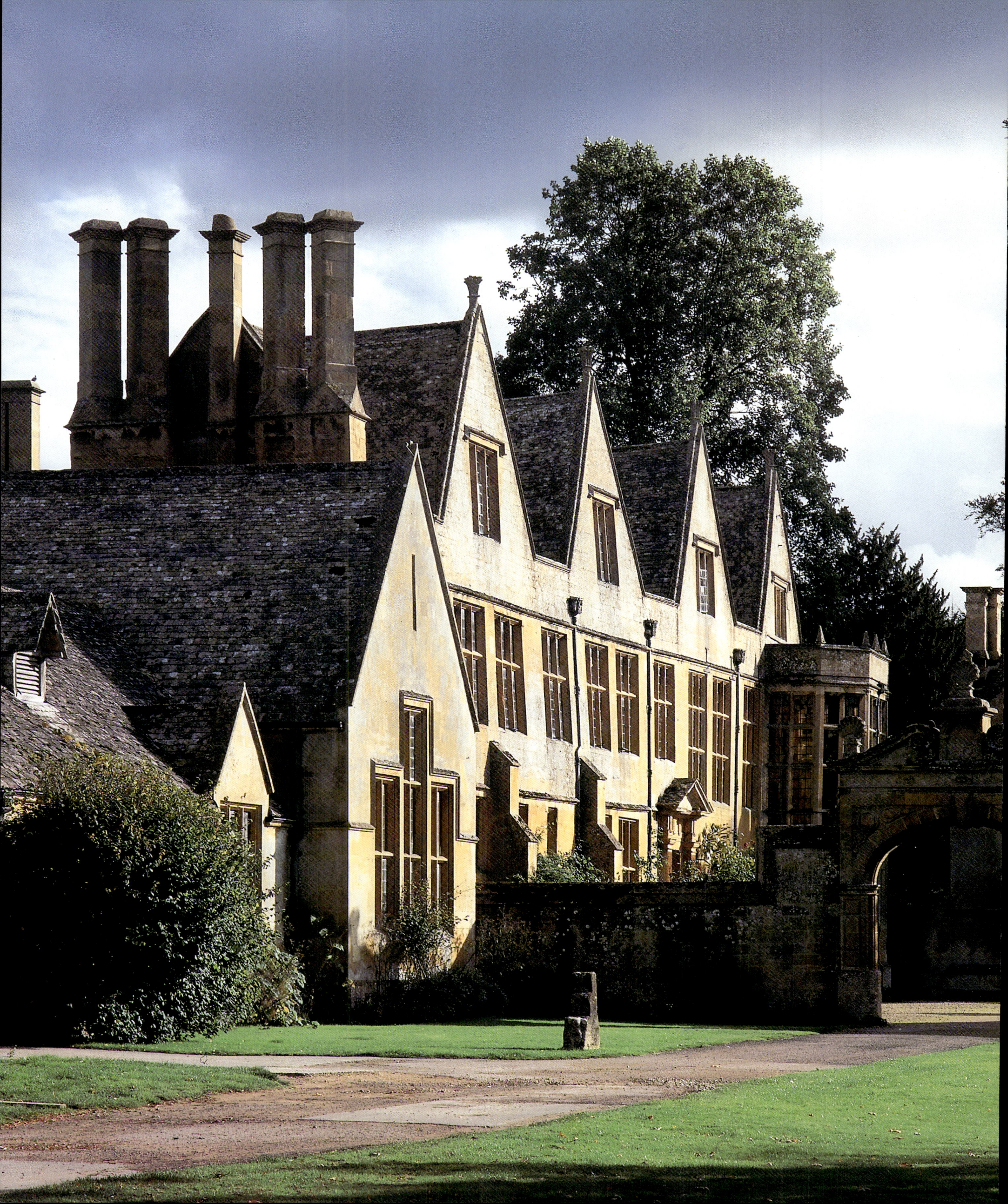

28

STANWAY HOUSE

GLOUCESTERSHIRE

'I CAN'T remember anyone who didn't fall under the spell of Stanway', wrote Lady Cynthia Asquith in her memoir, *Remember and Be Glad*, of her childhood home in the Cotswolds. The place features at the top of most people's lists of their favourite country houses. James Lees-Milne, for example, hailed it as 'incontestably one of the most beautiful and romantic in the British Isles'. Candida Lycett Green observed that 'its ancient and settled feel is absolute and although its buildings have evolved over 1,000 years, they form a glorious and golden whole'.

Stanway simply has everything – and more – you have ever dreamed of in an English squirearchical setting: an exquisite Jacobean Gatehouse (in itself a gem of Cotswold architecture), a Norman church, a medieval tithe barn, and a late Tudor manor house, all built of mellow honey-coloured limestone. Everything the eye rests on affords aesthetic pleasure – from the complex of out-buildings and the recently restored Kitchen Court to the Georgian pyramid above the magnificent, Baroque, newly recreated Water Garden, with its cascade, upper pond, waterfall, grand canal and 70-foot-high fountain; from the evocatively 1920s thatched cricket and tennis pavilions (where Lady Cynthia's boss, J.M. Barrie of *Peter Pan* fame, used to take his ease) to the dogs' graveyard. Here the present owner of Stanway, Lord Neidpath, a witty and original scholar-squire who has done much to enhance the beauty of the estate, has erected a gravestone in the Classical style featuring a tin of dog food and crossed bones, together with a Latin epitaph beginning *'Memoriae fragranti* OLD SMELLY...'.

Jamie Neidpath, heir to the Earldom of Wemyss, whose family inherited Stanway from the Tracys in the early 19th century, describes it as 'a typical squire's manor house, an harmonious product of vernacular craftsmanship and landscape rather than metropolitan or cosmopolitan tastes and ideas'. One of the things that makes Stanway so special is that it is

PRECEDING PAGES 'A typical squire's manor house, an harmonious product of vernacular craftsmanship and landscape rather than metropolitan or cosmopolitan tastes and ideas' – Lord Neidpath's description of Stanway, his beloved family home.

LEFT The symmetrical south front (with church and Gatehouse to the left) added by Sir Humphrey Tracy, 3rd Baronet, who succeeded to Stanway in 1657.

emphatically still lived-in, with unpretentious domestic clutter, and entirely free of the dead hand of 'museumization'. The manor has, after all, changed hands only once, other than by inheritance, in nearly 1,300 years.

The original manor of Stanway (meaning 'stony way') was granted to the abbots of Tewkesbury as long ago as AD 715 by two Mercian brothers who rejoiced in the names of Odo and Dodo. During the Dissolution of the Monasteries some 800 years later the local landowning family of Tracy of Toddington led the rush to gather up the spoils. Described by Lees-Milne as 'a godless and ferocious breed', the Tracys descended from William Tracy, one of the four knights who murdered St Thomas à Becket. Sir Richard Tracy, who first attained a lease on Stanway as early as 1533, was notorious for declaring, in the course of dismantling the nearby Hailes Abbey, that the venerated vessel containing the Holy Blood of Christ was merely duck's blood tinted with saffron.

Sir Richard appears to have been too busy with his anti-papistical activities to engage in building work, and what we see today of the west front, with its four gables and immensely high oriel, was built by his son Sir Paul, who succeeded to Stanway in 1569, was created a baronet in 1611 and died in 1625. The Gatehouse – an amazing mixture of styles, combining late Gothic, Renaissance and Mannerist motifs – and the rusticated North Arch came towards the end of Sir Paul's reign at Stanway. Their ashlar stone is of slightly more orange hue than the west front (softened by centuries of silvery lichen), and Alec Clifton-Taylor suggested that it came from Guiting nearby. The design of the Gatehouse and the North Arch has been attributed to the master-mason Timothy Strong of Little Barrington.

The serenely symmetrical south front seems to have been added by Sir Paul's grandson, Sir Humphrey Tracy, who succeeded as 3rd Baronet in 1657, though the lead downpipes (like those on the west front) were installed by Sir Richard Tracy, 4th Baronet, in 1670. The elegant south doorway is an early Georgian afterthought, of 1724.

Inside the house, the rent table in the Audit Room is still functioning – Stanway must be one of the last estates to operate this traditional system of rent collection, whereby the tenants appear in person every quarter. 'It not only saves postage', explains Lord Neidpath, who has a well-deserved reputation as a philanthropic landlord, 'but also facilitates complaints about leaking roofs, etc'.

ABOVE Doorway on the west front seen from the churchyard gate.

OPPOSITE 'A vast honeycomb': Lady Cynthia Asquith's description of the stupendous oriel in the Great Hall. Through some of its thousand-odd panes we gain glimpses of the Gatehouse (left) and the church.

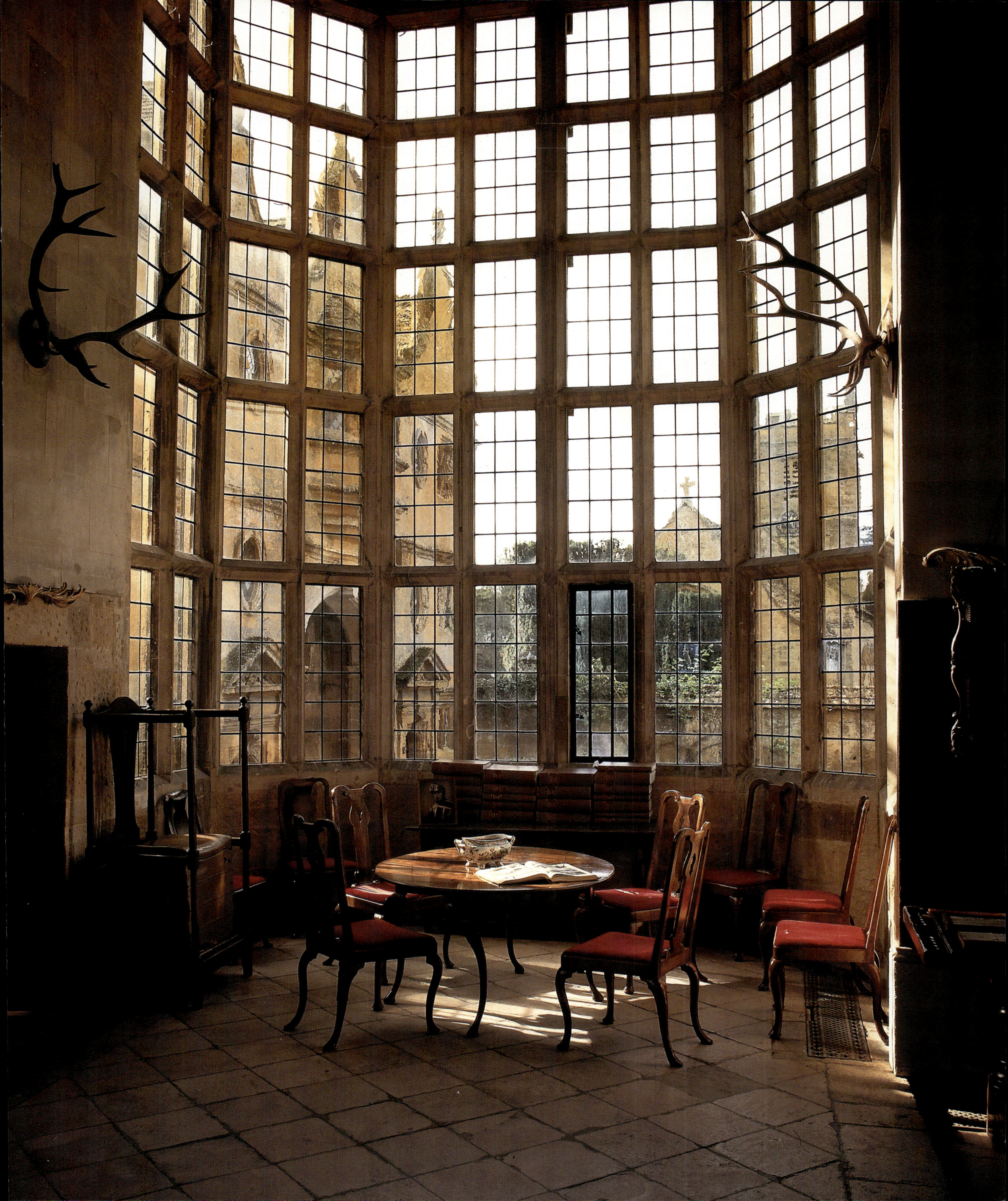

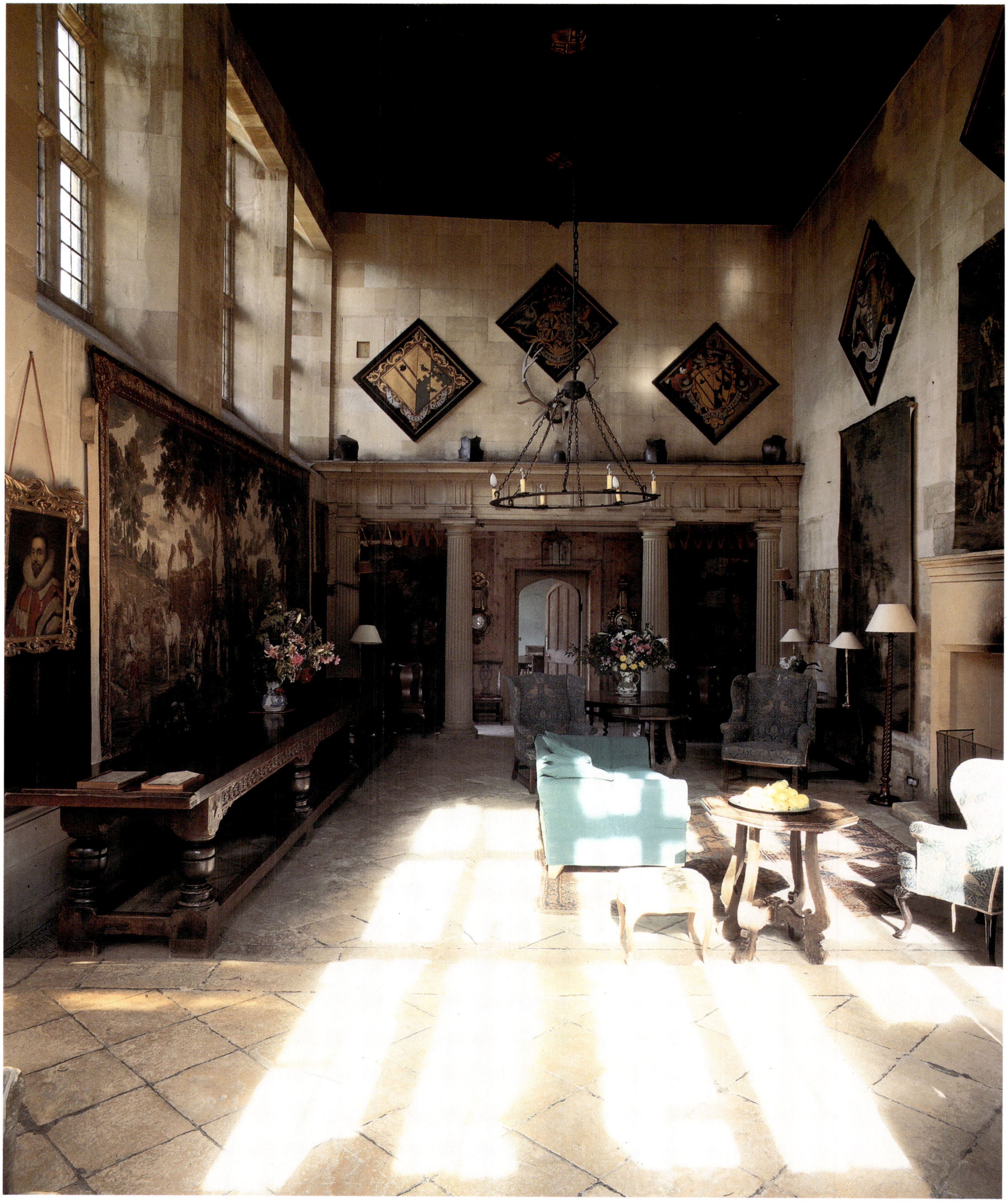

The Great Hall boasts a vast shuffleboard table (still in use) of about 1620, a Chippendale 'exercising chair' (half an hour's vigorous bouncing every day was supposed to be beneficial for the liver) and, above all, the stupendous oriel. Reaching to the height of the room, this wonderful window has more than a thousand latticed panes – 'so mellowed by time', as Lady Cynthia Asquith wrote, 'that whenever the sun shines through their amber and green glass, the effect is of a vast honeycomb and indeed at all times and in all weathers of stored sunshine'.

The Drawing Room has early Georgian panelling and a fireplace flanked by fluted pilasters. The room is dominated by a remarkable pair of 'Chinese Chippendale' day beds built about 1760 for the *de jure* 7th Earl of Wemyss. His son, styled Lord Elcho, married the Stanway heiress, Susan Tracy-Keck.

And so Stanway passed into the Charteris family, Earls of Wemyss, who brought in the Scottish architect William Burn to add the stable block and make various improvements to the house. In 1883 the 10th Earl of Wemyss made Stanway over to his son Hugo, Lord Elcho, on his marriage to Mary Wyndham and the house became celebrated as the Cotswold outpost of the late-Victorian and Edwardian intellectual and artistic coterie known as the 'Souls'. Its members included such luminaries as Mary's brother George Wyndham, Lord Curzon, Violet Duchess of Rutland, Harry Cust, Lady Desborough, Maurice Baring and Arthur Balfour. The Boudoir is something of a shrine to the Souls, with its portraits of Mary Elcho and her son 'Ego', Lord Elcho, killed in action in 1916.

Lord Neidpath, Mary Elcho's great-grandson, describes how her 'charm, extraordinary kindness and absent-mindedness endeared her to all who knew her'. Her spirit lives on at Stanway, where the spectacular Water Garden, triumphantly opened in 1998, can be visited by the public in the late summer months.

OPPOSITE The Great Hall, with its vast shuffleboard table of about 1620 (still in use).

RIGHT The Drawing Room, dominated by a pair of 'Chinese Chippendale' day beds of about 1760.

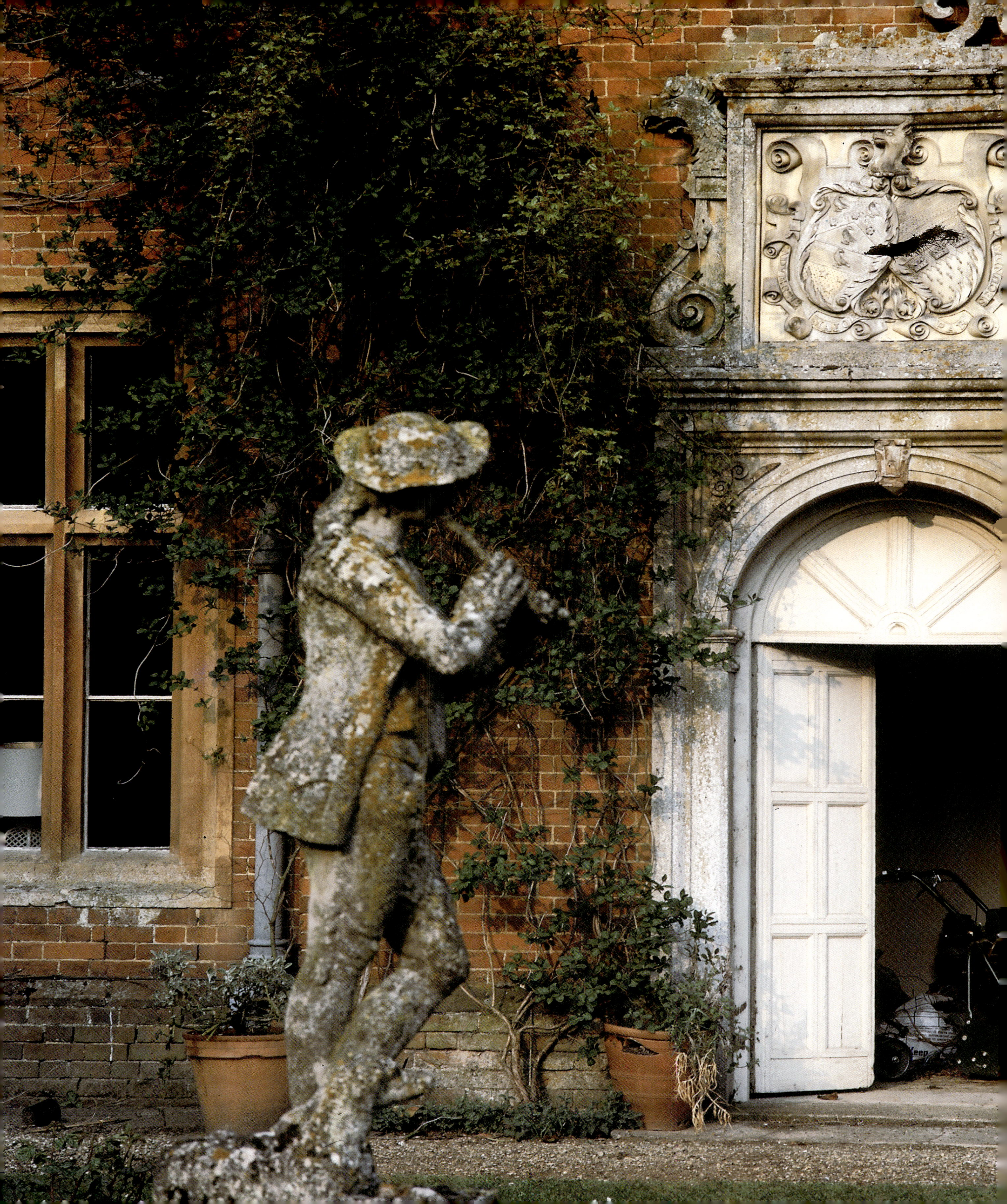

29
HEYDON HALL

NORFOLK

THE RECENT renaissance of Heydon is an inspiration to all who care about the country. Thirty-odd years ago the future of this late-Elizabethan manor house in a secret corner of north Norfolk seemed bleak. The heir to the estate, William Bulwer-Long, then serving with the 9th/12th Lancers, was given the 'sound advice' that he should demolish the house, which stood empty and decayed, its original charms largely obscured by unsympathetic 19th-century accretions, and sell off all the land.

Yet in 1970, when he came into the place, Captain Bulwer-Long and his bride, the former Sarah Rawlinson (whose father, Sir Frederick Rawlinson, 4th Baronet, had rented Heydon from the Bulwer-Longs in the 1950s), decided that they would ignore this policy of despair. They courageously determined to rescue his family seat and her childhood home, and to resurrect the estate. From the outset – with, as William Bulwer-Long used to recall, 'ten quid in the bank' – the new squire stuck to his principles. He hung on to his hedges when all over Norfolk others were ripping them out; he hung on to his water-meadows when others were reclaiming them for cereal-growing. He restored the houses and cottages in the beautifully unspoilt village (celebrated as the backdrop for the bucolic cricket match in Joseph Losey's languorous film of L.P. Hartley's *The Go-Between*) with a gentle approach; it became Norfolk's first Village Conservation Area in 1971. He let none of his estate houses to weekenders but to young married locals. He restored farm buildings for no immediate financial gain, but because he believed it was in the long-term interests of the estate and those who depended on it.

As for the big house, the Bulwer-Longs sensibly made it into a compact one, preserving its original Elizabethan essence. With the help of the architects Peter Miller and Stuart Taylor, and a grant from the Historic Buildings Council, a sympathetic reduction was carried out. The designer David Mlinaric played a key role in the restoration and redecoration of the interior, especially the Red Drawing Room and the Staircase Hall. Reflecting on what William and Sarah Bulwer-Long achieved at Heydon, Mlinaric observed: 'When dealing with the large-scale restoration of the Hall he never compromised; it was his own and

Sarah's vision of how to have the house for their stage in the story. For them it was not a burden, but a pleasure, individual and loved.'

This pleasure communicates itself to everyone lucky enough to experience the atmosphere of Heydon. John Cornforth of *Country Life* remarked that it was 'hard to think of a happier house'. He hailed the rejuvenated estate in 1982 as 'a remarkable enclave in what has become semi-ranching country: a unity of house and park, church and village, woods and farms'.

A few days before his untimely death in 1996, William Bulwer-Long heard that he had won the Royal Agricultural Society's Bledisloe Gold Medal for Estate Management. An obituary in the *Daily Telegraph* described him as 'one of the greatest countrymen of his generation and a quintessential Englishman. He stood and fought for what was at the heart of country life – landscape, farm, village, country house, country church and country sport – and his deep love of archetypal England was infectious.'

The history of Heydon goes back to medieval times when the Dynne family acquired the manor. The present gabled and pinnacled house was built by Henry Dynne, an Auditor of the Exchequer, in the early 1580s. It has the familiar Elizabethan shallow 'E' form of slim central porch and broader flanking bays with a pair of five-shafted chimneystacks rising behind them. Although the front door was altered twice in the 19th century, and the pinnacles and other details were also replaced, the recent reduction of the house has, as John Cornforth pointed out, 'had the happy result of emphasizing the felicitous quality of Henry Dynne's original design'.

At the same time as Heydon was being built, the Bulwer family were constructing Dalling Hall in nearby Wood Dalling, and two centuries later the estates were united when, in 1756, William Wiggett Bulwer of Wood Dalling married the heiress to Heydon, Mary Earle, whose ancestor, Erasmus Earle, had acquired the Heydon estate in 1640. Erasmus was a leading Cromwellian lawyer

PRECEDING PAGES Piping a song at Heydon: the front door of 1830, now on the west side of the house. The coats of arms displayed are those of Bulwer and Wiggett, Earle and Lytton.

BELOW Life imitates art on the doorstep of the present front door (dating from the 1840s).

BOTTOM The Elizabethan entrance front, now mainly free of its later accretions.

The comfortable Red Drawing Room as redecorated by David Mlinaric in the 1970s. The dog basks in the sunlight.

and served as one of the Counsel to the State during the Commonwealth. Oliver Cromwell himself was a frequent visitor to Heydon, and is reputed to have climbed the tree (still known as 'Cromwell's Oak') in front of the cottage in the park when chased by a bull.

In the late 18th century William Earle Bulwer of Heydon, who married Barbara Lytton, heiress of the Knebworth estate in Hertfordshire, made additions to the east end of the house (which partially survived the recent reduction). More substantial remodelling, including a tower to the west (which has gone), was carried out by his son William Earle Lytton Bulwer, who died in 1877. Among the architects this William consulted were Joseph and Richard Stannard and J.C. and G. Buckler, whose clock tower on the Stable Gatehouse is evocative of the cupola at Blickling, not far away.

Although somewhat overshadowed by the brilliance of his two younger brothers, the diplomatist Lord Dalling and the novelist and politician Edward Bulwer-Lytton (1st Lord Lytton), the Victorian squire of Heydon was a pillar of rectitude. His tenants revered him as a model landlord and his brother Edward (who transformed Knebworth into a Gothic fantasy house) described him as a man 'whose moral dignity and austerity of character… would be hard to equal'.

LEFT The Drawing Room: another stylish Mlinaric interior. The dog appears to be absent.

OPPOSITE Porter's chair and screen of exotic birds.

Today Sarah Bulwer-Long and her family carry on William's good work. The gardens, which are opened occasionally to the public, are noted for their azaleas, rhododendrons and old-fashioned roses. The splendid trees range from a recently planted avenue of clipped pink-and-white-blossomed hawthorns to ancient sweet chestnuts thought to date from medieval times. On the edge of the deer park is a deer shelter restored in memory of William Bulwer-Long. As the *Telegraph* obituary noted: 'Through the uncompromising example he set at his village and estate of Heydon in north Norfolk – as near to the pastoral idyll as anywhere in the land – he influenced politicians, landowners, farmers and local people in an understanding of the country and how it was possible to combine the best conservation practices with profitable farming.'

LEFT Here is the dog again in the warmth of the bow-ended Kitchen (formerly the library), with its William Morris wallpaper and display of horns. As John Cornforth wrote in *Country Life*, it is 'a magnetic room, where family and friends naturally look for each other and want to chat while the Aga gets on with its work'.

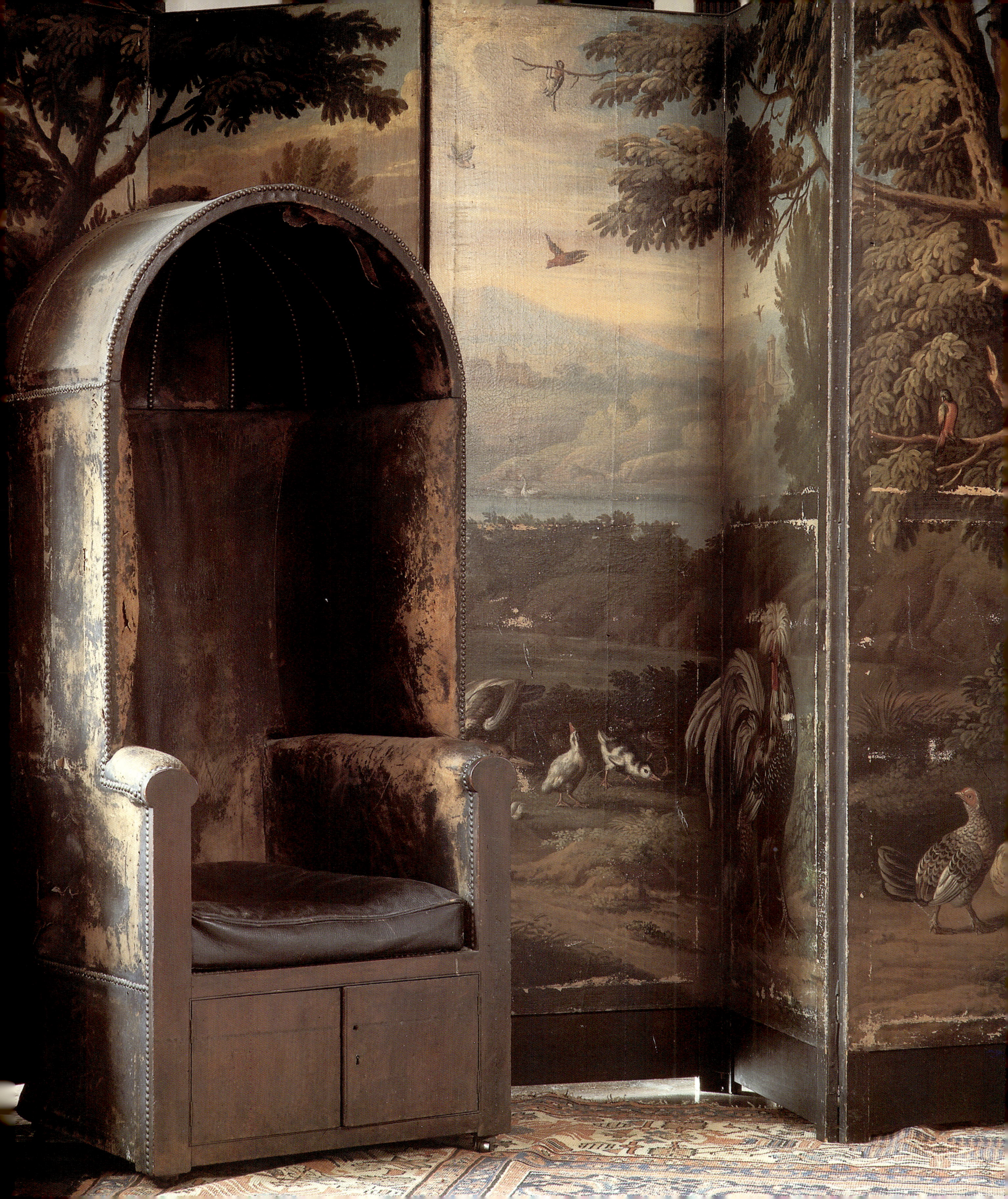

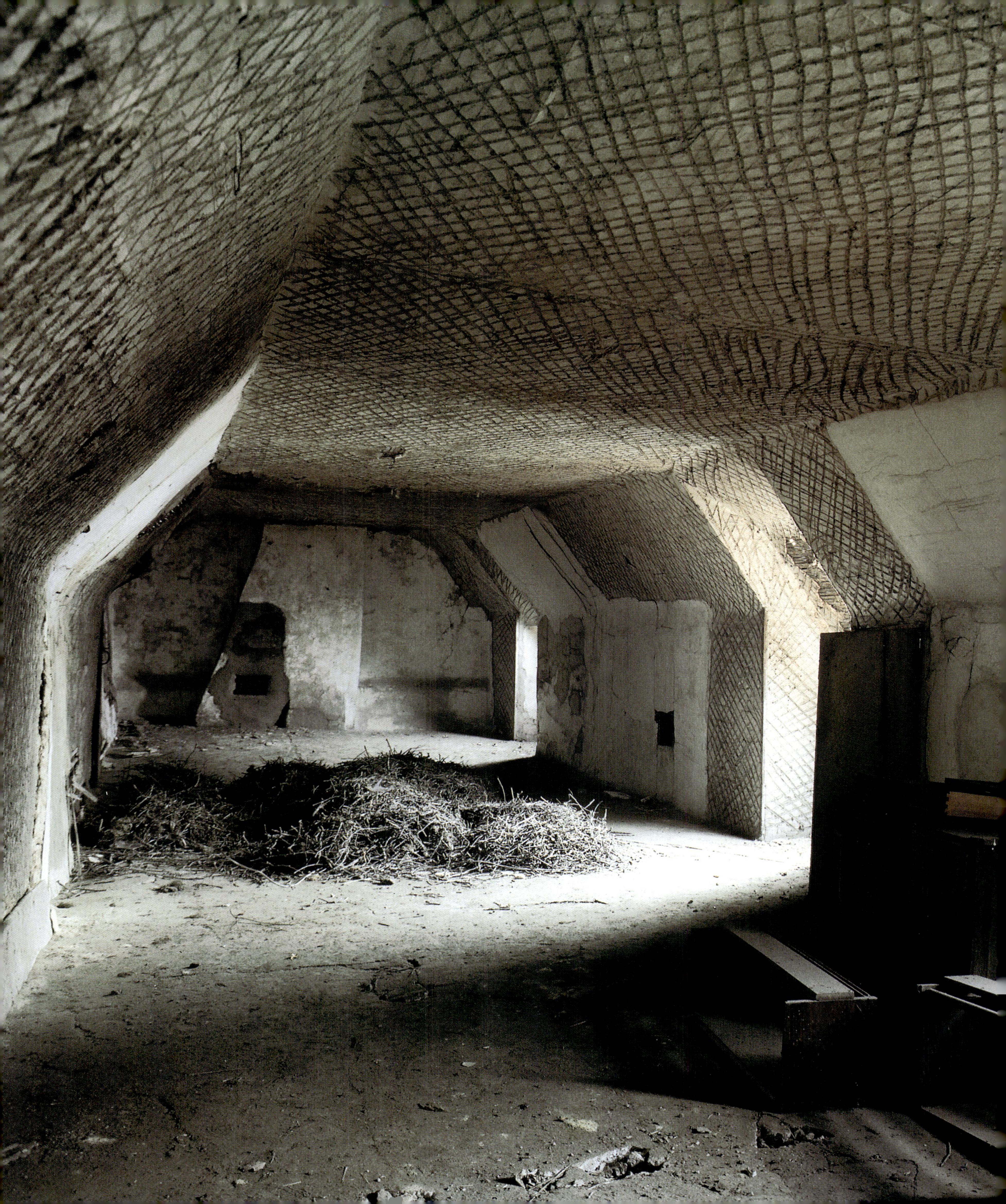

30

MARSTON HALL

LINCOLNSHIRE

'LINCOLNSHIRE', wrote the Reverend Henry Thorold in one of the numerous guides he compiled, 'is the second largest county in England and the least appreciated.' Yet no one did more to open people's eyes to its forgotten wonders than the scholarly 'Squarson of Marston', as he was known. In fact, this description of Henry Thorold, who died in 2000, was not strictly accurate, for though he lived in the Tudor manor house, took Holy Orders and was patron of the living, he was never the parish priest.

A memorable vignette of Thorold is given in James Lees-Milne's diaries:

A profile like George III's and a stomach like George IV's. Is rather greedy and hogs his food. An enthusiast. Madly keen antiquarian. His passionate interests are architecture and genealogy. Knows Lincolnshire backwards, and all the families that ever were, they being to a man his relations. Is fervently right-wing and deplores all that I deplore. Is in fact a most sympathetic being. He motors around the country in a large old Bentley motor-car and wears a dog-collar, an unexpected combination…. Is one of the last county historian squires. Should be an archdeacon.

As Lees-Milne intimated, the Thorolds are one of the longest-established Lincolnshire county families, supplying an unbroken succession of baronets, squires, parsons, squarsons, MPs, High Sheriffs and a Bishop of Winchester. They have owned Marston since the 14th century when Sir Richard Thorold married Joan de Hough, its heiress.

What we see today is but a fragment of the large Elizabethan E-plan house of the Thorolds, which was badly damaged during the Civil War when Sir William Thorold, 1st Baronet, was a prominent Royalist in a county well stocked with Cromwellians. In the 18th century, when the family decided to live at the grander Syston, a Palladian pile nearby, Marston was drastically reduced

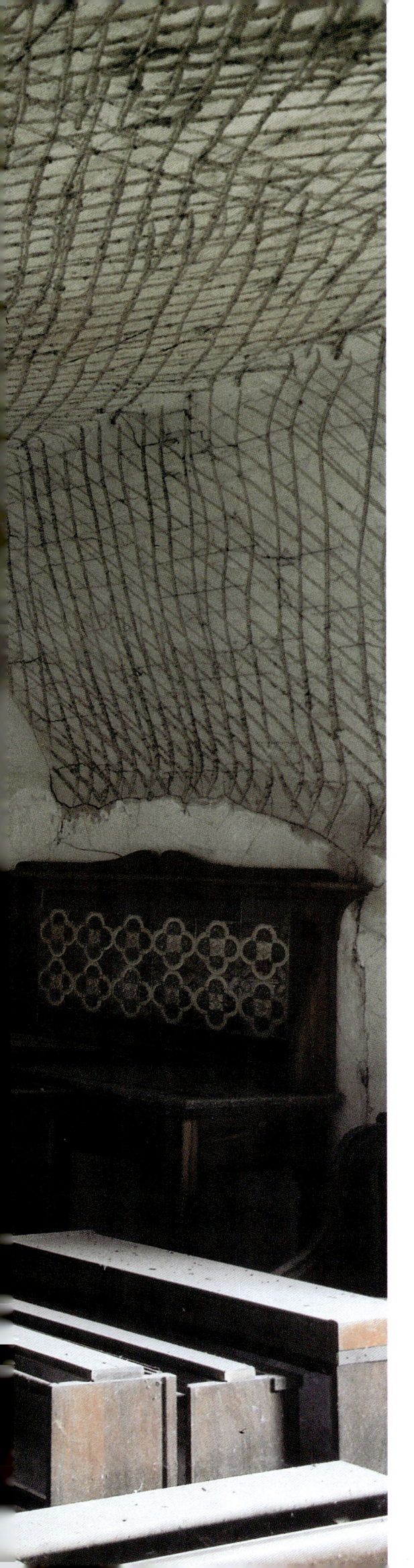

PRECEDING PAGES The atmospheric attic at Marston shows the possibility that a long gallery was intended at the top of the Tudor manor house – though it was never built.

LEFT The fragment of the large E-plan Elizabethan house that now survives.

in size. Its Elizabethan wings were demolished and the Great Hall split horizontally, to add bedrooms and a staircase. The original fireplace was moved to become the central feature of the new Hall; and in 1950 a 17th-century overmantel, carved with the Thorold arms, was brought from Blankney not far away when that house was demolished, and placed over the fireplace.

This was a characteristic embellishment made by Henry Thorold, whose father, the Reverend Ernest Thorold, Chaplain-General of the Forces, took on Marston in the 1920s from his cousin Sir James Thorold, 14th Baronet, and lovingly restored the old manor house to make it once more a family home. In the 18th century Marston was used as the estate agent's house and it had subsequently slumbered as a dower house or been let out. Now it became the centre of Henry Thorold's life: an evocative family shrine. Thorolds look down at you from almost every wall.

With the expert help of the distinguished architect Francis Johnson, Henry Thorold devoted himself to restoring Marston. Their most important addition was the Burston Room, a splendid bedroom which celebrates the 17th-century William Thorold of Little Ponton and his wife, Flora, for whom the exuberant plasterwork ceiling with its coats of arms of the female line, cherubs, fruits and flowers, had been a gift from her husband. It was transferred to Marston in the 1970s from Burston in Devon, Flora's family home. The centrepiece is a painting of the bare-breasted goddess Flora herself, complete with cornucopia. Her 18th-century namesake, only slightly more modestly clothed, stares haughtily from a portrait hanging against the contemporary panelling.

Besides re-creating this room Francis Johnson, from the neighbouring county of Yorkshire, was also responsible for the sympathetically designed overmantel installed in the Library above a marble chimneypiece brought in from Stillington Hall, near York. The Library chimneypiece accords with an illustration in Isaac Ware's study of *The Designs of Inigo Jones*. Francis Johnson's other delectable touches include a cupola on the Stables with a weathervane bearing the Thorold crest, *a roebuck passant argent*.

The Ancaster stone front of Marston, with its Elizabethan porch, looks out on to a romantic garden. There are the remains of a great elm tree on the lawn (twelve yards in circumference), and reputedly the oldest laburnum in England leans over the churchyard wall. At the back of the house, between tall clipped hedges forming enclosures, stands a tiny castellated Gazebo (with what John Harris described in the *Lincolnshire* volume of Pevsner's *Buildings of England* series as 'a piquant Gothick front'), built for Henry Thorold by John Partridge in 1962. The pinnacles are by Christopher Blackie. Inside this delightful garden building are murals of exotic birds and obelisks by Barbara Jones.

ABOVE The coat of arms on the front porch above the entrance. The three Thorold *goats salient* can be seen in the first quarter of the shield.

MARSTON HALL

RIGHT More heraldry: this time in the Burston Room, the splendid bedroom created in the 1970s with plasterwork brought from another Thorold property in Devon. The architect Francis Johnson carried out the work involved for the Reverend Henry Thorold, scholar-squire of Marston.

BELOW The Hall, a reduced version of the original Great Hall, though with the benefit of its fireplace. The 17th-century overmantel, carved with the Thorold coat of arms, was brought in from Blankney nearby when that house was demolished.

Stretching out into the landscape beyond the garden is the Lancing Avenue, a planting of Lombardy poplars presented to Henry Thorold on his retirement from the staff of Lancing College, where he was chaplain and a housemaster. The dramatic shape of the arching trees subtly echoes the lofty interiors of Lancing College Chapel.

Round every corner at Marston new vistas open up before you. A sculpture of Bacchus by Peter Ball fiercely surveys the central walk, between white trellis obelisks, and its recently added fountain. A cow may suddenly appear at a Gothick window cut into the hedge.

The gardens have been regularly opened to the public, chiefly in aid of the Lincolnshire Old Churches Trust, of which Henry Thorold was the chairman and prime mover. As he used to intone in his ringing, melodic voice: 'In a remote hollow of the Wolds, in a spruce village of the Stone Belt, in lonely Marshland or empty Fen, in town or city, the spires point to Heaven, the towers speak of faith in God.'

As John Piper said of Thorold, who was a much-valued contributor to the *Shell Guides* edited by Sir John Betjeman and himself, Henry was 'an undeterrable explorer and sound chronicler of old (and sometimes unwanted) churches, also a stout enemy of despoilers, destroyers and redundancy promoters'. Like Piper and Betjeman, Thorold was a born writer with an eye for the rare, the odd, the special and the forlorn. That eye found the perfect expression at his beloved Marston, where one can only salute his memory.

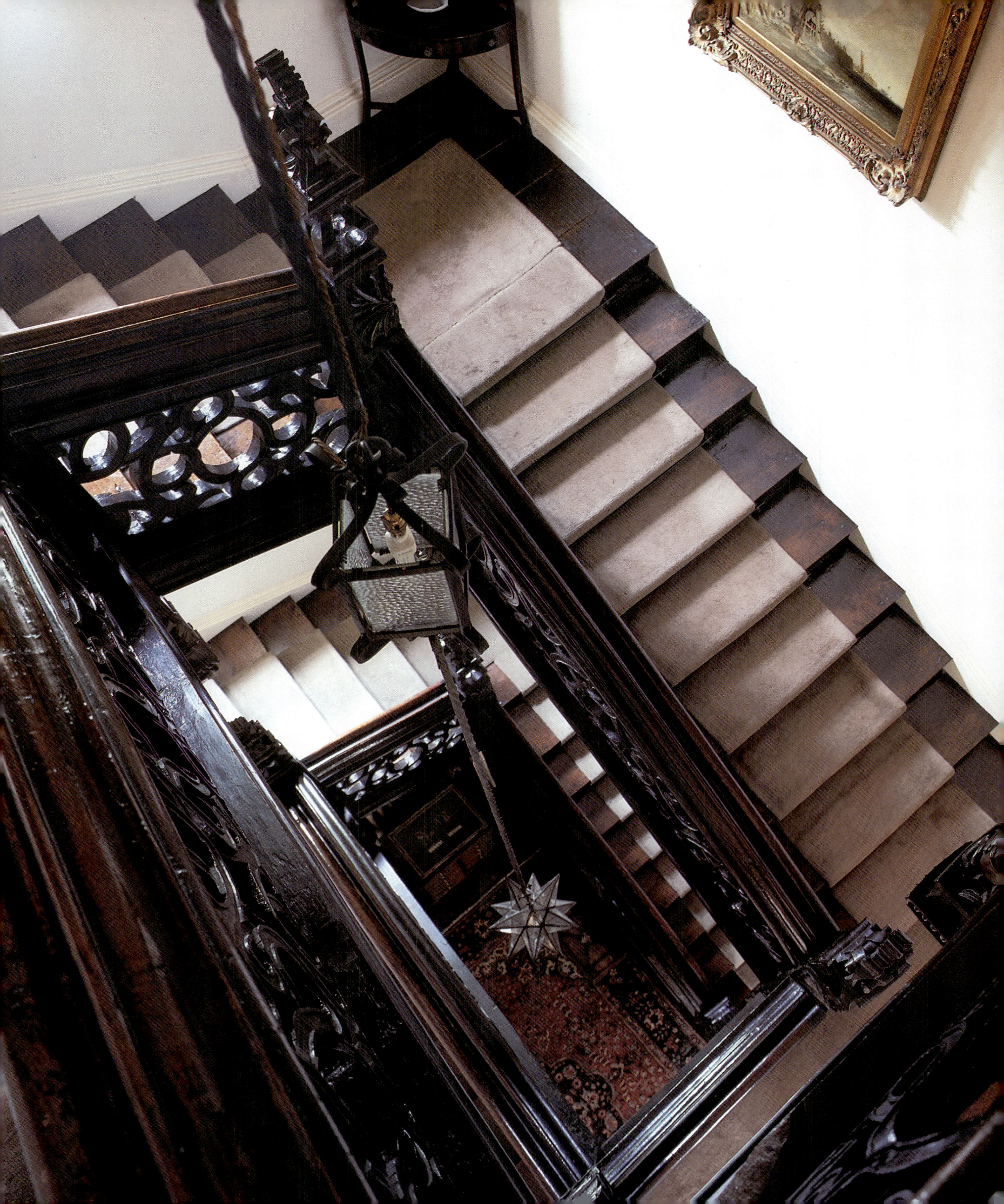

31

AUBOURN HALL

LINCOLNSHIRE

WITH HIS unerring eye the Reverend Henry Thorold of Marston (*qv*), the peerless county antiquary, described Aubourn in his book on *Lincolnshire Houses* as 'stately and at the same time homely'. It is certainly a strikingly unusual building and one of considerable architectural interest. The design of the early 17th-century rebuilding of the original Tudor house has been attributed by Mark Girouard to John Smythson, son of the great Robert Smythson of Longleat, Wollaton and Hardwick fame, as well as – more significantly – being the architect of Doddington Hall nearby.

Apart from stylistic grounds, the attribution of Aubourn to John is strengthened by the fact that he definitely drew up plans for altering a house called Grove in Nottinghamshire which was owned by the Nevile family, the in-laws of Sir John Meres, the builder (or rebuilder) of the manor house we see today. 'In a way', wrote Girouard in his study of Robert Smythson, 'Aubourn is typical of John Smythson, for it shows a certain sloppiness or indifference to symmetry, combined with a streak of individuality, which makes it unambitious, though it is a building that sticks in the mind.'

This 'indifference to symmetry' is reflected in the curiously haphazard arrangement of the windows and the off-centre placement of the doorway – even though its present position dates only from 1901, it had never been central. Girouard also noted that 'the transoms, sills and heads of the windows are extended like projecting teeth beyond the line of the jambs – a slightly unusual but by no means unique mannerism'. The façade we see today is predominantly Jacobean, though the present hipped roof must have been a later 17th-century alteration; the original may have been battlemented.

At the back of the house, however, there is evidence of Tudor building work, with bits of rubbed brick mullions visible in the north-east angle. The Meres family appears to have acquired the manor after the Dissolution of the Monasteries, that great bonanza for expanding dynasties of landowners.

PRECEDING PAGES From top to bottom, the interior of Aubourn is dominated by the astonishing carved oak Staircase, with its open strapwork panels (rather than balusters), open carved newel-posts and double handrail – a seemingly unique feature.

LEFT The entrance front: note the curiously haphazard arrangement of the windows and the off-centre placement of the doorway.

Previously Aubourn (the name derived from the Old English *alr-burna*, 'alder stream') had come under the sway of the Priory of Belvoir, itself a cell of the Abbey of St Albans, and was chiefly noted for its profusion of eels.

Little is known of the early Meres squires of Aubourn, save for the fact that Anthony Meres is recorded to have 'broken and defaced' the rood, vestments, altar-cloth, bells and other 'monuments of superstition' in Aubourn church in 1558, the year of Queen Elizabeth I's accession. Anthony's son, Sir John Meres, succeeded to the property in 1587 and served as High Sheriff of Lincolnshire nine years later.

Having rebuilt the house, whether or not with the help of John Smythson, Sir John sold the Aubourn estate to one Edward Osborn who, in 1628, promptly resold it for £5,000 to Thomas Thorold (a kinsman, needless to say, of the Reverend Henry's) and Sir John's own brother-in-law George Nevile. The Nevile share included the manor house, which happily remains in this family today.

According to a pedigree compiled by the Lincolnshire genealogist the Reverend W.O. Massingberd, the Neviles trace their descent from Jollan de Nevill, youngest son of Gilbert de Nevill, mentioned in the *Domesday Book* and traditionally 'Admiral' of William the Conqueror. The eldest brother, Gilbert, was ancestor of what the colourful herald Sir Iain Moncreiffe of that Ilk, Bt, hailed as 'the great historic house of Nevill... the most powerful family in the realm towards the close of the Middle Ages, making and unmaking Kings during the Wars of the Roses'.

For their part, the Lincolnshire Neviles were active in the Civil War, and Sir Gervase Nevile (George's son, upon whom Aubourn was settled) took part as a Royalist in the Siege of Newark. Consequently, the family was fined £1,737 in 1647. Sir Gervase's son, who became MP for Lincoln, was knighted like his father. His widow lived on at Aubourn until 1715, but after that the family based themselves at their grander 18th-century seat of Wellingore and Aubourn was let out as a farmhouse to the Lambe family for nearly 200 years.

Then, in the 20th century, it began to be used again by members of the Nevile family, including Isabel Lambert and her husband, Rear-Admiral R.C.K. Lambert. After the Second World War the squire of Wellingore and Aubourn, Henry Nevile (later Sir Henry, Lord Lieutenant of Lincolnshire), and his wife Jean decided to settle once more at the old manor house. With the help of a grant from the Historic Buildings Council, they carried out a sympathetic restoration, banishing the beetles that had eaten their way through much of the flooring.

It is the interior woodwork that gives Aubourn so much of its character. The panelling in the Drawing Room dates from about 1660 and was made specifically for the room, though some of the detail has since been altered. The panelling in the adjoining Study, Dressing Room and East Bedroom predates the rebuilding of the house and was brought in from an earlier family house. The original Hall would have included the present Dining Room and the passage behind it. The Dining Room was first formed when the additional chimneypiece was added at the beginning of the 19th century, and the room received a further remodelling a century later after the departure of the Lambes.

The most outstanding feature of the interior at Aubourn is the astonishing carved oak Staircase, which rises from the ground floor (complete with elaborate 'dog' gate) all the way to the top of the house. Not the least of its bewildering qualities is that it seems to become even grander the higher it goes. It also has very unusual open strapwork panels rather than balusters, open carved newel-posts and an apparently unique double handrail.

Hardly surprisingly, the Staircase baffles the experts. 'It cannot be Elizabethan, as has been suggested', noted the *Lincolnshire* volume of Pevsner's *Buildings of England* series. 'The decoration is grotesque: entwined leathery foliage and serpents all in a Gothic-Viking tradition. Yet the balustrade is avantgarde.... The question to ask here is whether it anticipates the maturer classical type of balustrade as at Ham House, Surrey, of *c*. 1638, or whether it is a provincial survival of the mid C17.'

Whatever the answer, it is a sensational example of the 'stately' style which blends so well with the 'homely' atmosphere of Aubourn. The late Sir Henry Nevile and his widow have enhanced its charms with the delightful gardens – including an orchard, rose garden, dell and pool – which surround the house. Today it is the home of their son Christopher, whose decorating credits include the phoenix-like restoration of the gutted Harrington Hall in the Lincolnshire Wolds, immortalized in Tennyson's line 'Come into the garden, Maud...'.

ABOVE Detail of open carved newel-post on the Staircase.

RIGHT Chimneypiece in the Hall, which originally would have included the present Dining Room and the passage behind it.

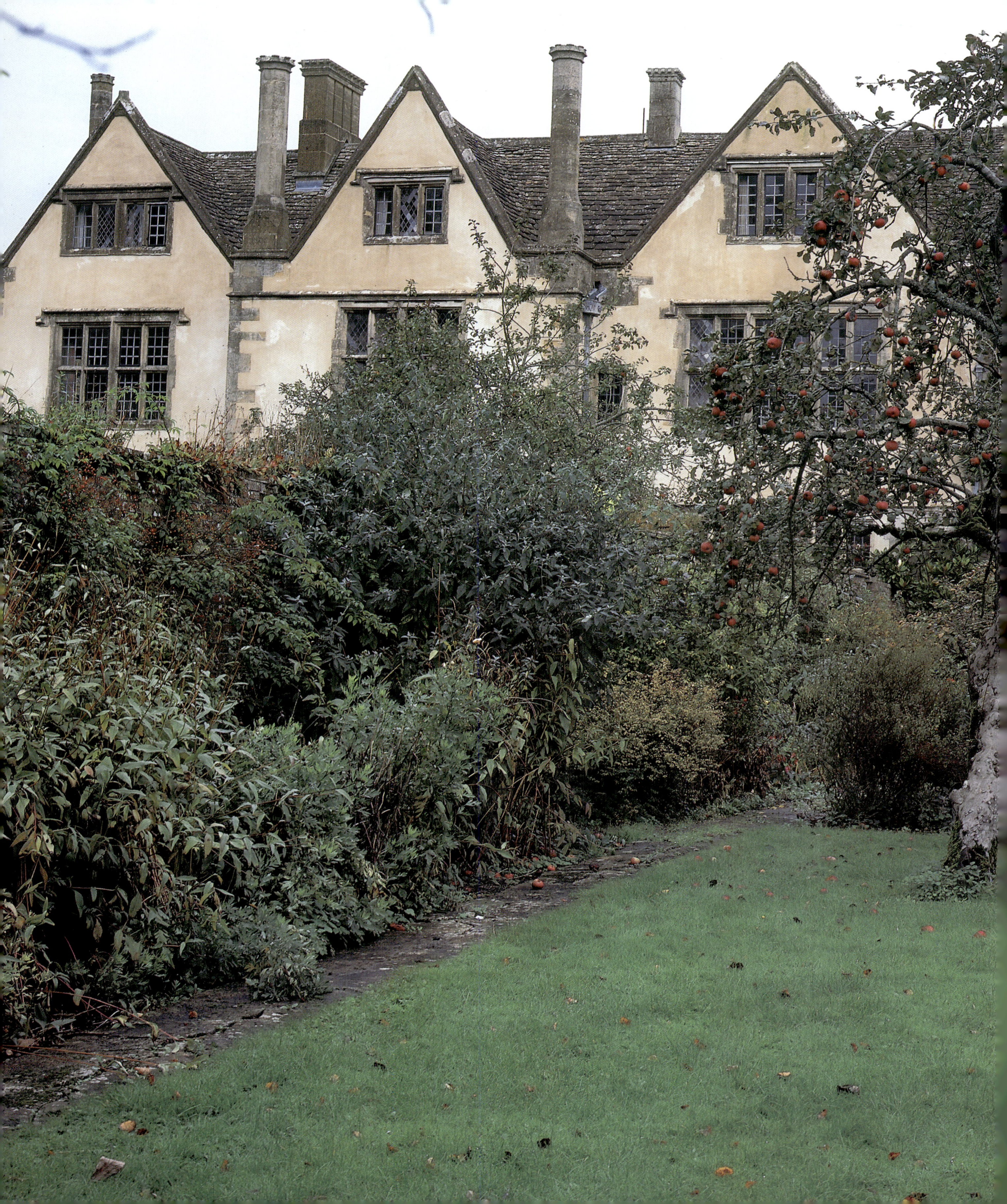

32

MELLS

SOMERSET

'ALL the counties of England have their own particular beauty, whether it be of nature, or art, or history,' wrote Lady Horner, grandmother of the present owner of Mells, the Earl of Oxford and Asquith, in her evocative memoir *Time Remembered*, 'but the county of Somerset seems to unite all these sources of enchantment. And Mells is one of the loveliest of its many lovely villages.'

The fine Perpendicular church of St Andrew which stands beside the manor house at Mells enshrines two unforgettable memorials: to Lady Horner's son, Edward Horner, and to her son-in-law, Raymond Asquith, two of the outstanding generation wiped out in the First World War. Young Horner, the tall, dashing heir to Mells, is portrayed as the very image of the chivalrous knight in a striking equestrian statue by Sir Alfred Munnings on a plinth designed by Sir Edwin Lutyens (who helped the Horners restore the manor house in the early 1900s). The inscription tells us:

> He was greatly loved in his home of Mells but with eager valour he left his heritage to fight in France. Severely wounded at Ypres, he recovered and returned to his regiment and fell at last in Picardy.... Thus in the morning of his youth he hastened to rejoin his friends and comrades by his swift and noble death.

Edward Horner had set off for war with the North Somersets, taking with him his mother's two best hunters, a valet and a cook. Munnings's statue captures him in the full flush of that crusading mood. Quite different is the memorial to his brother-in-law, Raymond Asquith, whose letters, edited by his grandson, John Jolliffe, give an absorbing picture of the world of the children of the 'Souls' we encountered at Stanway (*qv*). Below a bronze wreath of laurels (designed by Lutyens) is a Latin inscription, the lettering carved vigorously into the wall of the church by Eric Gill. As the novelist Anthony

PRECEDING PAGES The garden front of Mells.

LEFT The entrance front, with the church to the left.

OPPOSITE View through an upper window of the Perpendicular tower of St Andrew's Church, which contains two remarkable memorials of the Great War – to Edward Horner, heir to Mells, and his brother-in-law, Raymond Asquith, father of the present owner, the Earl of Oxford and Asquith.

Powell, who lived nearby, observed, this beautifully simple memorial brings back 'an overwhelming sense of the first war, its idealisms, its agonies, its tragedies'.

The early history of Mells is tied up with the church. Before the Dissolution of the Monasteries Mells belonged to the Abbot of Glastonbury. The pioneering Tudor antiquary John Leland noted in his *Itinerary* of a visit to Mells: 'a praty maner place of stone harde at the west ende of the chirche. This by likelihood was partely builded by Abbate Selwodde'.

This grange of the Abbots was duly extended, or rebuilt, by its new owners, the Horner family, who are recorded as living hereabouts in the late 15th century. Thomas Horner, who bought Mells in 1543, was already a

LEFT The Library.

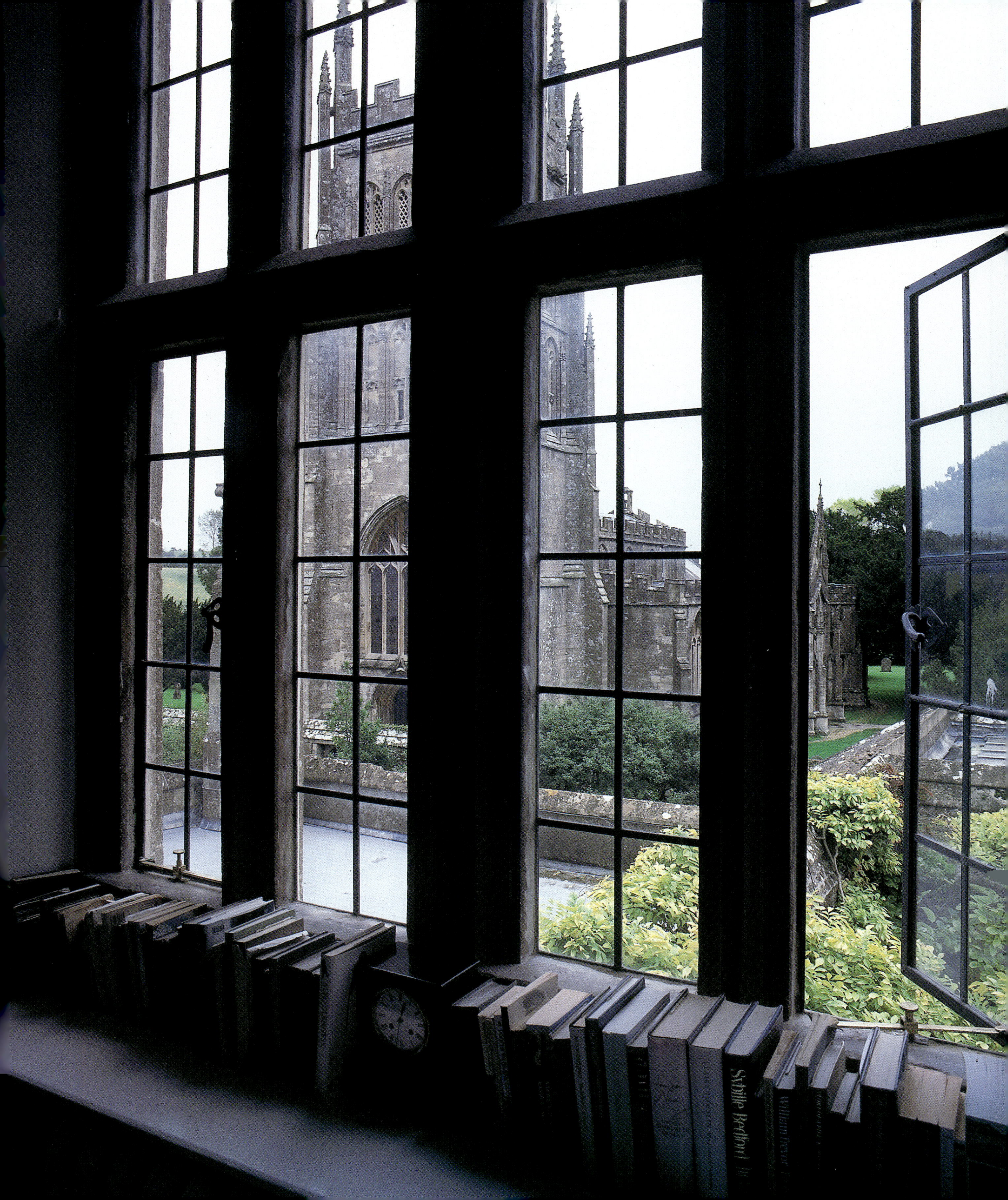
Sybille Bedford

local landowner. According to Leland, a Crown agent had occupied Mells after the Dissolution, pending a purchaser coming forward. The original conveyance confirms that Thomas Horner was the man who paid hard cash for the property.

Although Christopher Hussey of *Country Life* considered that there was some evidence that the Horners set about improving the 'praty maner place' in the later 16th century, recent research suggests that the main building work appears to have been undertaken in the early years of the 17th century. There is instructive confirmation of the layout in a drawing on an estate map of 1682 and in a diary of the Civil War which records that, in 1644, when the Cavaliers were moving from Bath to Devon: 'The King lay at Sir John Horner's house at Mells; a faire large house of stone, very strong, in the forme of a H; two courts.' The Royalist diarist, Symonds, went on to note that 'Horner is in rebellion; his estate sequestered'.

In Georgian times the family moved from the manor house to Mells Park at the other end of the village. Unfortunately, when they required stone for a block of stables, they pulled down the north wing and centre of the manor house for their materials. Only the south wing survived. It was not, of course, a period sympathetic to the preservation of old buildings; the revival of interest in manor houses had to wait another century or so. Happily, by then Mells had the perfect antiquarian squire, another Sir John Horner, a knowledgeable student of architecture and a member of the Royal Commission on Ancient Monuments.

In 1902 he and his wife Frances, the daughter of William Graham, MP for Glasgow, and their four children came back to live in the old wing of the manor house. Lutyens – whose friend and collaborator, the garden designer Gertrude Jekyll, was a connection of Lady Horner's – superintended the necessary alterations. These included the installation of such practical features as a new kitchen, bathrooms, heating and electric light, as well as the more aesthetic considerations of a loggia and a restyled garden.

The credit for the planting of the garden should, however, go to Lady Horner's friend, Mrs Harry Lindsay. As Lady Horner wrote in *Time Remembered*:

> The Manor House is so intimately joined to the garden that one hardly seems to exist without the other. Lupins and tall *Henryi* lilies nod at the windows of the sitting-rooms. It is small in size with homely flowers; with old apple trees still lingering among the flower beds, white with blossom in Spring, and scarlet and yellow in Autumn.

In her memories of Mells it was 'as if the sun always shone' and this nostalgic note is echoed in Christopher Hussey's lyrical description in *Country Life* of lunching with Lady Horner one summer's day, when he was brought to Mells by Lutyens. Hussey was struck by how Lady Horner's 'pale Botticellian grace (Rossetti had portrayed her as a girl), her irrepressible zest and humour and a baffling quality that... [the then] Rector of Mells has identified as "singular lack of self-esteem" combine in my memory with the summer scents and sunlight flooding into the white rooms from the garden'.

As Hussey wrote, that atmosphere of the sun always shining, and Lady Horner's personality, 'permeate the Manor House, rather than that of its four preceding centuries of existence'. That the peaceful serenity of Mells has survived into a new century owes much to the present Lord Oxford and his

ABOVE The Dining Room, originally a kitchen – hence the huge fireplace.

BELOW Bedroom.

The Staircase Hall.

family. His mother, the former Katharine Horner, widow of Raymond Asquith, inherited Mells as both her brothers predeceased her parents (Mark, the younger brother of the gallant Edward, died of scarlet fever aged 17). Lord Oxford, a former Governor of the Seychelles, succeeded to the earldom created for his grandfather, Herbert Asquith, Prime Minister at the outbreak of the Great War which casts such a haunting shadow at this beautiful place.

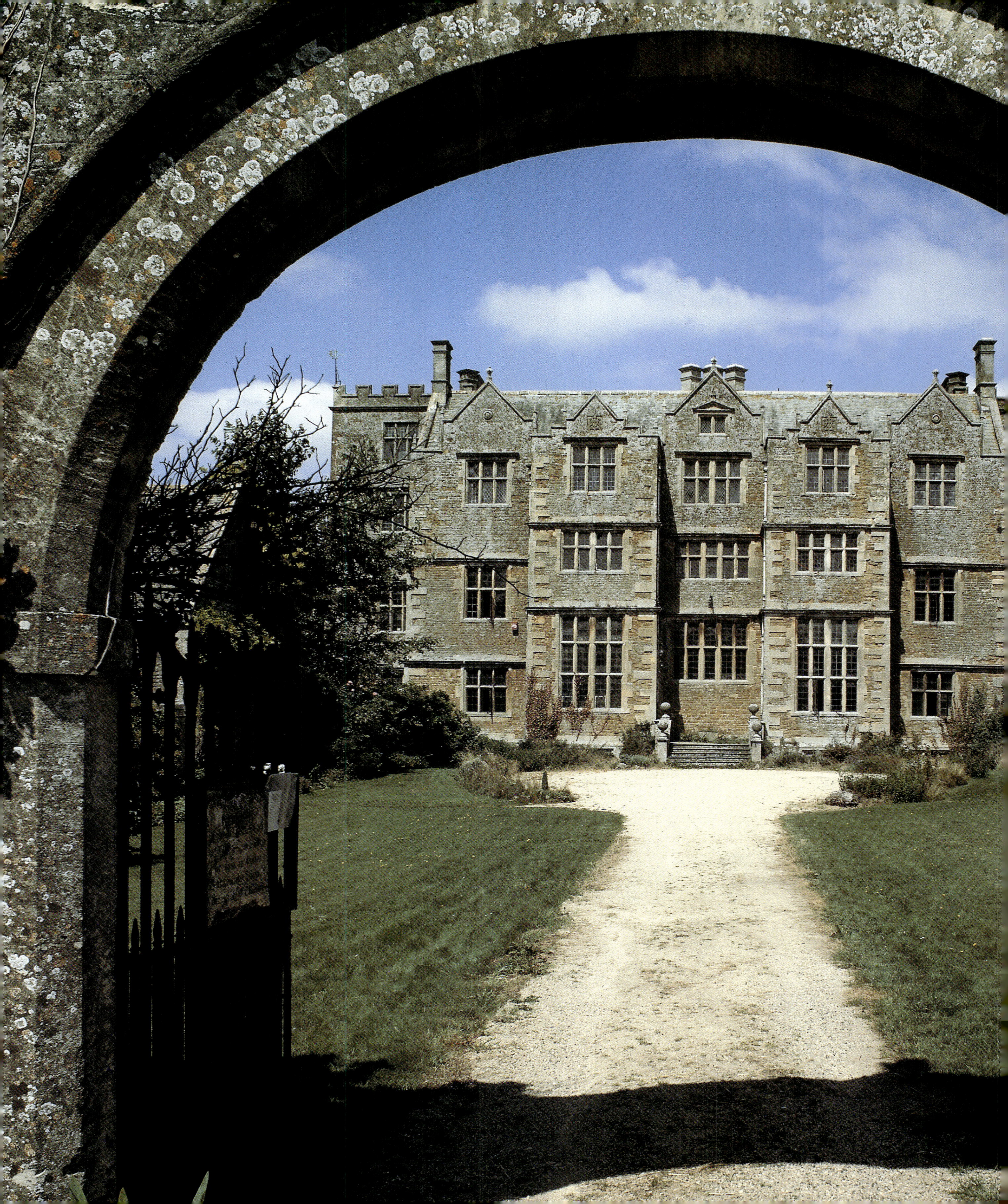

33

CHASTLETON HOUSE

OXFORDSHIRE

'POVERTY', Barbara Clutton-Brock, the last châtelaine of Chastleton before it was vested in the National Trust in 1991, used to say, 'is a great preservative'. The previous châtelaine, Irene Whitmore-Jones, who first opened this enchanting amber and greystone early Jacobean house in the Cotswolds to the public in the 1940s, would explain to visitors that the family in which it had remained since its creation had lost all their money 'in the war'.

The war Mrs Whitmore-Jones alluded to was not the recent World War but the Civil War, when Arthur Jones, whose grandfather Walter Jones had built Chastleton, was fined heavily for his Royalist sympathies. The story goes that Arthur fled to Chastleton after the fateful Battle of Worcester in 1651, when Charles II was defeated by Cromwell, and hid in the little room over the porch while his wretched wife, Sarah, was obliged to entertain the pursuing Cromwellian soldiers. After the Roundheads had retired to bed in the room next door to the closet where Arthur was concealing himself, Sarah is said to have brought them up a nightcap of ale heavily dosed with laudanum. As the drugged men snored away, Arthur slipped out into the night.

The Jones family's financial troubles, however, may have begun even earlier than the Civil War. Walter Jones, while usually described as *nouveau riche* and evidently a prosperous lawyer, possibly overreached himself in building and fitting up such a fine house as Chastleton. In fact, like several so-called 'new men' of that era, Jones's origins were not as jumped-up as the term *nouveau riche* implies. As with so many Welshmen, he could boast a long and respectable pedigree – even if not quite so illustrious as his claim of descent from Brutus, the ancient King of Britain, not to mention King Priam of Troy, would have us believe. His more immediate ancestors had been successful wool merchants at Witney in Oxfordshire.

Jones appears to have acquired the Chastleton estate, or at least part of it, through the good offices of his friend Ralph Sheldon, the tapestry manufacturer, who had earlier lent money to Robert Catesby, mastermind of the Gunpowder Plot, on the security of his Chastleton property. The Catesbys had come into Chastleton in the 15th century through marriage to the heiress, a descendant of the Trillowe family. The original history of the manor stretches back to AD 777 when Offa, King of Mercia, granted lands including Chastleton to the Benedictine Abbey of Evesham.

In 1602 Catesby and the mortgagees (including Sheldon) conveyed the manor to Walter Jones and his son Henry for £4,000, with the proviso that Catesby could redeem the property if he was ever capable of doing so. As it turned out, he was killed when resisting arrest after the failed attempt to blow up the Houses of Parliament, and in 1606 the Joneses concluded the Catesby connection with Chastleton by paying £550 to end an annuity payable out of the estate to Catesby's mother.

The building of the house probably began the following year and was completed by 1612. The authorship of its design remains an intriguing mystery. Mark Girouard has pointed out an interesting connection between Ralph Sheldon and his nephew-by-marriage Sir Henry Griffiths of Burton Agnes in Yorkshire; this could provide a possible link with the great architect Robert Smythson, who is known to have worked at Burton Agnes.

Although there is no documentary evidence, there are certainly instructive similarities between Burton Agnes and Chastleton in the arrangement of the courtyards, halls, staircases and front doors (both tucked away out of sight), as well as in the woodwork and the roofs of the long galleries. Moreover, Girouard, in his authoritative study of Smythson, shows how the main façade of Chastleton, with its battlemented projections, gables and towers, is curiously reminiscent of Hardwick. It is as if Chastleton is a slightly younger cousin of the Derbyshire pile of 'glass and wall'.

What strikes one about Chastleton is the endearing contrast between the sophistication of the design and the Cotswold vernacular style of the building work. As Robin Fedden and John Kenworthy-Browne concluded, in

PRECEDING PAGES A stately measure: view of the south front of Chastleton through the entrance arch.

BELOW Two of the haunting faces of Chastleton. The particularly ill-favoured person immediately below is portrayed in one of the grotesque plasterwork masks at the west end of the barrel-vaulted Long Gallery, which runs the length of the north front.

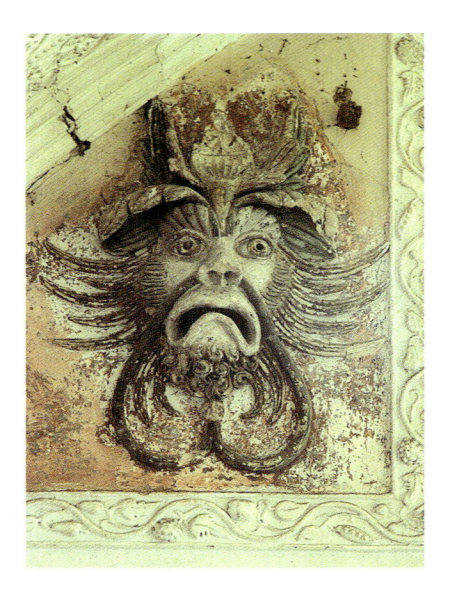

LEFT The Hall, with its carved oak screen and a strapwork overthrow. The screen was given a heavy varnish in the 1840s by J.H. Whitmore-Jones. The portrait above the chimneypiece is traditionally of Walter Jones, the builder of the house – though the Star Chamber petition he is holding suggests that it may in fact be of another Jones, Edward (no relation).

the entry in their admirable *Country House Guide*, the house may well have been designed largely by Walter Jones himself, 'for the Cotswold builders, like a well-trained orchestra, could work from the simplest of instructions'.

The musical analogy is apt, for the composition of the entrance front features narrow bays which advance and recede in a stately measure, topped by gables and anchored by higher staircase blocks that project on either side. Within we find a marvellously untouched series of Jacobean rooms – the special magic of Chastleton is that the house has changed hardly at all since Walter Jones's death in 1632. The provenance of many of the contents is authenticated by a probate inventory drawn up the following year. An almost incredible number of items – early lacquer cabinets, tapestries, fabrics and so forth – are still *in situ*, so that this is a veritable treasure-house for students of furniture, decoration and textiles.

The Hall has a gracious screen carved with columns, satyrs and acanthus scrolls. The panelled Great Chamber, Chastleton's outstanding interior, is adorned with paintings of prophets and rather beaky-looking sibyls, a richly heraldic chimneypiece and a copiously encrusted plaster ceiling. The two staircases, one in each tower at either end of the deceptively large house (in which it is easy to lose one's bearings), have impressive obelisk finials.

The Great Chamber, Chastleton's most lavish interior, with its richly carved heraldic chimneypiece, elaborately ribbed ceiling and frieze of prophets and sibyls.

ABOVE The Fettiplace Room, or state bedchamber, named after the landowning family into which Walter Jones's son Henry married in 1609. The Fettiplace arms take pride of place in the overmantel, flanked by niched figures of a king and queen (unidentified).

RIGHT The dais end of the Hall, with the White Parlour beyond. The curious creature above the door is known as the Chastleton Buck; its real antlers (from a North American caribou) and wooden head are joined to a painted body in only two dimensions. A payment is recorded in 1819 for painting 'the Buck in the Hall'.

Chastleton passed by descent from 1602 to 1991. In 1828 the male line of the Joneses died out and the house was inherited by John Whitmore, an enthusiastic antiquarian (he rebuilt the principal staircase, to the east), who assumed the additional surname of Jones and married Dorothy Clutton. Professor Alan Clutton-Brock, sometime art critic of *The Times*, succeeded his cousin Irene Whitmore-Jones in 1955 and his widow, Barbara, bravely kept Chastleton going as best she could until it was bought by the National Heritage Memorial Fund and vested in the National Trust.

There were those (including the present writer, I regret to say) who feared that the Trust would spruce the place up, but happily such fears have proved utterly misplaced. To its eternal credit the Trust has sensitively adopted an ultra-cautious policy of minimal repair and almost no modification. Wherever possible the venerable building and its contents have been allowed to show the marks of their age. By not tinkering, the Trust has imaginatively let Chastleton's intangible and fragile atmosphere of 'ancientness' speak for itself.

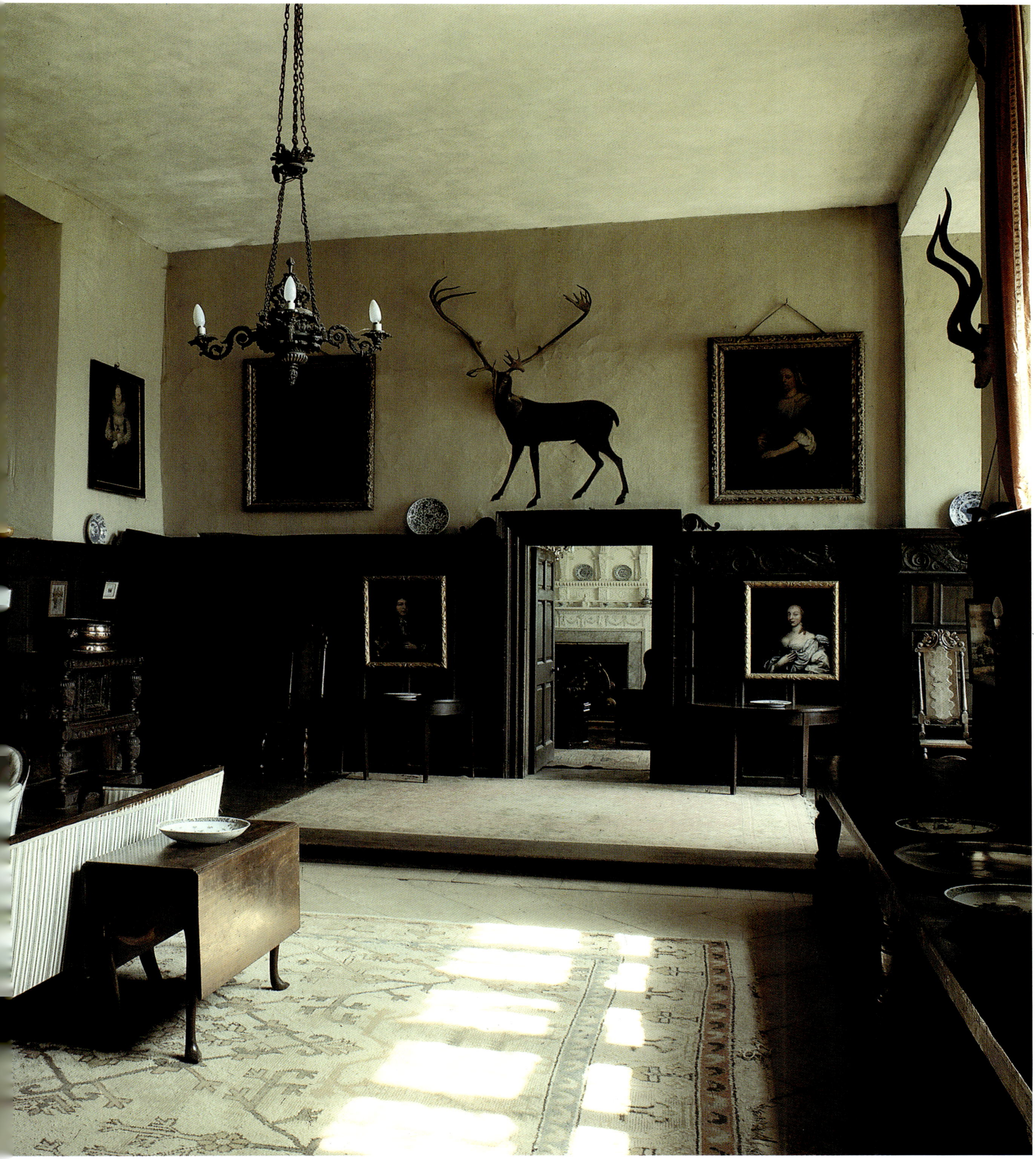

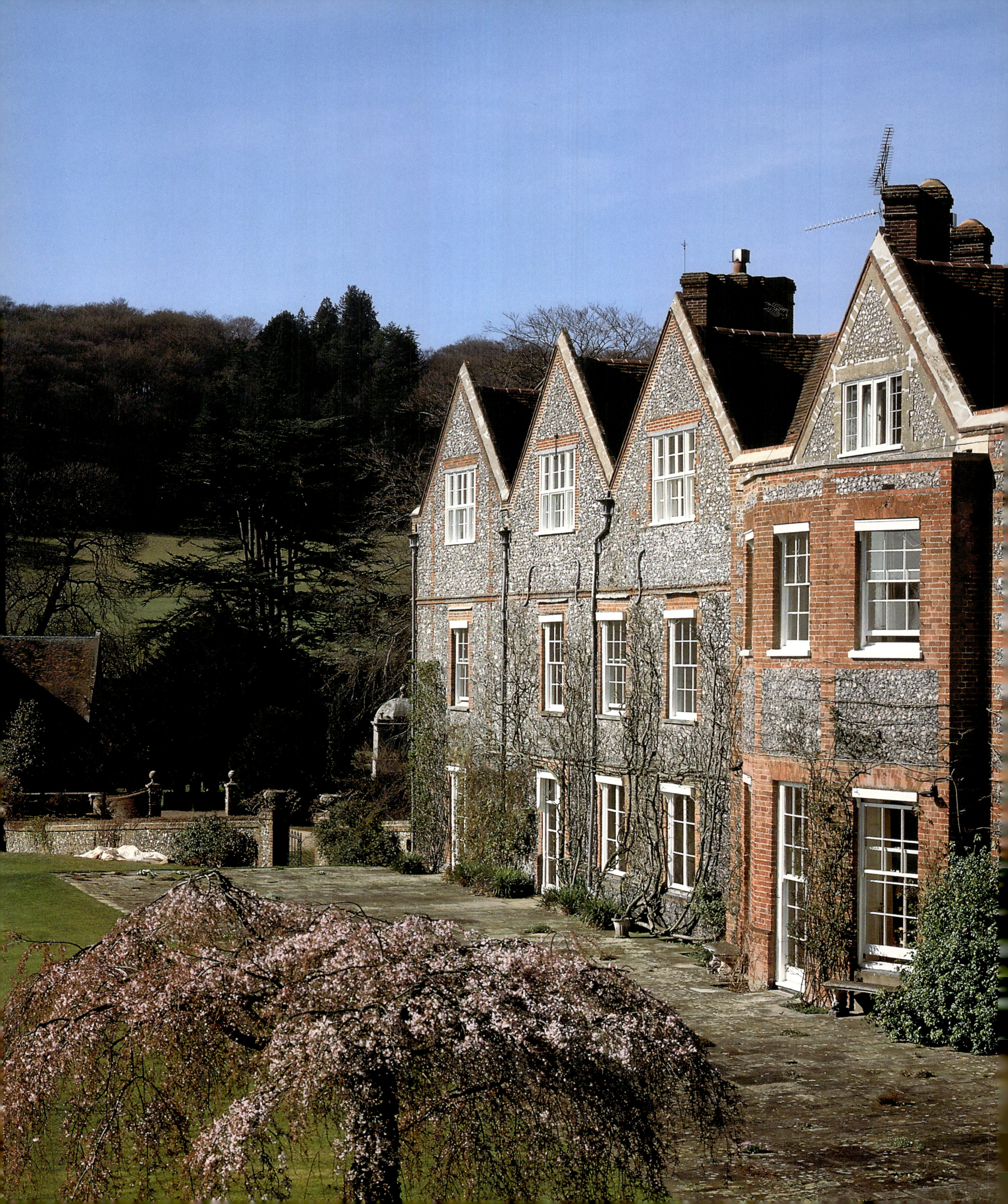

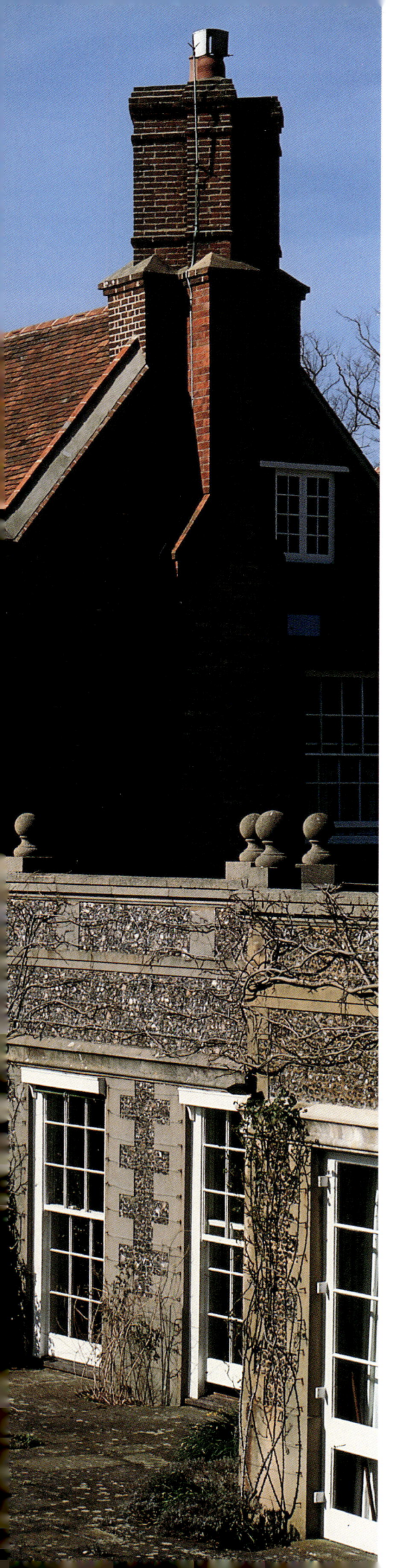

34

HAMBLEDEN MANOR

BUCKINGHAMSHIRE

DISCONCERTING as it may be to those who spent their formative years in that decade, the 1950s are now regarded as an historical 'period'. There could, though, be no more stylish or refreshing example of the country-house taste of the time than the brilliant restoration of Hambleden Manor by Viscount and Viscountess Hambleden and the interior decorator John Fowler. Maria Carmela Lady Hambleden is Italian by birth (her father Count Bernardo Attolico from Rome was Italian Ambassador to Russia and Germany), and the fusion of Italian *sprezzatura* and English taste achieved in this secluded valley of the Chilterns is a tonic to behold.

The manor house that faced Lady Hambleden on her marriage in 1955 to the 4th Viscount Hambleden, head of the celebrated W.H. Smith bookselling and stationery dynasty which has based itself hereabouts since the mid-19th century, proved an opportunity for a transformation that she was fully encouraged to take by her mother-in-law, the former Lady Patricia Herbert. Although the exterior is an attractive building of 1603 with gables, diagonal chimneystacks, brick string-courses and charming silvery knapped flints, the interior had been rendered gloomy by dark 19th-century panelling. John Fowler took one look at the panelling on the Staircase Hall and declared: 'It must be burned: it's Victorian and vulgar.' He and the Hambledens set about restoring the Georgian character of Hambleden's interior (a date of 1748 on the lead rainwater pipes on the entrance front suggests that the house was done up at that time). The walls and joinery of the Staircase Hall were duly painted in Fowler's favourite grey-blue. The low-proportioned Georgian panelled rooms – the Dining Room, Lady Hambleden's Sitting Room and the Ante-Room – were all repainted in clear, bright colours.

The old schoolroom was turned into a Library, additional bathrooms were installed and an attic room was joyfully transformed into a blue and white guest bedroom looking out over the lawn and cricket pitch. The climax of the restoration was the superb redecoration of the Regency Drawing Room with its canted bow window, added to the garden front in the early 19th century when Hambleden was in the somewhat surprising occupation of the 6th Earl of Cardigan (father of the colourful character who led the Charge of the Light Brigade, born in the house in 1797). As John Martin Robinson remarked in *Country Life*, the large Drawing Room at Hambleden is 'an example where the combined talents of Fowler and Lady Hambleden have given the original, elegant Regency architecture a dash of almost theatrical bravura'.

Fowler painted the walls a strong pink. When it was originally mixed and applied, Lady Hambleden complained that it was too strong and asked for it to be made paler. 'No,' replied Fowler (who always enjoyed spirited discussions with his clients), 'it will fade to a terrible yellow if you start with such a light colour.' Today, nearly 40 years on, it has faded to a luscious apricot, perfectly in harmony with the trim of apricot silk Fowler added to the bleached velvet curtains brought in from the family's Victorian Italianate pile of Greenlands nearby, which became a staff college after being requisitioned in the Second World War.

Fowler's own Italian sympathies blended creatively with Lady Hambleden's. Thus the chandelier of blue and clear glass was commissioned from Murano, near Venice, by the decorator, who skilfully absorbed his client's remarkable fan-shaped scenes of Rome into the scheme of this thrilling Anglo-Italian ensemble.

Away from the grandeur and formality of the Drawing Room, Lady Hambleden takes special pleasure in the jasmine-scented Garden Room, a delightful domed conservatory designed by the architect Sir Martyn Beckett, a family friend, in the early 1960s. Sir Martyn also reorganized the service side

PRECEDING PAGES The garden front of Hambleden. The canted bow window was added in the early 19th century by the 6th Earl of Cardigan (father of the Earl of Light Brigade fame, who was born here) and the conservatory, or Garden Room, to the right, was designed by the architect Sir Martyn Beckett in the early 1960s for Lord and Lady Hambleden.

BELOW The inside of the brick porch cheered up by a bold blue.

ABOVE The Hall: dark Victorian panelling banished in favour of Georgian yellow.

LEFT The west (entrance) front. The lower windows were sashed in 1748.

of the house as well as creating the Billiard Room, for which the Hambledens contrived a tent-like interior.

The protection of the Smith family, Viscounts Hambleden, together with the National Trust, has proved invaluable to the preservation of Hambleden as a blissfully unspoilt and picturesque village. The metropolis seems a thousand miles away, though the actual distance is barely 30. The brick and flint cottages, the medieval church, the domed Kendrick mausoleum and the gabled manor house form a quintessentially English group which has attracted artists and film-makers alike in search of authentic rural perfection.

William Henry Smith, MP and ultimately Leader of the House of Commons, grandson and namesake of the founder of the family firm, bought the Greenlands estate in 1868 and the family gradually expanded their property to embrace the whole valley, including the manors of Ewden, or Yewden, and Hambleden itself. 'Old Morality', as he was known, deserves a more honoured place in history than to be the butt of W.S. Gilbert in *H.M.S. Pinafore*, in which he is supposedly portrayed as Sir Joseph Porter, 'the Ruler of the Queen's Navee' (W.H. Smith was at one stage First Lord of the Admiralty). As Vicary Gibbs noted in *The Complete Peerage*: 'His career illustrates the success of stable, trustworthy character, immense business capacity, and solid intelligence.... In private life his kind heart and sterling work were universally appreciated; he was generous and hospitable, being quite free from ostentation or affectation.'

At Hambleden he built the attractive estate cottages and the village school, as well as enlarging Greenlands (which remained the principal seat of the family until the Second World War). 'Old Morality' died in October 1891, a month before the Viscountcy which had been conferred on him was formally gazetted, so it was granted to his widow, Emily, instead, with remainder to his male descendants.

The 2nd Viscount Hambleden acquired Hambleden Manor in 1923 from the Scott-Murray family, who had owned it since 1815. Originally the manor was held in the Middle Ages by the Scropes and descended through various families. The date of 1603 for the building was discovered during 19th-century repairs and, as John Martin Robinson has observed, 'this is convincing architecturally'.

The sumptuously Regency Drawing Room as decorated for the Hambledens by John Fowler. The glass chandelier was commissioned from Murano, near Venice.

The principal bedroom, with its Chippendale-style four-poster.

The mullions were replaced in the principal ground-floor rooms with sash windows in the remodelling of 1748. And although John Fowler may have deplored the Victorian 'improvements' made by the Scott-Murrays inside, their restoration work to the exterior helped retain its late-Elizabethan character. The Fifties flair which Fowler and the Hambledens, not forgetting Sir Martyn Beckett, added to the charm of this magical manor house deserves the highest praise.

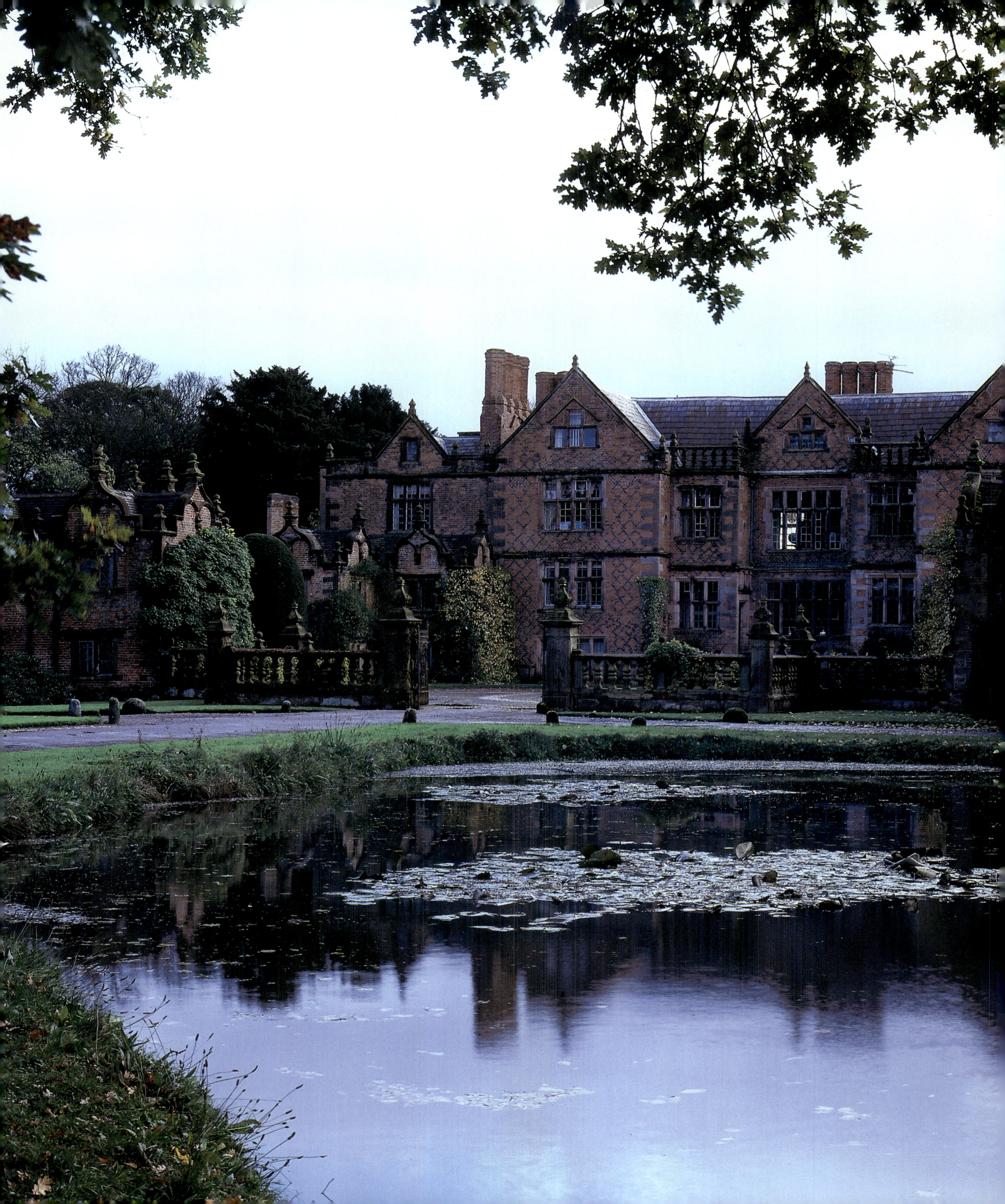

35

Dorfold Hall

CHESHIRE

AT DORFOLD, which by tradition is on the site of the ancient manor of Edwin, the last Saxon Earl of Chester (a grandson of Lady Godiva), we are comfortably into the Jacobean Age. As built by Ralph Wilbraham in 1616, it is a splendid example of Jacobean architecture: red brick with stone mullions, gables and octangular-shafted chimneys, a symmetrical entrance front, recessed centre, projecting wings and flanking subsidiary L-shaped pavilions with Flemish gables.

The plan, though, is unusual for a house of that date. At a period when manor houses of this type tended to be only one room deep, Dorfold is a 'double pile' with rooms behind the old hall (now the Dining Room) and the Great Chamber. Although some of the interior was subsequently altered in the 18th century, the Great Chamber, or Drawing Room, on the first floor retains its robustly Jacobean character. Dorfold's finest interior, executed in 1621, it has a coved stucco ceiling with geometrical patterns and hanging pendants. The cartouches contain varied forms of the Tudor rose, thistle and fleur-de-lys, emblematical of the hopes of peace arising from the unity of England and Scotland under King James I and VI. The panelling, of Mannerist design, the floor and the chimneypiece are also original. Among the other rooms upstairs that also contain plasterwork and panelling of the Jacobean period are the King James Room, with its elaborate armorial chimneypiece dated 1621 (tradition has it that the room was fitted out for the King himself but he never turned up), and the Oak Room, at the top of the richly balustraded Jacobean staircase.

The Jacobean formality of Dorfold's entrance front, however, is partially deceptive. While the main block and the two forecourt lodges are dated 1616 and are all of one build, the intervening replicas of the lodges were added in 1824. Moreover, the full-on approach was an ingenious 1862 scheme of William Nesfield's. An early map confirms that the original approach by

PRECEDING PAGES View of the north front of Dorfold from across the pool.

LEFT The garden front.

BELOW Autumnal view down the lime avenue planted as part of William Nesfield's improvements of 1862. These included the creation of the straight drive.

causeway was circuitous, skirting the north-east corner of the pool, which was then a fishpond, and much larger than it is now, extending in a crescent shape across the north side of the house. The present lodge on the main road and the straight drive with its double row of lime trees, the draining of part of the pool and the low balustrade wall at the entrance to the forecourt were all innovations of 1862. At the same time the front gates and the forecourt's sculptural group of a wolfhound and her cubs, both artefacts inspired by the Paris Exhibition of 1855, were also installed.

Dorfold's original builder, Ralph Wilbraham (whose portrait by Cornelius Jonson, together with other early Wilbraham portraits, hangs in the Drawing Room), came from a prominent Cheshire family with strong connections to the Law. These legal associations are reflected in a number of the heraldic features that adorn the house's interior. Far from settling into a steady squirearchical pattern, however, the new house was fortunate to survive the Civil War. The squire, Roger Wilbraham, supported the Cromwellian cause and consequently Dorfold was plundered by Royalist soldiers in 1643.

Eventually, after five generations of Wilbraham ownership, Dorfold was bought in 1754 by another lawyer, James Tomkinson of Nantwich nearby. A cultivated man, Tomkinson planted many of the fine trees in the garden and did up the downstairs rooms in contemporary style. Thus the old screens passage was enclosed, vaulted, and adorned with mid-Georgian plasterwork, and the old hall, now the Dining Room, acquired a goodly ceiling of the same period. The Adamesque ceiling in the Library is slightly later, having been designed by Samuel Wyatt (younger brother of the great James) to commemorate a Tomkinson marriage of 1772. In the centre are a pair of doves, billing with Hymen's torch and Cupid's arrows. The handsomely carved Adam-style chimneypieces in both the Library and the Dining Room are said to have been imported from an inn in the City of London.

ABOVE The Great Chamber, or Drawing Room, with its magnificent Jacobean ceiling. This, the panelling, the floor and chimneypiece are all original.

RIGHT Detail of the painted heraldic decoration above the chimneypiece in the Great Chamber. The three Gartered coats of arms are those of (left to right) Lord Burghley, the Earl of Derby and Sir Christopher Hatton.

LEFT The Georgian touch: groined vaulting with plaster enrichments.

BELOW Detail of the overmantel in the Oak Room. The coat of arms is that of Sir Thomas Delves of Doddington, who married a Miss Wilbraham of Dorfold. With their customary love of puns, the heralds devised a shield incorporating three sods of turf, or 'delves'.

Such provenance would have been not inappropriate, for during the Tomkinsons' time Dorfold was legendary for its convivial 'open house' hospitality. The estate enjoyed its own bakery, butchery and brewery, and was the last place in the area to relinquish them. Set as it is in open hunting country, Dorfold was a popular centre for the chase. The hunting parties were such a feature of the life of the house that it was found necessary to add an ungainly wing to the east to accommodate the large staff of those days, as well as stabling for 24 horses. Subsequently the major part of this wing, and the stables, were demolished.

In 1844 Ann Tomkinson, eldest daughter and heiress of the Reverend James Tomkinson, squarson of Dorfold, married Wilbraham Spencer Tollemache, scion of another well-known Cheshire dynasty and, as his first name might indicate, a descendant of the Wilbrahams. It was Tollemache who brought in Nesfield, the Victorian landscape gardener celebrated for his work at Windsor, Holkham and elsewhere, to alter the approach to the house and advise on changes to the vistas from both north and south.

DORFOLD HALL

The next squire of Dorfold, Henry Tollemache, was MP for West Cheshire and Vice-Lord-Lieutenant of the county, but he had no children and the estate passed to his sister's family, the Roundells, who happily remain here today. The present owner, Richard Roundell, and his father Charles before him, have carried out admirable restoration work and extensive repairs to the fabric in recent years. Ricky Roundell is an energetic champion of the smaller historic house and played a vital role in the setting-up of the 'Treasures of the North' exhibition, which opened many metropolitan eyes to the significance of such places and their survival. As well as being a chartered surveyor, he holds an important position with Christie's Fine Art.

In the best country-house tradition he commissioned the stylish portrait painter Howard Morgan to paint himself, his wife Anthea and their two children. These superbly bold portraits look very well in the Great Chamber alongside the heraldic decoration, landscapes and studies of such Elizabethan and Jacobean worthies as Burghley and Bacon.

The Roundells open Dorfold regularly to the public. The gardens include a magnificent Spanish chestnut (thought to be more than a thousand years old and the last survivor of Delamere Forest), herbaceous borders, a woodland garden (planted in the 1980s) and a water garden. And, by way of an eye-catcher, there is the old gateway from the Wilbrahams's almshouses in Nantwich – a jolly mid-17th-century Mannerist design with busts in niches.

ABOVE and RIGHT Two views of the Staircase, which has enriched Jacobean balustrading, repeated also as a respond against the walls.

– 225 –

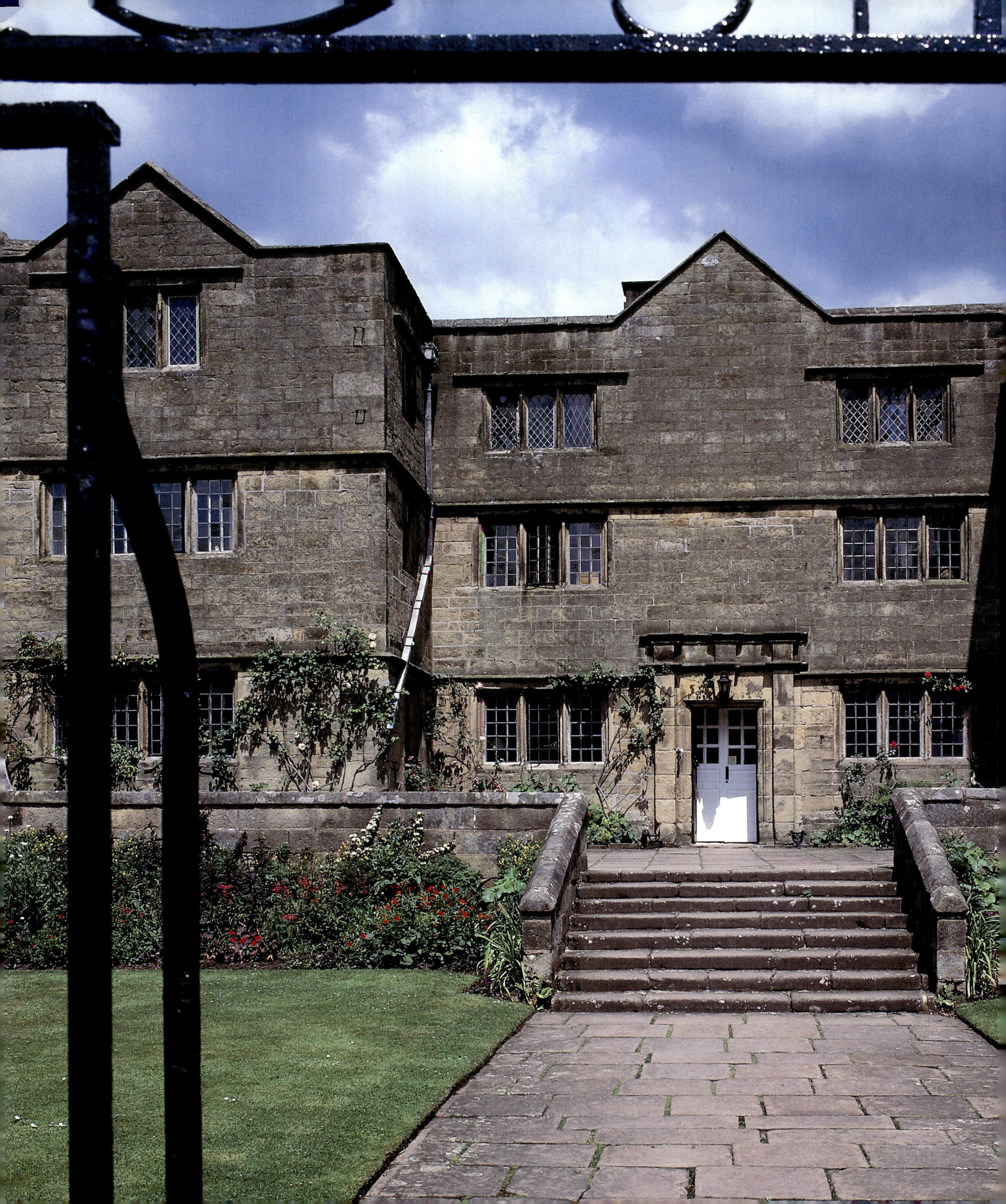

36

EYAM HALL

DERBYSHIRE

EVERYONE knows Chatsworth, the Devonshires' 'Palace of the Peak', but how many country-house enthusiasts have discovered the more intimate joys of its nearest historic house neighbour, Eyam, tucked away behind the hills that form Middleton Dale? As the Duchess of Devonshire herself said, when she formally opened Eyam Hall to the public in 1992, it is a very special place because Derbyshire has so few smaller manor houses of this type that are open – and what makes it all the more special is that Eyam is still the family home of the Wrights, who built (or rather rebuilt) it in 1671.

The first building on the site was the dwelling of a yeoman, John Wilson. Surviving features of this original house, such as some of the older windows (blocked up in some cases), can be discerned in the present structure. Then, in 1665 the plague came to Eyam, altering its history forever. The story goes that in September of that year a parcel of cloth arrived in the village from London, where the Great Plague was then rife, and brought the infection to the village. As it spread some residents fled, but the Rector, the Reverend William Mompesson, stood firm and declared a kind of quarantine, setting bounds around the village beyond which no one was supposed to pass. From Chatsworth, the owner at the time, the 3rd Earl of Devonshire, arranged for food and other necessities to be left at dropping points. In this way the infection was kept within the parish boundaries.

It was an act of heroic self-sacrifice. Mompesson, whose wife was among those to succumb, wrote that Eyam had become 'a Golgotha, a place of skulls; and had there not been a small remnant of us left, we had been as Sodom and Gomorrah. My ears never heard such doleful lamentations. My nose never smelt such noisome smells and my eyes never beheld such ghastly spectacles.'

The plague had done its worst by 1666 and life had to begin again at Eyam. In 1671 Thomas Wright, described in documents as a 'gent', second son of William Wright, owner of the Great Longstone estate nearby, began building Eyam Hall on the site of the old Wilson house for his son John. John's

PRECEDING PAGES View through the gates to the entrance front of Eyam, rebuilt after the Great Plague.

LEFT The Entrance Hall, with its pair of bacon settles on either side of the fireplace. The large conversation piece on the far wall is a family portrait of the Knivetons, whose daughter Elizabeth (the little girl in the bottom right of the painting) married John Wright, the builder of the present house.

BELOW View from the garden through to the forecourt.

wife, a local heiress called Elizabeth Kniveton, appears to have exercised considerable influence over its design. Hers as well as John's initials can be seen on the lead downpipe to the right of the terrace.

Set above an impressive forecourt, the house of attractive local millstone grit has four well-spaced bays, mullioned windows, parapets and shallow gables. This façade, along with the walled garden to the east and the Banqueting House, has altered remarkably little since its creation in the 1670s. The Kitchen wing, to the west, was added in about 1700, unfortunately constructed in an unsatisfactory combination of limestone and gritstone, which leads to a chemical reaction and eventual erosion of the gritstone. The Stable block was constructed in the same manner and has recently been the subject of extensive repairs; it now houses the Buttery, a licensed restaurant for visitors.

The tour of the interior begins in the Hall, with its diamond layout of local grit flagstones. There are portraits of John and Elizabeth Wright, for whom the house was built, and an unusual pair of 'bacon settles' (flitches of bacon were hung to cure in the tall cupboard sections), mentioned in the first inventory of the contents compiled in 1694. Shortly before opening the house to the public, the present owners discovered underneath the 18th-century fireplace surround an earlier 17th-century fireplace, but it was too damaged to reclaim.

The Hall also contains a portrait of perhaps the most prominent member of the Wright family, Major John Wright, who was ADC to General 'Gentleman Johnny' Burgoyne (himself a playwright and immortalized in Shaw's play *The Devil's Disciple*) during the American War of Independence. The Major's sword hangs in the room, above the fireplace.

The main Staircase, a robust affair, presents something of a puzzle. Its style appears to pre-date the rebuilding of the house; the stair tower is part of the original house and the relocation of the windows suggests that the present staircase was brought in and installed later.

ABOVE and RIGHT Two staircase views: the principal Staircase (right) is a robustly carved affair that appears to pre-date the present house and may have been brought in from elsewhere.

ABOVE Attic timbers (and homely clutter).

The most intriguing interior at Eyam is the Tapestry Room, with its striking floor-to-ceiling hangings. These range from a fine 15th-century Flemish tapestry, worked in silk and wool, to a couple of 16th-century Brussels tapestries, illustrating scenes of antiquity. Then there is a patchwork of pastoral scenes made up of 11 pieces, probably cut from the Flemish tapestry. Recently restored with great care, these wall hangings create a memorable effect of cosiness and colour.

Less cosy is a hair-raisingly gory book on display in the Library (originally the great chamber on the first floor) entitled *A Survey of the Microcosm or Anatomie of the Bodies of Man and Woman* (1675) by Michael Spaher, complete with fold-out sections not dissimilar to modern 'pop-up' volumes. More reassuringly, there is an evocative collection of old toys in the Nursery, including a rocking horse made by Ayres in the 1890s. The Bedroom on show boasts a splendid tester bed contemporary with the house and a rare set of 17th-century embroidered crewelwork hangings. These were recently restored thanks to the generosity of the Friends of Eyam Hall.

EYAM HALL

Robert Wright, a solicitor, inherited Eyam in 1990 upon the death of the widow of his cousin, Charles Wright (known as 'Daddy' to his pupils at King Edward VI Grammar School in Sheffield). Since then Robert and his wife Nicola have carried out a thorough and sympathetic restoration. Renovations in the Old Kitchen have revealed a fascinating array of old stone arches and flagstones. 'The most nerve-wracking moment', recalls Nicola, 'was when we discovered the live First World War German mortar bomb which Cousin Charles had brought home as a souvenir.' The bomb has been safely disposed of and is not on display, but there is much to admire in the way of embroidery, china, glass, silver and costume.

Eyam is full of life, with a busy summer programme of plays and concerts (Robert Wright and his daughter Felicity have a particular interest in the music contemporary with the house). It is well equipped for school visits, licensed for civil weddings (now a vital source of income for owners of historic houses), and the old farm buildings have been converted into a craft centre. This is a manor house where you can enjoy history in miniature.

BELOW Detail of ornate wood carving on the 17th-century tester bedhead. The bed has recently been hung with beautiful contemporary crewelwork bedhangings, restored thanks to the generosity of the Friends of Eyam Hall.

RIGHT A corner of the Tapestry Room.

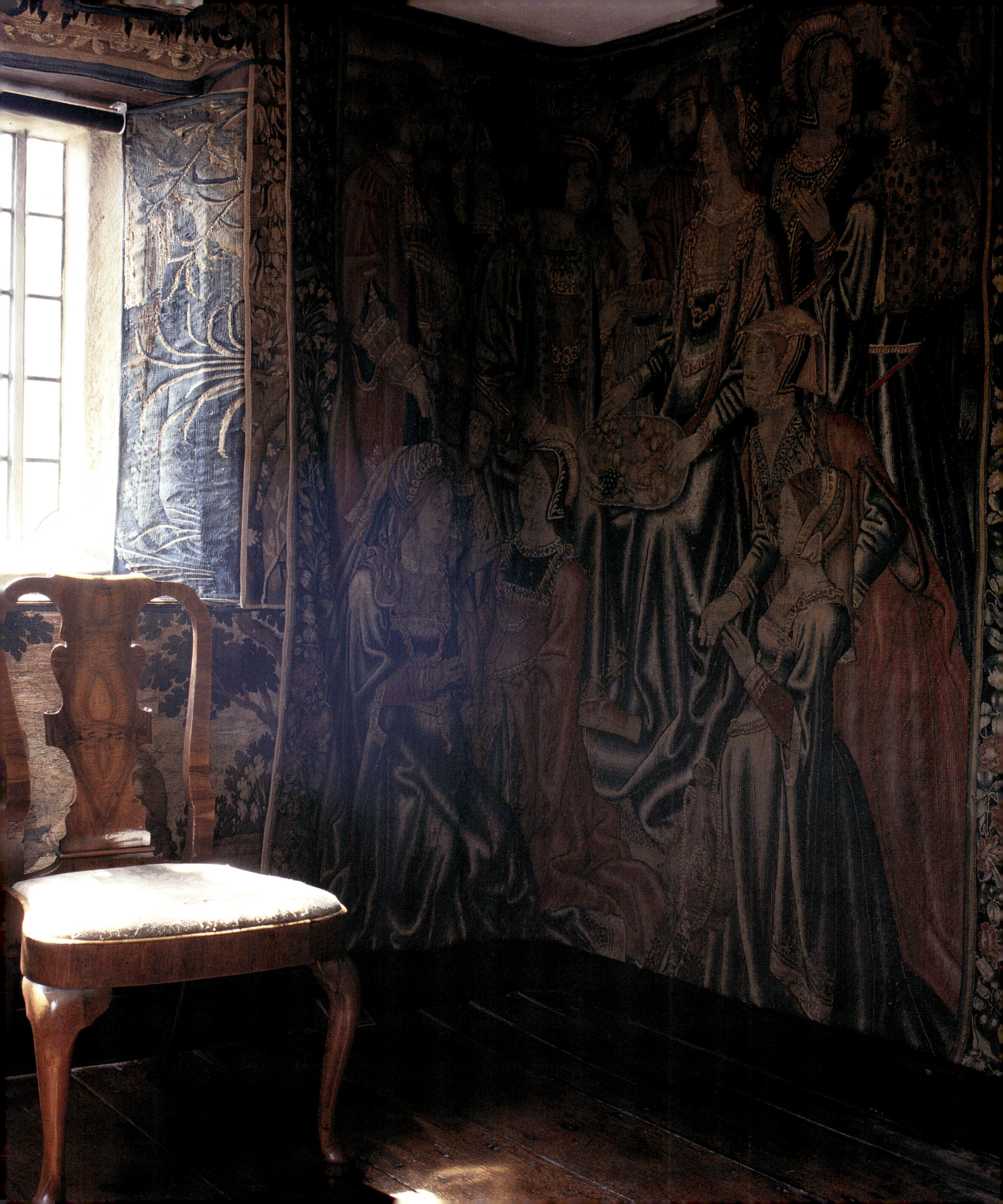

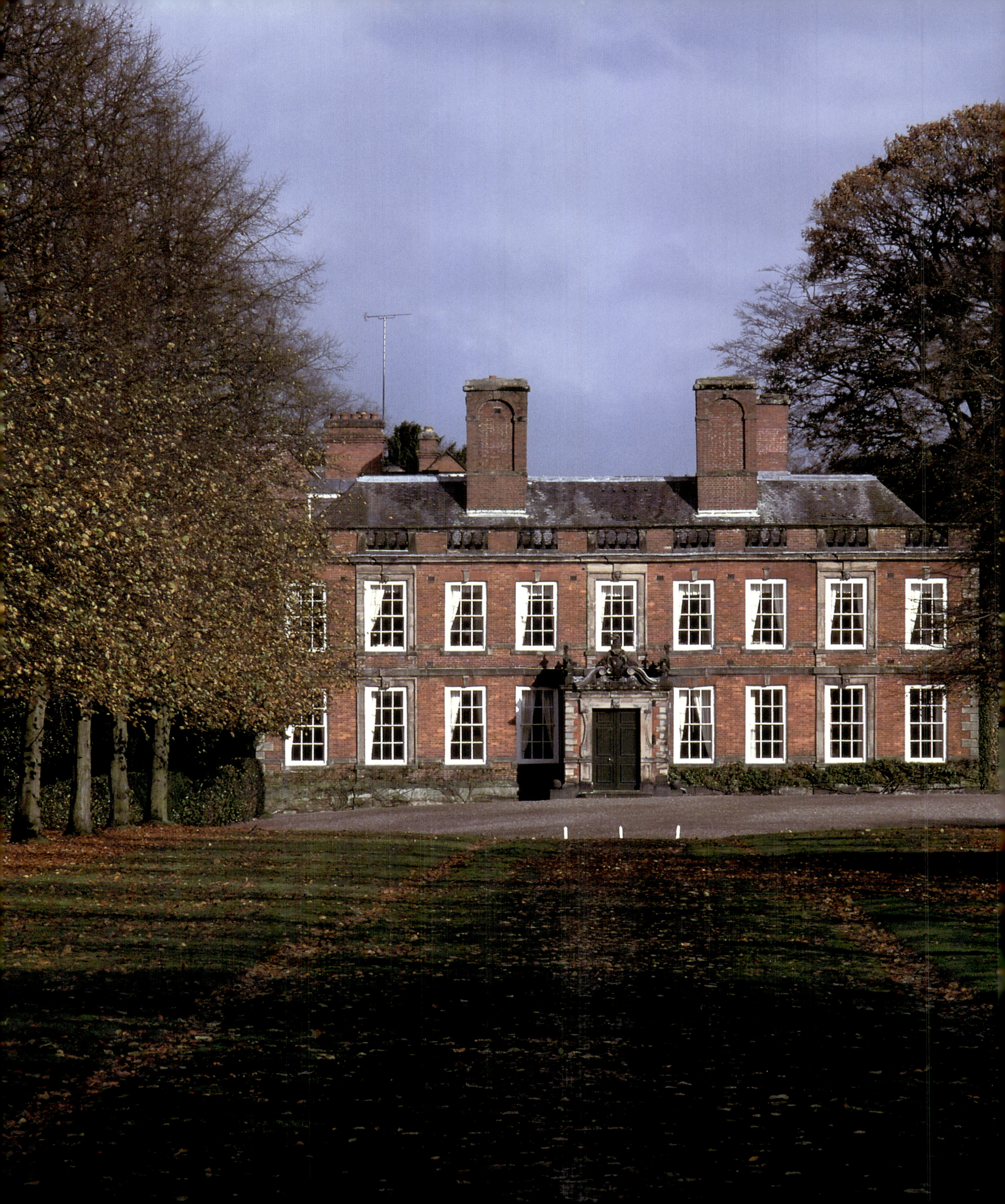

37

WHITMORE HALL

STAFFORDSHIRE

S TAFFORDSHIRE tends to conjure up images of an industrial landscape – the Potteries, Arnold Bennett's smoky 'Five Towns'. Yet its rural belt, near the point where the county meets Shropshire and Cheshire, remains remarkably unspoilt and well worth exploring. For any manorial enthusiast the highlight will be a visit to Whitmore Hall, near Newcastle-under-Lyme, which the Cavenagh-Mainwaring family opens regularly to the public.

In addition to the architectural interest – a Caroline manor house, incorporating a much older half-timbered building, and an outstanding early 17th-century stable block – there is the rare distinction that the estate has remained in the same ownership since Norman times. In his learned study of *The Mainwarings of Whitmore and Biddulph in the County of Stafford* (1933), Major J.G. Cavenagh-Mainwaring (grandfather of the present owner) traced a probable descent from Ricardus Forestarius (or Richard Forester), who held Whitmore at the time of the *Domesday Book* in 1086, having ousted the Saxon proprietor, one Ulfac. John de Whitmore, who held Whitmore in 1199, was probably a great-grandson of this Forester. The property remained in the de Whitmore family until the late 14th century, when it passed by marriage to the de Boghays or Bougheys. Following the death of Humphrey Boughey in 1540 Whitmore was settled on his granddaughter, Alice, who married Edward Mainwaring, a younger son of the Cheshire landowning dynasty of Mainwaring of Peover. It has continued to pass by descent in this family ever since.

The family history is rendered simple (or complex, depending upon how one looks at it) by the fact that there were eight squires, fathers and sons, between 1546 and 1825 all called Edward Mainwaring. From the time of Edward I (to adopt a kingly system, even if some of the Mainwarings were Cromwellians) an estate map of 1597 provides useful evidence that the manor house was a rectangular building with two projecting wings enclosing a narrow court (where the Entrance Hall is now) on the south side facing the church.

Significantly, though, the map does not show the Stable block of pink sandstone, which is often described as being late-Elizabethan, and looks it. For example, the original windows on the first floor have mullions and transoms of the Tudor rather than the Jacobean type. None the less, Gordon Nares in *Country Life* considered that the Stables were probably built during the tenure of Edward III, who succeeded to Whitmore in 1604 (a year after the death of Queen Elizabeth I) and died in 1647. He based this attribution not only on the grounds of the estate map of 1597 but also on the analogy that the stables at Over Peover, which clearly seem to have been inspired by those at Whitmore, were not built until 1654. In any event, whatever their precise date, the Whitmore Stables are a special treat, with their beautifully preserved turned columns and carved arches, nine cobbled stalls and arched hay-racks.

Edward III, who was an MP and a prominent Parliamentarian in the Civil War, fortified the manor house to enable it to survive the conflict. The present Caroline exterior was the responsibility of his son, Edward IV, an MP in the Restoration Parliament, who probably planted the splendid lime avenue that links the house to the church. The new façade, of plum-coloured brick and stone dressings, was flat; the Entrance Hall now occupied the courtyard space shown in the 1597 map between the two projecting wings. The porch in the middle was added in 1842 by Rear-Admiral Rowland Mainwaring, though he incorporated the old front door and its elaborate coat of arms (complete with the Mainwaring crest of an ass's head, a recurring motif at Whitmore), which had originally been flush with the façade. The door has a keystone bearing the date 1676 – presumably the year of the completion of the remodelling.

Edward IV had actually died the year before, but it seems right that the credit should go to him for the building work. The account books of his son, Edward V, do not mention large-scale constructions. The next significant changes came in the time of Edward VII, who marched with his tenantry against the Jacobite invaders in 1745 and married a Bunbury of the celebrated horse-racing family. It was this Edward who commissioned the architect William Baker of Highfields (*qv*) to survey Whitmore in 1756. The consequent improvements

PRECEDING PAGES View of the Caroline entrance façade of Whitmore down the lime avenue from the church.

ABOVE Detail of grotesque mask in the stone dressings of the redbrick exterior.

LEFT The Entrance Hall, which occupies the original courtyard space of the old house. The screen of Corinthian columns was probably added by the architect William Baker of Highfields (*qv*), when he surveyed Whitmore in 1756.

probably included the screen of Corinthian columns in the Entrance Hall; the curving staircase that rises behind them; the rebuilding of the northern part of the house; and the landscaping, in the 'Capability' Brown manner, of the serpentine lake that it overlooks at the back. Happily, Whitmore's sylvan park was protected from desecration by the new Newcastle to Market Drayton road in 1804 when Edward VIII insisted that the highway should be sunk in a cutting out of sight of the house.

After the death of Admiral Mainwaring (who added the porch) in 1862, Whitmore was inherited by a son living in Australia, and the house was let out for some years. During this interregnum, unfortunately, the rear part of the building was badly damaged by fire and had to be rebuilt. By the time Major J.G. Cavenagh-Mainwaring returned to take up his inheritance after the First World War the estate was in decline. He embarked on a thorough programme of restoration, faithfully carried on after his death in 1938 by his son, Rafe Cavenagh-Mainwaring, who rehabilitated the Stables and planted a new double avenue of limes to take the place of the 17th-century original.

Not the least of Rafe's achievements was the eradication of dry rot. Since his death in 1995, his son Guy Cavenagh-Mainwaring, together with his wife Christine and children Edward, Tara and Fleur, have undertaken a stylish renovation of Whitmore, which is a deservedly popular showplace. Visitors particularly enjoy the remarkable run of family portraits, which form a continuous line from 1624 to the present day. They include a fine double portrait by Michael Dahl of Edward VI and his wife Jemima Pye (great-granddaughter of John Hampden of 'Ship Money' fame) and a uniformed study of the Admiral by John Philip, which hangs above his sturdy sea-chest. The current Cavenagh-Mainwarings are depicted in the Dining Room by Gordon Wetmere; Guy represents the 34th generation of the family to live here.

BELOW Evidence of the original timber-framed structure behind a panel in an upstairs room.

ABOVE The early 17th-century Stables, with hexagonal cupola (a slightly later addition).

RIGHT Interior of the Stables, with their finely turned columns, carved arches, cobbled stalls and arched hay-racks.

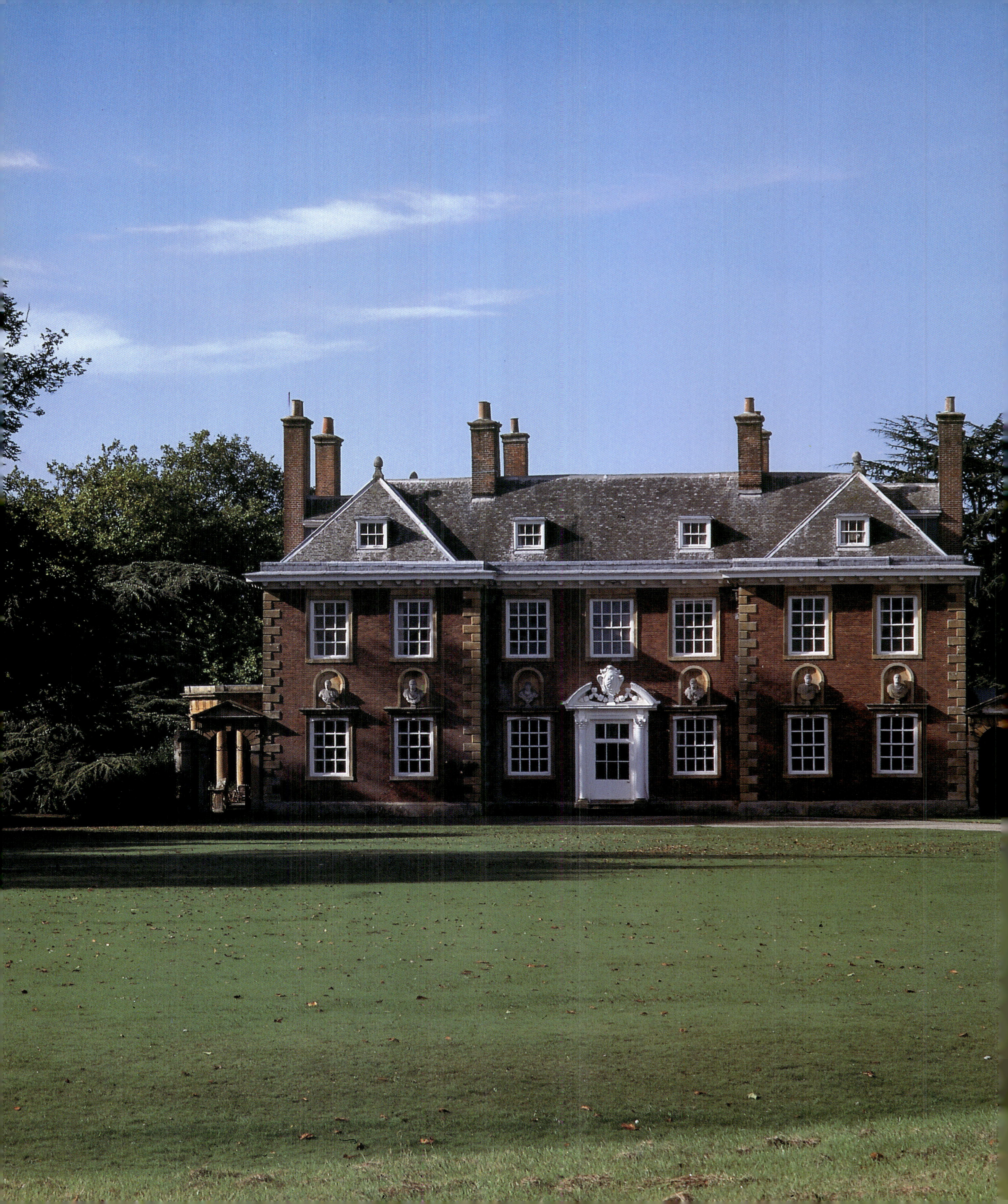

38

HONINGTON HALL

WARWICKSHIRE

THOSE in favour of the motion that England reached a high point of civilization in Good King Charles's Golden Days could hardly do better than to gaze at the glorious 1682 façade of Honington Hall, near Shipston-on-Stour. In Candida Lycett Green's selection of *100 Favourite Houses* for *Country Life*, Honington featured on the cover; she remarked on its 'utter, indefinable rightness of scale… built of brick the colour of mid-red wallflowers and just as rich, its stone dressings are golden, its elegance sublime'.

Honington, situated as it is in the heart of what Henry James called 'midmost England, unmitigated England', has been hailed as the 'perfect English country house'. Yet, paradoxically, it is better than that. As John Cornforth put it in *Country Life*, it has 'a slightly off-beat humanity that is wholly engaging'. The word 'perfect' somehow suggests sobriety, a lack of fun. But look at the richness of Honington's front door and the amusing round-headed niches containing marble busts of Roman emperors. And inside is an amazing surprise: early Georgian plasterwork of almost overwhelming exuberance. To quote Cornforth again, here is a 'felicitous synthesis… of Caroline domesticity with a Georgian sense of quality heightened by Rococo fireworks'.

If this were not enough, Honington also offers a secluded park approached by monumental Georgian gatepiers, the River Stour flowing just below the garden, a five-arched bridge with ball finials, some ravishingly pretty 17th-century stables and, of course, the exquisite church, which is reminiscent of a Wren building in the City of London. Unfortunately the architect of the house and the church (a remodelling job), presumably the same man, is not known. His patron, Sir Henry Parker, Bt, is commemorated with his son Hugh in a wonderfully vibrant monument on the west wall of the church which is so evocative of the late-Stuart age. Again, alas, the sculptor is unknown, though Cornforth (who nicely observes that the Parkers 'seem about to walk up the nave in conversation') wonders whether it could have been Francis Bird.

PRECEDING PAGES 'The perfect English country house': the entrance front of Honington, with, to the right, a screen that hides the stables.

LEFT The Stable gateway.

BELOW One of the dozen marble busts of Roman emperors which stand in oval-headed niches round the exterior of the house.

Sir Henry (who inherited the baronetcy from his uncle in 1696) bought the Honington estate in 1670 from the Gybbes family. They had acquired the property after the Dissolution of the Monasteries; previously it had come within the holdings of the Benedictine Priory of Coventry. Judging by the surviving outbuildings, which pre-date the Parker house, there must have been an earlier house on the site built by the Gybbeses, though there are no records to confirm this.

The Parker fortunes came from the City of London, where Sir Henry was a member of the Merchant Taylors Company and owned a coffee-house near the Temple. Possibly it was in this convivial establishment that he came across the architects and craftsmen who were to transform his country seat, for Honington has a curiously metropolitan air. The original façade of 1682 would probably have had casement windows; the sashes must date from the time of Joseph Townsend, who bought the estate from Sir Henry's grandson, the 3rd Baronet, in 1737.

Townsend, who became an MP, was the son of a London brewer and married Judith Gore, an heiress from Grimsby. They decided to make a serious splash at Honington, with plasterwork of the highest quality. The Hall was given an arabesque ceiling with a sunburst and representations of the Elements. On the end walls there are two Trojan scenes and four panels of the Arts, besides some delightfully Rococo brackets. On the Boudoir ceiling Aurora (or is it Flora?) scatters her morning flowers, and in the Oak Room (where the Caroline panels were spared by Townsend) the imposing doorcase is surmounted by two reclining cherubs. The plasterwork in the Hall has been attributed to Charles Stanley, an Anglo-Danish sculptor known to have been active in England until 1746.

The octagonal Saloon, Honington's outstanding interior, however, dates from about five years later and its authorship appears, from papers discovered in the Gloucestershire Records Office, to have been a somewhat uneasy collaboration between an amateur architect, John Freeman of Fawley Court in Buckinghamshire, and the professional William Jones, who evidently had strong views of his own. As so often in such cases of creative friction, the result is strongly stimulating – a thrilling fusion of Palladianism (Freeman) and Rococo (Jones). John Cornforth identified the corner 'drops' of Rococo as representing the Elements and Seasons, but those in the dome remain a mystery – as does so much in this marvellous house.

What is clear is that the original building along the usual Caroline 'thickened H' plan was modified in 1751 so that the octagonal Saloon could be inserted to fill the indent on its west side. At the same time changes were made to the positioning of the main Staircase. On the east (entrance) façade the Townsends substituted their coat of arms above the front for the Parkers' (which was transferred to the church) and flanked the front with a pair of pedimented doorways. The curved brick and stone screen extends to the north-west to hide the stables; another, almost linking the church to the house, is thought to have been pulled down in the early 19th century.

ABOVE Seeing double in the octagonal Saloon: the mirror above the chimneypiece reflects the overdoor on the other side of this spectacular interior (RIGHT), a thrilling fusion of the Palladian and Rococo styles.

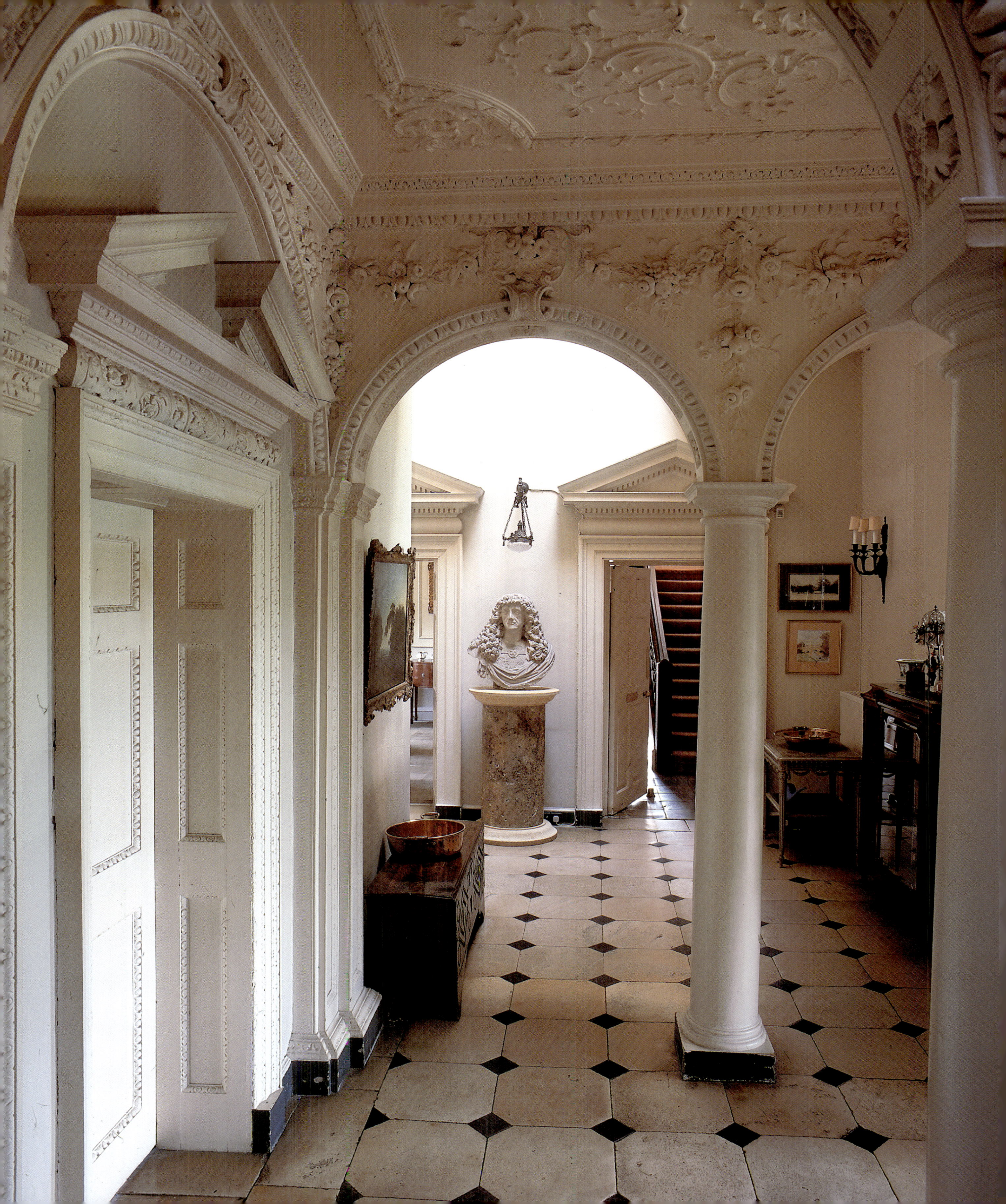

OPPOSITE The Inner Hall, as rearranged in the 1750s to accommodate the Saloon and the repositioning of the main staircase.

RIGHT The Hall, with its luscious plasterwork attributed to Charles Stanley. The overmantel depicts Venus appearing to Aeneas.

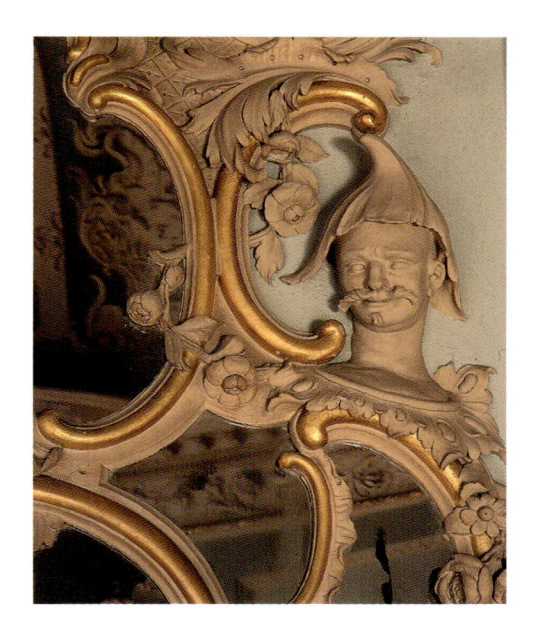

TOP and ABOVE Decorative details.

A Victorian service wing on the north-west side of the house had to be demolished in the 1970s when Honington was discovered to be riddled with dry rot. The late owner, Major Sir John Wiggin, 4th Baronet, dedicated himself to an extensive programme of repairs, restoration and modernization, with the help of substantial grants from the old Historic Buildings Council (precursor of English Heritage) and an expert team of craftsmen led by the conservation architect Jeremy Benson.

Honington had been bought in 1924 by Sir John's father, Colonel Sir Charles Wiggin, a legendary figure in the hunting field. Siegfried Sassoon described Sir Charles in his memoir *The Weald of Youth* as:

> One of the nicest people I had ever known, unfailingly good-humoured and companionable. The only complaint he ever made about anything was that he was compelled to miss one day's hunting a week. The reason for this was that duty called him three days a week to Birmingham, where he attended at the office of his father's business, which was concerned with the manufacture of nickel.

Happily, Honington remains the home of the Wiggin family, who open it to the public during the summer months. It is a joy to walk in the grounds, which were transformed by the Townsends in the 1750s (with advice from Sanderson Miller) into a blissfully romantic landscape.

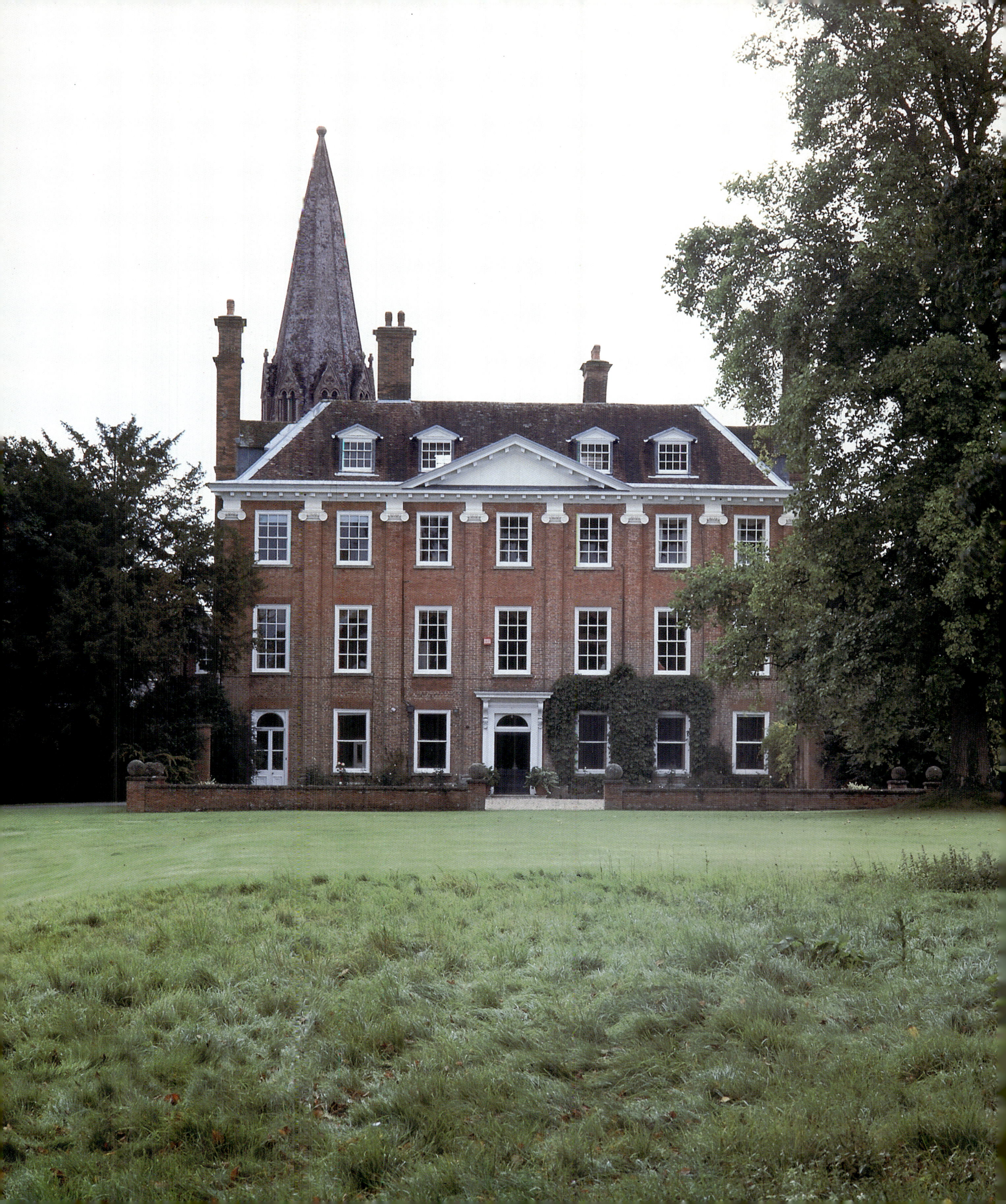

39

WELFORD PARK

BERKSHIRE

AT WELFORD, in the Lambourn Valley, we reach the end of our tour of medieval, Tudor, Jacobean and Stuart manor houses – save for the Victorian coda in the final chapter that follows, signalling the revival of 'Olden Times'.

In the early history of the site of this attractive late-Stuart 'dolls' house', Welford was first a monastic property and then, after the Dissolution, a hunting lodge of Henry VIII's. Subsequently it became vested in the Parry family; it seems likely that they built an Elizabethan manor house of some sort, as there is evidence of an earlier building in the cellar of the present house. Sir Thomas Parry, who first leased Welford from Henry VIII in 1546, went on to become Comptroller of the Household to Queen Elizabeth I, and his son, another Sir Thomas, was eventually Ambassador to France. Two years after the death of this second Sir Thomas, Welford was sold to Sir Francis Jones, Lord Mayor of London in 1620–1.

The present house was built, or at least begun, by the Lord Mayor's grandson, Richard Jones, who inherited Welford in 1652. In an undated contract recently discovered in the Welford papers in the Berkshire Record Office, Jones (or 'Jhones', as he is described) binds his workers on the new house to follow 'such modes manner or forme and direction as John Jackson of the Cittie of Oxon gent hath drawn described directed or set forth'. As Timothy Mowl has pointed out in *The Journal of the Georgian Group* (1994), John Jackson was originally a master mason and carver and did several significant works in Oxford, including the eclectic Canterbury Quad at St John's College, the exotic porch to St Mary's Church on the High and the sophisticated chapel and library at Brasenose College. The contract must have been drawn up some time between 1652, when Richard Jones came into the property, and Jackson's death in 1663. As Mowl argues, the likelihood was that 'it was nearer the first date of a young man coming into his inheritance, than the second'.

As built, the original entrance front was to the east, facing the church. The house would have been U-shaped, with two-bay wings projecting boldly on either side of the now hidden three-bay centre. Subsequently, the courtyard space in the centre of this façade was filled in with the present Dining Room and the entrance front was switched to the west, or garden, façade.

Before Mowl's attribution of the house to John Jackson, the hipped roof and 'extremely curious brick details' (some of the brick is in Flemish bond, some in English) had led Sir Nikolaus Pevsner in the *Berkshire* volume of his *Buildings of England* series to comment that Welford seemed to date from something like 1660–70. The windows (those on the ground floor lost their glazing bars in the 19th century) have remarkable raised frames vertically connected by a raised band standing in the centre of each lower window. Pevsner duly placed Welford in the school of provincial Classicism dubbed 'Artisan Mannerism' by Sir John Summerson.

Later in the 17th century, about 1680, the Jones heiress, Mary, married John Archer, whose family owned land in Essex. Their only child, Eleanor, married Thomas Archer (no apparent relation), a budding Baroque architect, who is thought – naturally enough – to have advised his parents-in-law on

PRECEDING PAGES The charming late-Stuart 'dolls' house' of Welford, with the church behind.

ABOVE The Hall.

the remodelling of Welford at the beginning of the 18th century. This involved the installation of eight giant Ionic pilasters – possibly, as Timothy Mowl points out, 'the earliest example of a giant Order used so confidently on such a large country house façade' – and the pediment on the new entrance front, as well as the addition of an extra storey.

Thomas Archer would barely have had time to finish his work at Welford before his wife died of smallpox in 1702, within a year of their marriage. He later went on, as Sir Howard Colvin notes in his *Biographical Dictionary of British Architects*, to design 'the most uncompromisingly Baroque buildings in England', including the north front of Chatsworth for the 1st Duke of Devonshire.

In 1706 Welford passed to a niece, Eleanora Wrottesley, who married William Eyre. William took the name of Archer and all subsequent owners of the estate descend from his second marriage, to Susanna, daughter of Sir John Newton, 3rd Baronet, of Culverthorpe, Lincolnshire, and aunt of the unfortunate heir, a baby boy who was thrown out of a top-floor window at Culverthorpe by a pet monkey.

Susanna eventually inherited Culverthorpe and the family came into another estate later in the 18th century, when her granddaughter and namesake married Jacob Houblon, of a distinguished Huguenot dynasty seated at Hallingbury Place in Essex. Consequently Welford became a subsidiary seat, but in 1831 a younger son, Charles Archer-Houblon (who changed his name to Eyre), came to live here and embarked on a series of improvements. These included the remodelling of the interior, which involved the enlarging of the Library and the Drawing Room and the construction of a new Staircase; the original staircase had risen up between these rooms. A new Dining Room, as we have seen, was inserted between the projecting wings on the east front and early Victorian plate-glass was substituted for the glazing bars in the ground-floor west front windows.

A model squire, Charles Eyre also rebuilt the church (to the designs of T. Talbot Bury) and erected the Stables. The grisly Eyre crest (a severed leg of a comrade-in-arms which according to tradition proved useful to an ancestor in battle) was placed atop the main entrance gates. The park was re-landscaped and greatly improved by the diversion of the Newbury–Lambourn road, which used to pass directly by the side of the house before stretching away in front of it.

Today, notwithstanding the proximity of the M4 and RAF Welford (on land taken over during the Second World War), the estate remains delightfully unspoilt. High above the park is an idyllic cricket ground, with serene views of the Berkshire Downs. This western corner of the county still has a beguilingly feudal air; now, as for the last few centuries, it is possible to walk from Newbury to Wantage (now, absurdly, dumped in Oxfordshire), traversing the land of only four families – three of which are closely interconnected.

The present squire of Welford, James Puxley (who took on the place in 1997 from his mother Aline, a great-granddaughter of Charles Eyre), farms all the land in hand and opens the house by prior arrangement in the summer. The grounds prove particularly popular with visitors, who enjoy walking along the River Lambourn as it flows through the garden. The waterfalls and fine collection of trees planted by Charles Eyre make a picturesque setting for this handsome late-Stuart manor house.

The Staircase, installed in 1831 by Charles Eyre. The large painting shows Sir Michael Newton, 4th Baronet, of Culverthorpe, Lincolnshire (brother of Susanna Archer, châtelaine of Welford), out with his hounds. Sir Michael's infant son was thrown out of a top-floor window at Culverthorpe by a pet monkey.

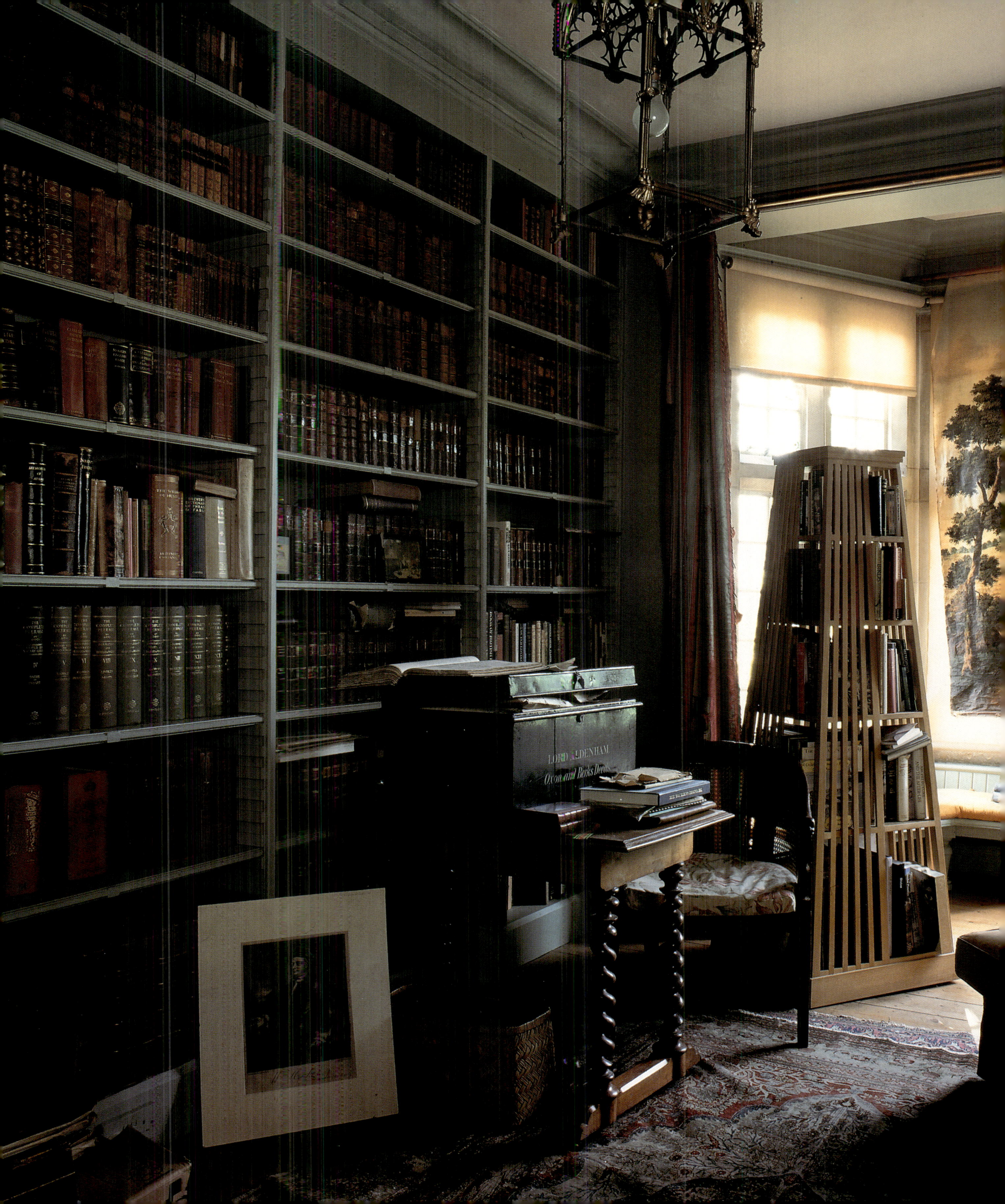

40

CLIFTON HAMPDEN

OXFORDSHIRE

WALKING along the towpath of the upper River Thames one is irresistibly reminded of Kenneth Grahame's evocatively Edwardian *The Wind in the Willows* and Jerome K. Jerome's jolly late-Victorian romp *Three Men in a Boat*. Jerome described Clifton Hampden, set beneath the two mounds known as 'Mother Dunch's Buttocks' and crowned with beech woods called the Wittenham Clumps, as 'a wonderfully pretty village, old-fashioned, peaceful and dainty with flowers… river scenery [that] is rich and beautiful'. In 2000 the great and inspiring collector Christopher Gibbs reflected, in the introduction to the Christie's catalogue for the sale of the contents he had imaginatively assembled at his family's beloved manor house, that 'the place is still of idyllic beauty and the river swells or dwindles with the seasons, transforming the landscape, mirroring church, bridge, manor and wooded cliff in unchanged beauty'.

The inclusion of Clifton Hampden as a coda to our tour of English Manor Houses is partly by way of a heartfelt tribute to Mr Gibbs and his genius for sympathetic, informal country-house interiors (our illustrations now serve as a record of his arrangement), and partly as an indication of how the manorial ideal was enthusiastically revived in the 19th century. For the ravishing composition we see today – bridge, parish church and manor house – is a Victorian creation commissioned by the Gibbs family from Sir George Gilbert Scott.

The Clifton Hampden estate had previously belonged to the Hucks family, a dynasty of prosperous brewers. Antony Gibbs, a London banker and trader, married, in 1784, Dorothea Hucks; and eventually, through this connection, Clifton Hampden and the other Hucks property, at Aldenham in Hertfordshire, were inherited by Antony's son, George Henry Gibbs, who died in Venice in 1842, having consolidated the family fortunes in the guano trade (as a wag put it, 'Mr Gibbs made his dibs/Selling the turds of foreign birds'). Among the

PRECEDING PAGES Christopher Gibbs's Library at Clifton Hampden, with *The Complete Peerage* handily placed. The oak table is attributed to A.W.N. Pugin; the obelisk bookcase, first exhibited in Paris in 1989, was designed by Alexis de Falaise. (Other versions are in the collection of Mick Jagger.)

LEFT The entrance front. The house was upgraded from parsonage (by Sir George Gilbert Scott, 1843–6) to manor house in the early 1900s for the 2nd Lord Aldenham.

BELOW St George stands sentinel in the porch. The plaster figure is a 19th-century replica of Donatello's early masterpiece (of about 1416), now in the Bargello, the National Museum, Florence.

OPPOSITE An enfilade to please the eye.

BELOW The marble figure of Sappho, holding a lyre, in a niche of the Dining Room. The sculptor was William Theed the younger, and the date 1848.

provisions of his will was that the church at Clifton Hampden should be fully restored and a parsonage built for his younger brother, the Reverend Joseph Gibbs, who had been incumbent there since 1830. The parsonage turned out to be a pleasingly modest, gabled house built of stone with ashlar dressings between 1843 and 1846 at a cost of £3,900. As Jeremy Musson wrote in *Country Life*, it was 'a good example of the smaller domestic work of George Gilbert Scott (who himself grew up in a Buckinghamshire rectory) after his conversion to Gothic in the 1840s'.

The principal attraction of the new parsonage was its glorious site, perched above the river. The Reverend Joseph Gibbs laid out the river walks in the gardens and planted many fine trees, including a Cedar of Lebanon and a *Magnolia grandiflora* which still grows on the south front of the house.

The Reverend Joseph died in 1864 and in the same year his nephew, Henry Hucks Gibbs, an enthusiastic Tractarian, scholar, banker, philologist, collector and builder, set about making improvements at Clifton Hampden. These included the addition of an east wing to the parsonage (including the present Library), by a member of Scott's office, Charles Buckeridge. The re-ordering of the chancel of the church and a splendid new brick bridge across the Thames were executed to Scott's own designs. All this work was carried out under the prolific Victorian architect's supervision.

Christopher Gibbs describes his colourful ancestor, Henry Hucks Gibbs, created 1st Lord Aldenham in 1896, as 'an awesome polymath who rode to hounds, blew off his right hand in a shooting accident and finished off the manuscripts which he was illuminating with his left hand'. Among his many other interests was genealogy, an absorbing addiction shared with his brother-in-law George Edward Cokayne, Clarenceux King of Arms and founder of *The Complete Peerage*, and with his third son, Vicary Gibbs, who amplified that superb work of scholarship into one of our most fascinating works of reference. This passion was certainly inherited by Christopher Gibbs himself, whose researches into family provenance netted so large a part of his brilliant collections.

In 1898 the 1st Lord Aldenham made Clifton Hampden over to his eldest son, Alban, already a widower, who preferred living here rather than at the principal seat of Aldenham. Four years later he remodelled the house to the designs of the architects Woodd & Ainslie and in the process upgraded Clifton

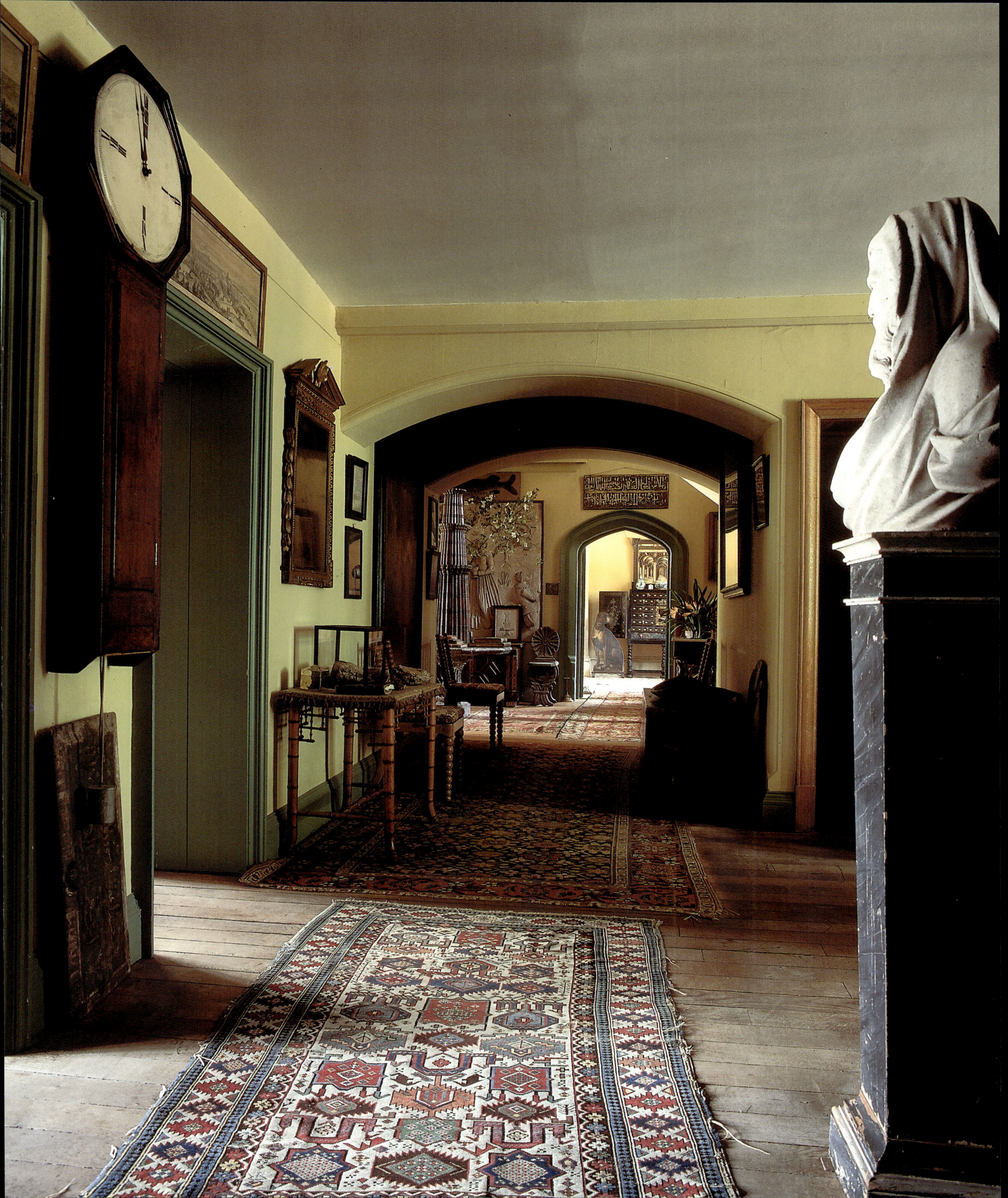

Hampden from a parsonage to a manor house. A substantial addition was made to the north-east approach, in matching materials, and a new porch was created. Furthermore, the house acquired two bay windows, one to the Drawing Room and the other to Buckeridge's extension, which is two-storeyed and crenellated. In the gardens Alban Gibbs was kept busy planting, as apparently his younger brother Vicary would bring cartloads of plants over from Aldenham.

  Alban, who succeeded as the 2nd Lord Aldenham in 1907, stayed on at Clifton Hampden until his death in 1936. After the Second World War the late Sir Geoffrey and Lady Gibbs (Christopher Gibbs's parents) came to live here, bringing, as their son put it, 'sweetness and light to the William Morris atmosphere of the house – and I, needless to say, have turned the clock back!' Sir Geoffrey and Lady Gibbs continued to develop the garden, and Lady Gibbs was responsible for the collections of snowdrops from Russia, Turkey and Greece which tumble down the banks of the river.

  Christopher Gibbs, as the youngest of five sons, did not expect to live at Clifton Hampden himself, but, as things turned out, found himself its owner in 1980 and, as he wrote at the time: 'It is a neglected corner of paradise that

A corner of the Garden Hall. On the marble table stands an Anglo-Indian mid-19th-century sandalwood model of the Qutb Minar Monument in Delhi. The plaster relief of figures in a landscape is early 17th-century.

RIGHT The Dining Room in use. Underneath the tablecloth could be found the diarist John Evelyn's late-17th-century mahogany table. The Gothic overmantel frames a Nativity scene in pen, black ink and watercolour panels of about 1800, after Sir Joshua Reynolds's stained-glass window at New College, Oxford.

BELOW A ceramic four-poster, with palm-wrapped pillars, made in William IV's reign by the Staffordshire Ironstone China factory established by Miles Mason.

I have to do something about.' That 'something', as John Harris said in his lyrical valediction for the Christie's sale catalogue, has been described as a 'paradise according to Gibbs', for Clifton Hampden is 'as celebrated for the magical garden he has made, as for the contents and ambiances within the house'.

After the depredations of Dutch elm disease, Christopher Gibbs created new viewpoints to the Chilterns from the circular walk. In front of the house's south façade he created a hornbeam 'room' and also added an ingenious lime-tree tunnel, rose-covered pergola walks, giant olive jars and a feast of sculptures, ranging from the 19th-century herm-heads of philosophers from the Sheldonian Theatre in Oxford to the pinnacle from Eton College Chapel, with its Latin inscription commemorating those, such as himself, who made early departures from that august seat of learning.

Yet though the objects Christopher Gibbs collected for the house have now been dispersed, it would be wrong to end on an elegiac note. Their dispersal affords new opportunities for antiquarian renewal in other places, just as the revival of the manorial ideal at Clifton Hampden in the 19th century heralded a new lease of life for the English Manor House.

GLOSSARY

BARGEBOARD A projecting decorated board placed against the incline of a gable of a building and hiding the horizontal roof-timbers.

BARREL VAULT A continuous semicircular arch.

BAY A division of a building marked by units of vaulting, arches, roof compartments or windows.

BOSS A projecting decorative feature at the intersection of vaulting ribs etc.

BRACE An inclined timber, straight or curved, introduced, usually at an angle, to strengthen other timbers.

BRACKET A projection designed as a support.

BRESSUMER A horizontal beam supporting a superstructure.

BUTTRESS Masonry or brickwork built against a wall to provide stability or to counteract the outward thrust of an arch or vault.

COLLAR-BEAM Tie-beam (*qv*) applied higher up the slope of a roof.

CORBEL A block of stone, or a piece of brickwork, projecting from a wall to support a floor, roof, parapet, vault or other feature.

CRENELLATE Fortify (crenellations are literally embrasures in battlements).

CROWN-POST A vertical timber standing centrally on a tie-beam (*qv*) and supporting a collar purlin (*qv*).

CRUCK(S) Pairs of inclined timbers, usually curved, which are set at bay-length intervals in a building and support the timbers of a roof.

CUSP Projecting point between the foils (*qv*) in a foiled Gothic arch.

DENDROCHRONOLOGY Study of chronology by carbon-dating of timber.

DIAPER An all-over pattern usually of lozenge, square or diamond shapes.

FIELDED PANELLING A wooden panel with a raised square or rectangular central area surrounded by a narrow moulding.

FINIAL The topmost feature, generally ornamental, of a gable (*qv*), roof, pinnacle or canopy.

FOIL (TREFOIL, QUATREFOIL, etc) A three-, four- or more-lobed ornamental infilling for a circle or arch-head.

GABLE Triangular portion of wall at the end of a ridge roof.

GARDEROBE Privy or lavatory.

HAMMERBEAM Beam projecting at right angles from a wall, to provide support for the vertical members and/or arched braces (*qv*) of a wooden roof.

HARLED Roughcast with lime and small gravel.

JAMB One of the vertical sides of an opening.

KING-POST A vertical beam standing centrally on a tie-beam (*qv*) or collar-beam (*qv*) and rising to the apex of the roof to support the ridge.

LINENFOLD Panelling carved to look like vertically folded linen.

LOGGIA A covered arcade or colonnade open on at least one side.

LOZENGE Diamond shape.

MULLION A vertical post or other upright dividing a window into lights.

NEWEL The central column from which steps of a winding staircase radiate, and also the principal posts at the angles of a square staircase which support the handrail.

ORIEL A window projecting from an upper storey.

PARAPET A low wall above the cornice.

PILASTER Flat representation of a Classical column in shallow relief against a wall.

PURLIN A longitudinal horizontal beam or pile supporting the common rafters of a roof.

QUEEN-POSTS A pair of vertical or near-vertical timbers placed symmetrically on a tie-beam and supporting side purlins (*qv*).

QUOIN Cornerstone; a stone or brick forming an angle.

ROLL MOULDING Moulding of part-circular section.

ROSE WINDOW Circular window with tracery (*qv*) radiating from the centre.

SCREENS PASSAGE Screened-off entrance passage between the Great Hall and the service rooms of a manor house.

SHAFT Vertical member of round or polygonal section, especially the main part of a Classical column.

SOLAR Parlour or private room, usually at first-floor level.

SPANDREL Roughly triangular space between the outer curve of an arch and the rectangle formed by the moulding enclosing it.

SQUINT A hole cut in a wall to allow a view of the Great Hall from a place where it could not otherwise be seen; often hidden by a mask.

STRAPWORK Flat interlaced decoration (16th- and 17th-century), seemingly derived from bands of cut leather.

TIE-BEAM Beam connecting the two slopes of a roof.

TRACERY Intersecting ornamental ribwork in the upper parts of Gothic windows, walls, screens and vaults.

TRANSOM A horizontal bar of stone or wood across the openings of a window.

TRUSS A group of strong timbers arranged as a supporting frame within the triangle formed by the sloping sides of a timber-framed roof.

UNDERCROFT A vaulted underground room or crypt.

WINDBRACE A diagonal timber brace, usually curved, crossing the rafters to strengthen the roof longitudinally.

SELECT BIBLIOGRAPHY

Aslet, Clive, *The Last Country Houses*, London, 1982
— 'Athelhampton, Dorset', *Country Life*, 10/24 May 1984
— 'Friston Place, Sussex', *Country Life*, 19 June 1986

Bailey, Brian, *English Manor Houses*, London, 1983
Bence-Jones, Mark, and Montgomery-Massingberd, Hugh, *The British Aristocracy*, London, 1979
Burke, Sir Bernard, *Burke's Peerage & Baronetage*, London, 1826–1999 (106 edns)
— *Burke's Landed Gentry*, London, 1833–1972 (18 edns)
— *A Visitation of the Seats and Arms of the Noblemen and Gentlemen of Great Britain and Ireland*, London, 1852–5 (4 vols)

Cecil, David, *Some Dorset Country Houses*, Wimborne, 1985
Chandler, John, *John Leland's Itinerary*, Stroud, 1993
Christie's catalogue: *The Manor House at Clifton Hampden*, London, 2000
Clifton-Taylor, Alec, *The Pattern of English Building*, London, 1972
G.E.C[okayne], *The Complete Peerage*, London, 1910–59 (13 vols); Gloucester, 1982 (microprint, 6 vols)
— *The Complete Baronetage*, Gloucester, 1983 (reprint, with Introduction by Hugh Montgomery-Massingberd)
Colvin, Howard, *A Biographical Dictionary of British Architects, 1600–1840*, London, 1995
Cook, Olive, and Smith, Edwin, *The English House Through Seven Centuries*, London, 1968
Cooper, Nicholas, *English Manor Houses*, London
— *Houses of the Gentry, 1480–1680*, London, 1999
Cooper, Nicholas, et al., *Chastleton House*, London, 1997
Cornforth, John, 'Heydon Hall, Norfolk', *Country Life*, 22/29 July and 5 August 1982
— 'Honington Hall, Warwickshire', *Country Life*, 21/28 September and 12 October 1978
Country Life: see Aslet; Cornforth; Hussey; Jackson-Stops; Marshall; Musson; Nares; Oswald; Tipping; Weaver

Dictionary of National Biography
Ditchfield, P.H., *The Manor Houses of England*, London, 1910

Fedden, Robin, and Kenworthy-Browne, John, *The Country House Guide*, London, 1979
Floyd, Robert, *Great Chalfield Manor*, London, 1998

Girouard, Mark, *Life in the English Country House*, London, 1978
— *Historic Houses of Britain*, London, 1979
— *Robert Smythson and the Elizabethan Country House*, London, 1983
— 'Arcadian Retreats from the Chase', *Country Life*, 26 September 1963
Greeves, Lydia, and Trinick, Michael, *The National Trust Guide*, London, 1989 (4th edn)

Heath, Sidney, *Some Dorset Manor Houses*, 1907 (Foreword by R. Bosworth-Smith)
Hussey, Christopher, *English Country Houses Open to the Public*, London, 1951
— 'Beeleigh Abbey, Essex', *Country Life*, 30 September 1922
— 'Ockwells Manor, Berkshire', *Country Life*, 12/26 January 1924
— 'Dorney Court, Buckinghamshire', *Country Life*, 26 July/2 August 1924
— 'Cothay Manor, Somerset', *Country Life*, October 22/29 1927
— 'Beckley Park, Oxfordshire', *Country Life*, 23 March 1929
— 'Markenfield Hall, Yorkshire', *Country Life*, 28 December 1940
— 'Stanton Harcourt, Oxfordshire', *Country Life*, 3/10 October 1941
— 'Mells, Somerset', *Country Life*, 23/30 April 1943
— 'Owlpen Manor, Gloucestershire', *Country Life*, 2/9 November 1951
Hutchins, John, *History of Dorset*, 1774

Jackson-Stops, Gervase, 'Norton Conyers, Yorkshire', *Country Life*, 9/16 October 1986

Lees-Milne, James, *Diaries*, London, 1975– (8 vols)
— *Some Cotswold Country Houses*, Wimborne, 1987
— *People and Places*, London, 1992
Lloyd, Rachel, *Dorset Elizabethans*, London, 1927
Lycett Green, Candida, *Country Life: 100 Favourite Houses*, London, 1999

Mandler, Peter, *The Fall and Rise of the Stately Home*, London, 1997
Marshall, J.M., 'Great Chalfield Manor, Wiltshire', *Country Life*, 18 June 1998
Montgomery-Massingberd, Hugh, *The Field Book of Country Houses and their Owners: Family Seats of the British Isles*, London and Exeter, 1988
— 'Heritage' articles in *The Field*, 1976–87, and *The Daily Telegraph*, 1987–96
Montgomery-Massingberd, Hugh (ed.), *Guide to Country Houses*, London, 1978–91 (4 vols)
Mowl, Timothy, 'Welford Park, Berkshire', *Journal of the Georgian Group*, London, 1994
Musson, Jeremy, *The English Manor House*, London, 1999
— 'Owlpen Manor, Gloucestershire', *Country Life*, 28 September 2000
— 'Clifton Hampden, Oxfordshire', *Country Life*, 26 October 2000

Nares, Gordon, 'Aubourn Hall, Lincolnshire', *Country Life*, 14 February 2000

— 'Whitmore Hall, Staffordshire', *Country Life*, 6 June 1957

NASH, JOSEPH, *Mansions of England in the Olden Time*, London, 1839–40

NEALE, J.P., *View of the Seats of Noblemen and Gentlemen in England, Wales, Scotland and Ireland*, London, 1818–23 (6 vols); London, 1824–9 (5 vols)

NICOLSON, NIGEL, *Ightham Mote*, London, 1998

OSWALD, ARTHUR, *Country Houses in Dorset*, London, 1935
— 'Bingham's Melcombe, Dorset', *Country Life*, 17/24 October 1947
— 'Wolfeton House, Dorset', *Country Life*, 6/13 August 1953
— 'Mapperton House, Dorset', *Country Life*, 4/25 January 1962

PEVSNER, NIKOLAUS (ed.), *The Buildings of England* series, London, 1950– (various edns and county vols)

ROBINSON, JOHN MARTIN, *Guide to Country Houses of the North-West*, London, 1991
— 'Hambleden Manor, Buckinghamshire', *Country Life*, 14 July 1994

SAYER, MICHAEL, and MASSINGBERD, HUGH, *The Disintegration of a Heritage: Country Houses and their Collections, 1979–92*, Wilby, 1993

SYKES, CHRISTOPHER SIMON, *Ancient English Houses*, London, 1988

TAYLOR, M.W., *Old Manorial Halls of Westmorland and Cumberland*, Kendal, 1892

THOROLD, HENRY, *Lincolnshire Houses*, Wilby, 1999

TIPPING, H. AVRAY, *English Homes*, London, 1921
— 'Layer Marney Tower, Essex', *Country Life*, 21/28 February 1914
— 'East Barsham Manor, Norfolk', *Country Life*, 5 January 1924
— 'Levens Hall, Westmorland', *Country Life*, 9/16 October 1926

TRISTRAM, E.W., *English Medieval Wall Painting*, London, 1944–55 (3 vols)

WALPOLE, HORACE, *Letters*, London, 1937–

WEAVER, LAURENCE, 'Cadhay, Devon', *Country Life*, 18 January 1913

WELLS-COLE, ANTHONY, *Art and Decoration in Elizabethan and Jacobean England*, London, 1997

WOLSELEY, VISCOUNTESS, 'Friston Place, Sussex', *Sussex County Magazine*, 1936

WOOD, M., *The Medieval English House*, London, 1963

INDEX

Adela, Queen 44
Alston, L.A. 154
Archer family 244-5
Archer, Thomas 244–5
Archer-Houblon family 245
Arundell, the Reverend F.V.J. 90
Aslet, Clive 81, 95, 96
Asquith family, Earls of Oxford and Asquith 203, 206–7
Asquith, Lady Cynthia 183, 184, 187
Athelhampton, Dorset 9, 76–81, 159, 160
Aubeney, de, *see* de Aubeney
Aubourn Hall, Lincolnshire 9, 198–201
Aubrey, John 126

Bagot family 177–81
Baker family 17, 167–9
Baker, William 167–8, 234–5
Ball, Peter 197
Bankes, Dame Mary 28
Bantock, 'Boots' 69
Barnsley, Ernest 69
Barnsley, Sidney 68, 69
Barry, J.M. 183
Barrow, Mr and Mrs Colin 157
Barry, Sir Edward, 2nd Baronet 58, 63
Batoni, Pompeo 87
Beauchamp, Sir Henry, Duke of Warwick 58
Beaufort, Sir Edmund, Duke of Somerset 58
Beaumont, Guillaume (William) 178–80
Beckett, Sir Martyn, 2nd Baronet 216, 219
Beckley Park, Oxfordshire 9, 138–45
Bedingfeld family 122, 153, 154
Beechey, Sir William 87
Beeleigh Abbey, Essex 9, 12–17
Bellingham family 177–8
Bellyse Baker family 167–9
Belwood, William 84, 86
Benson, Jeremy 241
Betjeman, Sir John 197
Biggs family 172–3
Bingham family 27–31
Bingham's Melcombe, Dorset 8, 9, 26–31
Bird, Francis 237
Blackie, Christopher 196
Blore, Edward 161
Bluett family 71–4
Bodrugan, Sir Henry 91–2
Bond family 30
Bosworth-Smith, Reginald 8–9, 11, 30
Boughey family 233
Brakspear, Sir Harold 51–2, 72
Brett family 133, 134
Brodrepp family 133, 135
Brontë, Charlotte 83, 84, 87

Broughton Castle, Oxfordshire 172
Brudenell family, Earls of Cardigan 216
Buckeridge, Charles 248
Buckler, J.C. 53, 191
Bulwer family 190–1
Bulwer-Long family 189–92
Burgoyne, General 'Gentleman Johnny' 228
Burn, William 187
Burrard family 51
Burston, Devon 196, 197
Butler, Sir James, Earl of Wiltshire 58

Cadhay, Devon 9, 146–51
Cadhaye, de, *see* de Cadhaye
Camville, de, *see* de Camville
Cant de Lafontaine, Alfred 81
Catesby family 210
Cavenagh-Mainwaring family 233–5
Cecil, Lord David 31, 109, 115, 125, 133, 136, 159, 163, 164, 165
Charles I, King 92, 206
Charlotte, Queen 89–90
Charrington family 123
Charteris family, Earls of Wemyss 183–7
Chastleton House, Oxfordshire 9, 11, 208–13
Chester, Hugh 167
Christie's 225, 247, 251
Clement family 33–7
Clifton Hampden Manor, Oxfordshire 9, 246–51
Clifton-Taylor, Alec 17, 184
Clutton-Brock family 209, 212
Cobbett, William 171
Cockrane, George 81
Cokayne, George Edward 248
Coleman family 119
Colvin, Sir Howard 245
Colyer-Fergusson family 33, 37
Compton family 133, 135
Condy, Nicholas 90
Conyers family 83
Cooke family 77–81
Cooper, Nicholas 117
Cooper, Lieutenant-Colonel Reginald 72–4
Cornelius, Blessed 126
Cornforth, John 190, 192, 237, 239
Cornwall, Richard, Earl of 139, 140
Corsellis family 123
Coteel, Sir Thomas 92
Cotehele, Cornwall 9, 10, 11, 88–93
Cothay family 71
Cothay Manor, Somerset 9, 10, 70–5
Cromwell, Thomas 15

Dahl, Michael 235
da Maiano, Giovanni 122

Dampier, Sir William 151
Danneggar, Chris 123
Daunt family 65–8
Day family 60
de Aubeney family 39
de Cadhaye family 147
de Camville family 44
Dee, John 17
de Falaise, Alex 248
de la Pole, Sir William, Duke of Suffolk 58
Delves family 224
de Redman family 177
de Turberville family 27, 134
de Veteripont family 39
Devonshire, Dukes of 99, 227
de Wolterton family 117
de Zoete, Walter 123
d'Ivry family 140
Dod family 167, 168
Doddington Hall, Lincolnshire 201
d'Oilly, Robert 140
Dorfold Hall, Cheshire 9, 220–5
Dorney Court, Buckinghamshire 9, 100–7
'Doublefees', Sir 'Bullface' (Fletcher Norton) 19–20
Du Cann, Sir Edward 74
Dynne family 190

Earle family 190–1
East Barsham Manor, Norfolk 8, 9, 11, 116–19
Edgcumbe family, Earls of Mount Edgcumbe 89–93
Edward VI, King 149
Elizabeth I, Queen 122, 149
Ellesmere, Lord 19, 20
Englefield family 58–60
Essex, Earl of, Harry Bourchier 14, 15
Evelyn, John 251
Every family 72
Eyam Hall, Derbyshire 9, 11, 226–31
Eyre family 54, 245

Falaise, de *see* de Falaise
Fedden, Robin 210
Feilding family 139, 140
Fermor family 117–19
Ferneley, John 84, 87
Fettiplace family 58, 212
Filiol family 110
Flemings Hall, Suffolk 9, 152–7
Fletcher, H.M. 151
Forsyth, James 34, 37
Fowler, John 215, 216, 218, 219
Foyle family 13–17
Freeman, John 239
Friston Place, Sussex 6, 8, 9, 94–9
Fuller family 51–5

Garrard family 101, 105, 106
Gascoigne, Ann 49

Gascoyne, Joel 161
Gate, Sir John 15–17
George III, King 89
Gibbs family, Lords Aldenham 247–51
Gibbs, Christopher 247, 248, 251
Gibbs, Vicary 217–18, 248
Gill, Eric 203
Gimson, Ernest 68, 69
Girouard, Mark 10, 90, 127, 139, 199, 210
Giuntini, G. 81
Graham family 83–7
Grahme family 177–80
Grantham, Captain F.W. 17
Grantley, Lady 20
Graves, Admiral Lord 150
Great Chalfield Manor, Wiltshire 9, 10, 11, 50–5
Grenfell family, Lords Desborough 60
Griffiths, Sir Henry 210
Grigg, F.L. ('Fred') 69
Grogan, Lady 30
Guinness, Sir John and Lady 119
Gurney family 54
Gybbes family 238

Hall family 54
Hambleden, Maria Carmela Viscountess 215–19
Hambleden, 4th Viscount 215, 218, 219
Hambleden Manor, Buckinghamshire 9, 214–19
Hanham family 54
Hapsburg-Lothringen, Count 119
Harcourt family, Viscounts Harcourt 43–9
Hardwick Hall, Derbyshire 210
Hardy, Thomas 27, 77, 125
Hare family 150–1
Harrington Hall, Lincolnshire 201
Harris, John 196, 251
Hasell family 40–1
Haut family 23–7
Haydon family 147–50
Henning family 127
Henry I, King 44
Henry VI, King 57, 58
Henry VIII, King 117, 149, 243
Herring family 109–10
Herringston, Dorset 9, 11, 108–15
Hewlings, Dr Richard 86
Heydon Hall, Norfolk 9, 188–93
Hicks, David 140
Highfields, Cheshire 9, 166–9
Hinchingbrooke, Huntingdon 136
Historic Buildings Council 241
Hobden, William 23
Honington Hall, Warwickshire 9, 11, 236–41
Horner family 203–7
Horseshoe Cloisters, Windsor 57
Houblon family 245

– 255 –

INDEX

Howard family 39–41
Hucks family 247
Hudleston, Nigel 39
Hungerford family 53
Hussey, Christopher 10, 14, 20, 21, 43, 57, 65, 71, 72, 102, 206
Hutchings family 161–4

Ightham Mote, Kent 5, 10, 11, 32–7
Inge, Isolde 34
Ionides, Basil 17
Ivry, d' *see* d'Ivry

Jackson, John 243–4
Jackson-Stops, Gervase 86
Jagger, Mick 248
James I, King 15, 36, 178, 224
James, Henry 37, 237
Jekyll, Gertrude 68, 206
Jewson, Norman 65, 68–9
Jolliffe, John 203
Johnby Hall, Cumbria 9, 38–41
Johnson, Francis 196, 197
Jones family 209–13, 243–4
Jones, Barbara 196
Jones, William 239
Jonson, Cornelius 222

Kastner, Michael 123
Kellock, Charles 169
Kenworthy-Browne, John 210
Kingston, 2nd Duke of 54
Knevet family 119
Kniveton family 228
Knole, Kent 7
Knoyle family 78, 159–61

Labouchere, Ethel 133, 135, 136
Lacey, Lady 174
Lane, Colonel George 119
Langham, Mr and Mrs John 27, 30–1
Layer Marney Tower, Essex 9, 11, 120–3
Leland, John 204
Le Strange family 119
Leech, Sir Stephen 58, 60–3
Lees-Milne, James 66, 89, 90, 92, 93, 195
Levens Hall, Cumbria 9, 11, 176–81
Leverton, Thomas 109, 115
Leyborne-Popham, Maud 40, 41
Lindsay, Mrs Harry 206
Lutyens, Sir Edwin 203, 206
Lycett Green, Candida 43, 133, 136, 183, 237
Lytton family 102, 190, 191

McBean, Angus 153–7
Maiano, Giovanni da 122
Mainwaring family 233–5
Maitland family 95, 99
Mander family 69
Mapperton House, Dorset 9, 132–7
Margaret of Anjou, Queen 58, 55
Markenfield family 19–23
Markenfield Hall, Yorkshire 9, 18–25

Marney family, Lords Marney 121–3, 154
Marston Hall, Lincolnshire 9, 194–7
Martyn family 77–81, 159
Mary I, Queen 149
Mason, Miles 251
Massingberd, the Reverend W.O. 200
Maynard, Allen 127
Medlycott family 159, 164–5
Mee, Arthur 154
Mells, Somerset 9, 10, 202–7
Meres family 199–200
Millar, Thomas 39
Miller, Peter 189
Miller, Sanderson 241
Mlinaric, David 189–190, 191, 192
Mohun family 131, 133
Mompesson, the Reverend William 227
Moncreiffe of that Ilk, Sir Iain, Bt 200
Montacute, Somerset 130
Montagu family, Earls of Sandwich 133
Morgan family 133–5
Morgan, Howard 225
Mornington, 4th Earl of 79
Mornington, 5th Earl of 81
Mowl, Timothy 243, 244, 245
Munnings, Sir Alfred 203
Musgrave family 39–41, 84
Musson, Jeremy 10, 248

Nares, Gordon 234
National Trust 33–7, 51–4, 89–93, 130, 165, 209–13
Neale family 51, 54
Neidpath, Lord and Lady 141, 183–4, 187
Nesfield, William 221–2, 224
Nevile family 200–1
Nevill, Lady Dorothy 81
Newton family 245
Norfolk, Dukes of 40–1
Norreys family 57–63
Norton family, Lords Grantley 19–23
Norton Conyers, Yorkshire 9, 82–7
Nussey, Ellen 83

Ockwells Manor, Berkshire 9, 10, 56–63
Oilly, d' *see* d'Oilly
Oswald, Arthur 130, 133
Owlpen family 65
Owlpen Manor, Gloucestershire 9, 11, 64–9
Oxburgh Hall, Norfolk 122

Palmer family 101–7
Palmer, General William Jackson 37
Parker family 237–9
Parker, John Henry 161
Parry family 243
Partridge, John 196
Paulet family, Marquesses of Winchester 135, 136
Pembroke, 2nd Earl of 172

Percy family 52
Pevsner, Sir Nikolaus 14, 17, 44, 57, 117, 133, 134, 142, 196, 201, 244
Philip of Austria, Archduke 126
Piper, John 197
Pole, de la *see* de la Pole
Pope, Alexander 43–4, 49
Potman family 98
Poulett family 148
Powell, Anthony 203–4
Pugin, A.W.N. 51, 248
Puxley family 245

Rawlinson family 189
Redman, Bishop 14
Redman, de *see* de Redman
Repton, John Adey 119
Robb, Mr and Mrs Alastair 74
Robinson, Charles Henry 33
Robinson, Fr Christopher 40
Robinson, John Martin 167, 180, 216, 218
Romney, George 87
Roundell family 225

Sackville-West, Vita 7, 11, 65
St Valery family 140
Sandford Orcas Manor, Dorset 9, 11, 78–9, 158–65
Sargent, John Singer 37
Sassoon, Siegfried 241
Scarfe, Norman 154
Scott, Sir George Gilbert 247, 248
Scott-Murray family 218–19
Scrope family 218
Selby family 23–7
Selwyn family 98–9
Shaw, Norman 34, 37
Shawcross family 95, 99
Sheldon family 209–10
Shuttleworth, Abraham 17
Skarlett, Thomas 14
Smith family, Viscounts Hambleden 215–19
Smythson, John 199
Smythson, Robert 199, 210
'Souls', the 187, 203
Southborough, 3rd Lord 30
Stanley, Charles 239, 241
Stannard, Joseph and Richard 191
Stanton Harcourt Manor, Oxfordshire 9, 10, 42–9
Stanway House, Gloucestershire 9, 182–7
Stapleton family 39
Stein, Brian and Jill 58
Stockton House, Wiltshire 9, 11, 170–5
Stoughton family 68–9
Strange, Le *see* Le Strange
Strong, Timothy 184
Summerson, Sir John 244

Taylor, Stuart 189
Theed, William 248
Thimbleby family 125, 131
Thomas, Mrs R.E. 17
'Thornfield Hall' (*Jane Eyre*) 83, 87

Thorold family 195–7, 200
Thorold, the Reverend Henry 195–7, 199
Tipping, H. Avray 117, 121
Tollemache family 224–5
Tomkinson family 222–4
Topp family 171–4
Torrigiano, Pietro 122
Townsend family 238–9
Tracy family 184–7
Trenchard family 125–31
Tristram, Professor E.W. 74
Trollope, Robert 86
Tropnell family 51–5
Tuke family 122
Turberville, de *see* de Turberville
Tyneham, Dorset 30

Verey, David 65
Verney family 72
Verity, Simon 66
Veteripont, de *see* de Veteripont
Villiers, Barbara, Duchess of Cleveland 105

Wade, Fairfax 60
Walbran, J.R. 23
Walker, Rob 174
Walker, Thomas Larkin 51, 52, 53
Ware, Isaac 196
Weaver, Laurence 68, 147
Webster, Francis 180–1
Webster, Sir Thomas 161
Welford Park, Berkshire 9, 11, 242–5
Wells, Paul 122
Weston, W.H.P. 127–30
Wetmere, Gordon 235
White Canons, Premonstratensian Order 13–15
Whitmore Hall, Staffordshire 9, 11, 232–5
Whitmore-Jones family 209, 210, 212
Wiggett family 190
Wiggin family 241
Wilbraham family 221–2, 224, 225
William-Powlett family 148, 151
Williams family 40, 109–15, 150
Williams of Thame, Lord 139, 140–1
Wode family 117–19
Wolfeton House, Dorset 9, 11, 124–31
Wolterton, de *see* de Wolterton
Wolseley, Viscountess 95–6, 98, 99
Wood, George 81
Woodd & Ainslie 248
Wright family 227–30
Wyatt, James 173
Wyatt, Samuel 222
Wyatville, Sir Jeffry 173
Wyvell, William 40

Yeatman-Biggs family 173
Young, Mrs 99

Zoete, de *see* de Zoete

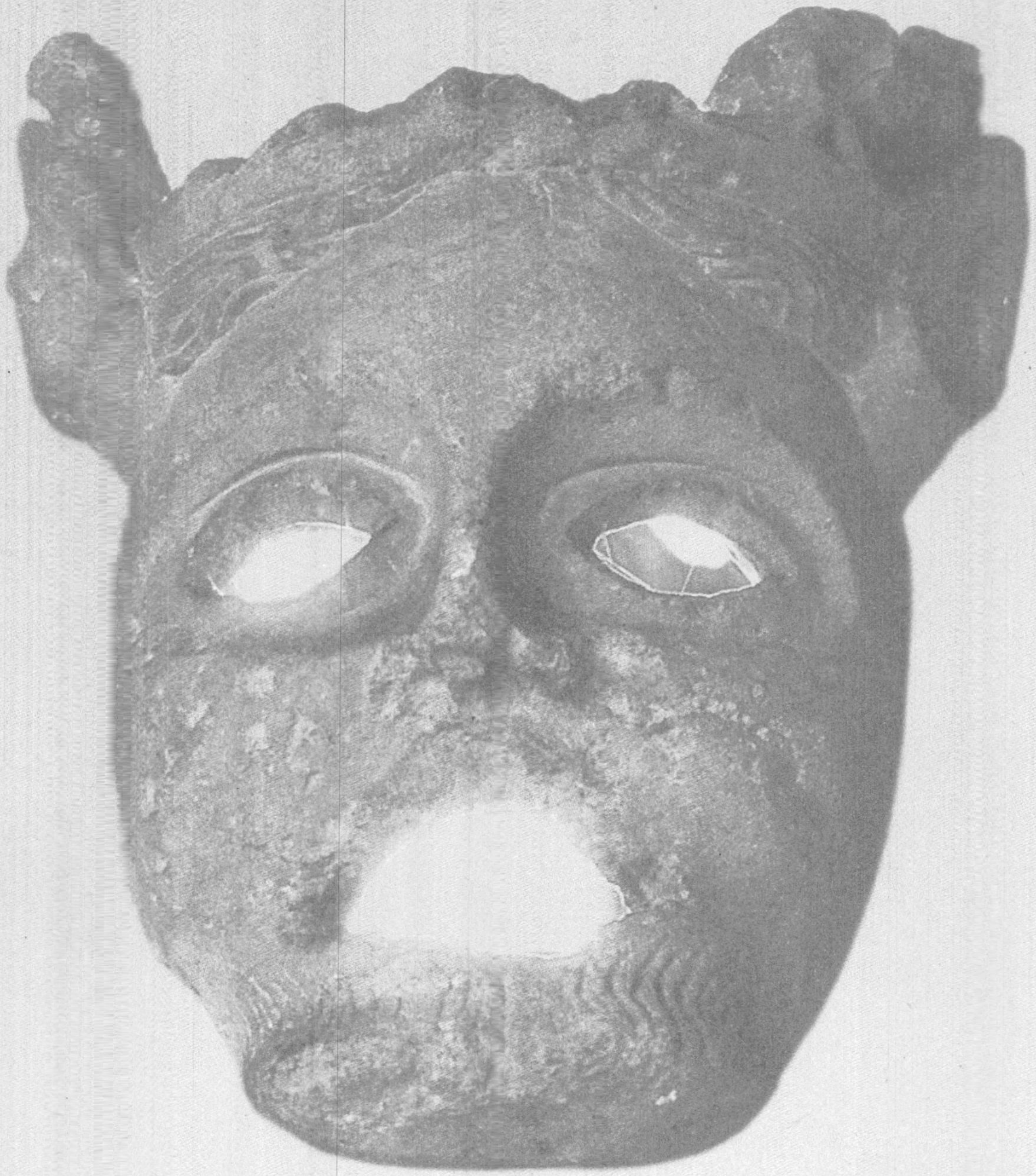